MEMORANDA

OF

PERSONS, PLACES, AND EVENTS;

EMBRACING

AUTHENTIC FACTS, VISIONS, IMPRESSIONS, DISCOVERIES,

IN

MAGNETISM, CLAIRVOYANCE, SPIRITUALISM.

ALSO

QUOTATIONS FROM THE OPPOSITION.

BY

ANDREW JACKSON DAVIS.

WITH AN APPENDIX,

CONTAINING ZSCHOKKE'S GREAT STORY OF "HORTENSIA," VIVIDLY PORTRAYING THE WIDE DIFFERENCE BETWEEN THE ORDINARY STATE AND THAT OF CLAIRVOYANCE.

SECOND THOUSAND.

BOSTON:

WILLIAM WHITE & COMPANY,

158 WASHINGTON STREET.

NEW YORK:

BANNER OF LIGHT BRANCH OFFICE, 544 BROADWAY.

1868.

McCrea & Miller, Stereotypers.

DEDICATION.

THIS VOLUME IS RESPECTFULLY DEDICATED:

FIRST,—TO PROUD MEN IN SCIENCE;

HAMLET.—Come hither, gentlemen....Once more, good friends.
HORATIO.—....But this is wondrous strange!
HAMLET.—And therefore as a stranger give it welcome. There are more things in heaven and earth, Horatio, than are dreamt of in your philosophy.

SECOND,—TO MORALISTS OF EVERY SCHOOL;

Thrice is he armed who hath his quarrel just—
And he but naked, though locked up in steel,
Whose conscience with injustice is corrupted.—*Shakespeare.*

THIRD,—TO ANTI-PROGRESSIVE CHRISTIANS;

Quench not the spirit; despise not prophesyings. Prove all things; hold fast that which is good.—*Paul.*

FOURTH,—TO RETICENT MEN OF IDEAS;

No object really interests us but man, and in man only his superiorities....Every man is entitled to be valued at his best moments....I look upon the simple and childish virtues of veracity and honesty as the root of all that is sublime in character. ...Speak as you think, be what you are, pay your debts of all kinds.—*Emerson.*

FIFTH,—TO TIMID MEN IN ALL PROFESSIONS;

Any theory, hypothesis, philosophy, sect, creed, or institution, that fears investigation, openly manifests its own error.—*Davis.*

SIXTH,—TO EXCLUSIVES IN ALL RELIGIONS;

Let no one call God, Father, who calls not Man, Brother.—*A Spirit.*

LASTLY,—TO ALL HUMAN KIND,

WITH THE FRATERNAL LOVE OF THEIR FRIEND AND BROTHER,

THE AUTHOR.

ORANGE, N. J., *March* 16, 1868.

PUBLISHERS' INTRODUCTION.

It has been said, and we fear, with too much truth, that all new discoveries are "treated with hostility by the generation to whom they are addressed."

Forty years ago railroads were considered as impracticable. In an article in the "Quarterly Review," the editor said, "*As to those persons who speculate on the making of railways*, generally throughout the kingdom —superseding all the canals, all the wagons, mail and stage-coaches, post-chaises, and, in short, every other mode of conveyance by land and by water—*we deem them and their visionary schemes* UNWORTHY OF NOTICE;" and in allusion to an opinion expressed of the probability of railway engines running at the rate of *eighteen* miles an hour (!) on a railway, then in contemplation, between London and Woolwich, the reviewer adds: "We should as soon expect the people of Woolwich to suffer themselves to be fired off upon one of Congreve's ricochet rockets, as trust themselves to the mercy of a machine going at such a rate."

It should be remarked that this volume is written in the interests of History—to put on record certain personal events and corroboratives in their chronological order which authentically reveal the rise, progress, and prospects of one of the grandest eras in the spiritual growth of mankind. The contents of the following pages are extracted from the author's private journal, and not before published in any of his many works on Spiritualism and Philosophy. He has kept memoranda of particular events, incidents, impressions, visions, correspondence, corroborations, etc., etc., embracing a period of over twenty-two years; during which time the most remarkable *facts* in Magnetism, Clairvoyance, and Spiritualism have been multiplied and established on both sides of the Atlantic.

All who want the author's philosophical explanation of the many strange facts and accounts which are presented in this volume, without comments, should consult his previous works, inasmuch as this book is designed chiefly as a semi-autobiographical contribution to the history of a new psychological epoch. This volume supplies links in the author's personal history which were omitted in the "Magic Staff."

In these plain, straightforward memoranda, it will be observed, the author has presented the "*pro*" and the "*con*," regardless of the bearing the quotations have upon himself, individually; therefore it is believed that this book will prove an excellent and reliable mirror, in which prejudiced opponents and calumniators may see themselves reflected at full length. With regard to opposers as a class, Mr. Combe remarks, that "if they are to profit by the lessons of history, they ought, after surveying these mortifying examples of human weakness and wickedness, to dismiss from their minds every prejudice against the present subject founded on its hostile reception by men of established reputation of the present day." And he adds, that, "if the new theory should prove true, posterity will view the contumelies heaped on its founders as another dark speck in the history of discovery; and that he who wishes to avoid all participation in this ungenerous treatment should dismiss prejudice and calmly listen to evidence and reason, and thus not encounter the chance of adding his name to the melancholy list of the enemies of mankind by refusing, on the strength of mere prejudice, to be instructed in the new doctrines when submitted to his consideration."

The appendix to this volume contains Zschokke's remarkable and instructive story of the "Transfigurations," illustrating the curative power of human magnetism, and the spiritual beauty and purity of the "superior condition;" and, also, a carefully compiled, instructive, and most cheering history of the introduction of the Harmonial Philosophy into Germany.

MEMORANDA.

1.

A JOURNEY IN THE DARK.

NEW YORK, *November 17th*, 1845.

I DO not mean to think myself over-taxed or discontented, for this is not true. But my life is immersed in a sea of uncertainty. Late this afternoon I returned from a toilsome journey,* the incidents whereof so soon have passed out of memory! I dimly recall mud-puddles, streets, ferry-boats, oil-barrels, sea-chests, a dismal vault, tobacco smoke, torches, and the features of gypsy-looking men and women. But it is vanishing while I write, like the "baseless fabric of a vision;" yet, incredible as it may seem to others, I have a feeling of *positiveness* that it was a real journey, and not a dream. It sometimes seems to me that I shall be the happiest boy in the world when the time comes for me to recollect and comprehend all the wonderful things I hear about myself.

* Further information concerning this experience may be found in the "Present Age and Inner Life," p. 181, *et seq.*

2.

TWO LIVES IN ONE BOY.

No. 92 Greene Street, New York, *November 28th*, 1845.

It is said that *I* am to begin a "Course of Lectures" to-night in the presence of witnesses! Why isn't my heart fluttering and palpitating beneath this overwhelming mysterious responsibility? Was any other boy ever so situated, and so uncomfortably perplexed about himself? I am sure that I have not a word of a "Lecture" in my mind. These two boys—or, rather, this one boy with his two lives—bother and confuse me. The boy in his natural state knows nothing of the same boy in the magnetic state. They tell me what was done when I am treating the sick, and they read to me the notes they took of what was said; but it seems like an account of the doings and speeches of a person living in a distant country. . . . . I am wondering every few moments whether it will be possible for that *other* boy to lecture to-night? And, if he does, what sort of a discourse will it be!

3.

PRESENTIMENT OF A SUICIDE.

TUESDAY, *November 30th*, 1845.

RETURNING from my customary walk this morning, I chanced to meet a large crowd of Irish women and children in the highest state of excitement. A by-stander said they were nonsensically quarreling and fighting because one of the women had in a fit of anger kicked another's barking cur down the stairs. But whatever the cause of the disturbance, the row-loving inhabitants ran out from their garrets and basements, and in a few minutes the street was so crammed with participants and spectators that the police had to interfere. But my attention was by some means attracted to a silent and sad-looking aged German woman standing on the opposite sidewalk, wrapped in an old worn-out shawl, her once rather beautiful features disfigured by disease and shriveled by poverty and despair. As I looked at her, all forgetful of the great fight going on about the kicked dog, I saw a thick mist, resembling a black crape veil, drop in the twinkling of an eye between her face and the outside world! "Poor, sad soul!" I instantly thought, "your hours on earth are numbered." The recollection of her unhappy face haunted me all the rest of the day. Taking up a recent morning paper, I read of a similar case: "An elderly woman, who resided with her two sons in Hester Street, committed suicide yesterday afternoon by hanging. The act was committed in her bedroom, by means of a piece of muslin, which had been torn from a sheet, one end of which was attached to a hook used for hanging up a looking-glass, and the other end was tied in a noose around the neck of deceased. When discovered, life was extinct. The coroner being notified, proceeded to the house, but, one of the sons being absent and the other drunk, he was unable to gain any particulars, and therefore postponed the inquest until to-day."

4.

VISIT FROM REV. SOLOMON SOBERTHOUGHT, LL. D.

NEW YORK, *December 4th*, 1845.

RESTORED to my ordinary state—from the ever-mysterious state of magnetic physical slumber, which with me is invariably accompanied by a peculiar mental transformation—the first word I heard spoken by a stranger in the room sounded like "*Anagosteleon.*"

On looking around the parlor, I was astonished and embarrassed because of the great number of strangers present, mostly patients, or applicants for treatment, as I supposed; and among them was a stout, red-faced, big-stomached, ancient, ecclesiastical personage, dressed in black, a white handkerchief around his neck, his scholarly face well-shaved, and his nose bearing aloft a pair of heavy gold spectacles. "The boy's clairvoyance," he said, addressing the gentleman at his elbow, "is absolutely of no importance." The other inquired, "Did the boy not correctly translate the words?" "Tolerably," he pompously replied, "but with innumerable misspellings, involving awkwardness of expression, with not the least accuracy as to the street, house, and situation of the furniture." . . . . .

Subsequently I asked the magnetizer (Dr. Lyon) who it was, and what it all meant. He said the gentleman was Rev. Dr. G———, of New York, who came with the avowed "intention" of demolishing clairvoyance as a monstrous invention of the devil. The Doctor said that I answered the questions of the round-countenanced and large-bodied minister in a foreign language, either Greek or Hebrew, he thought, which, at the time, the distinguished ecclesiastic seemed to understand, for his questions were apparently answered by me in his own tongue; but what was meant by the word "Anagnostos," or "*Anagosteleon*," which he pronounced erroneous, I did not learn. This large-bodied clergyman represents a class of prejudiced persons who resolve, before investigation, not to be influenced by any facts they may witness. Such visits are becoming frequent.

5.

EXTRAORDINARY MENTAL PHENOMENA.

24 Vesey Street, New York, *January 13th*, 1846.

The Lectures begin to excite a wide-spread interest in private circles. No person can be more excited with curiosity than myself. I have been stationed all this morning in my "sleeping chair," examining diseased strangers—women, men, children, whom I have never seen with my natural eyes, and may never meet again. It sometimes seems to me that I am situated half-way toward the center of an unknown world. I suppose that all this magnetizing for years is for some beneficent purpose. Possibly, I am gaining a knowledge of something which no other pathway could lead to. My toil does not weary my muscles, like the cold and dull work of earth-plodders, who take no soul-interest in what they do from day to day. Yet a darksome *uncertainty* occasionally envelops my mind, which is a weariness and a constraint; and sometimes I almost wish, with a good deal of impatience, that the *end* had come.

This morning, at 12, M., when the Doctor restored me from clairvoyance to full bodily wakefulness, a friend took from his pocket the *New York Tribune*, bearing to-day's date, and read aloud the following letter, written by the honored Scribe, thus:—

To the Editor of the Tribune:

Induction from tangible objects in the external world constituting, as it does, the common and habitual mode of reasoning, the public mind is naturally disposed to skepticism respecting alleged phenomena, the *causes* of which are not directly perceptible to the senses. At the back of all the *visible* operations of nature, however, there is a *hidden* cause, to which all mechanical and organic causes are but secondary and subordinate; and the admission of this *undeniable* fact should open our minds to conviction of *well-attested* phenomena, especially as connected with the mysterious economy of *mind*—whether these do or do not agree with previous experience, or point to a definite and adequate cause. Philosophers, for instance, have never succeeded in demonstrating to the senses any theory of the *cause* of *gravitation*; yet the *fact* undeniably exists. Physiologists have never demonstrated the cause of natural *somnambulism*, and the surprising phenomena usually attending it; yet these facts also exist, and are acknowledged by all. If, then, tangible and well-attested instances of the phenomena known as *Animal Magnetism* and *Clairvoyance* are produced, should not these, in like manner, be acknowledged as true, even though their *causes* could not be directly traced?

These considerations, superadded to the fact that many of the profoundest thinkers, both in this country and in Europe, have been forced to believe in the sciences last named, will, we hope, prepare the reader at least to bestow a *respectful attention* upon the following statements, to test the truth or falsity of which we earnestly invite the most searching investigation.

Mr. A. J. Davis, extensively known as the "Poughkeepsie Clairvoyant," is among the very few persons in the world whom magnetism places in a state entirely beyond the control of the operator's will, and all other influences of the external world. In the *less perfect* stages of magnetic somnambulism, the mental susceptibilities are so enhanced, and the imagination is so exalted, as to give the vividness of *real fact* to the mere conceptions of fancy; and hence the accounts of such clairvoyants are not always to be depended upon.

Mr. Davis explains these facts in his clairvoyant state, and claims, and shows by a process of connected reasoning, that he is in that highest state of magnetism, in which the physical system of himself and that of the operator form one being in all its magnetic forces; and that the vital action of the body being thus sustained sympathetically by the operator, the presence of the mental essence is not necessary to continue these functions; and that hence the mind, for the time being, is able to free itself from the organization, and to view existences both in the material and spiritual world, with that unclouded perception with which they would be viewed by a disembodied spirit. He says that the state in which he is placed is analagous to that of *death*—only that the mind is still connected with the body by an exceedingly rare and subtle medium, such as connects one thought with another; and by the same medium, the mind, after making an excursion for information, returns to the body to communicate its impressions.

I will not trouble you, Mr. Editor, with a recital of the wonders he performs while in the clairvoyant state. Suffice it to say, he seems to have access to every species of information. The human system particularly, it would seem, is perfectly transparent before him; and his examinations of its condition, and prescriptions for its diseases, evince a clearness of perception and accuracy of judgment truly surprising; and hundreds have experienced the benefits of his treatment. He uses the technical language of Anatomy and Physiology, and with the whole range of Materia Medica he seems perfectly familiar; though in his waking state his acquirements are singularly deficient, his education having been confined to five months' tuition in a common school! These statements, I grant, would at first view appear improbable; but if not *true*, they will be publicly contradicted by some one of the numerous persons who know Mr. Davis in his two states.

But the main object of this communication is to speak of a course of *Lectures* which Mr. Davis is now engaged in delivering, while in the clairvoyant state, concerning matters pertaining both to the material and spiritual world. These are delivered in the presence of Dr. S. S. Lyon, his magnetizer, 24 Vesey Street, the writer of this, who reports them for publication, and one or more of three witnesses, appointed to be present during their delivery, that they may testify to the medium through which the communication is given to the world. These witnesses are: Rev. J. Parker, 129 Avenue D.; Isaac S. Smith, M. D., 384 Broome Street; and Mr. Theron R. Lapham, 236 Canal Street.

Mr. Davis commences his work by a description of the evils which have in past ages, and which do still afflict society, and shows that these can not much longer continue. He shows that the remedy of these will, in general terms, consist in moral and intellectual progression. He opens a new field of progress in establishing a new ground of reasoning. He clearly and fully establishes the important conclusion, that the proper *reality* of all things consists in an *inward invisible principle;* and that the tangible objects of the external world are mere transient *forms* which this principle has assumed as its effects and ultimates. He clearly and intelligibly explains the phenomena of Animal Magnetism and Clairvoyance, and shows *where* and *how* he gets his information, stripping these subjects of much of their mystery. He shows that there is no such thing as positive *inertia* in matter, but that there is a perpetual, though invisible motion in the particles of the most solid rock; that matter was originally formed from a *spiritual essence*, and that in its progress of refinement, from the earth to the plant, from the plant to the animal, and from the animal to man, it will finally form *spirit individualized*—and that this is endlessly progressive in knowledge and refinement, continually approaching nearer and nearer to the great eternal *Positive Mind*—the Fountain and Controller of all existence. He shows that there is one general, unchangeable law of *development* in undeviating and eternal operation throughout the universe; and that each successive link in the great chain of progress bears a general correspondence with all other links throughout eternity, and that by knowing one, we may form a *general* conception of the *whole!* His generalizations are of the most stupendous kind, and his phraseology is surprisingly expressive, sometimes sweeping, as it were, the whole universe in a single sentence.

The first part of his work is mainly devoted to a discussion of natural principles. The second is to contain a *revelation*, touching both the material and spiritual world; and the third part is to consist of practical rules for the government of society, as deduced from what is to precede.

The writer of this is fully aware that the foregoing statements will subject him to the ridicule of the incredulous; but truth is omnipotent, and will sustain him. To us these facts are of intense interest, viewed merely as psychological phenomena, and considered simply as such it is proper that they should be familiarly known to the public, to say nothing about the *intellectual* pretensions of the Clairvoyant, in which much intercourse with him has compelled us *fully* to believe. We would, however, earnestly invite *investigation;* and for this purpose further inquiries may be made of the appointed witnesses, as named above, or of

WM. FISHBOUGH.

6.

SUFFERING FROM OVER-SENSITIVENESS.

VESEY STREET, NEAR BROADWAY, N. Y., *January* 18, 1846.

WHY is it that, like a flash of electric pain through the heart, I suffer with a strange, undefinable grief, whenever I pass certain individuals in the street? I *feel* their conditions, physically and mentally. This feeling of pity and sympathy becomes a *burden*, which I carry about with me for days, or until it is superseded by another impression of somebody's unhappiness. If a person is very poor, or very sick, or mentally out of balance, I seem to know it all instantly, whether I touch him or not; and ofttimes I am thus overpowered by the conditions of unknown individuals when I pass the dwellings in which they live. It is becoming painful, yes, almost intolerable, to walk through some of the side streets, and even in Broadway, where wealth, rank, education, and luxury abound. I can not understand what *good* there is in this overpowering impressibility. It often makes me very weary and strangely anxious, as though I had on my heart the great weight of the misery of whole families in the city. I am perfectly willing to help the poor and unhappy to the extent of my power; but I can not consent to waste my strength in *feeling* without benefiting somebody. Perhaps this great sensitiveness, so much increased of late, may result in something useful.

7.

PROF. GEORGE BUSH AND EDGAR A. POE.

NEW YORK, *January* 19, 1846.

THESE gentlemen are attracted by the Scribe's recent article published in the *Tribune*. It is said that they belong to that wonderful class of college-educated persons called "*literati.*" But to *me* they are simply human beings—sacred and fearful, as is every thing that represents the indestructible qualities of the human mind. Prof. Bush's face shines with a rare religious emanation. His presence causes one to think of a holy and profoundly learned man living in ancient Jerusalem. His eyes look into oriental mysteries, and his voice, although not unpleasant, sounds as from the bottom of a deep well. They whisper that he is Professor of Hebrew in the University of New York.

Edgar A. Poe's personal presence conveys me, in *feeling*, to a beauteous field, or to a kind of blooming valley, surrounded by a high wall of craggy mountains.

So high appear these mountains that the sun can scarcely shine over their summits during any portion of the twenty-four hours. There is, too, something unnatural in his voice, and something dispossessing in his manners. He is, in spirit, a foreigner. My sympathies are strangely excited. There are conflicting breathings of commanding power in his mind. But as he walked in through the hall, and again when he left, at the conclusion of his call, I saw a perfect *shadow* of himself in the air in front of him, as though the sun was constantly shining behind and casting shadows before him, causing the singular appearance of one walking into a dark fog produced by himself.

8.

DEMONSTRATION OF THE VISION OF A MEDICAL CLAIRVOYANT.

New York, *March* 10, 1846.

The newspapers and magazines are teeming with slashing discussions upon the subject of Magnetism and Clairvoyance. Miss Martineau's Letters on Magnetism give the materialistic solution of all these perplexing mental phenomena, which is generally received, showing that "it is neither imposture on the one hand, nor a revelation on the other." The religious press is unanimous in condemnation. The following paragraphs, from the pen of a distinguished magazinist, embodies the theory most generally accepted at this time (*i.e.*, twenty-two years ago), and it is doubtless the conviction of many at all times:—

"Coleridge preserved the anecdote of an ignorant Dutch chambermaid, who, when suffering from delirium, raved in excellent Hebrew, to the religious wonderment of all the simple neighbors. They thought the woman seized with 'the gift of tongues,' until some scientific visitors explained the miracle by tracing her former domestication with a worthy clergyman who used to read Hebrew aloud in his study, while his female servant dusted his books of a morning. It was then agreed by the wiser ones, that the mechanical impressions daguerreotyped upon the girl's senses in former years, were simply reproduced by congestion of the brain (just as the flame brings out letters traced with lemon juice on paper, thus hinting at the properties of a more appalling kind of fire), even as we have attempted to show how such images may recur, when commenting upon Admiral Beaufort's letter in a late number of this journal.

"The most startling phenomena of mesmerism, as now admitted by all intelligent observers to have a real existence, are, to our satisfaction at least, traceable to and explainable by the solution which these anecdotes offer to a most interesting problem. The testimony to the sympathetic influence of one brain upon another, in certain conditions of the system of the operator and patient, can not at this day be set aside; but the testimony as to any new impressions which were not before in the brain of the operator or patient, manifesting themselves from the mind of the latter when in an abnormal condition, stands by no means upon the same indisputable grounds of evidence. The phenomena of the one case, though not yet brought within the acknowledged pale of science, have been known to scientific men for ages. The preternatural claims in the other case, though not less old, have in every instance been set aside when carefully examined by the enlightened physiologist. Nor do we think that clairvoyance has necessarily any connection with the well-accredited phenomena of catalepsy as a natural malady, or as artificially produced by what is called mesmerism."

The hypothesis that clairvoyance is simply a reproduction of mental impressions, is overthrown by a *fact* which has just been made public. The clairvoyant disagrees with the surgeons concerning the position and inside dependencies of a tumòr on her own shoulder-blade. Her perceptions are proved correct, and the tumor is extracted while she is physically unconscious under the magnetic influence. The whole case is familiarly reported by a correspondent to the *Telegraph*, as follows:

I see there is a good deal about human magnetism in the *Telegraph*, especially in the last number, and not a few hesitate about believing all of it. Such things do appear strange; but then the mystery is, that people have not become acquainted with these natural powers of the human system before; and that they are so unwilling to believe the *vast amount* of evidence that is being accumulated on this subject. But the philosophy of the phenomena has not been satisfactorily explained; and we are so constituted as to be strongly inclined to disbelieve what we can not account for: unless the evidence of its existence comes to us through such a medium as to leave no room for the possibility of deception. And some of its developments are so very wonderful, and exhibit capabilities of mind so far beyond what has been heretofore considered the scope of the human intellect, that I should hardly write such *facts* as come under my observation, were it not for the expectation that some editor will ere long exhibit the *rationale* of the whole thing in such a light as to leave it as clear from mystery as the most simple manifestations of animated beings.

A few days since I was at Mr. Tuttle's, in Byron, Genesee Co., whose wife has created no little excitement by her wonderful clairvoyant powers, which have, for the most part, been manifested in examinations of diseases, and prescriptions for them; and I shall now give you something of an account of her, and her opinions in this department. You are aware that I called upon them last November, when, for the purpose of witnessing her powers, I had her make an examination of myself, which she did to perfection, commencing with the first causes of ill-health, and tracing their effects upon the system up to that time; mentioning particularly the time when the effect of too severe application to study obliged me to leave school with blighted hopes and dark prospects. Satisfied with her knowledge of the to us unperceivable works of the human system, I requested a remedy; and have used it since with quite as much benefit as she promised, and such as to open a door of hope for the future which had for a long time been pretty much closed.

The commencement of her clairvoyant operations was entirely accidental, or providential, she having been at first magnetized for a different purpose, and having no expectation nor desire for that celebrity which is beginning to result from it; having been, as she said, brought up in Tonawanda swamp, and desiring to live and die in the neighborhood of her nativity, unknown beyond the narrow circle of her early acquaintance. But being afflicted with a large tumor upon the left shoulder, which it was necessary to have removed, she was magnetized for that purpose by Mr. Joseph C. Walker, who was at the time engaged in teaching the common school in the vicinity. Among her first clairvoyant developments was a statement respecting the *position* of some parts of the tumor, in which she disagreed with the surgeons, which she could *not* have known from sensation, and which proved to be correct when the operation was performed. This was done while she was in the magnetized state, and without pain, though the tumor was from two to three inches in extent, and fast to the shoulder-blade, which was scraped, to insure the complete removal of all possible remnants of the tumor. On being awakened, this arm was left paralyzed, and it was some time before she became conscious of what had been done, she having been told before being magnetized that the operation was to be performed the next day, which was done to prevent her from being agitated, as this might have prevented a good sleep: but on coming into this condition she immediately undeceived herself, and told the hour at which Dr. Coates would arrive, and the object of his visit. This was on the 17th of February, 1846.*

She in this state prescribed the treatment for the wound, and also for her friends who wished her to do so; but this brought her in contact with the interests of certain professional men, who, because their craft was in danger, took all possible methods to destroy her influence, and who, finding all other means insufficient, hesitated not themselves, or by instigating others, to attack that character for virtuous integrity which all noble-minded females prize above all price. But dis-

* Although twenty-two years have elapsed since this test-case of clairvoyance was reported, I have the pleasure to record that I am personally acquainted with the celebrated clairvoyant, Mrs. Tuttle, and with her excellent magnetizer, Mr. J. C. Walker (my wife's half-brother), and can testify that her powers are giving daily satisfaction to the sick who apply. Her address is as above.

creet in the manner of transacting their business, the family exhibited no flaw upon which the approaching demon of slander could rest his polluted and polluting foot; and with full confidence in the noble nature of the mission, and in the ultimate triumph of truth, they kept steadily on their course, bravely stemming the strong torrents of abuse, obloquy, scorn, contempt, and derision with which the enemies of magnetic science endeavored to overwhelm them. And many are those who are and will be thankful that they did, for numbers are the cures they have performed, and which are being performed, through Mrs. T.'s prescriptions; many of which cases have baffled the skill of all medical practitioners, and for the cure of which hope had ceased to promise, until, by the aid of a mind in its unclouded independence of sensation, the nature of the diseases were pointed out, and the proper remedies prescribed.

And in her examinations and prescriptions it matters not whether the patients be present or absent, nor whether they send by their friends or by letter—all that is necessary being the knowledge that some person, somewhere, is desirous of being favored with such information and advice respecting his health, as she is capable of giving, while in that state of unclouded vision in which the wonderful workings of vitality become an unsealed book, and when not only are its present operations, but its past, and future, spread as on an open page before the mind. That she does perfectly read the history of disease, hundreds are ready to testify; and that she understands what remedies are suitable, very many of these are equally satisfied by having used them with success. And though she is rather averse to explore other departments, it is not because they are any the less clearly discernable, for the most subtile works of the mind are equally manifest to her; so that the most secret thoughts, whether present or past, are as clearly manifest to her as if transcribed in the plainest characters. It is therefore useless for persons to attempt to play a game upon her, for, perceiving their object, she is sure to give them any others than answers with which they could be pleased. Resting upon the consciousness of her own integrity, and standing far above the petty considerations which induce the groveling to deceive, she disdains to say aught for the purpose of convincing those who are unwilling to accord to her that honesty of purpose and power of perception of which she is so perfectly conscious.

9.

DISCOVERY OF AN EIGHTH AND NINTH PLANET BY AN INTERIOR LIGHT.

252 Spring Street, New York, *October* 30, 1846.

This glorious morning—the beginning of a great golden autumnal day—brought one of our patients, a distinguished Wall Street banker, earlier than was usual for our medical examinations to commence. He held in his hand Mr. Greeley's *Tribune*, which, he said, "contained a very interesting letter from the Scribe." It being agreeable to all present, he proceeded to read, as follows:—

To the Editor of the Tribune:—

From a paragraph in the *Tribune* of the 28th ult., credited to the *New Haven Palladium*, and bearing the signature " O." (doubtless Prof. Olmstead), I learn that news has, by a late arrival from Europe, been received at Yale College of the actual discovery of an eighth planet! It was first discovered by M. Galle, of Berlin, on the night of Sept. 23, and was seen at London, Sept. 30. The existence of this body was *inferred* a few months since by the French mathematician, Le Verrier, from certain disturbances in the motions of Uranus; but the announcement of this *inference* was not made in this country before some time in May or June last.

Not to deprive the discoverers of this body of their deserved honors, and with no attempt to excite the marvelousness of your readers, I would say that the existence not only of an eighth, but a ninth planet was distinctly announced in March last. I will explain: Your readers were informed, some time since, that A. J. Davis, while in an abnormal and exceedingly exalted mental condition, is engaged in the dictation of a book in explanation of the whole structure of the Universe, and developing that knowledge of the universal laws of Nature on which can be based an organization of society on principles of harmony and reciprocation, the same as pervade the celestial spheres. His abnormal condition (induced by the manipulations of another person), is analogous to *physical death;* when the spiritual principle is free from its shackles, and appears to have immediate access to every species of knowledge, and the reasoning power is entirely unclouded.

The following extracts concerning the eighth and ninth planets are from two lectures given by him, one on the 16th and the other on the 17th of March last. In order that what is said upon the planets may be understood, it is necessary to precede the extract with a few of his remarks upon the sun:—

"The wonderful sun or center to which our solar system belongs, may be understood as being a distant and extreme planet of another system, existing prior to its formation. And in accordance with the general plan of suns and worlds in the universe, its planets and satellites may be considered as satellites and asteroids belonging to a planet, and the planet as belonging to a sun.

"The constitution of the sun is an accumulation and agglomeration of particles thrown from other spheres; and these became united according to the law of mutual gravity and inherent and mutual attraction. Its igneous composition contains heat, light, and electricity, the successive developments of all primeval matter existing in an agglomerated condition, and subjected to the general and universal law governing all matter."

After explaining the *rotary* and *orbicular* motion of the sun (for the *causes* of which he accounts), he proceeds:—

"Therefore, the great internal portion or center of the sun is an immense body of liquid fire, evolving successively heat, light, and electricity, as developed and purified particles of the interior composition. The evolved atmosphere may be understood as being a part of the great body,—still an emanation of the internal by reason of its own constitution. This atmosphere, or immense zone of nebulous and accumulated particles extended to the circumference of the orbit that the immense planet occupies and traverses as a cometary body. This is one more planet than is now known, or has yet been detected by the observations made through the agency of the most powerful symbol of the human eye (the telescope).

"Eight planets have been recognized and determined as nearly beyond all doubt. Still the eighth and ninth are not recognized as bodies or planets belonging to our solar system. But the orbit that the last one occupies was the extreme circumference of the atmospheric emanation from the sun."

After proceeding with various remarks upon the laws of emanation, condensation, the origin of rotary and orbicular motions, the progression of primeval planetary matter to the development of the various (*so called*) *elementary* substances, &c., he continues:—

"The ninth planet, or cometary body, being composed of particles accumulated by the motion of the great sun, observed the same plane by the same specific force, but assumed a station in accordance with its magnitude; and obeying the laws of reciprocal gravitation, it occupied its assumed orbit at a distance proportionate to its rarity, and in accordance with its peculiar constitution.

"The eighth planet was next evolved, observing the same general law of motion and the same principles of formation; and was situated within the outer merely because its constitution was more dense than the first one evolved. Its occupying, therefore, the station and sphere thus described, is only in harmony with the established principles of gravitation, and general and rotary motions.

"By virtue of the two great motions which the sun has, the successive formations of the planetary bodies were produced. As the eighth and ninth planets have not yet been recognized as belonging to our solar system, there can be no conception of the original magnitude and diameter of the sun, as including its extended atmosphere."

After further philosophical remarks upon the peculiar elements, conditions, circumstances, &c., &c., as engaged in the formation of celestial spheres, he says:—

"But let it be deeply impressed, that the peculiar circumstances and conditions under which these elements may be situated will produce corresponding effects, according to the cause which occasions the manifestation of such consequences. This observation will lead to a proper understanding of the amount of heat and light which the *eighth* planet receives from the sun. The ultimate discovery of this celestial body, and its revolution and diameter being specified, will contribute greatly to the interesting subject of astronomy, particularly when the aberrations and refractions of light are known as they occur between it and the sun around which it revolves.

"Its density is four-fifths that of water; its diameter is unnecessary to determine. Its rotation and period of revolution can be inferred analogically from the period that Uranus observes in its elliptic and almost inconceivable orbit. The atmosphere of the eighth planet is exceedingly rare, containing little oxygen, but being mostly composed of fluorine and nitrogen. No organic constitution that exists upon the earth could exist there alive for one moment. The human eye would be a useless organ; for light there is of such a nature as to render its *darkness*, even at the darkest period, several hundred degrees above the present light emanating from the sun! It has, like Uranus, six satellites. These were evolved and formed by the two motions given this planet; the farthest from the primary being the extent of its original composition, and the nearest satellite being the accumulation of dense atoms near the planet. . . . . . It is wholly unfitted for the habitation of any organic constitution; yet life will ultimately cover its now undisturbed surfaces."

That the above extracts are genuine, satisfactory *demonstration* can be given to any one who may require it. Their existence in manuscript, as a part of Mr. Davis's course, has been known by many persons, and whose testimony will not be denied by any who know them. The lectures have, at promiscuous times, been witnessed by I. Kinsman, No. 1 New Street, T. Lea Smith, M. D., 9 Murray Street (now in Bermuda), H. G. Cox, M. D., 73 White Street, Theron R. Lapham,

308 Stanton Street, B. S. Horner, 9 Murray Street, and others.

In the same manner, Mr. Davis has revealed the formation, constitution, geological developments, *inhabitants*, &c., of all the other planets of our system. Indeed, his book aims to present in a *general* way, a knowledge of the constitution, laws, principles, and developments of the whole universe. He displays, while in his superior state, a power of analysis and generalization perfectly unparalleled and absolutely overwhelming; though while in the normal state he is almost entirely *uneducated*, and he is now only about twenty years old. If these are facts (and if not, their falsity *should*, *can*, and WILL be exposed,)the reflecting mind can not fail to recognize the *unspeakable* importance of their bearings. The only rational explanation of this psychological phenomenon is that which Mr. Davis himself gives, viz.: that his mind, while in the abnormal state, receives the influx of the science understood in the *spiritual spheres* with which his mind associates.

WM. FISHBOUGH.

10.

ANNA CORA MOWATT ON THE STAGE.

NEW YORK, *November* 10, 1846.

I HAVE been to witness a performance at the Park Theater, in which this singularly beautiful and spiritual lady played a part. She moves like one in the air, so well-governed and graceful are all her bodily expressions, and so fresh and intelligent are all her conceptions of the part she is to personate. . . While passionately portraying the profound grief of the character she had assumed, and at the very moment when her cheek grew pale and bosom heaved with the fullness of agony and despair, I had the happiness to behold the reality of beautiful influence (spiritual) descend upon her face and figure, imparting an energy and a marvelous brilliancy to her action and personal appearance, the effect of which everybody in the theater seemed to instantly recognize; for the applause immediately was universal and enthusiastic. . . It seems to me that the noble sentiments and profound feelings of human nature *attract* appreciable influences from the invisible sphere whence emanates "every good and perfect gift."

11.

MAGNETIC MARVELS IN NEW YORK.—LETTER FROM PROFESSOR GEORGE BUSH.

NEW YORK, *November* 15, 1846.

PROFESSOR BUSH's first letter, confirming the Scribe's, is published to-day, and reads as follows :—

To the Editor of the Tribune :—

The account given in the *Tribune* of the 10th, of young Davis's announcement of the existence of an eighth planet in our solar system, and even intimating that its elements had already been calculated months before any thing was known of the fact in this country, must be admitted to be, in any mode of explanation, exceedingly remarkable, especially when it is considered that in his normal state he knows almost nothing of astronomy or of any other science. As to the asserted fact that this announcement by Mr. Davis was made in March last, *I can testify that I heard it read at the time;* and numerous gentlemen in this city are ready to bear witness that I informed them of the circumstance *several months before the intelligence reached us of Le Verrier's discovery.*

This fact alone, if there was nothing else extraordinary in his case, would offer an astounding phenomenon to the world. But this is only one item of the many marvels which distinguish his mesmeric developments, and with which the public will in due time be made acquainted. Circumstances, which it is unnecessary for me to recite, having brought me into a peculiar relation to his revelations, and questions being almost daily proposed to me by friends respecting them, I am induced to seek the opportunity of stating through your columns that my forthcoming work on the "Relation of the Phenomena of Mesmerism to the Doctrines and Disclosures of Swedenborg" will contain a communication addressed to me by Mr. Davis, written by him in his abnormal or ecstatic state, and made up of a series of quotations, for the most part verbal, from a work of Swedenborg *which he had never read!* The evidence of this is decisive from the testimony adduced, and if any thing is lacking on this score, it is supplied from the fact that he is continually giving forth in his Lectures matter scientific, historical, theological, and philosophical, of a character so astonishing as to make entirely credible the narrative which I have related. On this head I remark as follows:—

"I can solemnly affirm that I have heard him correctly quote the Hebrew language in his Lectures, and display a knowledge of geology which would have been astonishing in a person of his age, even if he had devoted years to the study. Yet to neither of these departments has he ever devoted a year's application in his life. I can, moreover, testify that in these lectures he has discussed, with the most signal ability, the profoundest questions of Historical and Biblical Archæology, of Mythology, of the Origin and Affinity of Language, of the Progress of Civilization among the different nations of the globe, besides an immense variety of related topics, on all which, though the style is somewhat faulty, the results announced would do honor to any scholar of the age, even if, in reaching them, he had had the advantage of access to all the libraries in Christendom. Indeed, if he has acquired all the information he gives forth in these lectures, not in the two years since he left the shoemaker's bench, but in his whole life, with the most assiduous study, no prodigy of intellect of which the world has ever heard would be for a moment to be compared with him. Yet not a single volume on any of these subjects, if a page of a volume, has he ever read, nor, however intimate his friends may be with him, will one of them testify that during the last two years he has ever seen a book of science or history or literature in his hand. His daily life and habits are open to inspection, and if any one is prepared to gainsay in any point the statement now made, I will pledge myself to make a recantation as public as I now make the statement."

But this is not all; I say moreover: "In this state I do not perceive that there is any definable limitation to his power of imparting light on any theme of human inquiry. He apparently discourses on all subjects with equal facility and correctness. The range of his intuitions appears to be well nigh boundless." Indeed I am satisfied that, were his mind directed to it, he could solve *any* problem in *any* science. But he goes simply as he is led by supernatural guidance. On this head I observe:—

"The manner in which Mr. D.'s remarkable gift is, so to speak, *managed* and *overruled*, is no less extraordinary than the gift itself. It is uniformly held in entire subordination to some *important use.* He submits to no experiments prompted by mere curiosity. He makes no revelations, offers no advice, expresses no opinion, which would in any way give one person an undue advantage over another. Though evidently possessing in his abnormal state supernatural knowledge, no worldly inducement has the least effect toward persuading him to exercise it for any purpose which would not conduce to the *good of the whole.* The most urgent solicitations have been made to him to aid individuals in the accomplishment of schemes of private interest, but all in vain. He invariably turns a deaf ear to all such propositions. He refuses, because he says it would *not be right*, and because it would endanger the continuance of his clairvoyant power for higher and holier purposes.

"As to the Lectures in which he is engaged, he maintains that their grand scope aims directly at the regeneration of society; that a great moral crisis is impending in this world's history; and that he is selected as a humble instrument to aid, in a particular sphere, in its accomplishment."

Perhaps the most astonishing circumstance connected with these developments is the fact, that without ever having read a page of Swedenborg, he has reproduced, in the course of these Lectures, the leading features of his Philosophy of the Universe, and in several instances the coincidence is all but absolutely verbal. Of this I give a striking example in my work. Yet Swedenborg's philosophical writings, as distinguished from his theological, are of exceedingly rare occurrence in this country, and as they have been but recently translated into English, and as the exact number of copies imported is known, as also in whose hands they are, it is easy to reduce the matter to a moral certainty that he has never consulted one of them. Indeed, I should feel entirely safe in offering a reward of one thousand dollars to any person who will exhibit evidence that Mr. Davis has ever read or seen a copy of the "Principia," the "Animal Kingdom," or the "Economy of the Animal Kingdom" of Swedenborg, which are the works containing the ideas that he most frequently echoes in his Lectures. He has, moreover, in several instances, quoted his works by their Latin titles, some of which are not known to be in existence in the original on this side the Atlantic, and of which it is utterly incredible that he could previously have known any thing at all.

Viewed in any light whatever, the case of this young man presents a problem of the most astounding character, and one the solution of which will be seen to be indissolubly involved with that of the question of the truth of Swedenborg's alleged revelations of the spiritual world. This question, I am persuaded, can not be much longer staved off from consideration. It is pressing upon the general mind of Christendom in every direction with an urgency that can not be resisted, and there are a calmly-awaiting *few* who ask for no assurance beforehand as to the manner in which the question will be decided.

Respectfully, yours, &c.,

GEO. BUSH.

12.

VISIT FROM PROFESSOR TAYLOR LEWIS.

252 SPRING STREET, NEW YORK, *November* 27, 1846.

I HAVE just seen the particular acquaintance of Professor Bush. They have been long associated in the study and inculcation of Oriental Languages and Theology. They arrived together, and spent some time in our Examination room, talking about "mesmerism," "magnetism," "second-sight," "clairvoyance," and other subjects in psychology and theology that I do not comprehend. It is said that Professor Lewis teaches Greek and Latin in the University of New York, and that he is a very learned and distinguished man. He is rather small in stature, and not personally prepossessing; his head is large, and countenance expressive of erudition, and patient, laborious thoughtfulness. He impresses like a self-satisfied, but incessantly meditative mind; capable of persistent argumentation, with deficient appreciation of another's rights; although this fundamental lack would be, in a good degree, compensated for and concealed by the fiat of his scholarly attainments. . . . . Somehow, I can not feel personally attracted to the distinguished teachers of those unpronounceable languages. Perhaps the fault is in myself—in my sense of ignorance on all things in which they are chiefly interested—in my lack of education. Yet they seem to be as impoverished in what to *me* is Eternal Truth as I am poor in what they deem absolutely indispensable to a "classical education." What is education? And who are the truly educated? I wonder whether Professor Lewis will investigate the phenomena of mesmerism and clairvoyance. . . . Some patients have just arrived. The doctor is coming to ask me to be thrown into the state of medical clairvoyance. I shall not refuse, for the condition is increasingly attractive to me.

13.

THOUGHTS ON THE REVELATIONS OF MESMERISM.

NEW YORK, *December* 25, 1846.

IT seems that the gentleman who, one day last year, stood at the elbow of Rev. Dr. Solomon Soberthought, was a *man* as well as a clergyman; for, judging from the following, just from his pen, he was not *crushed* by the assumption of elephantine importance on the part of the immense-bodied ecclesiastic; but still lives, and what is better, *dares to think and investigate for himself*:—

"Good St. Paul wrote some things beside revelations. So may Swedenborg have done; so may Mr. Davis do. Shall I then swallow down all that comes from either of them; allowing their claims to supernatural vision to be just, simply because it comes from men sometimes inspired, without asking. Is it true? Is it in accordance with known principles of truth, that are immutable? Does it correspond to the All-Wise, who changes not? Verily not. While, then, I would exercise due caution against imposition upon the one hand, I would welcome with open heart and mind all that comes, from whatsoever source, in the name of truth and right. I have no fear of innovations or revolutions. I wish we had more of them. There is nothing to fear from the assumptions of any one. If they are true, they will be substantiated sooner or later; if they are false, truth will not suffer. Thus much in regard to the general subject.

In relation to the particular revelations of Swedenborg and Davis, I am free to confess, that, to me, they have an important bearing upon the progressive development of man. I have long, in common with many others, speculated upon the probable capability of spirit when separated from the body; whether it would survey at a glance an infinite extent, and know in a moment infinitely more than mortal ever conceived of here. I loved to think the mind, when disrobed of its earthly covering, would, like the bird uncaged, soar away on joyous wing, to revel in those exhaustless stores of wisdom, of which but little is seen in time; and I shall rejoice whenever any evidence is presented that goes to establish this favorite idea, though I can hardly trust myself to decide upon the validity of testimony in which I am so much interested. Swedenborg assumed to have had revealed to him the manner of life in the spirit world. He claimed for his revelations consistency with reason, philosophy, and scripture. Why, then, should there be any shrinking from an investigation of his claims? Mesmerism claims to unfold the hidden workings of creative and preservative principles in matter and spirit. It pushes the vision of the clairvoyant beyond the circle in which man has heretofore moved—marks out a new orbit for his future destiny, and bids him go where God and reason lead the way. Why should godlike beings fear or hesitate to attempt to follow? If there is a mistake at the bottom of the whole matter, somebody will find it out, while no one can be injured by it, if calm and prudent. If there is not, then glorious things are spoken of the City of our God. Who will take possession?"

14.

SUBSCRIPTION FOR A COUNTRY NEWSPAPER.

NEW YORK, *January* 3, 1847.

THE following is a copy of a letter I wrote this morning to the editor of a little newspaper published in the country. It is the first letter I ever had the courage to write to an "editor." I am as timid about it as a child, but I shall try to write correctly, and say what I think:—

MR. EDITOR:—With pleasure I have remarked several copies of your casket of valuable information.

The form, *freedom*, and freshness of Truth are captivating to, and congenial with, my reason, and to my supreme love of Nature and her divine soul! But for the purpose of establishing the *truth* that I have never read a *book, pamphlet, or paper* treating on any science, or theology, and in order to keep my mind free from the immensity of the first and the contamination of the latter, I have till this period positively refused to *read or subscribe* for *any* book or paper published. Inasmuch as the "Lectures" are near completed, in the development of which I have been and still continue to be an instrument employed, I am at liberty to subscribe a year for the present volume, including the already published numbers of your paper.

I have been three years engaged, as a subject of human Magnetism or Spiritual sympathy, and in some of the most novel, useful, and remarkable departments of terrestrial and celestial science. And manifesting a peculiar interior perception of external objects at any distance, or truths of great extent—comprehending, seemingly, the lowest and the highest creation at a glance—and yet *naturally* I am unacquainted with *any* of those vast and marvelous subjects so familiarly unfolded.

I am aware that *a change* is constantly going on between my natural and spiritual, or inner and outer being—one imperceptibly approaches and flows into the other—an elevation of the faculties and an unfolding of their *innate* possessions, which caused my inferior to ascend to my superior condition.

To Magnetism I owe unspeakable blessings; for by it I have been, am now, and shall be, I trust, a useful being to the conflicting world of mankind. If I can be this, my existence will be one of happiness and profit. This will be determined hereafter, when the book is presented to the public, and then the truth will shine forth amid the darkness that now pervades the mental world. I speak concerning the *lectures* I have given in my spiritual condition, with the same degree of wonder, as would any person uninformed of the circumstances; and I am seriously devoted to the interior manifestation of beautiful truths—feeling, as every mind should feel, a supreme *love* of truth, anxious to have it known and applied, the result of which will purify, unite, and elevate the human race.

Respectfully yours,

A. J. DAVIS.

15.

VISIT FROM A PHRENOLOGIST.

NEW YORK, *January* 16, 1847.

I BEGIN to wonder whether the science (or what may be one day called a science) of magnetism, and its resultant clairvoyance, will ever be delivered of false and shameless pretenders. To-day, a man called, making the largest professions to mesmeric skill, &c.; enough to disgust any common mind with the whole subject. And only yesterday a phrenologist visited us for the purpose of examining *my* head. He showed his "small bills" as well as his self-conceit, and pointed out a sentence which he understood to be a sort of editorial recommendation, to this effect: "It is not long since, in one of his lectures in the city of New Orleans, and also, I believe, elsewhere, a peripatetic head-reader demonstrated his ability to discover a man's religious tenets by the developments of his head; he could thus distinguish an Episcopalian from a Catholic, a Baptist from a Methodist, and a Presbyterian from the whole. We do not often speak respectfully of traveling phrenologists," &c. But, notwithstanding this "favorable notice" printed on his programme, I did not put my head under his hands. In fact, by experience, through great and painful sensitiveness to personal conditions and conflicting magnetisms, I am constrained to avoid, as far as possible, without seeming to be absolutely rude, all direct contact with the different individuals I meet in society.

There are phrenologists, however, such as Prof. O. S. Fowler, and others of his school, in Nassau Street, for whose personal qualities and reformatory efforts I entertain the profoundest respect. Possibly, one of these days, I may become better acquainted with the science they teach. The other day, when I met Mr. O. S. Fowler, I seemed to see an architect, whose plans are large, and various, and desirable, with an unusual number of windows and doors in his proposed superstructure, but either lacking the suitable building material, or else not properly and congenially assisted by efficient carpenters and masons.

16.

SEEING WITHOUT THE NATURAL EYES.

New York, *January* 18, 1847.

In order to show that the spiritual eye can read manuscript, without any outward contact, and independently of the bodily organs, I introduce the following voluntary attestation, from an interesting work, entitled, "Mesmer and Swedenborg," p. 179, by Prof. George Bush:—

"And what is remarkable, although I had my manuscripts with me, from which I wished to propose certain queries relative to the correctness of my interpretation, I found I had no need to refer to it, as he was evidently, from his replies, cognizant of its entire scope from beginning to end, though all the time closely bandaged, and unable to read a word by the outward eye. This will appear incredible, *but it is strictly true.* I had no occasion to refer to a single sentence in my papers; for it was evident that he was in possession of the whole, though he had not seen a line of what I had written, nor had previously known of the fact of my writing at all."

17.

COMPLETION OF THE CLAIRVOYANT LECTURES.

252 Spring Street, New York, *January* 25, 1847.

They say that my lectures are completed! Well—I do not feel any different. With the Doctor and the Scribe I share feelings of gratitude to the Immortal Power for blessings vouchsafed, and return thanks for the truths that have been imparted during the past few months. The world's millions know almost nothing of these remarkable experiences. A lecture would last forty minutes or longer, and the book, when published, will contain one hundred and fifty-seven of them. The first was delivered November 28, 1845, and the last, January 25, 1847. When delivering these lectures, I would receive impressions from the invisible world; and then, with my natural organs of speech, I would slowly, distinctly, and audibly deliver them to the Scribe, in order that they should be accurately recorded. I would then return to the invisible world for another impression.

If I were to write of the clairvoyant in the third person, I should say: In the personal appearance of

Davis, there is nothing to attract particular attention; his countenance indicates amiability and cheerfulness, rather than mental power; physically, he is slim, but well-formed; has very prominent features, black hair, a bilious, sanguine, nervous temperament; and, according to phrenology, small development of the animal powers.

This young man is so organized as not only to enter into what is called the ordinary mesmeric or somnambulic state, but to pass wholly into the spiritual world. In this condition, knowledge becomes a matter of direct intuition. In other words, whatever he is moved to seek to know, he *does know* at once, without any *à priori* or *à posteriori* process of acquisition. This clairvoyant and intuitive faculty has, generally, been employed in the examination of cases of disease submitted to his inspection, and to the prescribing of the proper remedies. Besides this daily application of his faculty, however, he has been delivering a course of lectures. These lectures, it is said, are of the most universal character. They profess to explain the origin, progress, and development of the Universe, and all things in it, from the Deity himself down to man, and the animal and vegetable worlds.

18.

JAMES VICTOR WILSON'S OBSERVATIONS ON CLAIRVOYANCE.

NEW YORK, *January* 26, 1847.

A FRIEND has just given me a newspaper containing the following testimony from the beloved Wilson, who has been spending several months in New Orleans. He is so pure, so good, so truthful. He is very dear to me:—

It is only in degrees far superior to somnambulism, where the manner of the subject's speech is so changed, and his style of expression is so much exalted above the ordinary, that you can implicitly confide in all his utterances. In this elevated state, his goodness of heart overflows every other sentiment, and no vast gregarious inducements can tempt him to employ his new faculties for sordid or mercenary ends. His diction is elegant and precise, yet easy, pure, and simple. His manner is unimpassioned, without enthusiasm, and ineffably tranquil, yet his tones and words are inimitably impressive. Having a distinct view of all he speaks, he proceeds with an entire conviction of the reality of what he says. There is an entire absence of the passions and opinions by which he is governed in his ordinary state, and even of all acquired ideas and talents; and though he can recollect them at pleasure, yet he attaches to them little importance. His judgment is quick and correct, and accompanied by an intimate conviction. He feels within himself a new light, whose rays are darted with an all-searching thoroughness, upon all that excites within him an interest; and the impressions and relations from without do not reach him.

The author has been personally acquainted with but two cases of clairvoyance so perfect as to be applicable to this description—the boy Leon (French), of New Orleans, under the case of M. Coulon; and the young Davis, of this city, to whom any description of this kind would not be justly adequate. There have been, and are, however, a few others, who have attained a similar perfection. The world will shortly be apprised of a triumph of clairvoyance through the celebrated Mr. Davis, which millions will be totally unprepared for. During the past year, this uneducated, unsophisticated, and amiable young man, has been delivering verbally, day by day, a comprehensive, well-planned, and extraordinary book—relating to all the vast questions of the age, to the physical sciences, to Nature, in all her infinite ramifications; to man, in his innumerable modes of existence; to God, in the unfathomable abysses of his love, power, and wisdom. No human author, in any department of literature or science, has ever electrified mankind to the degree that the eloquent, yet simple reasonings, the lofty and sublime disclosures will, that constitute this great compend of universal philosophy. Perhaps over four thousand different persons who have witnessed him in his medical examinations or in his scientific discourses, live to testify to the astonishing exaltation of mind possessed by Mr. Davis in his abnormal state. The two new planets of our system, recently conjectured, were described in Davis's manuscripts fourteen months ago. I have seen him discoursing in a most angelic manner for more than four hours in succession. The above, his first and least work, is, I believe, nearly ready to be issued.

19.

THE MAGNETIC SEPARATION.

NEW YORK, *April* 10, 1847.

I HAVE an indescribable feeling, amounting almost to melancholy, that *this day* ends my magnetic relations to the kind-hearted operator. A voice from the sacred mountain sounds the prophecy in my spirit's ear. What is before me as a person, or what I am hereafter to accomplish for the world, I have not the least notion. But my reliance upon the supremacy and triumph of truth is profound and immovable. Besides, I have a sovereign staff in my soul, invisible to my operator, and equally unknown to all my personal friends, with which I alone may journey into the hidden future.

20.

SEEING CLAIRVOYANTLY WHILE IN A STATE OF BODILY WAKEFULNESS.

POUGHKEEPSIE, *May* 16, 1847.

TO-DAY I begin a new psychological and personal career! As I supposed, a magnetizer will be no longer a necessity. But, Oh, how careful must be my employment of this faculty! I now begin to understand what Swedenborg meant when he wrote:—

"There are two kinds of visions, differing from those which are ordinarily experienced, and which I was let into, only that I might know the nature of them, and what is meant by its being said in the Word that they were taken out of the body, and that they were carried by the spirit into another place. As to the first, viz., the being taken out of the body, the case is this: Man is reduced into a certain state, which is mediate between sleeping and waking; when he is in this state he can not know but that he is wholly awake, all his senses being as much awake as in the most perfect state of bodily wakefulness, not only those of sight and hearing, but, what is surprising, that of touch, also, which is then more exquisite than it is possible for it to be in bodily wakefulness. In this state, also, spirits and angels are seen to the life, and are also heard, and, what is wonderful, are touched, scarce any thing of the body then intervening. This is the state described as being 'taken out of the body,' and in which they know not whether they are in the body or out of the body. I have only been let into this state three or four times, just in order that I might know the nature of it, and that spirits and angels enjoy every sense, even touch, in a more perfect and exquisite degree than that of the body. As to the other kind, viz., the being carried by the spirit to another place, the nature of this, also, was shown me, by lively experience, but only twice or three times. I will merely relate the experience. Walking through the streets of the city, and through the country, and being at the same time in discourse with spirits, I was not aware but that I was equally awake and seeing, as at other times, consequently walking without mistaking my way. In the mean time I was in vision, seeing groves, rivers, palaces, houses, men, and other objects; but after walking thus for some hours, on a sudden I was in bodily vision, and observed that I was in another place. Being greatly amazed at this, I perceived that I had been in such a state as they were of whom it is said that they were carried by the spirit to another place. It is so said, because, during the continuance of this state, there is no reflection on the length of the way, were it even many miles; nor on the lapse of time, were it many hours or days; nor is there any sense of fatigue; the person is also led through ways which he, himself, is ignorant of, until he comes to the place intended. This was done that I might know, also, that man may be led by the Lord without his knowing whence or whither."

21.

READING THE CONTENTS OF BOOKS AT A DISTANCE.

POUGHKEEPSIE, *August* 10, 1847.

PROFESSOR BUSH has been most cruelly misrepresented and constantly assailed for the indorsements and testimonies he published in the *Tribune.* In self-defense he has once more appeared in that paper as follows:—

"I confess myself to have taken a deep interest in this development from the outset, principally from its obvious relations with the psychological disclosures of Swedenborg, apart from which I am confident it can never be explained, but in connection with which the solution is easy and obvious. The *modus* of this it is not my purpose at present to dwell upon; whoever forms an acquaintance with Swedenborg, will soon find himself on the track of solving not only this, but all other psychological problems. My object is to advert to a particular passage in the Lectures, and examine its bearings upon the question of the *source* from which the information given by the so-called 'Clairvoyant' was derived. On p. 587 he has entered into a detailed and very accurate analysis of one of Swedenborg's scientific works, entitled 'The Economy of the Animal Kingdom,' in 2 vols. 8vo. He gives a minute account of the scope of each volume; and he could not well have been more correct had the volumes been open before him for the express purpose of exhibiting a summary view of their contents. The Lecture containing this passage I heard read shortly after its delivery. It struck me as very remarkable, as the work in question had but recently arrived in this country; and I was confident, from various reasons, that neither Mr. Davis nor his associates could have seen it. I put several interrogatories on this head, and received the most positive assurance that they had not only never seen it, but had never even heard of it. And, as a proof of this, on the part of the scribe, he remarked that he had noted the word 'Economy' as probably a mistake, as he had heard of a work of Swedenborg's, entitled simply 'The Animal Kingdom,' which was translated and published in England a year or two before, though he had never seen it. Yet this he supposed to be meant.

"My acquaintance with those gentlemen was sufficient to satisfy *me* that their disclaimer on this score was entitled to implicit belief; but, as I was aware that this would not be enough to satisfy others, I at once determined to institute an inquiry, the result of which should put the matter beyond all cavil. I saw clearly that if it could be shown that this young man had given a correct account of a work which neither he nor his associates had ever seen or heard of, it must be a strong point gained toward confirming the truth of his general claim to preternatural insight, for the establishment of which I was indeed anxious, but yet as subordinate to a still higher interest.

"I accordingly wrote to Mr. O. Clapp, bookseller in Boston, whom I knew to be the *only* person in this country who imported Swedenborg's scientific works from England. They are there published, not by individual enterprise, but by an association, from whom all the copies ordered from this country are consigned exclusively to Mr. C. I requested him to give me from his books, as far as possible, a detailed account of the disposal of every copy he had sold, as my object was to ascertain if any one of them could be traced to a point where it would be likely to fall into the hands of Mr. Davis or his companions. Mr. C. immediately replied, informing me of the number of copies he had imported, which was not large, as the book is costly, and the demand limited mostly to Swedenborg's adherents, and also of the direction which nearly every one had taken. Of these there were, in all, nine copies sent to this city to Mr. John Allen, of which all but three or four were disposed of to purchasers abroad. Of those that remained in the city, every one can be traced to individuals who will at once testify that they have never been purchased, borrowed nor consulted, by Mr. Davis or his friends. I have made diligent inquiry on this head, and am perfectly satisfied that it is morally impossible that either of these gentlemen should have had access to any one of the copies owned in New York.

"Still, I am perfectly aware that this statement will not, of itself, avail to overcome the rooted incredulity that opposes itself to such a demand upon faith. I now propose, therefore, to put this matter to a much more summary test, by applying a magnet of the highest potency in drawing out truth, as well as other things, from all weaker affinities. I am authorized to make a *bona fide* offer of $500 to any person who will produce a single iota of evidence, properly substantiated, that the work in question was ever seen, heard of, consulted, or in any way employed, by either of the gentlemen above mentioned, up to the time of the delivery of said lecture by A. J. Davis. I simply demand that such evidence shall be clearly and unequivocally made out; and I pledge myself, upon the truth of an honest man, that the above sum shall be punctually paid over, in the presence of witnesses, to the person who, on the condition specified, shall come forward and claim it.

"I can conceive nothing more fair or decisive than this proposition. If this book has been used for the purpose, it must have been obtained of *somebody*. It is not easily conceivable that such an one, if knowing to the fact, should have any motive for withholding it sufficient to counterbalance the inducement held out in the present offer to divulge it. A refusal to impart the information sought, by any one who possesses it, can scarcely be anticipated, except upon the ground of complicity in a grand scheme of imposture, which has been entered into by a knot of unprincipled men, with a view to palm upon the public a work charged as being of a 'directly undisguised infidel character.' But who are these men? Who can be named as possessing a copy of

Swedenborg's work that would be likely to lend either it or himself to such a contemptible piece of chicanery? Could such a man have any motive for this that would not be apt to yield to the certainty of pocketing the proffered reward? Has he more than five hundred dollars' worth of interest in bolstering up a pitiable delusion, which will be sure to be detected in the end, and cover with infamy the heads of all concerned? For myself, I am satisfied that there is not a copy of the 'Economy of the Animal Kingdom' in the city but is in the hands of those who have the profoundest respect for Swedenborg as a philosopher and a moralist; and no such man could be, knowingly, an accomplice in a scheme of pretended 'revelation,' the scope of a large portion of which is directly contrary to Swedenborg's teachings. What supposition more absurd? If it be said that such an one might have come into the junto without knowing precisely what would be the issue, or what use would be made of his Swedenborgian contribution, the fact is now palpable; he is undeceived, and what should prevent him from exposing the outrageous fraud, especially when he can spread the plaster of a $500 note over the sore of his chagrin?

The truth is, this whole supposition is incredible to the last degree. There is not a person in the community, who owns a copy of Swedenborg's 'Economy,' that could think for a moment of prostituting the book or himself to such a despicable fabrication; and I repeat, that the book is not to be found except with those who entertain sentiments in regard to this great and good man that would utterly preclude connivance at any clandestine procedure of the kind supposed. Should the offer now made—and which is made in the most positive good faith—fail to elicit any response contradictory to the assumption of the book, I would submit to every candid mind whether there does not arise from this source a powerful confirmation of its general claims. I do not say that such, considered in itself, is absolutely decisive. But it must surely be granted that it affords a strong proof of a collateral kind. The numerical count of probabilities is vastly on the side of the theory that the work in question has not been seen, if a generous premium fails of bringing to light the least evidence to the contrary; and yet, if the assumption stands good, what an astounding power is here developed! What can not a mind bring forth which is thus enabled to declare the contents of books never read or seen!

"On the whole, then, I venture the assertion that but one conclusion can finally be rested in in regard to the circumstance I am now considering. *Young Davis has correctly analyzed and characterized a work which he had never read nor heard of.* As this is directly claimed to be the fact, so it is, all things weighed, the solution which is attended with the fewest difficulties. No other than *presumptive* evidence can be adduced against it, nor will any other be attempted."

22.

PROFESSOR LEWIS ATTACKS PROFESSOR BUSH, AND DENOUNCES DAVIS'S REVELATIONS.

New York, *August* 15, 1847.

The battle has begun! I have just heard read the following very extraordinary letter by Professor Lewis, teacher of Greek and Latin in the University of New York:—

To the Editor of the New York Tribune:—

At the first announcement of the pretended revelations of Davis, I was requested by some friends, who knew that I had thoroughly examined the book and was familiar with the circumstances attending its production, to make some exposition of its true nature and merits. The fact, too, that it had been deemed worthy of six closely printed columns of commendation in the *New York Tribune* would also seem to have warranted such a course. It was, however, judged impossible that the boasted intelligence of the nineteenth century should be deceived by a work carrying on the very face of it such evidence of gross imposture. It was deemed incredible that a book abounding, not simply in philosophic skepticism, but in the lowest and most ribald infidelity of the school of Tom Paine—an authority whence a large part of it is evidently derived—could obtain any kind of countenance from a Christian community, or from any persons professing the lowest known form of belief in the inspiration of the Holy Scriptures.

For these reasons it was not deemed worthy of any extended notice, until the appearance of Professor Bush's indorsement in Friday's *Tribune.* He there speaks of it as a "work *justly* attracting a large share of public attention;" he recommends it to the community as a remarkable production, worthy of the most unprejudiced and candid examination; he exultingly speaks, in the style of a newspaper puff, of its remarkable sale of nine hundred copies in one week; regards this as evidence of a great increase of faith in that supernatural revelation which denies as impossible the miracles and resurrection of Christ; and, finally, makes a most remarkable manifestation of the high motives which should distinguish the scholar and the philosopher—to say nothing of the Christian teacher—in suffering himself to be the channel through which a reward of five hundred dollars is offered to any man who will swear that he has ever seen Davis reading a certain book of Swedenborg.

This gentleman is a Professor of Hebrew and Biblical literature, and a scholar and a writer of wide-spread reputation. This alone would render proper a notice of his communication in the *Tribune*, even if there existed no other reason. He is also a professed teacher of the Gospel of Jesus Christ; and this fact, too, of itself, would justify any severity of language which we have used or may use in relation to his strange course in this matter. Whatever delusions he may have been under in the *commencement* of this business, he *now* well knows that this book is thoroughly and unblushingly Infidel, in any, even the lowest, sense in which the advocates of the loosest form of Christianity would take the term. It attempts to disprove the very possibility of any supernatural revelation. It affirms that evil or sin can not possibly have any existence. It not only denies the supernatural of the Old Testament—some of the Professor's school might think this only a legitimate result of their doctrine of Progress—but pronounces false, and even affects to scoff at, all the miracles of the New. It denies the resurrection of Christ. It asserts that he was simply a moral reformer, but of an inferior kind, as being one who understood only effects, without that knowledge of *causes* and of the interior of things, which is now made manifest in these revelations of Davis. It speaks of his illegitimacy, and describes him in terms of inferiority to Fourier. It asserts that Prophecy and Miracles are, in the very nature of things, impossibilities; this, to be sure, by a most absurd and ridiculous attempt at reasoning, as we shall show; but the assertion is all with which we are at present concerned. It makes out Christ and his commissioned Apostles to be the weakest of all deluded enthusiasts, or the most wicked of impostors. It denies all human accountability to any higher power than Nature. It affects sometimes to be witty, and indulges in ribald scoffing at the claims of the Scriptures, and the sacred feelings which are associated with them in the believing soul. Every one of these positions we will prove most abundantly if Professor Bush dares to deny them. He knows, too, that the ribald objections to the Bible, and especially to the Gospels, which appear in the latter parts of this book, are identical, to a great degree, with the stale and oft-repeated blasphemies of Paine. With all this, he still—a professed teacher of Christ's Gospel—not only patronizes and encourages this avowedly Infidel production, but has done more than all other agents in the imposture combined, to give it currency with the public.

Prof. Bush may reiterate the declaration that he does not indorse the absolute truth of these pretended revelations; that he only views them as a remarkable psychological phenomena: he may even intimate, as he sometimes seems to do, that the contents are, to some extent, intrinsically evil and false, or the suggestions of evil spiritual agents—(certainly he must consistently deem them such, if they are blasphemies against that Being whom even he must in some sense regard as his Redeemer, and whom he professes to preach as the light of the world)—but what right, we ask, has he to aid the circulation of a work of the devil, whether that work be in the extraordinary way of a direct communication with the spiritual world, as claimed by Fishbough and Davis, or through those ordinary channels of Satanic suggestion, which, according to the universal faith of the Church, the devil has ever employed in instigating men to acts of wickedness and imposture? Suppose it *is* one of Satan's lying wonders; suppose, as the Professor has himself suggested, it *does* illustrate the remarkable psychological phenomenon, that the spirit of Tom Paine is yet engaged in injecting his infidel ribaldry into this world, whenever he can find a clairvoyant pipe for that purpose;—yet still, what right, even on the score of their marvelousness, has a Christian teacher to be puffing the devil's books, and so bravely offering $500 to any one who will prove that some man, and not the devil, wrote them?

But this argument will not avail. Whatever Prof. B. may say of the "sheer sophistry" of confounding some of the errors of the volume with the argument for its supernatural origin, yet still we are driven, by the very laws of the human mind, to make such connection. Nature teaches, and Christ and his apostles by their own course have sanctioned, the indelible lesson, that the fact of the "astoundingly supernatural" accompanying a revelation professing to be from the other world, is strong evidence of the intrinsic truth of the revelation itself. Whenever there has been the opposite manifestation, as in the case of the Egyptian Magicians (if there was in this instance a real intercourse with the agencies of the unseen world), there has ever been the higher supernatural triumphing over and preventing that delusion into which, without such aid, the human mind, by its own laws, would naturally run.

Prof. Bush has not yet made sufficient progress, consistently to believe all that Davis says about the impostures and delusions in Christ's pretended miracles; but he accepts of almost all the rest. This must be so, or there is no meaning at all in a great deal of the reason ing he has advanced on this subject. He believes that in the case of Davis there has really been most stupendously supernatural manifestation, a knowledge and use of languages which never came through the senses, or memory, or the reflective powers, or any innate ideas; nor were received as suggestions from other minds; and yet possessed and put forth as the soul's own consciously recognized furniture. Has the Professor ever seriously reflected on the astonishingly supernatural nature of this phenomenon, fully equal to, if not transcending, the miraculous gift of tongues imparted as evidence of the truth of the apostolical message? . . . .

The subject is an awfully serious one; and yet we can not well conceive of any thing, in the nature of an argument, more ridiculous than the one Prof. B. is so fond of employing in relation to this matter. The work, it is well known to him, denies directly the authority of the Scriptures, both Old and New; it blasphemes Christ on any supposition of His having been specially sent by God; it pronounces His miracles impostures and His resurrection a fable; in a word, it is an intrinsically bad and Infidel book; and yet, says the Professor: "It *justly* attracts public attention, and is to be recommended as a most valuable production, because it furnishes evidence of the existence of a devil and evil spirits." What is more wonderful and valuable still, it thereby confirms the Swedenborgian hypothesis in relation to these articles; as though such had not been the faith of the Christian Church in all ages, or as though we could not confidently rest on what is so clearly revealed in the Old and New Testaments, without the confirmation of Swedenborg! What crowns the absurdity is the fact, that nothing is more vehemently affirmed by Davis, nor more strongly held by the other parties who are united with Prof. B. in the promotion of the circulation of this volume, than the non-existence of devils and evil spirits, and the utter absurdity and even impossibility of any such notions having an objective reality.

There can be only three possible suppositions in this business: 1st. The book is true, and all the wonders in relation to it, extrinsically and intrinsically; or, 2d. Davis is obsessed by evil spirits, who make him the pipe through which they inject into this world their lies and blasphemies; or, 3d. It is, from beginning to end, a shameless and wicked imposture, practiced by evil spirits in this world, and for most wicked ends. The first position we will leave to the marvelous faith of the Infidel. If the second is correct, then every Christian man who has renounced the devil and his works, and who may happen to have the volume in his possession—having at the same time no better method of keeping it from doing harm to his children or others—*should immediately throw it into the fire.* If the last hypothesis is the true one, then all concerned in this nefarious juggle, and attempt to obtain money by false and impious pretenses, should be forthwith introduced to the acquaintance of the Grand Jury and District Attorney.

. . . . . The writer flourishes away with his "*therefores*," and his "*it follows*," and "*it is perfectly clear*," &c., when nothing follows, and nothing is clear, and nothing is proved but his own ignorance and impudence. He seems to be utterly unaware that in all this he is cheating himself with his own terms, ever assuming the very thing to be proved, and thus going round and round in an ever-revolving treadmill, in which the premises may continually become the conclusion and the conclusion the premises, and from which it seems impossible for him ever to get out. The very question is—Is there a power above Nature? He says no; because if so, it would be supernatural, and that which is supernatural is nothing; therefore, &c., &c. Had he had sense enough to understand his own sophistry, he might have made it look better by going a little farther back with his assumed position, and declaring that Nature is an *end in itself*, with no moral world above it. Then there would have been some shadow of ground for the argument that its processes are unchangeable, because God would have no reason more ultimate for ever interfering with them. As it now stands, the only real connection of thought (if it can at all be called thought) to be traced in this cloud of words, may be simply stated thus: "It is the very nature of Nature to be natural. Whatever is natural, *must* take place, because every effect, or thing caused, comes from something causing, and, therefore, *must* occur, because it is caused by a natural instigation. But alleged miracles are supernatural; whatever is supernatural is unnatural; and whatever is unnatural is contrary to the laws of Nature. It is, therefore, utterly unreasonable that a miracle should take place, and every one who is acquainted with these laws, must at once conceive, that such an occurrence is entirely opposed to these laws, and can not therefore possibly occur (Q. E. D.)." Is it not most clearand conclusive, and quite Swedenborgian beside? If he includes, in his word nature, God and the moral world, by such an abuse of the word he might have had the appearance of some more coherency of reasoning, but then his very clear conclusion would have been, that that which did not come from some cause, natural, moral, or divine, never could have been caused nor existed. In this case, however, it would not have been proved that what are called Christ's miracles never could have taken place, but only that they are excluded from his own absurd and arbitrary employment of the terms natural and supernatural. What makes this the very quintessence of all foolishness, is the fact, that while this very "remarkable" person is denying the miracles of Christ, on the ground of their being natural impossibilities which no rational mind can believe, or even conceive, he is asking, on his own assertion, our credence in states of being, and manifestations of knowledge far more wonderful than any of the exhibitions of Jesus in healing the sick and casting out devils, or even turning water into wine. He utterly denies the very possibility of prophecy or predictions for a few centuries; yet claims to know by intuition facts which took place fifty thousand years ago, and actually to have predicted discoveries in astronomy, by no natural observations, but by interior light! Another marvel, greater than all, is, that men should be found in this nineteenth century of progress, and a Professor of Hebrew among them, who can believe all this, while they find it so hard to rest on the martyr testimony of Jesus and his apostles, together with that immense mass of corroborating evidence which has been accruing in the Church for ages! T. L.

23.

A POPULAR NEW YORK EDITOR REPLIES TO PROFESSOR LEWIS.

NEW YORK, *August* 20, 1847.

THIS morning a friend handed me the New York *Sunday Dispatch*, containing the following rational remarks:—

Professor Lewis, a recognized champion of the Church, has taken up the cudgels against the meek and lowly A. J. Davis, and says, in almost so many words, that the shoemaker's apprentice is a cheat; that he knows nothing about Latin, Greek, and Hebrew; and that the reproduction of Swedenborg's philosophy through him, is the result of a *conspiracy* which, Professor Lewis intimates, Professor Bush is the master spirit of!

The champion of the Church denies, if we understand him right, the magnetic influence and clairvoyant power, notwithstanding the mass of evidence adduced to sustain both. Here he has committed a blunder, for which he deserves to lose his office and perquisites.

Christianity has, within a hundred years, suffered more from the stupidity of its defenders, than from the assaults of its opponents. The churchmen, fearful of losing their influence and their salaries, have looked with jealous eyes upon the progress of scientific knowledge. Every new discovery has awakened their apprehension lest it should overthrow one of the dogmas of their faith, and weaken the others in the public belief. . . . .

Never were the wrongs of the laboring classes—the oppressions and frauds practiced upon them—placed in a bolder light, than in 3d Part of Davis's Revelations. Allowing the correctness of Professor Lewis's favorite theory, *the Devil has a much greater sympathy for suffering humanity than we have ever given him credit for.*

The positions of the three learned professions—Law, Medicine, and Divinity, are then analyzed. The interest of each of these great and noble professions is shown to be contrary to the interests of society, so that these must inevitably prevent nearly all philanthropic action.

Thus it is actually for the interest of every lawyer, that there should be discord, contention, fraud, violence, and crime in every community.

It is for the interest of every doctor that there should be violations of sanitary laws, sickness, pain, distress, immorality, and vice.

And it is for the interest of clergymen, that people should be docile, obedient, superstitious—believing what they are taught, and exercising no independence of opinion.

For, were people all honest and peaceful, there would be little need of lawyers.

Were all so intelligent and virtuous as to regard the laws of life, there would be little need of doctors.

And, should all men exercise the right of private judgment in matters of faith, there would be, at all events, fewer preachers.

Thus, the interests of the members of these powerful

professions are, according to the work we are noticing, antagonistic to the interests of society—and in regard to lawyers and doctors, we suppose it will scarcely be denied.

24.

MORE GUNS FROM THE FORTIFICATIONS OF ORTHODOXY.

NEW YORK, *August* 24, 1847.

THE editor of one influential city journal replies to another editor, thus:—

The *Commercial Advertiser*, of this city, with an apparent anxiety to forestall opinion on the subject of "Davis's Revelations," gave, early in the week, a notice of a full column in length, which was of so queer a character as to deserve some comment. The *Commercial* says, literally or in substance:—

1. This is so large a book that we have not read it, and shall not.
2. It is absurd and ridiculous.
3. It is incomprehensible.
4. It is dangerous.
5. It teaches materialism.
6. It teaches infidelity.
7. It is false.

Finally, the *Commercial* is astonished that so many respectable men, both clergymen and laymen, should have given their names and influence to such a book.

It strikes us that this is a droll piece of criticism to come from such a paper. We are forced to look upon the writer of such a criticism as this as an arrant blockhead; a blockhead, for saying so much of a book he had not read; a blockhead for calling a thing dangerous which he had already pronounced absurd and ridiculous; and a very great blockhead for pretending to tell what doctrines are taught by a book which he has pronounced incomprehensible without reading!

If this is a sample of the criticisms of such papers as the *Commercial*, the fewer the better.

So much for the *first gun*, which begins the battle which is about to rage against this remarkable work.

25.

THE CLAIRVOYANT'S BOOK AND THE "COMMERCIAL ADVERTISER."

NEW YORK, *September* 2, 1847.

I AM more and more surprised at the great war that is raging among editors. The following review has just come into my hands:—

We are too well assured of the interest connected with the remarkable work above mentioned, to fear that our readers will grow weary of a discussion of its merits. We know too well what hold such a book must have upon the mind of every intelligent person, not to be convinced that there is no subject with which we could occupy our columns to more advantage. Whatever may be the ultimate conclusion of the world in respect to this work, there can be no question of the importance of its pretensions.

The *Commercial Advertiser*, a few days since, under

the head of "Religious Intelligence," contained a second attack upon this work, of a column and a half in length, some points of which we propose to notice.

The *Commercial* says:—

"A revelation having already been made to man from the Divine Being himself, as is unanswerably demonstrated by both fact and argument, no subsequent revelation from an inferior being can be received by men as authoritative. The minor can not overrule the major, the inferior the superior. What God has revealed neither men nor angels may gainsay, qualify, improve upon, or add to; when the Source of all being has made known his law, the profoundest investigations of the highest order of created intelligences, with their influences and conclusions, are of no account whatever, and are lighter than the small dust of the balance."

The *Commercial* refers, we suppose, to the Bible—which is a collection of the revelations of various individuals, supposed to be more or less inspired, and in which one adds to another, and the New Testament overrules the Old, as certainly as the Gospel has displaced the Law. Such a revelation, then, complete, indisputable, and satisfactory, has never existed. Whatever may be thought of the Bible, in other respects, it must be conceded, that men can not understand it alike, and that it does not impress itself upon men's minds, as the clear and direct revelation of the Supreme Intelligence. A direct revelation from God, could not be mistaken by those for whom it was intended.

The *Commercial* then narrows the question to this:—

"Is Mr. Davis's book a revelation from God, or is it not?"

We should answer: it is rather a revelation of God—than from him. God is revealed in his works, and it is these works which are revealed in the book in question. The truths of Astronomy, of Geology, of Natural History, are revelations, and of necessity, truthful revelations, of the Supreme Being.

Defining further what a revelation is, or should be, the *Commercial* says :—

"What it *reveals* must be authentic, a dictum, an absolute, authoritative making known of the truth. It can take no cognizance of falsehood, and enter into no controversy. A revelation from such a source can not argue. The moment it does so, it ceases to be a revelation.

If this rule be applied to the Bible, it is fatal to its claims as a revelation; for there is scarcely a book between its covers, which does not contain arguments of all kinds. Where is to be found a more elaborate reasoner than St. Paul, or a more pointed one than Christ himself? The *Commercial* says :—

"An argumentative exposition of that which is professedly received by *revelation* from the great source of truth, volunteered by the relator, is indeed an anomaly—it disproves either the relator's avowed instant perception of the truth, or his confidence in the perception of the source whence he professes to have received it.

How any one believing in the inspiration of Paul and Peter, could make such a sweeping assertion, passes our comprehension. But, in reality, the revelations of Davis have a wider scope than this critic seems to understand. He reveals not only processes of nature, but processes of thought. He does not merely say, God exists, but he reveals a process of logical reasoning, which demonstrates that sublime fact. And this, though an argument, is no less a revelation, because that Davis in his natural state is quite incapable of conceiving of such an argument. Thus, this is a revelation not merely to the credulity of man, but to his reason, and such a revelation must be argumentative and logical in the highest degree. Such a revelation as the *Commercial* describes is only fit for those who are incapable of reasoning. The *Commercial's* objection to this work, therefore, seems to us one of its highest merits.

The *Commercial* insists that the evidence of the reality of this revelation is not sufficient. The evidence is not only superior to that connected with any other revelation that we know of, but is of the most absolute character. The names of some fifty to a hundred persons now living, as witnesses of this revelation, are subscribed to its manuscripts.

These are, many of them, persons of high standing, and all men whose evidence is good in any Court of Justice. Have we any such evidence as this of the genuineness of St. John's gospel, which is doubted by profound theologians? This will not do. The evidence in regard to Davis's revelations, is complete and overwhelming.

The *Commercial's* next objection is, that these revelations—

> "Professing to come directly from the 'focus' of truth, have no feature in common with a prior revelation proved to have emanated from the same source."

The writer of this sentence, it appears, has not read the work which he is criticising; for Davis reveals, among other things, the degree of truth and authority which belongs to all prior revelations, and shows how far, and in what sense they can be said to have emanated from the same source.

The intimation of the *Commercial*, that this work absolutely contradicts, assails, and denies the whole Bible, from Genesis to Revelations, and impinges the honesty and veracity of each of its writers, from Moses to St. John, is a *falsehood of the grossest character;* and proves conclusively, either that the writer of the article has not read the book, or that he is a *deliberate falsifier!*

In short, the whole column and a half of this "religious intelligence" of the *Commercial* is a tissue of misrepresentations and falsehoods; the offspring of inexcusable ingorance or of a disregard of moral principle, which we refrain from characterizing in such terms as seem to us necessary to convey a proper idea of its baseness.

The case of attempted imposition on Davis, by a clergyman, to which the *Commercial* alludes, is of little importance, and is susceptible of a very simple explanation. Besides, a clergyman who would lie to Davis, would lie to any body else, and is not worthy of credit.

26.

PARKE GODWIN'S OPINION OF THE BOOK.

POUGHKEEPSIE, *September* 19, 1847.

A GENTLEMAN has just called to read and leave with me the following paragraph, taken from an influential New York journal:—

Parke Godwin, Esq., of this city, a son-in-law of William Cullen Bryant, and long associated with him in the management of the *Evening Post;* an author of deserved celebrity; a translator of some of the greatest works that ever appeared in the German language; in a word, a gentleman of fine taste and distinguished ability, in a letter published in the London *People's Journal*, says of this work of Davis, that "it is written with great coherence and profundity"—that it "unfolds a true method of reasoning which any reader will confess is ingenious and profound"—that it contains "the most rigid and unflinching logic;"—and that "as a mere work of speculation, to consider it in no other light, it is of the highest interest;"—that it is an "extraordinary work in every light in which we may regard it;"—that "it displays astonishing, almost prodigious powers of generalization;" and Mr. Godwin asserts that hundreds of the most respectable and sound-minded men in this city, are, after deliberate inquiry into all the circumstances of the case, most profoundly convinced of the claims of this work as the unaided production of Davis while in a state of mesmeric or magnetic clairvoyance.

Such is the testimony, and such are the opinions, of Parke Godwin respecting a book, which the long-eared critic of the *Commercial* and *Columbian* calls "an impudent bamboozlement."

In view of such stupidity, we blush for the press, and humbly trust that it has very little to do with guiding and governing public opinion.

27.

MR. N. P. WILLIS, EDITOR OF THE HOME JOURNAL

NEW YORK, *October* 28, 1867.

I FIND myself becoming more and more *curious* about notable people, who fill the conspicuous places in art and literature. An *editor* occupies to me an unknown station among men; and an *author*, of high reputation, is beyond my comprehension! I begin to wonder whether I shall ever behold such renowned and world-stirring men as Bryant, Greeley, Bennett, Godwin, &c.? Whether it will ever be possible for me to speak to them, and to know them as fellow-members of the human race? Whether, when I meet them, and look at them with my intense curiosity, I shall have sufficient self-possession, and the requisite degree of spiritual tranquillity, to obtain a correct "impression" of their most interior qualities and ruling characteristics? For this, after all, is the secret spring of my wishing to meet them.

A few days since somebody presented me a printed slip from the pen of Mr. N. P. Willis. It was the preface to a lengthy and appreciative review in the *Home Journal* of the "Lectures," and it read as follows:—

"To an unbeliever it will be a most delicious and far-reaching work of imagination, written with a vast background of scientific and philosophical knowledge, while to the believer it will be, of course, like converse with an archangel on the comparison of other worlds with ours. We simply propose to enrich our columns with an extract or two from the work, and to inform both believers and unbelievers in clairvoyance, of the existence of a book which will be a 'witch's broom' to the imagination, enabling a dreamer to visit the past, to visit stars, to measure his own value in creation, and his own stage of progress between chaos and perfection, and, in short, to forget care and trifles very effectively and go off on a revel of intoxicating and elevating imaginations. A more suggestive and *edifying* book, at the same time let us say, could scarcely come after the Bible. But without further introduction let us proceed at once to the work itself."

To-day I have, for the first time, seen Mr. Willis! He was standing (when a friend kindly pointed him out to me) on the steps of the Astor House. He appeared to be about six feet in height; was easily and gracefully dressed; a profusion of beautiful brown, curly hair; and a countenance, the expression of which gave me, as I slowly walked by, a peculiarly exuberant atmosphere of magnetism, emanating, seemingly, from a remarkable combination of eccentric but noble qualities, in a state of energetic impulsiveness—altogether a singular mentality, and the thought awakened in my mind was: "What a shower of rich sunlight falls from Nature's beautiful flowers and forms into this man's feelings, but he is not quiet long enough at any one time to grow a field of wheat." He neither attracted nor repelled me.

28.

INTERVIEW WITH THE SPIRIT OF A SAILOR.

POUGHKEEPSIE, *October* 30, 1847.

As I was strolling in the grove on the western declivity of "College Hill," musing rather than thinking, a blaze of keen-pointed magnetism suddenly enveloped my entire body. It was a primitive sensation; recalling the first time I experienced the mesmeric influence. With singular distinctness, clearness and purity, a voice said: "Jackson—hear this child of misfortune! He passed out of earth a gray-haired and wild-eyed, strong-voiced, broken-hearted, and broken-headed sailor."

The remarkable sweetness of the petitioning voice, emanating from unseen lips in the air, immediately secured my undivided attention. I became a spirit—unconscious of a physical existence; and thus I both saw and heard him who was called "The Child of Misfortune." He was an enthusiastic-looking man; with an expression of fervid sympathy in his large eyes; and around his mouth a smile of humor and universal good nature.

"True," he said, in a voice melodious with a sort of impulsive tenderness—"true, I am a broken-headed sailor."

"Your head is not broken," I replied, with a tone of playfulness.

"No, sir, no; it is not broken *now.* Although I left the earth through an opening a comrade made in my skull."

Vividly and vigorously, as though he held the pencil of the most masterly artist, and with great emotion, he pictured before me in the air, as on a vast sheet, the living identities, the likenesses of persons once in flesh and blood, with the time, place, circumstances, &c., which entered into his personal recollections, and which, by their immense combination and power, made up the catalogue of unfortunate causes and miserable effects visible in the very life of his existence.

The picture was a merchant-ship at sea; a plot, a quarrel, and a mutiny; officers and sailors disputing and wrestling together, and pummeling one another in the most unmerciful manner; fists, handspikes, swords, bloody faces visible all around; and the burly figure of the man then before me (as he appeared when a sailor), sinking down, lower and lower; he was sinking in the sea. A ruffianly-looking sailor, violently striking him on the head with a heavy club, fractured his skull, and threw him overboard during the tempestuous excitement of the fight.

"Oh, I understand now," said I, "how you left the earth through a broken head." And, I added: "Do you seek revenge? Would you *punish* the man who broke your skull?"

A noble, generous smile illuminated his face, as he replied, firmly: "No, sir, no; not that, sir, not that; for that sailor was once a kind-hearted boy. We were boys together. In many a street fight he stood by me and I stood by him. One of these days, 'Dug' will write the experience of that sailor-boy's brother; and I want *you* to promise me that you will read it, every word, and hand it around among your neighbors and chums, for it will soften their feelings toward us sailors, and help the unfortunate boys on land."

"Who is 'Dug'?" I asked.

"'Dug' is the lad that sailed on one voyage with us. He was the story-teller! When you spy his yarn about the boy going to the gallows, read every word of it; for it tells what is better than a rope for a poor boy."

I gave him my promise that if I ever found "Dug's" story in print, it should receive my immediate attention. Thus ended the interview. It seemed to me that I had been physically unconscious about two hours; but the distant clock, on the steeple of the old Dutch Reformed Church, had recorded the flight of only *twenty* minutes. This feeling was attributable to the mind's usual estimate of the amount of time consumed in the transpiration of a given number of events.

29.

FIRST NUMBER OF THE UNIVERCŒLUM.

POUGHKEEPSIE, *November* 4, 1847.

THE ship is launched. It is the first step in a new experience. The public will now have a fair opportunity to learn something of the principles of the new "Spiritual Philosophers."* And my name is put in

* The reader of this volume is referred, for numerous important, singular events in the author's personal psychological history, to his Autobiography, "The Magic Staff."

as one of the editors! The Scribe's editorial, in the first number, now before the world, embodies the only true position. Read and remember these two paragraphs:—

But though the book entitled "The Principles of Nature," &c., by Mr. Davis, the clairvoyant, is, as we confess, the immediate cause which has led to the creation of this journal, we would not be understood as receiving this or any other *mere book* as *infallible authority* in matters of faith and practice. To erect this, or any other book, as an *infallible standard*, and to bow slavishly to its teachings, without boldly inquiring into their intrinsic propriety, would be at once to sacrifice the high prerogatives of Reason, and to do violence to those principles of free and unrestricted thought inculcated on almost every page of this same book. Mr. Davis's book, therefore, will be regarded as a *light* rather than as an *authority;* and whatever devotion we may manifest toward its teachings will be exhibited because those teachings are presented to our *reason* in a reliable form.

The word "*Univercœlum*," which we have selected as our title, means, literally translated, "the united revolving heavens." It was coined by the youthful clairvoyant in the dictation of his wonderful book, and was used by him as significant of all things, terrestrial and celestial, existing in infinite space. We adopt this title, therefore, as an appropriate indication of the most expansive possible sphere of inquiry; and consistently with its import, *we shall know no party save the whole human race, and no restriction of thought save that which is prescribed by the laws of nature and the capacities of the human mind.*

The complete reasonableness of this position must be apparent to every rational and unprejudiced intellect. This signifies true and lasting freedom from all arbi trary standards in religion.

30.

BRENKENHOF'S TRUTHFUL DREAM.

POUGHKEEPSIE, *November* 6, 1847.

A CORRESPONDENT sends me, by to-day's mail, a translation of what he deems an interesting illustration of "Special Spiritual Providence." It is called the "Dream of the celebrated Mr. Von Brenkenhof," which has already been fully published and widely circulated. The truth of it is beyond a doubt, and it is related as follows :—

"This gentleman dreamed one night that he was in a desert and very dreary region, from which he longed to depart. He, however, saw a man who induced him to remain there, and he soon after saw this person, to whom he felt attached, expire. At the same time he saw a long train of people in a strange and unusual dress, and then he awoke. The countenance and the whole exterior of the man whom he saw in his dream made such an impression upon his imagination, that he almost saw him when awake. The whole scene was never obliterated from his memory, during his whole life. Some time afterward, he received a commission from Frederick II., king of Prussia, to proceed to Pomerania, in order to succor those provinces which had been devastated by the Russians in the seven years' war. Brenkenhof journeyed thither, but found the wretchedness so great, and the more closely he examined into it the greater he found it, that, despairing of being able to render any assistance, he determined to write to the king and inform him that he could not devise any means, nor give any advice how the country might be restored to its former state, particularly because of the deficiency of inhabitants.

"Occupied with these ideas, and while traveling to a certain place, a person came up to his coach, the sight of whom struck him with the greatest astonishment, for his appearance answered most exactly that of the man whom he had seen in his dream. It is easy to suppose that he was highly pleased at the sight of him, and immediately placed great confidence in him. He was the magistrate of that part of the country, and spoke to Mr. Von Brenkenhof in an encouraging manner, promised to assist him with his advice and co-operation, and thus induced him to commence the benevolent undertaking.

"Some time afterward, Brenkenhof learned that his friend was dangerously ill; he hastened to him, and witnessed his dissolution. That very day, or the following one, he saw a great number of men, women, and children, and whole families, arrive. They were colonists from Poland, who intended to settle in the devastated province, and were thus instruments by which Brenkenhof could carry his benevolent plans into execution.

"Now, what was the real object of this presentiment? It was not a warning from danger, nor did it give any hint either to do any thing or to leave something undone. At first sight, this dream, although it was a true presentiment, appears devoid of any definite object; but if the matter be more closely examined, a very remarkable predetermination of Providence is observable. If Brenkenhof had not seen, in a dream, the image of his subsequent benevolent friend, and if it had not made such an impression upon him, the sight of the man himself at his coach-door would not have struck him so forcibly, nor have given his whole soul such a lively impulse to act for the prosperity of that country. The whole dream was, therefore, an efficacious preparation for a most benevolent undertaking."

31.

ROBERT OWEN, THE REFORMER.

NEW YORK, *November* 9, 1847.

AN impression came through the air this morning from a high-minded philanthropist, long a resident of the Second Sphere, to the effect that Robert Owen is destined to hold "open intercourse" with the benevolent of the higher world. I hope this prophecy will be fulfilled. Last spring I chanced to see Mr. Owen, and was strongly attracted to his spirit. He was in excellent health and spirits, rode all night on the way from Washington to Albany without minding it, and though over seventy years of age, was perfectly sanguine in his expectation of witnessing a complete social transformation before his lamp of life burns out. Though I can not see through his spectacles, yet I deeply respect and honor him, and every one who devotes his life to the unselfish promotion of what he deems the highest good of mankind. There was a pure radiance on his face, and a singular glory in the atmosphere over his head when he said:—

It is now my intention—an intention created for me by the great Creating Power of the Universe—to leave this new true religion as a legacy for the human race, through all succeeding generations.

Its principles are the unchanging laws of God; easy—when the mind shall be freed from local ignorances—for all to understand.

Its practices will be highly beneficial for all of the family of man.

The few and simple, yet beautiful laws of God, on which this new religion is based, are: 1st. That the moving power of nature, the spirit of the universe, God—or by whatever other name this incomprehensible creative essence may be called, has created the general qualities of humanity, and made one man to differ from another by giving to each his own peculiar compound of these human qualities.

2d. That this ever-acting spirit of the universe so forms all men that they are compelled to believe or disbelieve, not by their own will, but according to the strongest evidence at the time made upon their minds; and to feel, not as they may desire, but in accordance with the instincts also thus forced upon them by this universal creating power.

3d. That man is thus made to be what he is without his knowledge, or possibility of merit or demerit on his part, and that, as the created, he must have power only to think and act as it has been given to him.

4th. Therefore, whatever may be man's individual qualities; whatever may be his thoughts or his actions; they all, directly or indirectly, emanate from God; from the unknown creative power of the universe.

5th. That this power, and not that man, the created, is alone the author of whatever is done upon the earth and throughout the universe. It is, therefore, the essence of ignorant presumption for any man to pretend that he knows any thing of the will or intentions of this power, or to speak and write of it, as do the pärrot-taught-unthinking in all countries. The will or intentions of this unknown power may be conjectured by man, from feeling, seeing, and considering the effects of creation as they exist within himself, and the circumstances around him; but, until more facts shall be discovered, these imaginations will be vague and most uncertain.

6th. That these principles, fully comprehended, are abundantly sufficient to direct all men to wisdom, goodness, and happiness. The practices of this new religion will be the reverse of that which has so far prevailed over the world, and made it a chaotic pandemonium.

Last summer I saw in a vision, and wrote out a chart of "The History and Destiny of the Race."* The leading idea makes me think that Robert Owen will not realize his beautiful and desirable hopes in this world.

32.

TESTS OF THE CLAIRVOYANT FACULTY IN EUROPE.

NEW YORK, *November* 15, 1847.

IT is truly refreshing and encouraging to hear that foreigners, men of science and authority, have investigated and indorsed the facts of clairvoyance. A friend of psychological progression kindly translates and sends me the following account, which was contained

* See full description in the "Magic Staff."

in a Strasburg paper, called the *Courier of the Lower Rhine*, No. 31, 12th of March, 1807:—

"The history of the somnambulist of Lyons," says the *Journal de Paris*, "presents an assemblage of such striking facts, that we should be inclined to regard the whole as charlatanry and deceit, if credible eye-witnesses had not vouched for the truth of it. People may smile on hearing it asserted, that an hysterical woman possesses the rare gift of revealing future things to those with whom she stands in *rapport*, but such is the case; the wise man believes without precipitation, and doubts with caution. M. Petetain, an esteemed physician in Lyons, who has long watched the progress of the disorder with which the lady is afflicted, is occupied in arranging the facts he has collected, and in preparing them for publication. Previous to the appearance of M. Petetain's announced work, we will adduce the following facts, which are related by a respectable eye-witness, M. Ballanche.

"The catalepsy of a lady in Lyons, had been for some time the subject of conversation in that city; and M. Petetain had already published several very surprising facts relative to it, when M. Ballanche became desirous of being an eye-witness of the astonishing effects of this condition. He chose the moment for visiting this lady when she was approaching the crisis (the time of the magnetic sleep). At the door he learned that not every one, without distinction, was permitted to approach the patient's couch, but that she must herself grant the permission. She was therefore asked if she would receive M. Ballanche; to which she replied in the affirmative: upon this he approached the bed, in which he saw a female lying motionless, and who was to all appearance, sunk into a profound sleep. He laid his hand, as he had been instructed, on the stomach of the somnambulist, and then began his interrogatories. The patient answered them all most correctly. This surprising result only excited the curiosity of the inquirer. He had with him several letters from one of his friends, one of which he took, with whose contents he imagined himself best acquainted, and laid it, folded up, on the stomach of the patient. He then asked the sleeper if she could read the letter, to which she answered yes. He then inquired if it did not mention the name of a certain person whom he named. She denied that it did. M. Ballanche, being certain that the patient was mistaken, repeated the question, and received a similar answer in the negative; the somnambulist even appeared angry at his doubting it, and pushed away the hand of the inquirer and the letter from her. M. Ballanche, struck with this obstinacy, went to one side with the letter, read it, and found to his great astonishment that he had not laid the letter he intended to have selected on the stomach of the sleeper; and that, therefore, the error was on his side. He approached the bed a second time, laid that particular letter on the place; and the patient then said, with a certain degree of satisfaction, that she read the name which he had previously mentioned.

"This experiment would, doubtless, have satisfied most men; but M. Ballanche went still further. He had been told that the patient could see through the darkest substances, and read writing and letters through walls. He asked if this were really the case, to which she replied in the affirmative. He therefore took a book, went into an adjoining room, held with one hand a leaf of this book against the wall, and with the other took hold of one of those that were present, who, joining hands, formed a chain which reached to the patient, on whose stomach the last person laid his hand. The patient read the leaves that were held to the wall, which were often turned over, and read them without making the smallest error.

"This is a faithful and simple relation of what M. Ballanche saw. An infinite number of objections may be brought against it, but a hundred thousand substantial arguments can not overthrow one single fact. The lady still lives, is seen by many impartial persons, and was long attended by an expert and respectable physician who attests the same. The individuals give their names. Who is bold enough still to deny it?"

So far the translation from the Strasburg paper.

This narrative contains nothing that is not confirmed by

numberless experiments: one circumstance is, however, remarkable, that the lady in question *can read at a distance*, without coming into immediatecontact, when a line of persons take hold of each other's hands, the first of whom lays his hand upon the pit of the heart—not of the stomach, which has nothing to do with the matter—and the last holds the letter: however, she reads through neither the partition nor the wall, but through the soul of him who holds the book or letter. By a similar connection or chain, electricity, or the electric shock is communicated. All this is still obscure, but in the sequel it will become clearer.

Equally remarkable, and perhaps still more important, is the observation, to which all confidence may be attached, that somnambulists, when they have attained to a certain high degree of clearness of vision, manifestly and distinctly perceive the thoughts and ideas of him with whom they are placed in *rapport*. He, therefore, who intends to magnetize another, should himself be a person of pure heart, of piety and integrity.

Among so many experiments of this kind, I will only adduce one, which Gmelin relates in a work on the subject. He states that, in the year 1780, he went to Carlsruhe to collect facts relative to magnetism, and found what he was in search of. He was told there was at that time a somnambulist living there, whose inward vision was so clear that she could distinctly read what passed in the souls of those with whom she was placed in connection: If he would, therefore, bring the patients, whom he had then under cure, distinctly in succession before her, she would tell him what his ideas were. He followed this advice, and found the fact was really so: she told him, distinctly, every thing that he imagined. He adds:—

Another individual, of great integrity, and to whom I am much attached, told me that his wife had once a housekeeper, who had also been magnetized on account of illness, and had at length, during her magnetic sleep, attained an extraordinary degree of clearness of vision. In this state she had communicated remarkable and important discoveries concerning the invisible world, which were in exact accordance with a work of mine, entitled "Scenes from the World of Spirits," although she had never seen my book, nor knew, nor could have known, of its existence.

She brought intelligence from the invisible world respecting certain important personages, enough to make the hearer's ears tingle. She once said to her master, in the crisis, "Your brother has just expired at Magdeburg." No one knew any thing of his illness, and, besides this, Magdeburg was many miles distant. A few days after, the news arrived of his death, which exactly agreed with the prediction.

According to our common conceptions of human nature, the fact is astonishing, incomprehensible, and most remarkable, that most somnambulists, even the most vulgar and uneducated people, begin clearly to recognize their bodily illness, and even prescribe the most appropriate medicines for themselves, which the physician must also make use of if he wishes to gain his end. Even if they do not know the names of the remedies, yet they describe their qualities so minutely that the physician can soon ascertain them. In this state, also, they speak high German, where this is the language of the pulpit and the written tongue.*

It is also very remarkable that somnambulists, who have often been in this state and at length attain this clearness of vision, arise, perform all kinds of work, play on an instrument if they have been taught music, go out to walk, &c., without their bodily senses having even the smallest perception of the visible world: they are then in the state of common sleep-walkers. Thus it happened, that while I was at Bremen, in the autumn of the year 1798, a young woman came to me to ask my advice respecting hereyes. She was a somnambulist, and had herself decided upon consulting me in the crisis; her mother accompanied her, but she awoke in my presence, and I was therefore obliged to prescribe the appropriate remedies alone and without her assistance.

All these incidents, and others still more wonderful, may be found in the writings of the above mentioned authors. The most eminent physicians, and, generally speaking, every learned and rational thinking person, who has had the opportunity and the will to examine, with precision, the effects of animal magnetism, will attest that all that has been now advanced is pure truth, and confirm it by their testimony. But how is it that no one has hitherto attempted to draw hence those fertile inferences by which the knowledge of human nature might be so much increased? To the best of my knowledge, no one has yet done so. Truly, so long as materialism is considered as the only true system, it is

* In most parts of Germany, the middle and lower classes speak low German, which varies considerably from the written language.

impossible to comprehend such wonderful things; but, according to my system of theocratic liberty, not only is the whole comprehensible, but we are also led by magnetism to the most important discoveries, which before were only mysterious enigmas. I entreat a candid and impartial investigation of the following conclusions.

Every naturalist knows, and it is generally acknowledged truth, that there is a certain extremely rarefied and active fluid, which fills the whole creation, so far as we are acquainted with it. We call this fluid rarefied celestial air; or, in one word, ether. Newton was acquainted with it, and called it *Sensorium Dei—the organ of Divine sensation.* Euler believed that the bodies of light gave a tremulous motion to this fluid, which extended itself till it reached the sight, and thus formed the light: which opinion I also regarded for a long time as the most probable; but, on close examination, I find it impossible. The million different intersections of this tremulous motion must, necessarily, confuse their direction. Even the definition of sound, by the progressive motion of the atmosphere, is untenable; for if we attentively observe how many thousand tones—sometimes all at once, and at another following each other in rapid succession—are distinguished by the ear in a variously-composed concerto, each of which tones must, therefore, occasion its appropriate motion in the atmosphere: I say, how can such a material motion be possible, without confusing itself a hundred, nay, a thousand times?

It is also acknowledged, further, that this ethereal fluid penetrates through the most compact bodies, so that it fills all things, and is itself perfectly penetrable; for if it were not so, it could not penetrate through the densest bodies. Light, electricity, galvanism, and perhaps also the magnetic power of iron, are, very probably, nothing else than different exhibitions of this one and the same fluid.

33.

CAZOTTE'S PROPHECY FULFILLED DURING THE FRENCH REVOLUTION.

WILLIAMSBURGH, *November* 20, 1847.

A GENTLEMAN, who writes me that he has been "absorbed" in reading the large book of Lectures, thinks I might like to read some demonstrations of the power of prophecy. He writes that a most remarkable instance of the development of the faculty of presentiment is incontestably the prediction of M. Cazotte, at a dinner in Paris. A favorite German periodical work has taken the liberty to ascribe the whole narrative to the invention of some ingenious idler; but this assertion is destitute of proof. Jung Stilling says:—"I can prove, on the contrary, that it is literally and minutely true. I have spoken upon the subject with a person of rank, who sincerely loves the truth, and who was well acquainted with Cazotte: and this individual assured me that Cazotte was a man of great piety, and endowed with a high degree of knowledge; that he frequently predicted the most remarkable things, which were always fulfilled; and that he testified, at the same time, that they were communicated to him by means of intercourse with spirits."

The narrative was found among the papers of the late M. La Harpe, in his own handwriting. This La Harpe was a member of the Royal Academy of Sciences in Paris.

I will first relate the narrative in La Harpe's own words, and then add a few remarks respecting its authenticity. He writes as follows:—

"It seems to me as if it were but yesterday, although it happened at the beginning of the year 1788. We were dining with one of our colleagues of the academy, a man of genius and respectability. The company, which was numerous, was selected from all ranks—courtiers, judges, learned men, academicians, &c., and had done justice to the ample, and, as usual, well-furnished repast. At the dessert, Malvasier and Constantia heightened the festivity, and augmented, in good society, that kind of freedom which does not always keep itself within defined bounds.

"The world had at that time arrived at such a pitch, that it was permitted to say any thing with the intention of exciting merriment. Chamfort had read to us some of his blasphemous and lascivious tales, and noble ladies had listened to them even without having recourse to their fans. After this, followed a whole host of sarcasms on religion. One person quoted a tirade from Pucelle; another reminded the company of that philosophical verse of Diderot's, in which he says, 'Strangle the last king with the entrails of the last priest!'—and all clapped applause. Another stood up, elevating a bumper, and exclaimed, 'Yes, gentlemen, I am just as certain that there is no God, as I am certain that Homer is a fool;' and, in reality, he was as certain of one as the other, for the company had just spoken of Homer and of God, and there were among the guests those who had spoken well of both the one and the other.

"The conversation now became more serious. The revolution that Voltaire had effected was spoken of with admiration; and it was agreed that it was this which formed the principal basis of his fame. He had given the tone to his age; he had written in such a manner, that he was read in both the ante-chamber and the drawing-room. One of the company related to us, with a loud laugh, that his hairdresser, while powdering him, said, 'Look, sir, although I am only a poor journeyman, yet I have no more religion than another!' It was concluded that the revolution would be completed without delay, and that superstition and fanaticism must make way for philosophy. The probable period was calculated, and which of the company would have the happiness of living during the reign of Reason. The more aged lamented that they dared not flatter themselves with the idea; the younger ones rejoiced at the probability that they would live to see it; and the academy, in particular, was congratulated on having prepared the great work, and for being the focus, the center, and the prime mover, of liberty of thought.

"A single individual had taken no part in all this pleasant conversation, and had even very gently scattered some jokes upon their noble enthusiasm. It was M. Cazotte, an amiable and original man, but who, unfortunately, was completely taken up with the reveries of those who believe in a superior enlightening. He now took up the discourse, and said in the most serious tone: 'Gentlemen, rejoice; you will all become witnesses of that great and sublime revolution which you so much desire. You know that I apply myself a little to prophesying: I repeat it, you will all see it.'

"'There requires no prophetic gift for that purpose,' was the reply.

"'True,' rejoined he, 'but perhaps something more for what I am now going to tell you. Do you know what will result from this revolution' (that is, when reason triumphs in opposition to revealed religion)? 'what it will be to you all, as many as are now here? what will be its immediate consequences, its undeniable and acknowledged effects?'

"'Let us see!' said Condorcet, putting on an air of simplicity; 'it is not disagreeable to a philosopher to meet with a prophet.'

"'You, M. Condorcet,' continued M. Cazotte, 'you will give

up the ghost, stretched out on the floor of a subterraneous prison. You will die of poison, that you will have swallowed, in order to escape the executioner—of poison, which the happiness of those times shall compel you always to carry about with you!'

"This, at first, excited great astonishment; but it was soon remembered that the worthy Cazotte sometimes dreamed waking, and the company burst out into a loud laugh. 'M. Cazotte,' said one of the guests, 'the tale you relate to us is not near so amusing as your "Devil in Love."' ('*Le Diable Amoureux*' is a pretty little romance, written by Cazotte.) 'What devil has suggested to you the dungeon, the poison, and the executioner? What has this in common with philosophy and the reign of reason?'

"'This is just what I tell you,' replied Cazotte. 'In the name of philosophy, in the name of humanity, liberty, and reason, will it come to pass, that such will be your end: and reason will then certainly triumph, for she will have her temples; nay, at that period, there will be no other temples in all France than the temples of reason.'

"'Truly,' said Chamfort, with a sarcastic smile, 'you will be no priest of these temples.'

"Cazotte answered: 'I hope not; but you, M. Chamfort, who will be one of them, and are very worthy of being so, you will open your veins by twenty-two incisions of the razor, and yet you will die only some months afterward!'

"The company looked at each other, and laughed again.

"Cazotte continued: 'You, M. Vicq. d'Azyr, will not open your veins yourself, but will afterward cause them to be opened six times in one day in an attack of the gout, in order to make the matter more sure, and you will die the same night!

"'You, M. Nicolai, will die upon the scaffold!—

"'You, M. Bailly, on the scaffold!—

"'You, M. Malesherbes, on the scaffold!'

"'God be thanked!' exclaimed M. Raucher, 'it appears that M. Cazotte has only to do with the academicians: he has just made dreadful havoc among them. I, Heaven be praised—'

"Cazotte interrupted him: 'You!—you will die on the scaffold also!'

"'Ha! this is a wager,' resounded from all sides; 'he has sworn to exterminate us all!'

"*Cazotte.* No, it is not I that have sworn it.

"*The company.* Shall we be then under subjection to Turks and Tartars? and yet—

Cazotte. Nothing less. I have already told you that you will then be under the government of philosophy and reason. Those that will treat you in this manner will be all philosophers; they will be continually making use of those very expressions which you have been mouthing for the last hour; they will repeat all your maxims, and, like you, will quote the verses of Diderot and Pucelle.

"The guests whispered into each other's ears: 'You see clearly that he has lost his reason' (for while speaking thus, he continued very serious). 'Don't you see that he is joking, and in all his jests he mixes something of the wonderful?'—'Yes,' said Chamfort, 'but I must confess his wonders are not very pleasing; they are much too gallows-like. And when shall all this take place?'

"*Cazotte.* Six years shall not pass over before all that I have told shall be fulfilled!

"'You tell us many wonderful things'—it was this time I (La Harpe) that spoke—'and do you say nothing of me?'

"'With respect to you,' answered Cazotte, 'a wonder will take place that will be at least quite as remarkable. You will then be a Christian!'

"A general exclamation! 'Now I am at ease,' said Chamfort; 'if we only perish when La Harpe is a Christian, we are immortal.'

"'We of the female sex,' said the Duchess de Grammont, 'are fortunate in being reckoned as nothing in revolutions. When I say as nothing, I do not intend to say that we do not interfere in them a little; but it is a generally-received maxim that we, and those of our sex, are not deemed responsible on that account.'

"*Cazotte.* Your sex, ladies, will be this time no protection to you; and however little you may be desirous of interfering, yet you will be treated precisely as the men, and no difference will be made with respect to you.

"*The Duchess.* But what is it you are telling us, M. Cazotte? You certainly are announcing the end of the world!

"*Cazotte.* That I know not; but what I do know is, that you, my lady duchess, will be drawn to the scaffold—you, and many other ladies with you—upon a hurdle, with your hands bound behind you.

"*The Duchess.* I hope, however, in that case, that I shall have a mourning-coach.

"*Cazotte.* No, madam! Ladies of higher rank than you will be drawn upon a hurdle, with their hands bound behind them.

"*The Duchess.* Ladies of higher rank? What, the princesses of the blood?

"*Cazotte.* Of still higher rank!

"A visible emotion now manifested itself through the whole company, and the master of the house assumed an air of displeasure. It began to be evident that the joke was carried too far.

"The Duchess de Grammont, in order to dispel the cloud, let the last reply drop, and contented herself with saying, in a most jocular tone, 'You shall see he will not even leave me the consolation of a confessor!'

"*Cazotte.* No, madam; none will be given, either to you or any one else. The last sufferer to whom the favor of a confessor will be granted—(Here he paused a moment.)

"*The Duchess.* Well, who will be the fortunate mortal to whom this privilege will be granted?

"*Cazotte.* It will be the only privilege he will retain, and this will be the king of France!

"The master of the house now hastily arose from the table, and the whole company with him. He went to M. Cazotte, and said with deep emotion, 'My dear Cazotte, this lamentable joke has lasted long enough. You carry it too far, and to a degree in which you endanger yourself, and the company in which you are.'

"Cazotte made no reply, and was preparing to depart, when the Duchess de Grammont, who still endeavored to prevent the matter being taken in a serious light, and labored to restore hilarity, went to him and said, 'Now, Mr. Prophet, you have told us all our fortunes, but have said nothing of your own fate.'

"He was silent, cast his eyes downward, and then said: 'Have you ever read in Josephus, madam, the history of the siege of Jerusalem?'

"*The Duchess.* Certainly; who has not read it? But do as though I had never read it.

"*Cazotte.* Well, madam, during this siege a man went seven successive days upon the walls round the town, in the sight of both the besiegers and the besieged, and cried out incessantly, with a mournful voice, 'Woe to Jerusalem! Woe to Jerusalem!' On the seventh day he cried, 'Woe to Jerusalem, and woe to myself also!' and in the same moment he was crushed to death by an immense stone, hurled from the enemy's engines.

"After these words, M. Cazotte made his bow and departed!"

It is certainly true, that all those who were present at the dinner lost their lives precisely in the manner here predicted by Cazotte. The person who gave the entertainment, to whom Cazotte prophesied nothing, and who was most probably the Duke de Chuiseul, was the only one that died a natural death. The worthy and pious Cazotte was guillotined. . . . . . . If it be supposed that a fanatic or an enthusiast had invented it for the purpose of saying something striking, the nature of the narrative itself, which bears no resemblance to fiction, contradicts such a supposition, to which must be added the certainty that M. La Harpe wrote it with his own hand. It may be found in the

"*Œuvres Choisies et Posthumes*" of M. La Harpe, celebrated member of the French Academy, published at Paris by Mignerol, in four volumes octavo, 1806.

34.

MINISTRATIONS OF REV. T. L. HARRIS.

WILLIAMSBURGH, L. I., *November* 25, 1847.

ABOUT eleven o'clock this morning I entered clairvoyance.* My object was: the present location and prospective condition of the hard-working Brother Harris. He is growing exceedingly nervous and impressible, and will become strangely susceptible to the psychological play of spirits—a very painful and unprofitable form of mediumship, from which I would most gladly shield him. But I see that he is lengthening the distance between us, and presently it will be impossible for me to help him. What an electrical imagination! He looks like an apocalyptic angel! Through him, or by the imaginations of his spirit-touched faculties, Hades will open and send into the world generations of crushed and dumb victims of social sins; the crust of society (he thinks) will crumble under the enormous pressure of his pen; the heavens will send down the fire of destruction upon guilty govern-

* The reader should bear in mind that since the 16th of May last, when the author, without the aid of a magnetizer, passed into the "Superior Condition," he has enjoyed perfect recollections of his various perceptions and investigations.

ments; and the tainted atmosphere of hell will surround all who do not voluntarily forsake their sins. . .

This picture I get out of his present *status*. And yet his mental powers have a large promise of health in them, and energy and practicality; and in years to come he may recover his self-possession, and retire to calmer views of truth and humanity.

35.

SWEDENBORG AND DAVIS COMPARED.

New York, *December* 3, 1847.

An amiable and well-educated gentleman, of the New Jerusalem persuasion, put in my hand this morning an article from the pen of Theophilus Parsons, Esq., of Boston. The gentleman politely said that, in his opinion, it very correctly shows the *difference* between the disclosures of Swedenborg and those which have been presented by Davis and other mesmeric clairvoyants. Mr. Parsons thus proceeds:—

"Now let us compare this case with that of Swedenborg. We perceive at once this important point of difference. Mr. Davis's normal, or natural, or common state, has no apparent connection whatever with his clairvoyant state. Doubtless there is a connection which we can not perceive, between the peculiarities of his constitution—physical, intellectual, or moral—and this extraordinary clairvoyance. But it is certain that neither the amount nor the character of his knowledge while clairvoyant, have any perceptible relation whatever with the amount or character of his knowledge in the natural state. These two things do not differ *in degrees;* that is, Davis does not know a little of cosmogony and philosophy, and think a little about them in his natural state, and then know and think a vast deal more on the same subjects while clairvoyant; but in this last state he has a marvelous quantity of knowledge on topics whereon in his natural state he has never in his life known or thought any one thing great or small.

"In the next place, it does not at all appear that Davis's fitness or capability for this clairvoyance, or for the learning he there acquires or utters, is the result of any intellectual training. He has never been a student, never a practiced and logical thinker; and has never acquired, by careful discipline and sustained endeavor, the power of profound and coherent meditation. It is not by reason of these things, or of any of them, in any degree, that he is able to learn and tell in a state of clairvoyance the wonders of cosmogony, or of any branches of science or philosophy.

"The next thing to observe (and it is one of great importance) is, that Davis, *in his natural state*, knows nothing whatever of his magnetical state. They who looked on and saw can tell him what was done to him and what he did; they who listened and took notes can repeat to him what he said; but of all this he knows nothing himself; absolutely nothing more than if the Davis of the one state and the Davis of the other were two persons, living in distant countries, without any intercourse with, or any knowledge of, each other. And when they who heard him repeat to him what he had said, they repeat it for the most part in vain, for he can comprehend it but very imperfectly; his own reason has not the preparation nor the power required to ascend to this lofty elevation. Thus it is with Mr. Davis; and all of this is in accordance with the usual phenomena of mesmeric clairvoyance, of which Mr. Davis may well be regarded as a type.

"And now how is it with Swedenborg? In the first place, he was prepared for his illumination not only by a thoroughly moral and religious character, but by very many years most diligently and most successfully devoted to the acquisition of a vast fund of knowledge. And this learning, immense in its extent, and embracing most of the branches of science, was nevertheless closely and definitely related to the higher learning which he afterward acquired. It in fact became the foundation of his spiritual knowledge, and served him in comprehending spiritual truths in all their relations, and in illustrating them for the minds of others. In the next place, he was prepared for his illumination by a long and careful intellectual discipline. Naturally a close and steadfast thinker, he became, by study, one of the first mathematicians in the world; and the effect of this exact and rigorous science was to give clearness, precision, and accuracy to his reasoning powers. And all this was for the end that he might use these powers in understanding spiritual truth when it should be opened for him. It was designed for this end, and it had this effect. His eyes were opened, and he saw things of the spiritual world; his ears were opened, and he heard its wisdom; and because of the thorough preparation of his wonderful mind, he understood what he saw, and drew just inferences from the phenomena around him, and grew in the wisdom of heaven while yet an inhabitant of earth. Lastly, and most importantly, between the state of Swedenborg when under illumination, and his normal, natural, or common condition, there was no separation, no disunion, no impassable abyss. What he saw or learnt while under spiritual illumination, *made him wiser in his natural condition.** It was for the purpose of becoming wiser in his natural condition, that his eyes were opened, and his preternatural condition induced; because it was in and through his natural and normal faculties, and by his own laborious exertion of these faculties, that the effect of his own growth in knowledge and wisdom was to be produced upon the world.

"But Swedenborg and Davis agree in this, that their knowledge comes to them in ways which are not the common ways of human nature. Just so far as this goes, there is an analogy between them; but here is its precise limit; for if we go a step

* Judge Parsons wrote this criticism in January, 1847, at which time my state, when magnetized, was precisely as described by him; but on the 16th of May, 1847 (the same year), my two conditions became blended, and still continues precisely analogous to that of Swedenborg.

further; if we look to see whether the ways are the same or similar in the two men, we shall find, instead of resemblance or analogy between them, the marks of difference, of contrast, of opposition. . . . In a few words, and to use an important distinction, made by Swedenborg himself, it is not accurate to say that the wisdom of the heavens came *through* Swedenborg to the earth; but that it came first *to* Swedenborg, and being possessed *by* him, came forth *from* him, by his own act, done *as of himself*.

"We suppose nothing of this kind, and nothing at all like it is true in the case of Davis, or of any mesmeric clairvoyant. There, the rationality of the individual is silenced, superseded, suppressed; or, it is occupied and used by others; his freedom is annihilated. In some cases, the hands and limbs move in obedience to the will of another, and the tongue tastes, the eyes see, the ears hear, and the nose smells, as if the soul of that other was within them; and in other cases, the subject is invigorated with a life not his own, his eye brightens, and his lips pour forth the knowledge and thoughts of other minds, while the subject himself has no more to do with all this than the air whose undulations make the sounds he utters—no more than if he were dead, and it were possible to reanimate his corpse, and make it vocal by galvanism or magic. After a while this possession passes away. The subject returns to his normal state; he is no longer a subject in any sense, but free; no longer another, but himself. And then how is it? Every man who heard him speak has somewhat of what he said when mesmerized; the sense, if it were comprehensible, or the sound of the words at all events in his memory; but the subject, or he who was the subject and then poured forth this utterance, has of it all now, now that he is *himself*, NOTHING. What else, then, can we conclude, than that the state of Swedenborg is as opposite to the state of a clairvoyant, as earnest of a high rationality is opposite to its inaction; as being one's own is opposite to being another's; as freedom itself is opposite to the absolute control of another; as the full and rejoicing exercise of all that constitutes the free, rational, conscious individual, is opposite to its sleep, suspension, or suppression?"

36.

MYSTERIOUS DEVELOPMENTS IN WESTERN NEW YORK.

WILLIAMSBURGH, *March* 31, 1848.

ABOUT daylight this morning, a warm breathing passed over my face, suddenly waking me from a profound slumber; and I heard a voice, tender and yet peculiarly strong, saying: "*Brother! The good work has begun—behold, a living demonstration is born!*" . . . . The breathing and the voice ceased immediately, and I was left wondering what could be meant by such a message.*

37.

REMARKABLE WARNINGS AND PROVIDENCES.

POUGHKEEPSIE, *May* 4, 1848.

A FRIEND has sent me this extract from Jung Stilling: The proof of the truth of the following statement, taken from the *Courrier de l' Europe*, rests upon the fact that the whole occurrence is registered in the judicial records of the criminal trials of the Province of Languedoc. We give it as we heard it from

* Afterward I learned that, at this time, spirit communication was established at Hydesville, New York.

the lips of the dreamer, as nearly as possible in his own words.

As a junior partner in a commercial house at Lyons I had been traveling for some time in the month of June, 1761. I arrived at a town in Languedoc, where I had never before been. I put up at a quiet inn in the suburbs, and being very much fatigued, ordered dinner at once, and went to bed almost immediately after, determined to begin very early in the morning my visits to the different merchants.

I was no sooner in bed than I fell into a deep sleep, and had a dream that made the strongest impression upon me.

I thought that I had arrived at the same town, but in the middle of the day instead of the evening, as was really the case—that I had stopped at the very same inn, and gone out immediately as an unoccupied stranger would do, to see whatever was worthy of observation in the place. I walked down the main street into another street, crossing it at right angles, and apparently leading into the country. I had not gone very far when I came to a church, the Gothic portal of which I stopped to examine. When I had satisfied my curiosity, I advanced to a by-path which branched off from the main street. Obeying an impulse which I could neither account for nor control, I struck into this path, though it was winding, rugged, and unfrequented, and presently reached a miserable cottage, in front of which was a garden covered with weeds. I had no difficulty in getting into the garden, for the hedge had several gaps in it wide enough to admit four carts abreast. I approached an old well which stood, solitary and gloomy, in a distant corner, and looking down into it I beheld distinctly, without any possibility of mistake, a corpse, which had been stabbed in several places. I counted the deep wounds and the wide gashes whence the blood was flowing.

I would have cried out; but my tongue clove to the roof of my mouth. At this moment I awoke with my hair on end, trembling in every limb, and cold drops of perspiration bedewing my forehead—awoke to find myself comfortably in bed, my trunk standing beside me; birds warbling cheerfully around the window; whilst a young, clear voice was singing a provincial air in the next room, and the morning sun was shining brightly through the curtain.

I sprang from my bed, dressed myself, and as it was yet very early I thought I would seek an appetite for my breakfast by a morning walk. I went accordingly into the street and strolled along. The further I went the stronger became the confused recollection of the objects that presented themselves to my view. "It is very strange," I thought, "I have never been here before, and I could swear that I have seen this house and the next, and that other on the left." On I went till I came to the corner of the street crossing the one down which I had come. For the first time I remembered my dream, but put away the thought as too absurd, still, at every step I took, some fresh point of resemblance struck me. "Am I still dreaming?" I exclaimed, not without a momentary thrill through my whole frame. "Is the agreement to be perfect to the very end?" Before long I reached the church with the same architectural features that had attracted my notice in the dream, and then the high road, along which I pursued my way, coming at length to the same by-path that had presented itself to my imagination a few hours before—there was no possibility of doubt or mistake. Every tree, every turn; was familiar to me. I was not at all of a superstitious turn; and was wholly engrossed in the practical details of commercial business. My mind had never dwelt upon the hallucinations, the presentiments that science either denies or is unable to explain, but I must confess that I now felt myself spell-bound as by some enchantment—and, with Pascal's words on my lips—" A continued dream would be equal to reality," I hurried forward, no longer doubting that the next moment would bring me to the cottage, and this really was the case. In all its outward circumstances it corresponded to what I had seen in my dream. Who then could wonder that I determined to ascertain whether the coincidence would hold good in every other point! I entered the garden and went direct to the spot on which I had seen the well; but here the resemblance failed—well there was none. I looked in every direction, examined the whole garden, went round the cottage, which appeared to be inhabited, although no person was visible, but nowhere could I find any vestige of a well.

I made no attempt to enter the cottage, but hastened back to the hotel in a state of agitation difficult to describe; I could not make up my mind to pass unnoticed such extraordinary coincidences—but how was any clue to be obtained to the terrible mystery?

I went to the landlord, and after chatting with him for some time on different subjects, I came to the point and asked him directly to whom the cottage belonged that was on a by-road which I described to him.

"I wonder, sir," said he, "what made you take such particular notice of such a wretched little hovel. It is inhabited by an old man with his wife, who have the character of being very morose and unsociable. They rarely leave the house, see nobody, and nobody goes to see them; but they are quiet enough, and I never heard any thing against them beyond this. Of late, their very existence seems to have been forgotten; and, I believe, sir, that you are the first who, for years, has turned your steps to the deserted spot."

These details, far from satisfying my curiosity, did but provoke it the more. Breakfast was served, but I could not touch it, and I felt that if I presented myself to the merchants in such a state of excitement, they would think me mad; and, indeed I felt very much excited. I paced up and down the room, looked out at the window, trying to fix my attention on some external object; but in vain. I endeavored to interest myself in a quarrel between two men in the street—but the garden and the cottage pre-occupied my mind; and, at last, snatching my hat, I cried—"I will go, come what may."

I repaired to the nearest magistrate, told him the object of my visit, and related the whole circumstance briefly and clearly. I saw directly that he was much impressed by my statement.

"It is indeed very strange," said he, "and after what has happened, I do not think I am at liberty to leave the matter without further inquiry. Important business will prevent my accompanying you in a search, but I will place two of the police at your command. Go once more to the hovel, see its inhabitants, and search every part of it. You may perhaps make some important discovery."

I suffered but a very few moments to elapse before I was on my way, accompanied by the two officers, and we soon reached the cottage. We knocked, and after waiting some time an old man opened the door. He received us somewhat uncivilly, but showed no mark of suspicion, nor, indeed, of any other emotion when we told him we wished to search the house.

"Very well, gentlemen, as fast and as soon as you like," was his reply.

"Have you a well here?" I inquired.

"No, sir; we are obliged to go for water to a spring at a considerable distance."

We searched the house, which I did, I confess, with a kind of feverish excitement, expecting every moment to bring some fatal secret to light. Meanwhile, the man gazed upon us with an impenetrable vacancy of look, and we at last left the cottage without seeing anything that could confirm my suspicions. I resolved to inspect the garden once more, and a number of idlers having been by this time collected, drawn to the spot by the sight of a stranger with two armed men engaged in searching the premises, I made inquiries of some of them whether they knew any thing about a well in that place. I could get no information at first, but at length an old woman came slowly forward, leaning on a crutch.

"A well!" cried she. "Is it the well you are looking after? That has been gone these thirty years. I remember it as if it was only yesterday, how, many a time, when I was a young girl I used to amuse myself throwing stones into it, and hearing the splash they used to make in the water."

"And could you tell where that well used to be?" I asked, almost breathless with excitement.

"As near as I can remember; on the very spot on which your honor is standing," said the old woman.

"I could have sworn it," thought I, springing from the place as if I had trod upon a scorpion.

Need I say that we set to work to dig up the ground. At about eighteen inches deep we came to a layer of bricks, which being broken up, gave to view some boards which were easily removed, after which we beheld the mouth of the well.

"I was quite sure it was here," said the woman. "What a fool the old fellow was to stop it up, and then have to go so far for water!"

A sounding-line furnished with hooks was now let down into the well; the crowd pressing around us, and breathlessly bending over the dark and fetid hole, the secrets of which seemed hidden in impenetrable obscurity. This was repeated several times, without any result. At length, penetrating below the mud, the hooks caught in an old chest, upon the top of which had been thrown a great many large stones, and after much time and effort, we succeeded in raising it to daylight. The sides and lid were decayed and rotten; it needed no locksmith to open it, and we found within what I was certain we should find, and which paralyzed with horror all the spectators who had not my pre-convictions—we found the remains of a human body.

The police officers who had accompanied me, now rushed into the house, and secured the person of the old man. As to his wife—no one could, at first, tell what had become of her; after some search, however, she was found hidden behind a bundle of fagots.

By this time, nearly the whole town had gathered around the spot, and now that this horrible fact had come to light, everybody had some crime to tell of, which had been laid to the charge of the old couple. The people who predict after an event are numerous.

The old couple were brought before the proper authorities and privately and separately examined. The old man persisted in his denial most pertinaciously, but his wife at length confessed, that in concert with her husband she had once, a very long time ago, murdered a peddler whom they had met one night on the high road, and who had been incautious enough to tell them of a considerable sum of money which he had about him, and whom, in consequence, they induced to pass the night at their house. They had taken advantage of the heavy sleep induced by fatigue, to strangle him, his body had been put into the chest, the chest thrown into the well and the well stopped up.

The peddler being from another country, his disappearance occasioned no inquiry; there was no witness of the crime; and as its traces had been carefully concealed from every eye, the two criminals had good reason to believe themselves secure from detection. They had not, however, been able to silence the voice of conscience; they fled from the sight of their fellow-men; they thought they beheld wherever they turned, mute accusers; they trembled at the slightest noise, and silence thrilled them with terror. They had often formed a determination to leave the scene of their crime, to fly to some distant land, but still some undefinable fascination kept them near the remains of their victim.

Terrified by the deposition of his wife, and unable to resist the overwhelming proofs against him, the man at length made a similar confession, and, six weeks after, the unhappy criminals died on the scaffold, in accordance with the sentence of the Parliament of Toulouse. They died penitent.

The well was once more shut up, and the cottage leveled to the ground; it was not, however, until fifty years had in some measure deadened the memory of the terrible transaction, that the ground was cultivated. It is now a fine field of corn.

Such was the dream and its result.

I never had the courage to revisit the town where I had been an actor in such a tragedy. The story was told again by me last winter in a company where it gave rise to a long and animated discussion upon the credibility to be attached to dreams. Ancient and modern history was ransacked to find arguments on both sides. Plutarch was quoted in what he says of a certain Lysimachus, grandson to Aristides, who embraced the profession of interpreter of dreams, and realized wealth by the trade—Cicero states that a dream of Cecilla, daughter of Barbaricus, appeared to be of sufficient importance to be a subject of a decree of the Senate. One of the most indefatigable commentators of the sixteenth century, Cœlius Rhodizinus, when laboring to correct the text of Pliny which he has singularly obscured, was stopped by the word *ectrapelis.*

In vain did he work at the meaning for a whole week—he ended by falling asleep—and in a dream the solution of the difficulty came into his head. It was during sleep that Henricus Van Heeres, a Dutch writer, very celebrated in his day, but very obscure in ours, composed all his works; once awake, he had but to transcribe from memory.

38.

RETURNING TO THE PULPIT.

POUGHKEEPSIE, *May* 9, 1848.

YESTERDAY'S mail brought me a kindly note from a New York artist. He informs me that Brother Harris, the brilliant preacher and poet, is already returning to the pulpit. He says that the exercises on Sunday afternoon, in the Coliseum, were attended by a large and highly intellectual audience. Among those present, he noticed Rev. W. H. Channing, of Boston, Horace Greeley, and Freeman Hunt, and many other eminent citizens. The discourse was on the "Religious Tendencies of the Age." Arrangements will be made during the week for obtaining a hall in Broadway, and the poet will preach at least once on every Sunday. It is believed that one of the largest and most intellectual congregations in the city will speedily be gathered around the inspiring minister. . . . . . This news does not surprise me, neither would it astonish me to hear that Brother H. had renounced the spiritual idea of infinite progression, and returned to the bosom of the endless punishment church.

39.

AGREEMENT BETWEEN SWEDENBORG AND DAVIS.

POUGHKEEPSIE, *May* 15, 1848.

MY impression this beautiful morning is to call the world's attention to fundamental agreements between the teachings of clairvoyance and those of Swedenborg. Let his "friends" read the following :—

THAT THE END OF CREATION IS A HEAVEN OUT OF THE HUMAN RACE.—That heaven consists only of such as were born men, ... and as heaven does not consist of any others, it follows that *the end of creation is a heaven out of the human race.* But the same will be still more manifestly seen from an explanation of the following points: 1. That every man is created to live to eternity. 2. That every man is created to live to eternity in a state of happiness. 3. That every man is created to go to heaven. 4. That the divine Love can not do otherwise than desire it, and that the divine Wisdom can not do otherwise than provide for it. Since, from these considerations it may also be seen that the Divine Providence is no other predestination than to heaven, and that it can not be changed into any other, it is here to be demonstrated, in the order proposed, that the end of creation is a heaven out of the human race.—D. P. 323, 324.

THAT TO SUPPOSE THAT THOSE ONLY ARE SAVED WHO ARE BORN WITHIN THE CHURCH, IS AN INSANE HERESY.—Those who are born without the Church are men, as well as those who are born within it; they are of the same heavenly origin, and are equally living and immortal souls; they have a religion by which they acknowledge that there is a God, and that they ought to live well; and he that acknowledges that there is a God, and lives well, becomes spiritual in his degree and is saved.

THAT TO SUPPOSE ANY OF THE HUMAN RACE ARE PREDESTINED TO BE DAMNED, IS A CRUEL HERESY.—For it is cruel to think that the Lord, who is Love itself, and Mercy itself, would suffer so vast a multitude of men to be born for hell, or that so many myriads of myriads should be born condemned and devoted, that is, born devils and Satans; and that he would not out of his divine wisdom provide, that those who live well and acknowledge a God, should not be cast into everlasting fire and torment. . . . . He alone leads all, and wills not the death of any one. Therefore it is cruel to think and believe that so great a multitude of nations and people under his auspices and inspection, should be predestined to be delivered as a prey to the devil.—D. P. 330.

THAT THESE ARE THE COMMON ESSENCE OF ALL RELIGIONS BY WHICH EVERY ONE IS SAVED.—To acknowledge a God, and not to do evil because it is against God, are the two things by virtue of which religion is religion. If one of them is wanting, it can not be called religion; for to acknowledge a God, and to do evil is contradictory, as well as to do good and not acknowledge a God: one does not take place without the other. It is provided by the Lord that there is some religion almost everywhere, and that in every religion there are these two essentials.—D. P. 326.

40.

DUG'S STORY OF THE LIVES OF TWO BOYS.

POUGHKEEPSIE, *June* 4, 1848.

A CURIOUS circumstance occurred about two hours ago. Passing a newspaper and periodical store on Main street, idly musing as I went, all at once I heard a tongue distinctly speak near my left ear:—"*Read Dug's Yarn! Remember your promise! Read Dug's Story of the Two Boys!*" Instantly, the incidents of the visit from the old sailor, last year, came back into my mind. I entered the store. On looking and handling over the papers, a *hot* sensation from one attracted my attention. I examined the paper, and found a part of a story, by DOUGLAS JERROLD, giving the history of the lives of two boys, of whom one was born to wealth, rank, education, respectability, and luxury; the other to famine, ignorance, shame, vice, and crime. "St. Giles," has been tried for stealing the pony of "St. James," and found guilty. It will be keeping my promise to read "Dug's Story," of which the following is the fragment:—

"GUILTY—DEATH!"

What familiar syllables were these in the good old times—the time of our history! In those happier days, how many goods and chattels, live stock and dead, were protected, watched by Death! Death was made by law the guardian of all things. Prime agent, great conservator of social security—grim keeper of the world's movables. Death, a shepherd, avenged the wrongs of stolen mutton: Death stood behind every counter, protector of chapman's stock; Death was the day and the night guard of the highway traveler against the highway thief; Death watched ox and ass; the goose on the common, the hen on the roost. Even at the altar, Death took his cautious stand, that Hymen might not be scoffed, defrauded by wicked bigamist. Turn where he would, the rogue's path was dug with graves. Nevertheless, the world grew no better; made no visible return to that happy state, ere hemp was made a sovereign remedy for wrong. And so by degrees, Death lost somewhat of his reputation with the members of the world; and by degrees many things were taken out of his charge. It was found that—sheep were stolen—tradesmen's goods lifted—pockets picked—hen-roosts forced—and maids wickedly married by men already bound—it was seen that these abominations continued and increased, ay, in the very face of the great ghastly bugbear, Death, and so his watch and ward were made a lighter task; he was gradually relieved of many of his social duties; the world, to the astonishment of some folks, still spinning on its axis, though the life of immortal man was not, as in the good old times, offered to stolen colt, to the king's gracious face unlawfully stamped in counterfeit metal, to a hundred other sins all made mortal by the wisdom of untaught humanity. Truly, Justice, turning back the leaves of the jail calendar, might sit awhile in sackcloth and ashes, penitent for past transgressions—past wrongs committed in her moral blindness! The sword of justice! An awful weapon, truly: a weapon working out the will of highest Providence: a solemn interest which man solemnly acknowledges. This has been, and may be. Yet, thinking of the world's mistakes; of the cruel blunders worked by law on man, the sword of justice—of so-called Christian justice robed and ermined—may sometimes seem to the eye of grieved humanity as terrible as the blood-dripping tomahawk of the wild, revengeful savage. The sword of justice! May not the time come—it *will* come, as surely as the sun of far-off years—when Justice shall lay down her sword—when, with better wisdom, she shall vindicate her awful mission to mankind, yet shed no drop of blood!

Let us return to St. Giles; to the boy in his fifteenth year, spawned upon the world and reared by daily wrong and ignorance, a morsel for the hangman. Now, a condemned thief, palsied and aghast with terror, upon the very threshold of the world; to be flung therefrom, an offering to the majesty of offended law. Grim majesty—ghastly Moloch! Stately wickedness, with robes dyed in the blood of sinning ignorance! A majesty that the principle of all evil may too often smile upon as its working genius here on earth. A majesty as cold and pulseless as the idol whose wooden nostrils know not the sacrifices its darkened worshipers prepare it. But St. Giles will now know there is a government—a knot of the wise and good, whose harmonious souls combined make up the music of the State; the moral melody that softens and refines the rugged, dull-eared mass. He will now know this; the hangman will teach it him. A sharp, short lesson; the first and last prepared him by a paternal State.

"Guilty--death!" Such was the verdict. Tom Blast breathed heavily, and a faint smile flickered at his lips as he felt assured of his escape. Still, he durst not turn his eye toward his boy-victim in the dock. Conscience was at the felon's heart; and seared, withered as it was, it felt the sudden horror of remorse. His features grew pale, then dark; were for a moment convulsed; then instantly—daring no look at St. Giles—he disappeared from the dock. The boy stared about him with a foolish gaze, and then began to sob. There was no terror--no anguish in his face. It was the grief of a boy doomed to a whipping, not the gibbet; and it was such sorrow—such seeming childish ignorance of the impending horror—that to those who looked upon him made his condition more terrible. And then again it seemed impossible that the sentence, so sonorously uttered, should be carried out. Could it be that such an array of judges--such wisdom, such learning, such grave and reverend experience--should be opposed to a miserable child, of no more self-accountability than a dog? Appalling odds! Could it be thought that the scene was a frightful reality of daily, breathing life? Was it not a grim farce--a hideous foolish mockery? Could the wise hearts of men—fathers of well-taught, well-tended, happy children—doom that child to death? That miserable item of human ignorance--that awful reproach to those who made laws to protect property, but left the outcast poor a heedless prey to their own unbridled instincts? Nevertheless, the law would hang St. Giles; and grave, respectable, church-going men, in the very cosiness of their ignorance, would clasp their hands, and raise their eyes, and pity and wonder at the wickedness of the new generation. . . . .

And young St. Giles lay in Newgate, sinking, withering, under sentence of death. After a time, he never cried, or clamored; he shed no tear, breathed no syllable of despair; but, stunned, stupefied, seemed as if idiocy was growing on him. The ordinary—a good, zealous man—endeavored, by soothing, hopeful words, to lead the prisoner, as the jail phrase has it, to a sense of his condition. Never had St. Giles received such teaching! Condemned to die, he for the first time heard of the abounding love of Christianity—of the goodness and affection due from man to man. The story seemed odd to him; strange, very strange; yet he supposed it was all true. Nevertheless—he could not dismiss the thought, it puzzled him. Why had he never been taught all this before? And why should he be punished, hanged, for doing wrong; when the good, rich, fine people, who all of them love their neighbors like themselves, had never taught him what was right? Was it possible that Christianity was such a beautiful thing—and being so, was it possible that good, earnest, kind-hearted Christians would kill him?

St. Giles had scarcely eight-and-forty hours to live. It was almost Monday noon, when the ordinary—having attended the other prisoners—entered the cell of the boy thief. He had been separated, by the desire of the minister, from his miserable companions, that their evil example of hardihood—their reckless bravado—might not wholly destroy the hope of growing truth within him. A turnkey attended St. Giles, reading to him. And now the boy would raise his sullen eyes upon the man, as he read of promises of grace and happiness eternal; and now his heart would heave as though he was struggling with an inward agony that seemed to suffocate him—and now a scornful, unbelieving smile would play about his mouth—and he would laugh with defying bitterness. And then he would leer in the face of the reader, as though he read to him some fairy tale, some pretty story, to amuse and gull him. Poor wretch! Let the men who guide the world—the large-brained politicians who tinker the social scheme, making themselves the masters and guardians of their fellow-men—let them look into this Newgate dungeon; let them contemplate this blighted human bud; this child-felon, never taught the path of right, and now to be hanged for his most sinful ignorance. What a wretched, sullen outcast! What a darkened, loathsome thing! And now comes the clergyman—the State divine, be it remembered—to tell him that he is treasured with an immortal soul; that—with mercy shed upon him—he will in a few hours be a creature of glory before the throne of God! Oh, politicians! Oh, rulers of the world! Oh, law-making masters and taskers of the common million, may not this cast-off wretch, this human nuisance, be your accuser at the bar of Heaven? Egregious folly! Impossible! What—stars and garters impeached by rags and tatters! St. James denounced by St. Giles! Impudent and ridiculous! Yet here, we say, comes the reverend priest—the Christian preacher, with healing, honeyed words, whose Book—*your* Book—with angelic utterance, says no less. Let us hear the clergyman and his forlorn pupil.

"Well, my poor boy," said the ordinary, with an affectionate voice and moistening eyes: "well my child, and how is it with you? Come, you are better; you look better; you have been listening to what your good friend Robert here has been reading to you. And we are all your friends, here. At least we all want to be. Don't you think so?"

St. Giles slowly lifted his eyes toward the speaker. He then slowly, sullenly, answered,—"No, I don't."

"But you ought to try to think so, my boy; it's wicked not to try," said the ordinary, very tenderly.

"If you're all my friends, why do you keep me here?" said St. Giles. "Friends! I never had no friends."

"You must not say that; indeed, you must not. All our care is to make you quiet and happy in this world, that you may be happier in the world you're going to. You understand me, St. Giles? My poor, dear boy, you understand me? The world you're going to?" The speaker, inured as he was to scenes of blasphemy, of brute indifference, and remorseful agony, was deeply touched by the forlorn condition of the boy; who could not, would not, understand a tenderness, the end of which was to surrender him softened to the hangman. "You have thought, my dear—I say, you have thought of the world"—and the minister paused—"the world you are going to?"

"What's the use of thinking about it?" asked St. Giles. "I knows nothing of it."

"That, my boy, is because you are obstinate, and I am sorry to say it, wicked,—and so won't try to know about it. Otherwise, if you would give all your heart and soul to prayer——"

"I tell you, sir, I never was learnt to pray," cried St. Giles, moodily; "and what's the use of praying?"

"You would find it open your heart, St. Giles; and though you see nothing now, if you were only to pray long and truly, you would find the darkness go away from your eyes, and you'd see such bright and beautiful things about you, and you'd feel as light and happy as if you had wings at your back—you would, indeed. Then you'd feel that all we are doing for you is for the best; then, my poor boy," said the ordinary with growing fervor, "then you'd feel what Christian love is."

"Robert's been reading to me about that," said St. Giles, "but I can't make it out nohow. He says that Christian love means that we shouldn't do to nobody what we wouldn't like nobody to do to ourselves."

"A good boy," said the ordinary, "that is the meaning, though not the words. I'm glad you've so improved."

"And for all that, you tell me that I must think o' dying—think of another world and all that—think of going to Tyburn, and, and"—here the boy fell hoarse, his face turned ash-color, and reeling, he was about to fall, when the ordinary caught him in his arms, and again placed him on a seat. "It's nothin'—nothin'—nothin' at all," cried St. Giles, struggling with himself—"I'm all right; I'm game."

"Don't say that, child; I can't hear you say that:

I would rather see you in tears and pain than trying to be game, as you call it. That, my boy, is only adding crime to wickedness. Come, we were talking of Christian love," said the ordinary.

"I knows nothin' about it," said St. Giles; "all I know is this—it isn't true; it can't be true."

"Tell me, why not! Come, let me hear all you'd say," urged the clergyman, tenderly.

"'Cause if it means that nobody should do to nobody what nobody would like to have done to themselves, why does any body keep me locked up here? Why did the judge say I was to be—you know, Mister?"

"That was for doing wrong, my boy: that was for your first want of Christian love. You were no Christian when you stole the horse," said the ordinary. "Had the horse been yours, you would have felt wronged and injured had it been stolen from you? You see that, eh, my boy?"

"Didn't think o' that," said St. Giles, gloomily. "But I didn't steal it: 'twas all along 'o Tom Blast; and now he's got off; and I'm here in the Jug. You don't call that justice, no how, do you? But I don't care; they can do what they like with me; I'll be game."

"No, my dear boy, you must know better: you must, indeed—you must give all your thoughts to prayer, and——"

"It's 'o no use, Mister; I tell you I never was learnt to pray, and I don't know how to go about it. More than that, I feel somehow ashamed to it. And besides, for all your talk, Mister, and you talk very kind to me, I must say, I can't feel like a Christian, as you call it,—

for I can't see why Christians should want to kill me if Christians are such good people as you talk about."

"But then, my poor boy," said the ordinary, "though young, you must remember, you're an old sinner. You've done much wickedness."

"I never done nothing but what I was taught; and if you say—and Bob there's been reading it to me—that the true Christian forgives everybody—well, then, in course, the judge and all the nobs are no Christians, else wouldn't they forgive me? Wouldn't they like it so, to teach me better, and not to kill me? But I don't mind; I'll be game; see if I don't be game—precious!"

The ordinary, with a perplexed look sighed, deeply. The sad condition of the boy, the horrid death awaiting him, the natural shrewdness with which he combated the arguments employed for his conversion, affected the worthy clergyman beyond all past experience. "Miserable little wretch!" he thought, "it will be worst of murders, if he dies thus." And then, again, he essayed to soften the child felon, who seemed determined to stand at issue with his spiritual counselor; to recede no step, but to the gallows foot to defy him. It would be his ambition, his glory—if he must die—to die game. He had heard the praises bestowed upon such a death—had known the contemptuous jeering flung upon the repentant craven—and *he* would be the theme of eulogy in Hog Lane—*he* would not be laughed, sneered at, for "dying dunghill." And this temper so grew and strengthened in St. Giles, that, at length, the ordinary, wearied and hopeless, left his forlorn charge, promising soon to return, and hoping, in his own words, to find the prisoner "a kinder, better, and more Christian boy."

"It's no use your reading that stuff to me," said St. Giles, as the turnkey was about to resume his book. "I don't understand nothin' of it; and it's too late to learn. But I say, can't you tell us somethin' of Turpin and Jack Sheppard, eh? Something prime, to give us pluck!"

"Come, come," answered the man, "it's no use going on in this way. You must be quiet and listen to me; it's all for your good, I tell you; all for your good."

"My good! Well that's pretty gammon, that is. I should like to know what can be for my good if I'm to be hanged? Ha! ha! See if I don't kick my shoes off, that's all." And St. Giles would *not* listen; but sat on the stool, swinging his legs backward and forward, and singing one of the melodies known in Hog Lane—poor wretch! it had been a cradle melody to him—whilst the turnkey vainly endeavored to soothe and interest him. At length the man discontinued his hopeless task; and, in sheer listlessness, leaning his back against the wall, fell asleep. And now St. Giles was left alone. And now, relieved of importunity, did he forego the bravado that had supported him, and solemnly think of his approaching end? Did he, with none other but the eye of God, in that stone cell, upon him—did he shrink and wither beneath the look; and, on bended knees, with opened heart, and flowing, repentant tears, did he pray for heaven's compassion—God's sweet mercy? No. Yet thoughts, deep, anxious thoughts were brooding in his heart. His face grew older with the meditation that shadowed it. All his being seemed compressed, intensified in one idea. Gloomily, yet with whetted eyes, he looked around his cell; and still darker and darker grew his face. Could he break prison? Such was the question—the foolish, idle, yet flattering question—that his soul put to itself. All his recollections of the glory of Turpin and Sheppard crowded upon him—and what greater glory would it be for him if he could escape! He, a boy, to do this? He to be sung in ballads—to be talked of, huzzaed, and held up for high example, long after he should be dead—passed forever from the world? The proud thought glowed within him—made his heart heave—and his eyes sparkle. And then he looked about his cell, and the utter hopelessness of the thought fell upon him, withering his heart. Yet again and again—although to be crushed with new despair—he gazed about him, dreaming of liberty without that wall of flint. And thus his waking hours passed; and thus, in the visions of the night, his spirit busied itself in hopeful vanity.

The Tuesday morning came, and again the clergyman visited the prisoner. The boy looked paler, thinner—no more. There was no softness in his eyes, no appealing glance of hope; but a fixed and stubborn look of inquiry. "He didn't know nothing of what the parson had to say, and he didn't want to be bothered. It was all gammon!" These were the words of the boy felon, then—such was the humanity of the law; poor law! what a long nonage of discretion has it passed!—then within a day's span of the grave.

As the hour of death approached, the clergyman became more assiduous, fervent, nay, passionate in his appeals to the prisoner; who still strengthened himself in opposition to his pastor. "My dear boy—my poor child—miserable, helpless creature!—the grave is open before you—the sky is opening above you! Die without repentance, and you will pass into the grave, and never—never know immortal blessings! Your soul will perish—perish, as I have told you—in fire, in fire eternal!"

St. Giles swayed his head to and fro, and with a sneer, asked, "What's the good o' all this? Haven't you told me so, Mister, agin and agin?"

The ordinary groaned almost in despair, yet still renewed his task. "The heavens, I tell you, are opening for you: repent, my child; repent, poor boy, and you will be an immortal spirit, welcomed by millions of angels."

St. Giles looked with bitter incredulity at his spiritual teacher. "Well, if all that's true," he said, "it isn't so hard to be hanged, arter all. But I don't think the nobs like me so well as to send me to sich a place as that."

"Nay, my poor boy," said the ordinary, "you will not, can not understand me, until you pray. Now, kneel—my dear child, kneel, and let us pray together." Saying this, the ordinary fell upon his knees; but St. Giles, folding his arms, so placed himself as to take firmer root of the ground; and so he stood, with moody, determined looks, whilst the clergyman—touched more than was his wont—poured forth a passionate prayer that the heart of the young sinner might be softened; that it might be turned from stone into flesh, and become a grateful sacrifice to the throne of God. And whilst this prayer, in deep and solemn tones, rose from the prison-cell, he for whom the prayer was formed seemed to grow harder, more obdurate, with every syllable. Still he refused to bend his knee at the supplication of the clergyman, but stood eying him with a mingled look of incredulity, defiance, and contempt. "God help you—poor lost lamb!" cried the ordinary, as he rose.

"Now, I hope we shall have no more of that," was the only answer of St. Giles.

The ordinary was about to quit the cell, when the door was opened, and the governor of the jail, attended by the head turnkey, entered. "My dear sir, I am glad to find you here," said the governor to the ordinary. "I have a pleasing duty to perform; a duty that I know it will delight you to witness." The ordinary glanced at a paper held by the governor; his eyes brightened; and clasping his hands, he fervently uttered—"Thank God!"

The governor then turned to St. Giles, who suddenly looked anxious and restless. "Prisoner," he said, "it is my happiness to inform you that his gracious majesty has been mercifully pleased to spare your life. You will not suffer with the unfortunate men to-morrow. You understand me, boy"—for St. Giles looked suddenly stupefied—"you understand me, that the good king, whom you should ever pray for, has, in the hope that you will turn from the wickedness of your ways, determined to spare your life? You will be sent out of the country; and time given you that, if you properly use, will make you a good and honest man."

St. Giles made no answer, but trembled violently from head to foot. Then his face flushed red as flame, and covering it with his hands, he fell upon his knees, and the tears ran streaming through his fingers. "Pray with me; pray for me!" he cried, in a broken voice, to the ordinary.

41.

CLAIRVOYANT PERCEPTION OF JESUS.

WILLIAMSBURGH, *August* 10, 1848.

SOME instances of a miraculous knowledge in the life of Jesus may remind us of the "*clear-and-long-sightedness*" of persons in a magnetic state, or of those in a similar condition. As Jesus saw Nathaniel under the fig-tree, so magnetic persons see their physician, their relatives, and sometimes even indifferent individuals, in distant houses and remote parts of the country; as he spoke to the woman of Samaria of her six husbands, so magnetic somnambulists (adds Strauss) have frequently read the most secret concerns in the hearts of those with whom they were conversing; and as he knew in what part of the lake a quantity of fish had crowded together, unnoticed by his disciples, though they were experienced fishermen, so there are persons who are able to tell where metals or bones are buried, where water is concealed under thick layers of earth, and some even, to whom the body of others is transparent as it were, so that they can see its innermost parts, and describe their condition or ailment, as the case may be.

42.

IMPRESSIONS OF HORACE GREELEY.

WILLIAMSBURGH, *October* 18, 1848.

TO-DAY I ventured into the presence of Mr. Horace Greeley. My only object was to call his personal attention to my just published Chart of the "History and Destiny of the Race," and to ask him if he would have the goodness to give it a little editorial notice. He was writing, when I entered, on a slanting board projecting from the wall, sitting uncomfortably in a very old chair; his right arm and hand on a level with his shoulder; his face almost touching the "copy" and his hand as he wrote. I coughed a little, and stepped about the floor quite emphatically for a few moments, and so got his attention. He leaned carelessly back in his chair, turned his pure and honest face toward me, squinted his eyes as if trying to see, and extended his left hand with an air of supreme indifference, signifying as plainly as if spoken: "Shake my hand if you want to, but don't bother me long." Advancing timidly, I shook his lazy-feeling left hand. At once I showed him the Chart, and hoped he would have time to look it over, and to give it a little notice in his *Tribune*. He put his eyes close up to the sheet as I held it unrolled before his face, and, seeing the caption:

"Progressive History," said, bluntly and decisively, "Don't believe that! Society in New York is no better than it was in the days of Charlemagne." After one or two more similar expressions, he said: "You can leave it. I'll look at it when I get time." Accordingly, I left the Chart in his editorial corner, and gladly withdrew.

I came straight to this room, and these are my impressions of Horace Greeley, to wit: Under pressure and excitement, he is firm as a rock. Will not give up a cherished idea; will do what seems right for him to do, though the heavens fall; unless he is peculiarly approached by the magnetism, rather than by the reasoning, of gentle and trustworthy friends. His mind, on one side, is hard as flint; on the other, his mental nature is tender and sympathetic as a child. He is, therefore, an inconsistency. His efforts and his prayers are benevolently for the millions. If aware, or if he imagines, that a person or party is trying to control him, he is immovable. His creed is, "Give to all their natural rights!" Clear in what he sees, and faithful to the suggestions of his own flinty intelligence, he yet has not the philosophical capacity to grasp the spiritual springs within the growth of individuals and nations. He distinctly sees that the earth-toiler was not meant for a throne, or for despotic power, nor that it was God's intent that man should ever become a victim or a criminal; but how to organize industry and exalt labor, and especially how to overcome fraud in high places, is too frequently beyond Mr. Greeley's comprehension. Yet, his ruling principle is, to try every available and logical remedy that looks like a genuine reformation for the people; and through his life, as a stain of ink seen in the beauty of a white garment, will ever stream this palpable misapplication of remedies. . . .

A feeling possesses me this moment, amounting to a kind of sadness, with respect to Mr. Greeley, namely: His long devotion to journalism will be a loss to literature; and what he has done, or may do, in politics, can never be to mankind a sufficient compensation. When I stood by his side, only two hours ago, I was conscious of an access of intellectual strength. His mind is capable of large industry not only, but of gaining and imparting the greatest fund of practical knowledge. A hint, a single word, a suggestion, teaches Mr. Greeley many great lessons. There is, too, an undefinable tenderness of expression in the atmosphere of his face, so to speak, which says to me: "Behind the editor—within the intellectual faculties, and beneath the moral energies of this every-day man—there lives a genius, a rare and beautiful mind, which could multiply itself many times in poetry and literature." But, alas! the god of UTILITY, the practical Benjamin Franklinism of turning every thing into account in this day, and in this hour, has found in him a perpetual worshiper.

43.

A DEAD BODY FOUND BY CLAIRVOYANCE.

NEW YORK, *December* 6, 1848.

MY attention has just been called to the following account published in the Boston *Chronotype*:—

About the 20th of February, 1846, a young man named John S. Bruce, aged about 18 years, son of Mr. Lewis Bruce, a respectable farmer in Westford, Middlesex County, Mass., started from his father's residence with a span of horses and a sled-load of straw, for the purpose of selling the latter in this city. The distance being only twenty-five miles, he was expected to return the following day. Days, weeks, and months passed, however, and no tidings were heard of him by his anxious family, though diligent search and inquiry were made—and his friends accordingly remained in a distressing quandary, whether it was possible he had left for parts unknown or some fatal evil had befallen him.

We will here mention an apparently trifling incident, but one which resulted in furnishing the first clue to information concerning young Bruce.

It appears that Mr. Otis Hildreth, a neighbor—who subsequently removed from Westford to Salem, N. H., —arranged with Bruce to take to Boston a small keg to be filled with molasses for him—which, of course, was never returned. Mr. Hildreth came to the city on business in the succeeding month of July, and happening to call in at the office connected with the stable of Edward Eastman, in Deacon Street, *saw his keg there*, and identified it by several marks. On inquiry, he was told that it had been left there during the winter previous, together with a span of horses, which, after being kept seventeen days without being called for, were advertised by Eastman and sold at auction, and that there was a balance of between five and six dollars after deducting expenses, due the owner of the horses when he should make his appearance. From the accounts given, Mr. Hildreth was satisfied that the horses were those driven by young Bruce, but of the latter he could gain no intelligence except a faint remembrance that a person of singular description had been seen around the stable sometime the previous winter.

Upon his return to Salem, Mr. Hildreth wrote to Mr. Bruce at Westford, stating the above circumstances—which very naturally excited in the mind of the father a revival of hope that he might trace from them some knowledge of his absent son. He accordingly promised soon to come to Boston for the purpose of making inquiries, but could learn nothing further than that his son was last seen on the sidewalk near the stable referred to. His name was also found recorded on the hayweigher's book, but another name was registered at the stable as the person by whom the horses were left.

Some time after this, Mr. Bruce was induced by the solicitation of friends—though himself an unbeliever in Mesmerism—to come to the city and employ the clairvoyant power of Mrs. Freeman, in Lyman Place—a practitioner somewhat celebrated for her success in similar cases—in further inquiry respecting his son. The clairvoyant made some startling developments, which were repeated at subsequent examinations attended both by Mr. Bruce and a daughter who resided in Lowell; and from the investigations which they were able to make, it was conclusive to them that there was much truth in the statements, although, from the nature of the case, it was difficult to ascertain certain things thus revealed, or even to connect the several links of evidence so as to form a tolerably complete chain.

The principal features of the clairvoyant's revelations—drawn out in fragments at different times—comprised the known facts detailed above concerning young Bruce's journey to Boston, with the declarations that shortly after his arrival he was induced by certain persons to take something to drink, which threw him into convulsions, of which he died—that his body was concealed for some time under a manure heap, but afterward taken by a colored man in the night time, carried out upon the water and sunk in the harbor—that it was subsequently discovered, and was *to be found in a certain tomb in the City burial-ground on the Neck!* The clairvoyant also stated that the drug was administered to Bruce for the purpose of obtaining money, &c., which he was supposed to possess, and that a certain individual cognizant of these transactions had since been dangerously ill, and came near divulging them, &c., &c.

These representations so inflamed the curiosity of Mr. Bruce and others to inspect the cemetery, that on Tuesday afternoon last, accompanied by Mr. Franklin Smith, one of the city undertakers, they proceeded thither for an examination. Abiding by the minute instructions he had received from the clairvoyant, Mr. Bruce requested that Tomb No. 15 might be opened, and if the remains of his son were not in the lowest coffin in that tomb, he would be satisfied without further search. Mr. Smith accordingly pulled down some dozen or fifteen coffins, and on prying up the lid of the lower one, *mirabile dictu!* the father recognized the dress of his son within the coffin!—he having been entombed with his clothes on, as is usual when bodies are found in a decayed condition. Of the remains nothing was left save a portion of the stomach, which appeared to be in a singular state of preservation, some locks of light auburn hair, and teeth, two of which were also identified by the father from some peculiar appearances. A wallet was also found about the clothing, which contained no money, but a few buttons, needles and thread. A pocket-book which the deceased brought with him to the city was not found. It was evident he was buried under a false name, as his proper name was not to be found on the Superintendent's books, and but one—a colored man—had been interred as "unknown."

Mr. Bruce took from the coffin a piece of the pantaloons, the vest, and the other articles described, and returned home. As soon as it was seen, the clothing was recognized by members of the family, and a storekeeper identified the buttons, needles, and thread as sold by him to young Bruce the day before he left Westford.

The identity of the remains being thus clearly established, the father, on application to Mr. Lincoln, Superintendent of Burials, was granted a permit to remove them, and on Friday afternoon he conveyed them home, stating that he would have the stomach analyzed; and thus this singularly mysterious case rests at present.

44.

J. G. WHITTIER'S ACCOUNT OF MESMERIC REVELATIONS.

BOSTON, *May* 7, 1849.

I HAD the pleasure to-day of seeing in a Cambridge stage the plain-looking man who wrote "The Reformer," parts of which my old friend Ira Armstrong used to quote with such enthusiasm. In Mr. Whittier's "Stranger in Lowell," p. 102, he says:—

It is too late now to regard mesmerism wholly as charlatanry and imposture—to rank its phenomena with the tricks of Cagliostro and Count St. Germain. Grant, if you will, that the everlasting and ubiquitous quack has taken advantage of it—that he has engrafted upon its great fact the fictitious and shallow legerdemain of common jugglery—still a FACT remains, attested by unnumbered witnesses, which clashes with all our old ideas and our habitual experience—which throws open the door for "thick-coming fancies," and interminable speculations—a miracle made familiar—an impossibility realized—the old fable of transfusion of spirit made actual—the mysterious trance of the Egyptian priesthood reproduced. This first fact in mesmerism dimly reveals a new world of wonder—a faint light falling into the great shadow of the mystery which environs us like an atmosphere of night. It affords us a vague and dim perception of the nature of what we call Life; it startles the Materialist with phenomena fearfully suggestive of the conditions of a purely spiritual being. In the language of another, when we plant our first footfall upon the threshold of the portal to which this astonishing discovery introduces, long and deep are the reverberations which come forth from the yet dark depths which lie beyond it. Having made this first step, we are prepared to go "sounding onward our dim and perilous way," passing from one wonder to another, like the knight of the nursery tale, in the Enchanted Castle—

> "His heart was strong,
> While the strange light crept on the floor along."

Without assenting in any respect to this theory, I have been recently deeply interested in reading a paper from a gentleman who has devoted much of his leisure, for the last seven years, to a patient investigation of this subject. He gives the particulars of a case which occurred under his own observation. A young girl of great purity of character, in a highly exalted state of what is called clairvoyance, or animal electricity, was willed by the magnetizer to the future world. In the language of the narrator, "The vision burst upon her. Her whole countenance and form indicated at once that a most surprising change had passed over her mind. A solemn, pleasing, but deeply impressive expression rested upon her features. She prophesied her own early death; and when one of her young friends wept, she said: 'Do not weep for me; death is desirable, beautiful! I have seen the future, and myself there. O! it is beautiful, happy, and glorious!—and myself so beautiful, happy, and glorious! And *it is not dying*, only changing places, states, and conditions, and feelings. O! how beautiful!—how blessed!' She seemed to see her mother, who was dead, and when asked to speak to her, she replied: 'She will not speak; I could not understand her. They converse by willing, thinking, feeling, without language.'"

All this may, in part, be accounted for on the theory of cerebral excitement—the disturbed over-action of a portion of the brain, or, to speak phrenologically, of the "religious organs." Yet the mystery even then is but *partially* solved. Why in this state of exaltation and preternatural mental activity should similar images and thoughts present themselves to persons of widely varied temperaments and beliefs, from the cold materialist to the too ardent spiritualist; from the credulous believer to the confirmed skeptic?

For myself, I am not willing to reject at once every thing which can not be explained in consistency with a strictly material philosophy. Who knows the laws of his own spiritual nature? Who can determine the precise conditions of the mysterious union of soul and body? It ill becomes us, in our ignorance and blindness, to decide that whatever accords not with our five senses, and our every day experience, is an impossibility. There is a credulity of doubt which is more to be deprecated than that of belief.

45.

VISIT FROM JAMES VICTOR WILSON.

BOSTON, *May* 29, 1849.

WITH the exception of a brief call from his spirit in December, 1847, this is the first I have heard and seen any thing of my dearly-beloved spirit-brother Wilson.* His personal affection is gentle, and there is an indescribable illumination enveloping his face and figure. He is learning all he can concerning the life and spheres beyond the grave.

46.

PREMONITIONS AND SPIRITUAL APPEARANCES.

BOONTON, N. J., *October* 10, 1849.

I RECORD the following account by one in whom I have entire confidence:—

My paternal grandfather was a man of that patriarchal mould of character that combines great benevolence and natural urbanity with a conscientiousness and firmness which, but for these tempering principles, would have been severe. He was not imaginative, and he had also a large share both of moral and physical

* See further information in Gt. Har., vol. I, p. 176, *et seq.*

courage. Hence his truthfulness was undoubted, and he was neither liable to be easily frightened, nor imposed on by any trick of fancy.

One summer evening, just before sunset, as he was returning from the neighboring town, and riding leisurely and thoughtfully through his front yard, he chanced to look into a garden adjoining, and there he saw two of his daughters walking along the central avenue, not side by side, but one following at a little distance after the other. These girls were then supposed to be sinking with the consumption, a malady which had carried off several of the family. Fearing they might take cold by exposure to the evening dew, my grandfather called them by name, and desired them to come directly into the house. Upon this they quickened their pace; and passing through a gap in the wall, that opened into a large peach-orchard beyond, they disappeared from his view. There was a row of trees standing along the wall between the garden and peach orchard, and these, as well as the garden itself, were covered by a luxuriant grape-vine, which in fact nearly closed the passage, also, with the delicate tracery of its young and tender branches; so that all beyond the space where the figures seemed to enter, lay in deep shadow. My grandfather thought this conduct very strange; for he was accustomed to strict obedience and respect from all the members of his family. Full of anxiety, he hurried into the house, and proceeding directly to my grandmother's sitting-room, he earnestly addressed her, in his accustomed manner:—

"Mother, why do you let the girls stay out so late? Don't you think they will take cold?"

"What girls?" she asked.

"Why Susan and Hetty," he replied. "They are walking in the garden, and in very thin white dresses."

"What makes you talk so?" returned my grandmother; "they are not in the garden, and have not been there for a long time. Nor are they dressed in white. They are up stairs."

"Why mother!" he responded, "I saw them with my own eyes, and just as plainly as I see you at this moment. They were walking in the garden; and when I called to them to come in, they turned round and looked at me; and then they went off into the peach orchard, when I lost sight of them. I certainly thought their conduct very strange."

"You *must* be mistaken, father. They have not been down stairs for several hours. I will go and speak to them, in order to convince you of your mistake."

As she spoke she stepped into the hall, and called the girls to come down, when they immediately came, and both of them in dark dresses. They looked very pale and miserable; and my grandfather found it difficult to conceal his secret anxiety on their account. But he questioned them very closely, whether they had been out walking, or had lately changed their dresses; when they both averred that they had not changed their clothes since morning, or been in the garden during the day.

In a very short time these girls fell a prey to the disease which was then corroding their vitals; and the order of their death was that of the appearance and disappearance of their forms as seen by my grandfather.

This story was often told in the family, as one of those unaccountable events which were in those times, called very strange, and wondered at—but never accounted for. The character of the witness precluded all question of the fact; but no one, in those days, ever dreamed that the occurrence might be explained on philosophical principles.

To the above account I will now add another, which was related to me by a friend, who well knew the circumstances; for they occurred in her own family. My narrator had an aunt, who was the wife of a sea-captain, residing, I think, in Bristol, R. I. One day, while her husband was away at sea, as a little girl of six years old, daughter of the above lady, was standing in a chair by the window, suddenly her eyes were fixed, and her whole person became rigid, as if she were about passing into a fit, when she uttered a fearful screech, her whole countenance wearing the expression of one who was looking on some fearful and distressing scene. Her mother, and other friends, hurried to her relief; and inquiring what ailed her, strove to withdraw her from the window. But she clung to the casement, begging not to be taken away. In the mean time, redoubling her screeches, she cried out in the intervals: "Oh, my father! he is drowning in the water!—he is drowning in the water!" In this state she remained half an hour: and during this time no effort could soothe or pacify her; but afterwards she sank to sleep from mere exhaustion. The circumstance was so remarkable that the exact time of the paroxysm was noted down; and when the next news from the ship arrived, it was found that the father of the child had, at the precise time of the attack, fallen overboard in a storm. For one half hour he was swimming after the vessel; and those on board being unable to save him, he was drowned.

The little girl who manifested this high degree of natural clairvoyance, was a very beautiful and precocious child—one of those sweet angel natures that sometimes shine over the dark ground of life, a ray of peerless light, which is too soon absorbed by the heaven. from whence it had stolen away. She died very early.

47.

THE WORLD MOVES.

HARTFORD, *March* 6, 1850.

THE managers of periodicals begin to acknowledge the law of progression, at least in things temporal. It is freely admitted that—

"Philosophy, since it was directed to the attainment of a knowledge of the properties and laws of matter, has already discovered and performed so much, that the commonest necessaries of life are now the production of the most complicated and wonderful inventions: and the condition of the humble peasant in point of solid comfort and luxury, is superior to that of the wealthiest noble three centuries ago; the conveniences and splendor of the rich are such as the monarchs of old never imagined even in their wildest dreams, and the common and daily spectacles of life are of such a character that would have startled our ancestors as the work of supernatural agency.

. . . Let these magazine editors keep their eyes open, and let them look far enough into the essential nature of things, and they will as freely admit that the progressive law operates with equal power and success in realms spiritual and eternal.

48.

INJUSTICE TO SWEDENBORG.

BRIDGEPORT, *May* 17, 1850.

On returning from Stratford to-day a gentleman, a very ardent friend of Swedenborg's, showed me a copy of the London *Athenæum*, which, in the course of a very long and elaborate review of Davis's Revelations, contains the following:

> "Time will roll on, and the revelations of Andrew Jackson Davis will be put on their proper shelf, in that curious museum which men call human nature. One man, we foresee, will be treated with injustice—we mean Emanuel Swedenborg. Davis and he will be classed together. Against this we protest. We have read enough of Swedenborg to justify us to ourselves in declaring that we would rather believe his supernatural communications upon his own word, than Davis's upon any possibly attainable amount of evidence."

. . . It seems to me that the "friends" of Swedenborg are the worst enemies that noble Seer ever had. For example, recently, one of his "friends" wrote this curious sentence:—

> "No small proof of Swedenborg's claims, is the fact that such a person as Davis has arisen; for history informs us that when a new dispensation has been given, a counter one of evil has appeared."

. . . So long as the receivers of the doctrines of

Swedenborg plant themselves upon such ground, they need not expect to grow in love and wisdom, to say nothing of "Charity" which is the brightest angel virtue in the heaven of their Master.

49.

SOMETHING WORTH REMEMBERING.

NEW YORK, *May* 24, 1850.

A YOUNG merchant, doing business in Cortlandt Street, is very anxious to bring his neighbor to grief through the law. He went to the "rappings" for in struction, and to find out whether he would succeed. The judicious spirits, much to my joy, would not "rap" for him! But a gentleman present told the young merchant the following facts, which I think are well worth remembering:—

"A farmer cut down a tree, which stood so near the boundary line of his farm that it was doubtful whether it belonged to him or his neighbor. The neighbor, however, claimed the tree, and prosecuted the man who cut it, for damages. The case was committed from court to court. Time was wasted, temper soured, and temper lost; but the case was finally gained by the prosecutor. The last my friend knew of the transaction was, the man who 'gained the cause' came to the lawyer's office to execute a deed of his whole farm, which he had been compelled to sell to pay his costs! Then houseless, and homeless, he could thrust his hand into his pocket, and triumphantly exclaim—'I'VE BEAT HIM!'"

50.

MR. GEORGE RIPLEY, LITERARY EDITOR OF THE TRIBUNE.

NEW YORK, *June* 8, 1850.

IT was my good fortune to-day to meet, or rather to see, Mr. Ripley, with two other gentlemen, investigating the "phenomena" occurring through the magnetic mediumship of the "Fox Family," now holding daily sessions at Barnum's Hotel, in Broadway. While the rappings, like the clickings of Morse's telegraph, are spelling out messages in answer to questions put by strangers gathered around the table, I am constrained to take "impressions" of Mr. George Ripley; but, happily for him, it is all going on *in me* without his knowledge, and it sums up as follows:—

Here is a marked and thoughtful man—a conscientious scholar; possessing great sweetness of disposition; in full sympathy with the advanced thoughts of his own generation, grasping with gloved hands the great problems of social ethics, religion, and philosophy; a warm friend to all who sincerely work for humanity, although he may regard them as vitally mistaken; independent of authorities in matters of literature and religion, and firmly advocating the principle that "unlimited liberty of speculation ought to be universally tolerated." For some reason, unaccountable as yet, I can not but think that Spinoza, the great German thinker of the seventeenth century, is Mr. Ripley's true intellectual counterpart and occasional guardian. I seem to see Mr. Ripley writing the *Ethica*—or editing and publishing some immense book, possibly the *Tractatus Theologico Politicus* of Spinoza—and I seem further to see that he will be, unlike the great metaphysician, fully appreciated by the people among whom he labors. . . . . But, why is this gentleman such a foreigner to me? It seems that I can never talk with him. . . . . . He is to me a stranger!

51.

ANOTHER VISIT FROM ANGEL WILSON.

HARTFORD, CONN., *November* 25, 1850.

TO-DAY I am overflowing with an inexpressible grateful joyousness. Through the solemn stillness, as comes a seraph's song from the stars, Brother Wilson floated down to me in this very house. He is a wingless being, as are all the inhabitants of the higher spheres, and yet he soars aloft with air-pinions I can not discern. He walked unheeded by others into this little room, and, with beautiful human eyes and tender language, gave me his second message.*

* This account was subsequently published in "Philosophy of Spiritual Intercourse," p. 157.

52.

FRANKLIN'S DISCOVERY OF THE RAPPING TELEGRAPH.

HARTFORD, *January* 6, 1851.

I HAVE just written out a *verbatim* report of a communication received this morning from the illustrious American philosopher, Benjamin Franklin, whose great personal influence yet lingers upon me, and seems to fill every object in the room with a profound presence.* . . . . . I am physically weary, or sleepy, perhaps, and so will not now write what I had in my mind.

53.

THE FACTS INCONTROVERTIBLE.

HARTFORD, *February* 9, 1851.

A DISTINGUISHED professor in one of the New York institutions of learning, has had the courage to make the following acknowledgment in a lecture to his class :—

"If the circumstances in respect to Davis had occurred at a distant period, then might they have been doubted; but this is

* This communication was printed in "Philosophy of Spiritual Intercourse," p. 77, *et seq.*

not the case, as they happened, as it were, but yesterday, and in a city where, if any fraud had been practiced, it could not have failed to have been detected; for not only did the various incidents have to bear the rigid scrutiny of its bitter opposers, but at the same time the potent agency of money was invoked, and a reward of five hundred dollars was offered to detect, if possible, the so-called imposition. Though six months were allowed for this purpose, yet it was in vain; the proof was wanting, and to this day the facts of the case remain incontrovertible. . . . . After this, who will not have faith in the Galileo affirmation that "*the world moves!*"

A writer in the Quarterly Theological Review, adverting to the great religious and governmental agitation of the times, says: "The fountains of the great deep have been broken up, and a deluge of information—theological, scientific, and civil—is carrying all before it, filling up the valleys and scaling the mountain-tops. . . . . . A spirit of inquiry has gone forth, and sits brooding on the mind of man."

54.

TALK WITH A DECEASED FRIEND.

HARTFORD, *October* 19, 1851.

THE following minutes of a conversation held with the spirit of a departed friend, who left this mortal state in June, 1849, is not published as any evidence of the *truth* of the remarkable phenomena of alleged intercourse with disembodied spirits.

The object of publishing the colloquy is simply to refute the common assumption that *nothing is ever com-*

municated from the spirit world by these new agencies that is of the slightest importance. The responses, it is said, are uniformly frivolous, useless, and uninteresting.

Here is a specimen, copied *verbatim* from notes hastily taken down as the words were uttered by the clairvoyant: The deceased, Mr. C., was a man of decided intelligence, energy, and philanthropy, and these responses are very like his manner of speaking while on earth. But to the questions and answers:—

Question. Mr. C., had the human race a conscious existence before we came on this earth?

Answer. Soul-matter had an existence, but not a conscious existence.

Q. Are there any spirits which exert an evil or malignant influence on human actions and conditions?

A. Yes: But not because they desire to do so, but because of their inferior or gross organization.

Q. Are there are any human spirits which have passed from earth which are not in a state of progress or improvement?

A. No: But some progress slowly, having a very gross organization to begin with.

Q. Do you know Edgar A. Poe, the poet?

A. Yes.

Q. In what sphere is he?

A. I have a different classification from others.

[Question pressed.]

A. He is in [what I consider] the third society, second sphere.

Q. Are there any spirits in a state of misery or pain, so as to feel their existence a burden?

A. There are some who have a mental suffering,

because they did not improve [or misused] their advantage while on earth.

Q. Are there any so separated from their friends as to cause them unhappiness—not being allowed the society of those they love best?

A. If they might [now] have been associated with those friends by improving their advantages [when] on earth, then they are unhappy.

Q. Are there any who despair of ever attaining the condition of the blest?

A. They may at times, but not lastingly.

Q. Does the state in which Mr. C. now is seem more immediately, palpably, under the Divine Government than *our* condition?

A. Its inhabitants see more clearly, as they have progressed further.

Q. Are there any in that state who disbelieve the existence of the Deity?

A. They do not disbelieve it, but some do not comprehend it.

Q. Then the Deity is not visible from that sphere?

A. He is nowhere visible. We receive impressions from Him, but do not see Him.

Q. Are the Apostles and founders of Christianity visible to Mr. C.?

A. No: none who are in a higher sphere are visible to those in a lower.

Q. Can those in a higher sphere communicate to those in a lower?

A. Yes.

Q. When Clairvoyants suppose they see Apostles, &c. are they deceived? or do they really see as they suppose?

A. Many of them think they see the Apostle Paul, or whoever else they wish to communicate with, when *they really do not.*

Q. When a mother, who dearly loves her good child, but who has lived unworthily, goes to the spirit world, is she, or is she not, permitted to see her child before she has attained his sphere?

A. She does not see him, but receives impressions from him.

Q. Does *he* see *her?*

A. Yes; he communicates to her, and watches over her.

Q. Have former generations passed away, so that they can not be seen from Mr. C.'s present sphere?

A. Some have, and some have not.

Q. Could Mr. C. see Adam and the ancient patriarchs?

A. No.

Q. Is this new ability on our part to communicate with the spirit world a consequence of any change or improvement in the human family?

A. Yes: The human race have become more refined and susceptible [to impressions from the spirit world] than formerly.

[It was here casually stated by some one present that Mr. C. had stated, on a former occasion, that idiots have no immortal existence. The present querist demurred to this, and asked]:—

Q. Do children who die in conscious infancy, live in the future state?

A. The moment an infant has been ushered into the world, an individuality has been formed, which continues to exist, provided the physical constitution was perfected—not otherwise.

Q. Then why do not animals also have an immortal existence?

A. Man has a peculiar formation, which animals have not. To all who have that formation, Soul adheres—not to others.

Q. Can Mr. C. give us any idea of his present locality in space—whether it is on any particular planet, or around this earth?

A. Human spirits love to hover around this earth, but they are not confined to it.

Q. Do those born on the several planets usually remain each on that which was his birth-place?

[Answer not taken down, but believed to have been affirmative.]

Q. Are the planets visible to Mr. C.?

A. Yes.

Q. Does Mr. C. see this outer, material earth? Does he see it as we do, with our material eyes?

A. He perceives the earth as a highly material body.

[The above is all that we noted down, though a few other questions were asked and answered, which were not noted at the time. On another occasion, it was stated, in reply to a question, that *all* created existences are first clothed in material bodies, passing thence into purer and more spiritual forms, and that the inhabitants of the higher planets, like Saturn, pass through a change from the material to the purely spiritual state equivalent to our Death, but one unattended by pain, and which is desired, not dreaded.]

55.

THE NEW ENGLAND RELIGIOUS HERALD DENOUNCES THE SUPERIOR CONDITION.

HARTFORD, *October* 20, 1851.

In the New England *Religious Herald* of this week is to be found a somewhat lengthy review of what it calls "superior illumination." The writer strikes out quite energetically, and makes several vigorous comments upon "Nature's Divine Revelations." The whole matter, in the reviewer's opinion, is summed up and logically disposed of, by stating that the "superior state" is very *inferior*, "compared with that of vigorous health and activity of the bodily powers." This opinion may be confidently entertained by all who have not studied the principles and phenomena of the human mind; but by the enlightened psychologist and metaphysician a vastly different opinion is obtained and cherished.

The reviewer says: "In all ages of the world, those persons who have claimed these remarkable powers of looking into the future, reading destiny, and seeing things afar off, have been almost entirely *persons of inferior mental power, connected with low tribes of gypsies and vagrants*, and having almost no knowledge of the best truths of being." Now history records a *different* verdict, and the writer of the article in question should have known it. Thucidydes, in speaking of Themistocles, (see Dæmonologia, page 128,) says: "By a species of sagacity peculiarly his own, for which he was *in no degree* indebted to early education or after study, he was supereminently happy in forming a correct judgment in matters that admitted but little time for deliberation; surpassing, at the same time, all his common *deductions of the future from the past.*" Tacitus foresaw the dire calamities which desolated Europe on the downfall of the Roman Empire, and predicted them in a work 500 years before they came to pass. Bishop Williams, in the time of Charles the First, could "see things afar off," and predicted the ultimate success of the Puritanic party; and so certain was he, that, when success was scarcely believed by any one beside himself, he abandoned the Government and joined the obscure party. (See Rushworth, vol. I, page 420.) Solon, the great Athenian, could "look into the future, and read destiny," &c. When contemplating on the port and citadel of Munychia, he exclaimed, "Oh, how blind is man to futurity! Could the Athenians see what mischief *they will do*, they would even eat it with their own teeth to get rid of it." The *dreams* or previsions of Joseph, Pharaoh, and Nebuchadnezzar, the records of which there seems no reason to dispute, can scarcely be considered as the subjective *fancies of their own minds*, considering their remarkable fulfillment.

In the same article the writer says: "Fancy a world of *noble* beings . . . . with tongues lolling out of their mouths, their muscles rigid, their faces clothed in the pallor of death, and they all *dreaming* out glorious visions and gewgaw vagaries, &c. . . . . . Say! would it not rather be a race of fools?" Let me ask, how will the reviewer explain the mental conditions of Ezekiel and Daniel? These prophets, who could see "into the future, read destiny," &c., described their condition as something similar to what is now-a-days denominated "the mesmeric state," and their mental state as analogous to the "superior condition." Ezekiel generally prefaces his "visions" by such expressions as, "The Heavens were opened," or, "The hand of the Lord was upon me." (See Ezek. i. 1–3.) Daniel, too, could enter this half-dying or superior state, and see spiritual things. He was generally, according to his own affirmations, in a deep sleep, while obtaining his *impressions* of interior and truthful realities. (See chap. x. v. 7.) "And I, Daniel, alone saw the vision . . . and there remained no strength in me, for my comeliness was turned in me into corruption, and I retained no strength. Yet I heard the voice of the words; and when I heard the voice of the words, then I was in a *deep sleep on my face, and my face toward the ground*." In the phraseology of our day, this "deep sleep" which fell upon Daniel would be called the "magnetic condition," allowing the mind an opportunity to exercise its higher powers. But the reviewer, doubtless, would consider Daniel's state very *inferior*, "compared with that of vigorous health and activity of the bodily powers."

A new field of investigation is thrown open by the magnetic marvels of this era, which all intelligent minds should be willing to explore; and may we not expect from the writer in the *Religious Herald* something more relative to the question of the inferior and "superior" conditions? The effort may introduce his mind into new regions of thought, and his condition may thereby experience an improvement. He should remember that the same identical methods of explaining away the trance state, will equally and as forcibly apply to the solution of all "dreaming," "visions," "prophecies," and other psychological phenomena recorded on the pages of profane and ecclesiastical history.

56.

DOCTOR JOHN F. GRAY, OF NEW YORK.

HARTFORD, *Oct.* 26, 1851.

YESTERDAY, having business in New York, I called upon the justly celebrated homeopathic physician, Dr. J. F. Gray, and found him in his office, opposite the Astor Library, in Lafayette Place. . . . Of him my impressions are: A searcher and perceiver of subtile and occult truths; sees fine shadings in the panorama of truth; appreciates the spiritual in the natural; knows more by intuition than by reasoning, but can think logically and profoundly; loves the Greek and Latin and German coverings of thought; is a foreigner to me, and keeps me at a long distance from him, as much as to say, "Not too familiar, if you please." He is a medium for the intellectual and intuitive perception of truth. Some remarks were as follows:—

He said, that I, by being magnetized, entered the spiritual legitimately. Everybody, he thought, should be magnetized, if they would scientifically approach the inner life. Substantially he said, that "there is one truth which mesmerism teaches, without which it would be difficult, if not impossible, for many to receive the Scripture doctrine concerning the ministration of spirits, and of their intercourse with this world.* . . . The mesmeric phenomena prove that such intercourse is quite possible; for in the experiments which have been made, it is shown that one's mind, while on this earth, can be put into such a state of quiescence, as to be completely under the control of another. Thus, it has been repeatedly exhibited, that a subject can be so acted upon as to think what the magnetizer thinks; to see what the operator beholds, even though his eyes are bandaged; to taste what the other partakes or appears to take; and so far has the transfer been made, that if the operator was pricked with a pin, the subject instantaneously felt the pain, and precisely as if it had been in his own body. In these experiments and others of like nature, it is exhibited that the magnetizer's mind or spirit is connected and forms one with the mind of the subject—so much so, that it would appear that the subject's intellect had disappeared, and the magnetizer acted upon and put in action a lifeless body. Now if this is so, if it is true that one man's spirit can possess another, so that the subject's own consciousness is destroyed, and he at the time thinks and fully believes that he is acting from himself, then it is evident that it is possible for spirits from the hidden world to act upon mankind in the same manner."

* Dr. Gray was, at the time of the author's first visit, a reader and receiver of Swedenborg.

57.

CHEERING PROPHECY BY A SPIRIT.

HIGH ROCK TOWER, LYNN, MASS., *October* 22, 1852.

A KIND friend writes that at a meeting of a circle in Williamsburg a few evenings since, Mr. B— having been carried into the magnetic state delivered the following prophecy dictated by a spiritual intelligence:—

"Brethren; be of good cheer. The stone is not yet rolled from the sepulcher. There are many truths which will yet descend on the wings of angelic love, and there are many voices which will be heard above the din and strife of earth. A mighty spiritual flood will yet sweep over the bosom of the human world; a heavenly power shall descend, in whose presence the tongue of slander shall cease its whisperings, and the pen shall write no longer the things which are not true. Then shall the press be turned into a mountain of light, within whose glowing beauty the truths of angels shall find a dwelling-place. The theologian whose interest has been to reveal a smoking pit, will preach a new doctrine; and the physician that seeks for gain will heal for gold no longer, when spirits act as physicians to the diseased body. Behold the star of righteousness is arising, and the truly wise men of earth will go forth to welcome it."

58.

BENJAMIN F. WADE AND JOSHUA R. GIDDINGS, MEMBERS OF CONGRESS.

JEFFERSON, ASTRABULA CO., O., *November* 30, 1852.

MY engagement to give a lecture in this place brought me here just in time to shake hands with the Hon. B. Wade, who, accompanied by his affable and intelligent wife, is on the point of leaving for the Capitol at Washington. I had less than ten minutes chat with him and his lady; yet, of him, I carry away these impressions: A solid, strong, stormy, positive intellect. Is not selfish, but is self-reliant. Perceives quickly, reasons much (for reason is his guiding principle), and decides and *stands!* Has much benevolence; worships justice and reality; entertains feelings of universal good-will; but can *despise* what displeases him with unflinching firmness and frankness. Enjoys domestic comforts; loves children, friends, and household pets; is orderly, studious, industrious, and punctual; enjoys simple music and instructive amusements; hates pretensions and shams with a perfect hate; and would make "his mark" in any public or private position. . . . God speed him!

Of Hon. J. R. Giddings, in whose house I am now visiting and writing, I think: He is not a sectarian, and he can not be one, for his intellect is broad, and his ideas extend far beyond the age in which he lives. He possesses the true principles of liberty, and must manifest them throughout his public life. Freedom of thought and freedom of speech, must be his motto. Possessing strength of character and purpose, he is naturally firm and decisive in his actions; although an appeal to his sympathies would affect him, even to vascillation and weakness. He is conscientious, and is governed much by intuitive perceptions of right. When surrounded by opposition his character is most fully displayed. He is not attractive in either his appearance or conversation: yet, nevertheless, when aroused by what deeply *stirs* his ruling thoughts and noblest feelings, there are few men who have a more manly deportment, or a larger personal influence for good. . . . . In his family I find education, pleasing manners, and a *welcome* that is manna upon my heart.

59.

R. P. AMBLER AND S. J. FINNEY IN HARTFORD.

CLEVELAND, O., *December* 23, 1852

So we change places. . . . . I have been long laboring in Hartford. Now, for the first time, I venture far out into the field. As I look back in thought to the friends in that old New England city, I seem to realize how the timid ones shrink from the terrific storm from the lips of our young Brother Finney, the impetuous torrent of whose fiery invective, flashing against the errors and prejudices of Theology, with the fearful lightnings of justice and truth, is sufficient to alarm all heedful citizens. Happily, I hear, that Brother Ambler is speaking to the same audiences. His milder presentation, although lacking in both the qualities of force and depth, will, nevertheless, beautifully calm the troubled waters.

. . . . . This morning a letter comes, printed in the "Spirit Messenger," dated Hartford, Ct., December 8th, only two weeks ago, in which I read:—

Mr. Finney and myself have delivered several lectures in this city, which have been exceedingly well attended. Thus far our lectures have been devoted chiefly to the pulling down of strongholds, and the dispelling of theological darkness from the minds of the people. It is clearly seen by spirits that the time has now come, when an open and fearless exposure of mythological errors is essential to the reformation which they are seeking to accomplish. Hence they will cause the mediums whom they control to speak plainly on theological questions. The ground which has been falsely deemed too sacred for mortal feet to tread shall be examined by the light of Reason; and the creeds and dogmas which are unable to endure the light shall be dissolved thereby, and sink back into their native darkness. There is no compromise to be made with error. The sun does not fear to rise when night has thrown her mantle on the earth; but its rising dispels the shadowy gloom and reflects the smile of God.

Through the mediumship of Mr. Finney, the spirits have made a bold attack on the errors of the Church, and have even gone so far as to invite the clergy of this city to a public investigation of theological and spiritual subjects. To timid and shrinking minds, this course might seem to indicate a want of earthly policy and a lack of just discrimination and judgment. But on careful reflection it will be seen by all true harmonial philosophers that the world has been deceived and darkened long enough by doctrines whose very tendency is to absorb the life of the soul, and that if truth has been revealed from the Heavenly Sphere which will bless humanity, this truth should be spoken—freely, boldly, and fearlessly spoken—even though it should be opposed to the sensitive prejudices of the blinded mind. I believe with Mr. Davis that 'we need more independence of soul;' and I rejoice to know that he, with others, has been sufficiently independent to manifest the freedom which the truth imparts. In a recent lecture by the seer,* entitled "What will the people say?" he takes the bold and truthful position that, "From the New Testament alone you may find the entire vocabulary of the profane man." Of course, in this expression Mr. Davis does not implicate the original writers of the New Testament, but simply refers to the expressions in this book as they now stand before the world and are uttered from the pulpit, and, in doing so, exposes to the public view a significant and notable fact. How true and forcible is the following sentiment:—"The village pastor talks about the devil and hell; shows how and upon what rigid laws of retributive justice God will damn the souls of certain persons; and so the child and the thoughtless man learn to employ the same terms and epithets, in the same emphatic, God-

* The lecture here referred to was published in *The Harmonial Man*, p. 115, *et seq.*

like manner as the minister of the Gospel." In the light of this truth does it not become evident that to prevent profanity in the streets, we must first stop the use of the same expressions in the pulpit? And how shall this be accomplished without an open and fearless exposure of the wrong?

My friends may, perhaps, be pleased to know that in my public lectures I speak entirely under the control of an unseen Intelligence, usually not knowing even the subject on which I am to speak previous to my appearance before the audience. . . . .

Thine as ever, R. P. AMBLER.

6.

SPIRIT VOICE HEARD BY A FERRYMAN.

CINCINNATI, O., *January* 8, 1853.

A GENTLEMAN of this city, an artist *con amore*, and a banker of large wealth, has just brought me a remarkable tale of circumstantial evidence. It seems that a farmer in one of the western counties of England was met by a man whom he had formerly employed, and who again asked for work. The farmer (rather with a view to be relieved from his importunity than with any intention of assisting him) told him he would think of it, and send word to the place where the man told him he should be found. Time passed on, and the farmer entirely forgot his promise. One night, however, he suddenly started from his sleep, and, awaking his wife, said he felt a strong impulse to set off immediately to the county town, some 30 or 40 miles distant, but why he had not the least idea. He endeavored to shake off the impression and went to sleep again, but awoke a second time with such a strong conviction that he must start that instant, that he directly rose, saddled his horse, and set off. On his road he had to cross a ferry, which he could only do at one hour of the night, when the mail was carried over. He was almost certain that he should be too late, but nevertheless rode on, and when he came to the ferry, greatly to his surprise, found that though the mail had passed over a short time previously, the ferryman was still waiting. On his expressing his astonishment, the boatman replied: "Oh, when I was on the other side I heard you shouting, and so came back again." The farmer said he had not shouted; but the other repeated his assertion that he had distinctly heard him call. Having crossed over, the farmer pursued his journey, and arrived at the county town the next morning. But now that he had come there, he had not the slightest notion of any business to be transacted, and so amused himself by sauntering about the place, and at length entered the court where the assizes were being held. The prisoner at the bar had just been, to all appearance, proved clearly guilty, by circumstantial evidence, of murder; and he was then asked if he had any witnesses to call in his behalf. He replied that he had no friends there, but looking around the court amongst the spectators, he recognized the farmer, who almost immediately recognized in him the man who had applied to him for work; the farmer was instantly summoned to the witness-box, and his evidence proved, beyond the possibility of a doubt, that at the very hour the prisoner was accused of committing murder in one part of the county, he was applying for work in another. The prisoner was, of course, acquitted, and the farmer found that, urged on by an uncontrollable impulse which he could neither explain nor account for, he had, indeed, taken his midnight journey to some purpose, notwithstanding it had appeared so unreasonable and causeless. "This is the Lord's doing, and it is marvelous in our eyes."

Is it a mere idle imagination to suppose that the spirit of some departed friend should have perceived the extreme danger of the poor laborer, and also the only means by which his innocence could have been established; and, hurrying on the wings of love to the sleeping farmer, suggested a journey to the scene of interest and danger, reiterating the impression with a dictate of imperative authority? This must have been so—and what songs of joy rang through the echoing aisles of Heaven, at the redemption of the innocent from the bondage of a cruel and unrighteous law!

61.

A PHRENOLOGICAL DESCRIPTION BY A BLIND PROFESSOR.

CINCINNATI, O., *January* 12, 1853.

THE accompanying delineation of my character by F. Bly, a perfectly blind phrenologist, was given this day, and is recorded as a kind of curiosity. Possibly some of it is correct:—

Temperament—nervous bilious; brain full size, favorably balanced for contentment and happiness.

The scale, in numbering the various organs or faculties, is from one to twenty, as follows:—1, very small; 4, small; 7, moderate; 10, medium; 13, full; 16, large; 20, very large. Here is the size of each individual function or organ:—

1	Amativeness,	9	22	Imitation,	16
2	Philoprogenitiveness,	10	23	Mirthfulness,	11
3	Adhesiveness,	19	24	Individuality,	20
4	Inhabitiveness,	7	25	Form,	13
5	Concentrativeness,	15	26	Size,	15
6	Combativeness,	3	27	Weight,	12
7	Destructiveness,	5	28	Color,	16
8	Alimentiveness,	8	29	Order,	11
9	Acquisitiveness,	7	30	Calculation,	17
10	Secretiveness,	9	31	Locality,	15
11	Cautiousness,	14	32	Eventuality,	16
12	Approbativeness,	10	33	Time,	15
13	Self-Esteem,	11	34	Tune,	8
14	Firmness,	19	35	Language,	18
15	Conscientiousness,	18	36	Causality,	12
16	Hope,	20	37	Comparison,	19
17	Marvelousness,	6	B	Sublimity,	19
18	Veneration,	15	C	Suavity,	12
19	Benevolence,	17	D	An intuitive disposition to know human nature,	20
20	Constructiveness,	14			
21	Ideality,	19			

This combination of phrenological development will give one of the most wonderful characters of the age. He is sensitive and impressible to a high degree; yet his mind and body work in unison and harmony. No man whom I have ever examined has more control over his passions than himself. No circumstances, however annoying, can irritate or ruffle the even tenor of his way, because the intellectual faculties preponderate, and the moral principles of the mind guide the reasoning powers in the channel of love and charity. He has not the spirit of revenge, however much he may be injured or reviled, though he ever has a resolute desire to promote general good. This feeling has ever actuated him from the earliest period of his life up to the present. He has not the love of ambition or personal fame. Selfishness is not a part of his disposition; ever kind and affectionate; warm and ardent in his attachment for his friends; no particular love for place, but can make himself at home wherever his friends or labors call him; always friendly and social to ever one, yet he seeks not the applause of men. It is natural for him to be devotional, watchful, and prayerful, though with this organization of mind it is impossible to believe and advocate the popular religious faith, as it is taught by the orthodox churches. His intuition, presentiment, and foresight, are preeminent; his penetration and perceptive faculties enable him to understand and appreciate life as it is, and the laws of nature governing mind and matter. His originality of thought and reflection, combined with the observing powers, qualify him to study the books of nature with success and interest to himself and others. Possessing great application in the accomplishment of his purposes, always looking forward with great anticipation to the Spirit-world. Not easily discouraged by disappointment of any kind; could bear misfortune well; always the same in feeling and manner—yesterday, to-day, and forever; humorous and good-natured; mathematical talent remarkably good; enjoys music and might execute some, if cultivated; language well-developed, conveys his ideas to others plainly and distinctly, at the same time his style of speaking is easy and fluent, well calculated to please others; his expression is mild but forcible; no man of mind can hear him and not be interested; memory generally good. This description, according to my science and judgment, is true. But much more might be said of this character.

62.

A SPIRIT-MOTHER CURES HER SON.

HARTFORD, CT., *September* 6, 1853.

A NEW YORKER called upon me to-day to relate an interesting *test* of the idea that death does not necessarily sever the ties that bind parents to children, but that guardianship is natural. It seems that in the summer of 1850, Mr. Edward Tyler had a tumor formed in the roof of his mouth, which, though small at first, was exceedingly painful, and gradually increased in size, till it assumed an alarming appearance, so much so that he was compelled to apply for medical advice—he then residing near Boston. The doctor told him it must be probed, which was consented to, but he either could not or would not tell him definitely what the disease was. After the probing, it was for some time less painful, but ere long it assumed a more formidable appearance, and his anxious friends thought (though they did not tell him) that it must be a cancer. At this time he resorted again to medical skill, but did not consult the same physician as before, thinking that another professional man would give him more satisfactory assistance. The tumor was again opened, but with no better permanent results. Of course, day by day and week by week the pain and inconvenience increased, and the want of his regular food, which he was unable to masticate, reduced him very much.

It was now the summer of 1852, when, in this state, he came with his family to reside in Astoria. Soon after his removal to this place, his friends advised him, as a last resort, to apply for admission into the New York Hospital. Every thing was arranged for his going there; but two or three days before the time appointed for his removal to the hospital, he visited Mrs. Snyder's circle, accompanied by his wife and sister, who also reside in Astoria. On this occasion no one intended to consult the spirits respecting Mr. T.'s mouth, although he and most of his family had attended the circle before; but as they sat with the circle, and the spirit of his departed mother was communing with them, his sister asked, "Mother, do you know how bad Edward's mouth is?" She answered by raps, "Yes." "Do you know that he is going to the hospital?" Ans. "No." "But he *is* going." Ans. "No." All were very much surprised, as every one in the room (and there were eight or ten persons present) believed that he *was* going to the hospital. This, by the way, is one striking illustration of the fallacy of the opinion that the answers are at all times in accordance with the mind of the medium, or the parties present.

In this instance, the medium (Mrs. Snyder) was as much astonished at the positive "No," as any one in the room. Then the question was asked, "Shall he apply to any other physician?" Ans. "No." "Is he then to linger out a miserable existence, and die with the disease?" Ans. "No." "Is there a cure for it?" Ans. "Yes." "Will you tell us what he is to do?" Ans. "Yes." At this time one of the company was impressed to say, "I have known burnt alum to be used with good effects in some cases." Immediately three violent raps were heard, indicating that that was the remedy intended. It was accordingly applied, and its good effects were in a few days satisfactorily felt—first in lessening the pain, then in decreasing the size of the tumor; and finally, without any other physical application, an effectual cure was performed.

63.

VISION OF WILLIAM AND MARY HOWITT.

PORTLAND, ME., *March* 10, 1854.

I AM delivering a course of lectures in this city. . . . Henry C. Wright is here,* and the "Hutchinson Family" of natural singers. . . . We spent hours together in the hospitable parlor of the intelligent Widow Dennett, whose house is ever open to reformers of the pure Garrisonian stamp.

What keen, cold weather! The very atmosphere seems to sparkle and crackle like a silk dress loaded with diamonds. . . . There is something mysteriously delicious in this frosty, crispy air; it fills me with live

* The author's estimates of the character and works of Mr. Wright may be found in "The Reformer," Vol. IV., Gt. Har.

lightning, so to say, and promotes lucidity of clairvoyant vision.

Yesterday I had a trans-Atlantic observation. . . . Saw many places and persons of renown. I penetrated the shadowy walls, and had a pleasant view of William and Mary Howitt, the noted authors and translators of several volumes from the German. . . . There was a sick person in the house, and a child. I could not clairvoyantly approach Mr. Howitt without feeling an influence from his sphere. He possesses a wonderful concentration of mind—few things disturb him; yet he is remarkably sympathetic, and alive to the nobler impulses. Music imparts a sense of pleasure to his mind, but chiefly phenomenal displays of divine guidance, with some philosophical investigations absorb his thoughts. He is a very excellent judge of human nature; and sometimes can almost perceive and scan the motives of men. The organization of his person is extremely well balanced. His mind is deep and reflective; and the spiritual and intellectual nature predominates over the public and social. He seems to be a bright and beautiful spirit, and his sphere delights me. . . . He could have been a kind-hearted and much-beloved minister of the Established Church. He has a keen appreciation of true wit; takes a peculiar delight in what others term "vagaries;" he sincerely loves the fine arts and good society; and the Truth he worships, but is not independent of precedents and accredited authorities.

Another person I perceive. . . . Mrs. Mary Howitt, a self-poised, lady-like, matronly, finely organized woman. Her round body is wearing away somewhat under the industry of her feeling, sentiments. and thinking powers.

Not selfish, but is rather easily absorbed in the comfort and education of others. She causes others to feel brighter, happier, better than herself. Her magnetism is stimulating, and acts tonically upon those she is moved to aid. Is fond of retirement; is spiritual (religious) in feeling; loves poetry better than philosophy, and beautiful word-pictures better than either. . . . I see harmony and much independence in the life of these noble persons.

My visit to-day over the Atlantic was of short duration—about thirty minutes. . . . I went entirely for another object, a *use*, to obtain a fact in geology for one of my lectures; but, incidentally, under invitation of their guardians, I could not refuse to look into that home. For some reason I did not observe London as a great city, but only this family by itself.

64.

A RICH LECTURE ON ASTRONOMY.

PORTLAND, *March* 12, 1854.

TO-DAY I have come within *one* of having a personal interview with the poet Whittier; that is, I have just had a long, pleasant talk with the poet's own brother. He is a rather solemn, quiet gentleman; smiles rarely and confidentially; converses with great caution, like a retired clergyman, and looks like one who seldom felt the emotions of humor. Fancy my great pleasure when a friend assured me that this same solemn, thoughtful, unsmiling gentleman is the celebrated

"Ethan Spike, Esq., of Hornby, Me." Not long since this grave man wrote the following letter to the Portland *Transcript and Eclectic*, descriptive of matters and things in his part of the country. All readers will enjoy his amusing report of

A LECTURE ON ASTRONOMY.

Perhaps in a litterary pint of view aour town haint been so forrered as she orter. While Polly-ticks and the millingtary interest has been carried furder perhaps than in any other place on the airth, yet excepting my own case, litteratoor hasn't gone beyond coarse hand-writing or the single rule of three. Ferlosofy has been quoted in this market below pork; syence hasn't compared with syder; string beans has generally sot higher than stronomy, letters led trigernometry and punkins was ahead of poetry. Naow, haowsever, the tables is turned bottom side under. Syence is riz!

We've got a Lie-see-um! The cry of Letters is begun, the tree of nollidge has sprouted, interlect biles over matter—that ere interlect which has been dormouse is naow raoused like a sleepy lion gittin away from Jordan.

The fust lectur of the season was gin last night by James Peabody, who's bin one quarter to an academary.

General subjek—STRONOMY.
Partickeler ditto—COMICS.

I haint time to gin you more'n a digestive or facsimelar of the lectur—

Jemes begun by observin that ef anybody supposed

that the stars warnt a heap bigger than they looked, they was almighty behind hand. Why, sez he, there's that ar little shiner called Satan, says he, don't look bigger than a tater, and yet according to Herklys—who knows the heavenly bodies jist as well as I know father—tis somewhat larger than the whole county of Oxford! An the leetlest star you can pick aout, is as big as a cart wheel. At this pint Dea. Elderberry ris an said this was goin too fur, twas regelar blasfeeme, contrary to scriptur, and agin common sense. Then he tuck his hat and cleared, fust spittin aout his terbaker cud as a testimony agin the doctrine.

After speaking of the milky way—which he said was longer than the Cumberland or Oxford canawl—an the moon, which the onlarned considered to be a green cheese, but which syence demonstrated to be a jacker-lantern on a large scale, the lecterer proceeded to the pertickeler part of his subjek.

COMICS, OR BLAZIN STARS.

Comics, says Jemes—says he—are of two kinds, the Tame and the Wild. The fust is peaceable—tother aint. The fust ones is made of old moons as aint fit for service, and is called by the oneddikated shootin stars, but we of the schools call em meters. This difference led the speaker to remark that larnin is every thin.

The wild kind, says Jemes, is a different crittur: bein composed of nebulous matter, hyfolution gass, ox-side of cast iron, an salts of harmonia, makes it highly salvage and onsartan. They fust appeared about

Deuteronomy or perhaps a little later in the year six, and was diskivered spontaneously from Portland Observators and Pompey's pillow in Rooshy. They are pesky things, says he, ollers gittin up wars, hurrykanes, and airthquakes, &c. Oneasy and restless, travelin about faster than a rale road, but never reachin anywheres in pertickeler. Kinder loominated Peter Ruggs. Mighty onsartin, they ar—can't be depended on. Father Miller engaged one to do a pertickeler job in '43, but it probably got better tarms somewheres else, and that ere job remains ondone to this day.

But now, says Jemes, we come to consider their tails. Them, says he, is raal numerous. Talk about the moon's wondrous tale! Why the tales of all the planics in the cideral heavings wouldn't make one for a fust rate wild comic! Longer than the magnetic paragraph and wider than Sebago pond, they stretches aout over the universal kanerpy in the unlimited nugacity of either, now sweepin' down among the elongate concavities of diurnal convexities and agin sorein upwards till lost in the grate hyperion!

Jemes was so used up by this peoration that he had to be carried home on a cheer. This morning, however, he was as well as could be expected, and ef convalescence don't set in he'll be about in a day or two.

65.

THE RAG PICKER'S STORY.

NEW YORK, *November* 8, 1854.

A FRIEND gives me a report of a *sceance*, during which occurred the following manifestations:—

L., was influenced and, in the tone and manner of gentle girlhood, she said:—

I'm happy now. I guess I am. I'm in Heaven I guess. I hain't got any bare feet any more neither. Ain't I happy! Nobody scolds me any more neither. Ain't I happy! Guess I am. I wish I could find mother tho'. I tell you what—these cold stones ain't agoing to hurt my feet any more, are they?

I heard the doctor say when I was dying, "The poor little wretch is dying." What did he call me wretch for?

I used to go round the streets in hot weather and cold weather getting pieces of bread and picking up rags. I used to be sorrowful and hungry sometimes. I used to hook an apple when I could find one and couldn't get any thing else. I used to tell God to look another way. At that time I had been told God was looking at me.

I was took sick. But say! What's the reason you don't tell me to go away? You let me come in and don't say go away! Oh! I know. You can't see me and I've got the better of you. I feel kind ashamed to talk before you, but I feel so kind, so happy, I can't help it.

Mother cried a peck when I died, I know. I guess baby will miss me tho', won't she? I went home after picking up rags and felt kind-o-bad all over. Mother said I'd got cold; and every day when I come home my legs grew stiffer and stiffer and would ache dreadful bad.

I wanted to go out one morning 'cause I'd promised some girls we'd go round the streets down town and have a good pick, for a fellow had been moving and thrown his dirt in the street. I couldn't go, I felt so bad.

Mother used to take the rags, wash 'em out, dry 'em, and sell 'em. She couldn't go a picking, for she had a baby. I thought the baby might as well know how to pick rags as I, and I used to give it the poker and teach it how. It thought it fine fun. It was black too—had black hair and eyes, but I had light. Why was this?

Well! I got kind-o-sick and the baby used to take me for rags and poke me. I guess she warn't far from right to look at my petticoats. I lay there in the corner. The rats used to make such a noise I couldn't sleep and I wanted to poke them.

[Hear she was speaking too fast for me to write, and I said, "wait a minute." She said, "I guess you're waiting to cross Broadway."]

She then resumed:—

As I was laying one night in the corner—dreadful sick, I tell you my head ached like fun, I heard a kind-o-noise and thought it was the nasty rats. I looked round and seen, oh! the prettiest thing right above me! It was a woman, so smiling and pretty? Oh, warn't she pretty! She looked so white and clean and there was no rags about her. And when she looked at me, her eyes were like two stars. It made me feel comfortable all over, and says I—"Where did you come from?" She says: "Mag, dear child! I've come for you to go home with me." "Oh, dear!" says I, "I don't look nice enough." She kissed me and told me never mind my clothes, God didn't mind if man did. She said she'd take me where I'd be real happy. I asked her if she knowed me? She said, Oh yes! she'd been with me ever since I was a little bit of a baby. Warn't she good! I told mother of it and I heard her tell some of the neighbors, I was out of my head, and she said I was going to die. She cried awful hard and I did die, and found myself right in the arms of that lady, and she says now I can come round the baby and mother and make mother better and happy and take care of baby better than I used to.

Where I is, is all a beautiful place. Tain't no cold where I am. I don't shiver nor hungry now. 'Cept I want to see mother sometimes. And then I can go and see her, and that lady's spirit round me says as how there is around a great many ragged children just such pretty faces as hers.

I asked her one time, who she was? and she says she once lived in our land and had a little baby and she loved that baby better than her Heavenly Father, she fears, and He took her baby home to Him. She felt very lonesome. She grew older and she went home. And they told her, before her baby could be always with her, she must go to earth and take care of some little child, and so she had picked me out 'cause she'd seen I was like her baby. She seen my mother had so many, she didn't care particular about me. And now, she says, she'll go where her little child is, and I'll be lonesome! Won't I? She says, if I'll be good, I'll come where she is and be her child with the other one.

She says, God ain't a great big angry man, but he loves every little child, if she is dirty and ragged, and if I'll only be good, I'll always be happy. She says God is all love. Well! I guess I'll turn it the other way, Love is all God. I'll remember it better that way.

When I come here to night, I thought I was going to mother. Now she says I may go to mother. If you ain't ashamed of me I'll come again.

[Here the communication seemed to cease, but L. remained under the influence. What had been said thus far, had been said continuously by her, without interruption. Now Mr. A. and Mrs. S, became influenced, and through the three mediums the following dialogue occurred:]

Mr. A. described her appearance—" She had on a check petticoat."

L. " Why! You can see me can't you?"

Mr. A. " Her petticoat was two or three inches longer than her frock—"

L. " So it was. The frock was given me but the petticoat was one of mother's. They used to say I stole– "

I asked. " Did you?"

L. " I did. I used to hook once in a while. What are you going to do, if you are hungry and see lots of things not eaten up?"

In answer to some questions, she said she was about ten years old, and lived in Centre Street, near Pearl.

I asked her mother's name?

L. "Let that lady tell."

Mrs. S. "Her name was Katrina Moeglar. Her father used to get drunk, and once a big fellow came and took him away"—

L. "And I never seen him since."

Mrs. S. then had a vision of her mother's residence and described it, and, as she described, the child recognized it and added some particulars. It was a single room in a cellar. It had a few chairs, a broken table, lots of rags, some shavings, a piece of broken looking-glass—

L. "That I stole, and used to look at myself in it. I wonder you can go down there, it is so dirty. Do you see mother?"

Mrs. S. "I see there a pale-looking woman—some one says she has the consumption."

L. "Do you see the baby?"

Mrs. S. "Yes, dear little thing! It is lying on some rags."

L. "Has it grown?"

Mrs. S. "It would be a pretty child if taken care of. I see a gray cat there."

L. "That was my pussy, I hope they give it enough to eat."

Mrs. S. "I see somebody else there—"

L. "It is one of mother's boarders."

Mrs. S. "She is an old woman and looks wretched. She has a basket filled with paper and rags."

L. "And a flat nose. It's old aunty. She used to lick me like every thing."

Mrs. S. "I see a boy there—"

L. "It's her son Peter."

Mrs. S. "I see a man there, a horrid looking man."

L. "Is he there yet? It's old aunty's husband. He hired one corner of the room."

Mrs. S. "Your mother won't live long—"

L. "Won't she? What'll be done with the baby?"

Mrs. S. "She coughs now and spits blood."

L. "This lady says I can then take mother in my arms. But what *will* they do with the baby?"

Mrs. S. "It will be taken care of."

L. "Who'll do it?"

Mrs. S. "A kind lady who belongs to a society—"

L. "Has she come again?"

Mrs. S. "Yes she takes care of your mother and sends her food. Your mother is not able to work now. She used to wash for the poor people around her and get two shillings a day, and since her strength failed her, her only means of living have been to let a part of her miserable room to lodgers, and a kind lady helps her as much as she is able to."

L. "Say, Misses, do you see the street that runs down near the house; it's awfully crooked—cow tracks, the boys called it."

Mrs. S. "The spirit here tells me to tell you, little child, your mother will soon be with you."

L. "Ain't I happy!"

[It is impossible to convey an adequate idea of the tone in which this was said. It was full of deep emotion and subdued joy. It was inexpressibly touching.]

Mrs. S. "Your father here to night is crying bitter tears of repentance and shame."

L. "Will he let me speak to him? I ain't afraid of him now"

Mrs. S. "He is not permitted yet."

L. "Why not?"

Mrs. S. "He is not able to answer you, my child."

L. "Has he lost his tongue? He used to have one long enough and talk loud enough."

Mrs. S. "Be patient my child. You'll meet again."

L. "Say, will mother be with me, then?"

Mrs. S. "Yes."

L. "O dear! I m glad of that."

[Here the influence seemed to be withdrawn, and the interview to end. But the spirit that attended the child then spoke to us:]

She said that she had as yet seen her own child but once since her entrance, several years since, into the spirit world. The reason was that her love for it was a selfish love. She had lived a common, ordinary life on earth, caring little for the future; and on her entrance there she found that she must return to earth and finish the task she had neglected while living here, by taking into her care some child, whom she could guide and protect until she should remove from her love all its earthly taint. Her task was now nearly performed. The child she had selected was now very dear to her, together they would progress, and soon she would again be united to her dearly loved child, and they three together advance onward toward their high destiny.

66.

IMPROVEMENT IN THE QUALITY OF COMMUNICATIONS.

AUBURN, N. Y., *January* 17, 1855.

PERHAPS some good may result from a few notes in regard to my daily paths. O, if I could only paint the changing scenes and pleasant places through which I pass in this TEACHING excursion. . . . . But the spirit of description is not upon me this morning. The incidents of my journey are interesting to me, but I have not the assurance that ——— could see in them a similar fascination. . . . . Since my departure from Hartford, I have addressed thousands of my fellow-men. . . . . Although I have, ere this, visited several of the localities, yet now my spirit beholds them as fairer than before. They are like familiar forms clad in new garments of brighter texture, . . perhaps, because a marked change, an internal improvement has occurred in the people since 1853. Then I found every audience alive only in the direction of Miracle and Mystery. Now, I find more solidity of thought, and more attraction manifested toward the truly philosophic departments of Harmonial Reform. . . . . In 1852–3, my observations led me to state publicly that only 40 per cent. of the occurring phenomena were traceable to spiritual causes. Now I can affirm truthfully that fully 70 per cent. is a legitimate emanation from the higher sphere of human existence. . . . . Another fact is remarkable. The *character* of the correspondence between the *two worlds* has been steadily progressing in purity and wisdom. True, here and there I encounter a medium, who, by organization, *invites* ordinary manifestation. But this class is rapidly finding its healthy limitations.

Many experiences on my trip are of too *interior* a nature to admit of hasty description; therefore, as I write these notes in haste, they must for the present remain untold. . . . . Occasionally, while discoursing, my perceptions are far beyond my audience. New views open before me, brighter and grander than when surrounded by witnesses in days of yore. Spiritual "new births" in the hearts of persons occur in all directions. I have seen many a crucified REASON resurrected, and the heart of an auditor suddenly awakened to newness of life, inspired with noble resolutions in favor of human redemption from discord, and in favor yet more of the unconditional emancipation of *slaves* in all climes and under all circumstances. In the light of Harmonial Gospel I now and then behold the things and dwellers of earth touched with a heavenly radiance, as the "morning dawn streams over the horizon of hope," and as the promises of eternal progression come to my soul, indorsed unmistakably by Nature's every principle. . . . . Steadily my spirit is approaching the westward localities. But I fear my time is too limited to visit them all. The southern tier of towns in the State of New York I must pass entirely by, in consequence of engagements in cities.

. . . . Rev. J. H. Fowler is on the same path with me. He is a graduate of Cambridge, was a clergyman for a few years, but is now in the field of the New Dispensation. Of course he is preaching *Reform*. . . .

67.

ORTHODOX OPPOSITION TO REFORM IN THE MARRIAGE RELATION.

BROOKLYN, *August* 24, 1855.

THIS forenoon was spent in writing and meditation. . . . . Returning from the customary afternoon trip to New York, the mail-carrier met me at the door, and delivered into my hand a copy of the N. Y. *Independent*, edited by Henry Ward Beecher, containing the following not remarkable specimen of Dr. George B. Cheever's Christian fairness and liberality :—

> "'THE GREAT HARMONIA.'—Somebody has sent us volume four of a series issued by that impudent pretender, Andrew Jackson Davis. The course of our duty has compelled us to form some acquaintance with many bad books, but with none *more* dedestable than this."

Yet Henry Ward Beecher himself is believed, *by the majority* of "Christian clergymen" to be a dangerous man, and his paper of course is considered a "dangerous" sheet. . . . . . Only a few days ago, very soon after the publication of this Fourth volume, I chanced to take up an influential weekly journal, containing a somewhat different notice by the Editor thus :—

"We would earnestly call attention to the fourth volume of the 'GREAT HARMONIA,' by A. J. Davis, recently published. Perhaps there are some of our readers who have not read it; and our appeal is to them, that they do so at once. It contains suggestions of wisdom that should be appropriated by every lover of his kind. Says the author upon the title-page—'Absolute purity of heart and life is the richest human possession; and perfect obedience to the highest attractions of the soul is the only means of its attainment.' This is a key to the work. Oh, that this comprehensive treatise upon physiological vices and virtues could be universally read and digested by the youth of our land. The true field of the Reformer is this. Scatter the seed *among the youth*, where it will surely find a genial soil, and germinate to profit."

And in another paper, only yesterday, I noticed this appeal:—

"Reader, have you read this excellent book? If not, do not delay procuring it and reading it carefully, deliberately, repeatedly, especially if you have or belong to a family. You will find the price of it one of the best expenditures you ever made. Do not lose time by pleading poverty or want of money; do without tobacco, tea, coffee, meat, or even bread for the body, until you secure this bread for the soul. It is the best, because it is the most practical of that excellent author's works; it teaches the true theory of life—especially of conjugal and parental life. Every family who has a copy of the Bible, should have a copy of this book by its side, and read it as often, until the best teaching of the Bible, or Christianity, has become practical, and improved upon by a living reform."

On the other hand, by way of variety to spice up public thought, the evangelical editor of the Hartford *Courant* says:—

"This fourth volume of the gospel according to Andrew Jackson Davis, contains the physiological vices and virtues, and the seven phases of marriage. We think it one of the worst books ever published; calculated, if followed up, to overthrow all that the laws and the gospel of Christ have ordained concerning the sacredness of marriage."

68.

AN ORTHODOX EDITOR ON THE ORIGIN OF FREE LOVE.

HARTFORD, *October* 25, 1855.

THE respectable orthodox editor of the respectable Hartford *Courant* appears this morning in the following atrocious love story:—

One of the consequences of the "Gospel according to Andrew Jackson Davis" is the introduction of the new, sensual, abominable doctrine of Free Love. It would break up all the benefits which God ordained should arise from the family circle to children in their education in purity and usefulness, and to the domestic happiness of man. It would make society one complete brothel, and all men and women its unprincipled inmates. It is time that men who value the purity of the domestic home, the chastity of uncontaminated woman, and the preservation of the next generation in virtue, should lift up their voices against this most abominable doctrine. The following is but one of many of the instances of this fatal doctrine—catering to the very lowest and worst passions of human nature: "A lady residing in Ainslie street, Williamsburg, appeared before Colonel Ming, at the Mayor's office, yesterday morning, and entered a complaint that her husband for a year past has been a member of a spiritual circle which meets at 193 Bowery; and he says that he has received a communication informing him that it was just and proper that he should form new associations with females whenever he saw fit, and with as many different ones as his spirit might move him to. He also endeavors to persuade her to receive the visits of different men, assuring her that there is no harm in her doing so, notwithstanding she has two children by him." So much for departing from the faith of the gospel of Christ and going astray after the delusions and errors of Spiritualism! "By its fruits ye shall know it." If it has any origin beyond that of living humbuggery, it is that of the Infernal Regions!

69.

"JUSTITIA" WEIGHS THE "COURANT" EDITOR IN THE BALANCE.

HARTFORD, *October* 27, 1855.

To the Editor of the Courant:—

AN article in your paper of the 25th, under the above title, is calculated to do great injustice from its misstatements, unintentional, no doubt, and which you will gladly see corrected. You associate with what the public have chosen to call Free Love, the name of Andrew Jackson Davis, and the body of the believers in Spiritualism, making the Spiritualists responsible for the opinions of Mr. Davis, and asserting that Mr. Davis was the introducer of the doctrine of Free Love. *Both these statements are entirely incorrect.* Mr. Davis did not introduce the doctrine of Free Love. It had been advocated in various forms before he ever uttered a word to the public. I do not know that he even accepts it. But I do know that he did not originate it; that it was taught long ago, and is still, by those having no connection whatever with him. But for his views on this or any other matter, Spiritualists are not responsible. Spiritualism did not originate with Mr. Davis, nor does it indorse his opinions. His "Revelations," so-called, were published before Spiritualism was heard of, and never claimed to have been dictated by spirits, but to have been uttered by him in a state of trance. As a believer in Spiritualism, which he subsequently became, he is but one of hundreds of thousands, many of whom have no sympathy with, or even knowledge of, his opinions. He is not in any measure the founder of the faith, nor of the body accepting it.

As to the relation of Spiritualists to Free Love, it is to be said, first, that the doctrine, so-called, did not originate with them. The Socialists, before them, were charged with it, and with equal injustice. Second, the Spiritualists have never indorsed the doctrine. The story which you quote, if true, only shows how a sensual man may abuse Spiritualism to promote his sensual ends, even as others have actually perverted the Christian Scriptures for the same purpose. But it is an old, and still a true saying, that the abuse of a thing is no argument against its use. Third, the avowal of this doctrine has not been peculiar to Spiritualists. The club in New York City, about which there has been so much excitement, was not made up of Spiritualists. Indeed, no evidence has been furnished that any considerable portion of it consisted of this class. And lastly, the doctrine numbers very few advocates among the Spiritualists. They are an insignificant minority, numerically speaking, some few score, perhaps, among hundreds of thousands; while among the majority opposed to the doctrine, there have been frequent condemnations of its tendencies, and that long before any of the public prints thought fit to stir in the matter.

It is quite time that the public were candid enough to recognize what has been often asserted by the Spiritualists themselves, viz: that they have but one article of faith, in which they all unite, and for which they, as a whole, are responsible, which is, "that spirits can and do communicate with man," and that for all abuses of this doctrine, and for all other opinions or practices entertained by individuals, individuals only are to be held accountable.

I have written the above, Mr. Editor, not as an indorser of Mr. Davis, or a believer in Spiritualism, or an advocate of Free Love. For I am neither, least of all, the last; but as one bound to obey Christ's injunction to "judge righteous judgment." I hold it neither just nor right to make a body of individuals, among whom are to be found, as I know, some of the purest minds, responsible for the vagaries or the vices which a few of their number, in common with many more not of their number, may display; especially when such responsibility has been repeatedly, in private and in public, repudiated.

JUSTITIA.

70.

ABIGAIL MOSES, A TYPE OF THE FREE LOVERS.

BROOKLYN, *December* 6, 1855

IT is said that a certain clique of New Yorkers, mostly socialists and retired *literati*, have organized a kind of private Drawing-room Association for the purpose of of discussing freely questions not elsewhere admissible . . . . It is also reported that the majority of these persons are Spiritualists . . . . Whether this is true, or not, I do not know, for I have only to-day heard any thing definite concerning the Society. I have just read, with considerable amusement, the following

Letter from Abigail Moses to the New York Evening Post, Explanatory of how she found out what her "Innard Natur'" required.

I raily haint a minit of time, dear neighbor, Mrs. Baldwin, to devote to nobody, but I do recon I'd better jest let you know somethin' about this here society of associationers I'm contemplatin' joinin'. Afore I begin I'd like to menshun that if you'd just step in and see to husband's stockin's I'd take it agreeable. I hadn't no time to mend 'em, for Professor K——h had such a heap to tell me about the innard development, and of his spiritual coalition with my spiritual witals, that I sat a good bit longer than I meant to, with him; an' somehow or other he ketched a hold of my hand an' said he didn't know when he'd been so monstrously drawed to any body afore. He hadn't nothin' to say agin my husband; he might be a very clever person; but yet he felt convinced my natur was sich an elevated one, he raily believed my wants hadn't never been met.

I told him sure enough they hadn't, but I reckoned the reason was, we were too poor to go to further expense, buying things. But I did confess, if there was a want I had, it was for a new parlor carpet, ourn was a gittin' so dreadful shabby. The Professor gin me an awful nudge then, and said I must excuse him, if he didn't feel disposed for joking that morning; he was a sufferin' most tremenjous innard tortures, 'cause he'd been misunderstood the day afore by a person who wasn't great enough to comprehend him. Of course I let on *I* understood him, and pretended I'd been jokin', but afterwards, when I went to the meetin', I found out all about what it meant; and I'm real miserable, neighbor Baldwin, to think I've been a livin' these sixteen years with Hiram Moses, an' he's never yet comprehended what my natur' required.

I know my hull bein' haint called into play; there's only one set of faculties a goin', an' I might as well be a livin' mummy, as to be mated with such a noodle. Brother B—e ses he's convinced me and him has sich a sympathy for one another, that we must have played together when we was children in some other state of existence, an' though I don't remember ever bein' in that state, yet I s'pose it's jest so. Brother B—e is a very spiritual soul, an' is jest as developed as he can be. Me and him has sich good times together, and sich beautiful attractions to one another, that we don't think no more of kissin' than if we was two females. He sed I needn't tell Hiram, though, for it wasn't likely he'd understand how our spirits met, an' he was one of those common-place beins who might go and kick up a rumpus about me a kissin' another woman's husband.

I do declare it's too bad to be forced into sich a position as I am with Hiram; but Dr. C—s ses that's just the way with him an' his wife; she haint no understandin' of the ideal beauty of sich friendships, and don't begin to fill up the measure of his soul's yearnin' after perfection. Poor fellow! he's so often cast back upon himself that it is enough to crush his too sensitive natur'. The meetin's on thursday nihhts is all the comfort I have. There's been Professor K—h an' S—, Dr. E—y, an' Mr. H— an' Mr. H—s, that's all situated just in the same uncomfortable way in their domestic relations, besides several females that's studyin' medicine and 'natomy so hard that they partake quite of the natur' of skeletons. Their souls is developed at the expense of their poor, frail, perishable bodies.

E— B— don't think no more of dissectin' dead bodies than she would of cuttin' up a roast chicken. I don't know as I'd trust her to treat my neuralogy, but Hiram might just as well employ the poor thing for his rheumatiz as not. She looks as though she might handle a right gripin' case pretty severe. But the best of all is the principles we purfess. There we sit the hull evenin' and jest discourse about the poor oppressed creatures that have to git their livin' at shovelin' snow, handlin' wood, and so on. It would raily do your marrow bones good to see the benevolence and charity that prevails, an' how they remarks, they don't want no body to do nothin' that don't agree with 'em—an' I'm sure mendin' stockin's don't agree with me.

An' they tell sich lovely anecdotes about them who go on an' git every thing done as cheap as they can, so as to cheat folks, an' grind down the poor. And then, besides all this active goodness an' a strugglin' to redeem their feller bein's, they have a festival about onst a year, so as to hear the remarks of them as comes from the furrin cities—such as Boston and Philadelphia—consarnin' the wickedness of people in not payin' their workmen; an' Brother C— often draws tears from the female members regardin' the tramplin' down of their blessed privileges. He's lovely, an' there aint one of us females, ugly or otherwise, but what he's willin' to embrace in gospel love.

I do hope, neighbor Baldwin, that I'm as virtuous a person as there is in the world; but I must say, I can't see a bit of harm in relievin' my full sympathies in the buzzums of them that are my spiritual partners—'cause wat's the body, any how? 'Taint no more than a wet blanket throw'd over the sperrit—a squenchin' the yearnin' after that soul communion that every well-developed person feels. Mr. R—— says 'I'm a great soul,' and that sich sentiments has inaugurated me more tangibly into his best feelin's than any paltry takin' on of what the world calls 'modesty.' Ses he to me, a standin' on the steps t'other night, 'Would we was in the blessed Philanstery!' My sperrit whispered 'Without Hiram,' tho; an' his'n immediat elyresponded in an audible 'Yes.' So completely do we meet one another.

We have been readin' Jacque together. I recon you wouldn't be pleased with his observations on this, but it's the very epitome of morality and virtue, we think. I'm come to the end of my sheet, and here's Hiram just come in—ugh? My soul revolts from him. But I'm doomed to misery. Pity my unfortunate organization that requires sich different associations.

Yourn,

ABIGAIL MOSES.

P. S.—I send you some verses which I've bin a ritin' to try to settle the commotions that's continually ragin' in my breast when I think of my contrary attractions:

VERSES BY ABIGAIL MOSES.

I aint a doin' nothin else,
  But walking paths that's thorny,
For him that needs my werry soul
  Is going to Californy.
And now I'm left to bear the brunt
  Of life with Hiram Moses;
He's just as different from me,
  As poppies is from roses.

He eats and drinks, and works and sleeps,
  An' aint a bad provider,
But nectar's all the same to him
  As so much beer and cider.
I hate this way of doin' life,
  In sums of vulgar fractions;
My spirit yearns for sympathy,
  And 'passional attractions.'

My spiral natur's innard self,
  Has gone and bin divided;
Of course I can't be nothin' else,
  But innardly lop-sided;
I keep a graspin' after things
  That's neither here nor yonder,
Just like a goose that's yoked for life
  To him that aint her gander.

I know we'll meet in sperrit yet,
  But some how human natur',
Let's try to squelch it all we can,
  Develops soon or later.

And if it's true, 'All flesh is grass,'
  It's time ole Hiram Moses
Was greenin' in the pickle now,
  For that Metempsychosis.

He haint got no ideal life,
  And 'pivotal revolvin',
He don't begin to comprehend,
  Or even think of solvin';
I sometimes wish my views of things
  Was all confined to wittals,
To makin' bread and pumpkin pies,
  An' scourin' pots and kettles.

And then I shouldn't feel so bad,
  Because I ain't rewealin',
To some one else's t'other self,
  My undeweloped feelins;
I wonder when the time'll come,
  That in association,
A studyin' of the beautiful,
  I'll follow my vocation.

71.

SPIRITUALISM OVERTHROWN BY THE PROFESSORS OF HARVARD UNIVERSITY.

NEW YORK, *July* 10, 1857.

THE Boston controversy respecting "Spiritualism," growing out of an offer of $500 by *The Courier* to any one who could exhibit in the presence and to the satisfaction of certain eminent Professors of the Natural Sciences, in Harvard University, any such marvelous, phenomena as were commonly reported by Spiritualists as having transpired in the presence if not through the agency of certain persons designated "mediums," has resulted, after a week's investigation, in the following award:—

"The Committee award that Dr. Gardner, having failed to produce before them an agent or medium who 'communicated a 'word imparted to the spirits in an adjoining room,' 'who read a 'word in English written inside a book or folded sheet of paper,' who answered any question 'which the superior intelligence must 'be able to answer,' 'who tilted a piano without touching it, or 'caused a chair to move a foot;' and having failed to exhibit to the Committee any phenomenon which, under the widest latitude of interpretation, could be regarded as equivalent to either of these proposed tests, or any phenomenon which required for its production, or in any manner indicated a force which could technically be denominated Spiritual, or which was hitherto unknown to science, or a phenomenon of which the cause was not palpable to the Committee, is, therefore, not entitled to claim from *The Boston Courier* the proposed premium of $500.

"It is the opinion of the Committee, derived from observation that any connection with spiritualistic circles, so called, corrupts the morals and degrades the intellect. They therefore deem it their solemn duty to warn the community against this contaminating influence, which surely tends to lessen the truth of man and the purity of woman.

"The Committee will publish a report of their proceedings, together with the results of additional investigations and other evidence, independent of the special case submitted to them, but bearing upon the subject of this stupendous delusion.

"Benjamin Pierce, Chairman,
"Ls. Agassiz,
"B. A. Gould,
"E. N. Horsfold.

"Cambridge, *June* 29, 1857."

It is most important to history, and should be recorded in full, that Dr. Gardner absolutely and unequivocally testifies that the four learned gentlemen insisted upon rejecting and violating *all* the *laws* and *conditions* by which spirits can influence mediums and demonstrate their presence and power.

If we mistake not, a similar investigation was had and a similar judgment rendered at Paris some seventy odd years ago, with regard to the alleged phenomena popularly known as Mesmerism or Animal Magnetism.

And if we mistake not, a similar opinion or judgment was pronounced by certain learned Jewish Doctors, some eighteen hundred and sixty years ago, with regard to those now known as the Founder and First Apostles of Christianity.

We wonder if the Harvard gentlemen ever heard of the Pope's bull against Galileo and the revolving planets!

72.

FATHER ROBINSON EXCOMMUNICATES THE BAPTIST CHURCH.

PROVIDENCE, R. I., *August* 10, 1857.

THE few months past, like all the months of the previous two years, have been full of opposition. The orthodox world has been extremely bitter and wicked. . . . But the progressive work is going forward. To-day's mail brings a telling letter from Mary's Father to the

Orthodox Church. It is entitled to a place in the history of this war:—

HOLLEY, N. Y., *June* 22, 1857.

To my brethren of the Second Freewill Baptist Church, in Clarendon:—

I wish you to give me a letter of dismissal from your church, for the following reasons:—

1st. I would not say to you that "Nature's Divine Revelations," by A. J. Davis, or the "Harmonial Philosophy," by the same author, are better moral guides than the Bible, or a truer history of the "Creation;" but I do say, that in my opinion, whatever good Orthodoxy may have done in a ruder state of the world, it has ceased to do any now. Sectarianism can do but little more good if it ever did any. The churches are a dead weight to all reform movements. They fought the Temperance cause till it was made popular by the "Infidel" world. Indeed, they never have taken hold unitedly in it. So with the Anti-Slavery cause and other reforms. Church members, priests, and laymen, are just as filthy—smoking, chewing, spitting, perhaps drinking and lusting after "filthy lucre" if not the flesh—as other men. Many of them make the Bible support and sustain Slavery, Polygamy, Intemperance, Popery, Protestantism, and all Sectarianism.

2d. So then I have come to the firm conviction that the world needs now a new race of Reformers—purer and holier than the Church affords, more philanthropic, loving, and harmonious, less sensual and selfish, requiring less money than it takes to move the sectarian machinery. A new Theology, too, more consistent and rational, more in harmony with natural laws and of more universal application than the Orthodox—more vital religion, with less formality, hypocrisy, sanctity and fanaticism—more honesty, with less craft and duplicity—drawn and held together by fitness and mutual attractions instead of creeds. This new class of Reformers should embrace all good and pure men and women, in and out of the Church.

C. ROBINSON.

73.

TOUCHING STORY OF TWO POOR LITTLE BOYS.

BOSTON, *August* 12, 1857.

A MORNING paper says that the Hon. A. H. Stephens, of Georgia, in a recent address at a meeting in Alexandria, for the benefit of the Orphan Asylum and Free School of that city, related the following anecdote:—

"A poor little boy, in a cold night, with no home or roof to shelter his head, no paternal or maternal guardian or guide to protect or direct him on his way, reached at nightfall the house of a wealthy planter, who took him in, fed him, and sent him on his way with his blessing. Those kind attentions cheered his heart, and inspired him with fresh courage to battle with the obstacles of life. Years rolled round; Providence led him on, and he had reached the legal profession; his host died; the cormorants that prey on the substance of man had formed a conspiracy to get from the widow her estates. She sent for the nearest counsel, to commit her cause to him, and that counsel proved to be the orphan boy long before welcomed and entertained by her deceased husband. The stimulant of warm and tenacious gratitude was now added to the ordinary motive connected with the profession. He undertook her cause with a will not easily to be resisted; he gained it; the widow's estates were secured to her in perpetuity; and Mr. Stephens added, with an emphasis of emotion that sent an electric thrill throughout the house, *that orphan boy now stands before you.*"

It is not always certain that every "poor little boy"

will reach the same goal; yet each should strive to deserve the best reward. Not long since we met a paragraph to the following effect:—

"I once knew an industrious boy whose parents were poor, but honest. He commenced life in the commercial metropolis without a cent; he had a wart on his nose, and a sore foot; but, nothing daunted, he worked with a determination and will, backed by perseverance and energy, and nobly fought his way along, surmounting every obstacle. . . . Mark the result: Last week I met him for the first time in ten years, and that little boy who commenced life only ten short years ago without a cent, hasn't got a darned cent yet."

74.

A SCIENTIFIC EXPLANATION OF THE CAUSE OF VISION.

PROVIDENCE, R. I., *August* 17, 1857.

THE learned and distinguished Professor Felton, of Harvard University, has just appeared in the editorial columns of the *Boston Courier*, as follows:—

"Some of the most conspicuous figures in the drama of Spiritualism, are the trance-mediums or speakers. This form of inspiration, so far as it is connected with the present state of things, was first introduced, we believe, by a famous Seer, who asserts that he can read the *London Times* across the ocean as well as a book in his hand. For aught we know, it may be true. We remember once sitting at the side of a singular-looking personage, at a hotel table. Our attention was drawn to him by the extraordinary speed with which the edibles on the table vanished down his capacious throat. The raps on the table for fresh supplies resembled in frequency and vehemence those which are heard in the best constituted spiritual circles. Soup, beef, mutton, poultry, fish, cabbage—in short, nearly every thing on the bill of fare—

came and were seen no more. We were filled—not with dinner, for wonder held our appetite in suspense—but with amazement. It seemed as if he must be a conjurer. It looked like the performances of Jack the Giant Killer, when he slyly thrusts the enormous pudding into a bag under his waistcoat. We do not usually inquire the names of those whom we chance to meet at hotel tables; but there was something so miraculous in this gentleman's performances, that curiosity gained the better of reserve, and we were told the great Devourer was *Andrew Jackson Davis*. This explained the matter. *His trances were now to be traced to their true cause.* They are the trances of an anaconda after he has swallowed an ox, horns, hoof, and tail. He has not only his own earthly organism to support, but the spiritualistic organisms of the innumerable higher intelligences."

I hope there is no person living who waits for my positive denial before rejecting the above as a total fabrication. . . . I make a note of the statement to show how vulgar a falsehood can emanate from a source high in the estimation of literary gentlemen in Boston. Verily, prejudice blunts the moral sense, and makes intellect an ally of bigotry.

75.

THE CONDITION OF NEW ENGLAND MOTHERS.

BUFFALO, N. Y., *September* 28, 1857.

WE know of no one cause more responsible for whatever there may be of physical degeneracy among the farming population (says a writer in the *Atlantic*) than the treatment of its child-bearing women; and this after all, is but a result of entire devotion to the tyrannical idea of labor. If there be one office or character higher than all others, it is the office or character of mother. Surely the bringing into existence so marvelous a thing as a human being, and the training of that being until it assumes a recognized relation to God and human society, is a sacred office, and one which does not yield in dignity and importance to any other under heaven. For a woman who faithfully fulfils this office, who submits without murmuring to all its pains, who patiently performs its duties, and who exhausts her life in a ceaseless overflow of love upon those whom God has given her, no words can express a true man's veneration. She claims the homage of our hearts, the service of our hands, the devotion of our lives.

Yet what is the position of them other in the New England farmer's home? The farmer is careful of every animal he possesses. The farm-yard and the stall are replenished with young, by creatures for months dismissed from labor, or handled with intelligent care while carrying their burden; because the farmer knows that only in this way can he secure improvement, and sound, symmetrical development, to the stock of his farm. In this he is a true, practical philosopher. But what is his treatment of her who bears his children? The same physiological laws apply to her that apply to the brute. Their strict observance is greatly more imperative, because of her finer organization; yet they are not thought of; and if the farm-yard fail to shame the nursery, if the mother bear beautiful and well-organized children, Heaven be thanked for a merciful interference with the operation of its own laws! Is the mother in the farm-house ever regarded as a sacred being?

Look at her hands! Look at her face! Loo at her bent and clumsy form! Is it more important to raise fine colts than fine men and women? Is human life to be made secondary and subordinate to animal life? Is not she who should receive the tenderest and most considerate ministries of the farmer's home, in all its appointments and in all its service, made the ceaseless minister and servant of the home and all within it, with utter disregard of her office? To expect a population to improve greatly under this method is simply to expect miracles; and to expect a farmer's life and a farmer's home to be attractive where the mother is a drudge, and secures less consideration than the pets of the stall, is to expect impossibilties.

76.

JERKS AMONG PRESBYTERIANS, METHODISTS, BAPTISTS, EPISCOPALIANS, QUAKERS, AND INDEPENDENTS.

DETROIT, MICH., *October* 2, 1857.

IT seems that the different popular religious sects, now *so* proud and *so* respectable, in their *juvenile days* out-jerked the spiritual mediums by considerable! A correspondent gives a description of these singular manifestations among the fashionable Christians. Most physicians regard these twitchings, swoonings, trances, visions, &c., as a nervous affection, produced by a strong impression upon the mind, and think there is a sympathetic influence making them contagious to some extent. The facts connected with their appearance are as follows:—

"Five or six weeks since, during a protracted meeting held by the Methodists at Indian Grove, several persons were seized immediately after conversion, with what are called the jerks; that is, a contraction and expansion of the muscles that caused the arms to move suddenly either horizontally, up and down, or obliquely, and with such a rapid motion that it convinced every one that it was done involuntarily.

"After the lapse of a few weeks, a similar meeting was commenced at Avoca, and with similar results. Each evening, for several evenings, the number of jerkers increased, until it is supposed that there were as many as fifty seized with this strange disease, and what makes it seem quite singular is, each one differed from another in jerking; no two jerked precisely alike. One was seen jumping violently with both feet—another dancing—another shaking the head—another reeling backward and forward—another still from side to side—some jerked both hands and feet, and others performed strange convulsions indescribable; some clapped their hands—one laughed heartily—another made a noise similar to a puppy, and yet another gave forth a chuckle similar to demoniac. The dancing, clapping of hands, and some other motions, were called forth generally only as the shouting and responding became boisterous.

"All this was witnessed by hundreds, and yet not one who was a close observer will declare that he thinks any of this feigned or within the power of the victim of these strange phenomena to control. Indeed, persons from time to time seized the jerkers by the arm and tried to prevent it, but found it impossible. Many of them, at home or abroad, asleep or awake, were in motion. None of them seemed at all insane—they were generally of a happy frame of mind, and some declared they were never so happy as when jerking hardest. So intensely were some of them exerted, and so violent the action of their limbs, that when in meeting, water had to be passed constantly to them, while the perspiration incessantly rolled down their cheeks."

Goodrich (Peter Parley), in his interesting "Recollections of a Lifetime," vol. I., page 200, &c., gives some curious items concerning the *jerks* which prevailed in the early days of Methodism in Kentucky and Tennessee, at the beginning of the present century.

"At the religious gatherings," says he, "whether in dwellings and churches, or in the open woods and fields, persons would be suddenly taken with certain irresistible spasms, inciting them to the most strange and extravagant performances. Some would bark like dogs, and attempt to climb the trees, declaring that they were treeing the devil. Some had delicious trances; others danced as if beset with sudden frenzy; others still were agitated by violent and revolting convulsions and twitchings, which obtained the popular name of *jerks*. All classes of persons who came within the atmosphere of the mania, Methodists, Presbyterians, and Quakers, men and women, became subjects of these extraordinary agitations. I recollect to have heard the late Thomas H. Gallaudet say that, when a young man, he visited one of the meetings where these phenomena were taking place, and that he felt within himself an almost uncontrollable temptation to imitate some of the strange antics that were going on around him."

Howe's *Great West* mentions the same occurrence, stating that the first instances occurred at a sacrament in East Tennessee, and that "the contagion even spread to Ohio, among the sober people of the Western Reserve."

The celebrated Lorenzo Dow has an interesting account of the *jerks*:—

"Sunday, February 19, I spoke in Knoxville, to hundreds more than could get into the court-house—the Governor being present. About one hundred and fifty appeared to have jerking exercise, among whom was a circuit preacher (Johnson), who had opposed them a little before, but he now had them powerfully; and I believe he would have fallen over three times, had not the auditory been so crowded that he could not, unless he fell perpendicularly.

"After meeting, I rode eighteen miles to hold meeting at night. The people of this settlement were mostly Quakers, and they had said, as I was informed, that 'the Methodists and Presbyterians have the JERKS because they SING and PRAY so much; but we are a still, peaceable people, wherefore we do not have them;' however, about twenty of them came to meeting, to hear one, as was said, somewhat in a Quaker line. But their usual stillness and silence was interrupted, for about a dozen of them had the jerks as keen and as powerful as any I had seen, so as to have occasioned a kind of grunt or groan when they would jerk. It appears that many have undervalued the Great Revival, and attempted to account for it altogether on natural principles; therefore it seems to me, from the best judgment I can form, that God hath seen proper to take this method to convince people that he will work in a way to show his power, and sent the jerks as a sign of the times, partly in judgment for the people's unbelief, and yet as a mercy to convict people of divine realities.

"I have seen Presbyterians, Methodists, Quakers, Baptists, Church of England, and Independents, exercised with the jerks. Gentleman and lady, white and black, the aged and the youth, rich and poor, without exception; from which I infer, as it can not be accounted for on natural principles, and carries such marks of involuntary motion, that it is no trifling matter. I believe that they who were the most pious and given up to God are rarely touched with it; and also those naturalists, who wish and try to get it to philosophize upon it, are excepted; but the lukewarm, lazy, half-hearted, indolent professor is subject to it; and many of them I have seen, who, when it came upon them, would be alarmed, and stirred up to redouble their diligence with God, and after they would get happy, were thankful that it ever came upon them. Again, the wicked are frequently more afraid of it than the small-pox or yellow fever. These are subject to it; but the persecutors are more subject to it than any, and they sometimes have cursed and swore and damned it whilst jerking. There is no pain attending the jerks except they resist them, which, if they do, it will weary them more in an hour than a day's labor, which shows that it requires the consent of the will to avoid suffering.

"I passed by a meeting-house, where I observed the undergrowth had been cut up for a camp-meeting, and from fifty to one hundred saplings left breast-high, which to me appeared so slovenish that I could not but ask my guide the cause, who observed they were topped so high, and left for the peeple to jerk by. This so excited my attention that I went over the ground to view it, and found, where the people had laid hold of them and jerked so powerfully, that they had kicked up the earth as a horse stamping flies. I observed some emotion both this day and night among the people. A Presbyterian minister (with whom I stayed) observed: 'Yesterday, whilst I was speaking, some had the jerks, and a young man from North Carolina mimicked them out of derision, and soon was seized with them himself (which was the case with many others). He grew ashamed, and on attempting to mount his horse to go off, his foot jerked about so that he could not put it into the stirrup. Some youngsters seeing this, assisted him on, but he jerked so that he could not sit alone, and one got up to hold him on, which was done with difficulty. I, observing this, went to him, and asked him what he thought of it. Said he, 'I believe God sent it on me for my wickedness, and making light of it in others;' and he requested me to pray for him."

77.

THE ABOMINABLE TEACHINGS OF SPIRITUALISM.

BATTLE CREEK, MICH., *October* 14, 1857.

A GREAT friend of Methodism, and one who edits a journal in the interests of Christ, opens thus:—

From a paper entitled the *Illuminati*, published under the auspices of the Spiritualists, we take the following:

The third annual meeting of a so-called Religious Association was held at North Collins, Erie County, New York, on the 25th, 26th, and 27th of September last. From the minutes of its proceedings, as published in the *Age of Progress*, we learn that Andrew J. and Mary F. Davis were prominent among the speakers on the occasion. The following among other declarations, or "testimonies," indicates the doctrine of Mr. and Mrs. Davis:—

WOMAN AND MARRIAGE. — *Resolved*, That woman, being the mother of the world and a coequal with man in the heritage of immortality, should be favored with every advantage enjoyed by her brother, for physical, intellectual, and moral education or development; that all civil and political privileges and emoluments should be as accessible to her as to man; that the same remuneration should be granted to her as to her brother for the same kind and amount of labor; and that, in the marriage relation, she should be fully secured in her natural rights to property, to the legal custody of her children, and to the entire control of her own person, that thereby fewer and better children may be born, and humanity be improved and elevated.

This same editor and follower of the New Testament, after quoting the above resolution, says:—" A. J. Davis claims to have sprung from monkeys and baboons; and certainly his doctrine is worthy of such an ancestry. Yet this wretch in human form claims to be a reformer, and it is a mournful commentary on the state of public morals that he has numerous followers. . . . The whole vile breed are fit only for a lunatic asylum. This miserable delusion is styled by its victims 'the new religion.' Such a religion is, in the strongest possible sense, 'earthly, sensual, and devilish.' To every pure mind it is loathsome and disgusting to the last degree. The man, and still more the woman, that will publicly teach such doctrines, should be shunned, as we would shun the devil, whose servants they are. When one is fairly drawn into the vortex of this abominable delusion, there is no hope for him. It is a leprosy which defies all cure. It is a signing, sealing, and delivering of the soul to Satan, beyond all redemption. When will the community have sense enough and moral principle enough to shun these 'filthy dreamers?' Their very touch is polluting, and the 'poison of asps is under their tongues.'"

78.

VARIOUS FORMS OF MAN'S CRUELTY TO WOMAN.

BATTLE CREEK, MICH., *October* 18, 1857

AN article in the last number of the *North British Review* contains some strong remarks on the outrages which women in all classes of society endure. The writer contrasts the so-called "brutality of the lower orders" with the heartlessness of "the higher orders," and shows that blows inflicted on the body are not always the worst forms of outrage. Brutality is a common trait among the ignorant and degraded poor of England, and wife-beating is an offense of daily report in the English police courts. But the writer in the *Review* draws a picture of a class, who, though they do not beat their wives, treat them still more cruelly :—

Men of education and refinement do not strike women ; neither do they strike one another. This is not their mode of expressing resentment. They may utter words more cutting than sharp knives ; they may do things more stunning in their effects on the victim than the blows of pokers or hammers ; they may kill their wives by process of slow torture—unkindness, infidelity, whatever shape it may assume—and society will forgive them. The law, too, has nothing to say to them. They are not guilty of what is recognized as an assault, because they only assail the affections—only lacerate the heart. They speak with horror of the "brutal wretches" who inflict on women blows, less painful at the time, and less abiding in their effects. But is their treatment of women any better than that of these ruffians? Have they any higher sense of what is due to womanhood? They would not besmear a fair face with blood; but they would set a tender heart bleeding until it can bleed no more. They would not mar the beauty of God's handiwork ; but they would soil the purity of a virgin soul.

And here is a terrible and true accusation, entirely outside and beyond the spiritualistic movement :—

There are various forms of man's cruelty to women, of which wife-beating, we are afraid, is not the worst. To seduce, betray, and desert a young and beautiful woman, in the first freshness and innocence of youth—to leave her to die slowly of hunger, disease, or gin, or suddenly, by a leap, on a cold winter's night, from the parapet of a bridge spanning the Thames, is to do what must be done amongst us on a much larger scale than wife-beating—else whence all these evidences of the "great sin of great cities?" and it is to do it quietly and deliberately, under no irresistible provocation, and with none of those attendant excuses or palliations which are not unfairly pleaded on behalf of the poor, uneducated, ignorant man, whose neglected childhood and misguided youth are naturally and necessarily followed by a brutalized manhood.

79.

WANTED—MORE KNOWLEDGE CONCERNING MARRIAGE AND PARENTAGE.

AURORA, ILL., *October* 22, 1857.

I WONDER why really just and intelligent mothers and fathers do not take more interest in the laws of true harmonial marriage. . . . . . I suppose they are frightened by Christian editors, who cry: "Behold! the abominable teachings of Spiritualism." . . . . . . O, when will the mass rise superior to their own foolish prejudices? Domestic vices and evils are to be totally *destroyed* by the teachings of Spiritualism. Read this testimony:—

In one of the New England States lives a lad, now about twelve or thirteen years of age, whose condition is a most remarkable demonstration of the natural law that, in every case, the child is a very faithful copy of his parents.

The boy is a natural drunkard. From his birthday to the present moment, he has given all the outward indications of being deeply drunk; and yet, so far as I know, or think it probable, he has never swallowed a drop of ardent spirits in his life. Though in good sound health, he has never been able to walk without staggering. His head is always upon his breast; and his speech is of that peculiar character which marks a person in a very low stage of intoxication. If, nevertheless, in the midst of his mutterings and reelings something is said to him in a way to pass through the thick atmosphere of his intellectual being, and penetrate his mind, he at once rouses, like a common tippler, and gives proof enough that he is not wanting in native talents, however his mental faculties are enshrouded. His disposition, also, seems to be extremely amiable. He is kind to every one around him; and I may add, he is not only pitied for his misfortune, but in spite of his lamentable condition, regarded with uncommon interest. He is looked upon as a star of no mean magnitude, obscured and almost blotted out by the mist in which he is doomed to dwell, until he shall pass from the present state of existence to another.

Now, as I understand the law of hereditary descent, there is nothing unnatural in this boy's case. Every individual ever born, is governed by the same principle which caused him to be what he is. Prior to marriage his father had been a secret but confirmed inebriate; and when the fact became known to the gentle and sweet-spirited being, who but a few months before had become his wife, the revelation was made suddenly, and in a way the most impressive and appalling. One night, when he was supposed to be the most unimpeachable of husbands, he staggered home, broke through the door of his sleeping apartment, and fell down on the floor in a state of wretched inebriation. For weeks he wallowed in misery. During the next six or seven months, seeing his domestic reputation had been forfeited, he kept up also a continuous scene of intoxication. When, at the end of this period, it was told him that he was the "husband of a mother," he reeled and staggered on without much abatement. Months passed away; but there occurred no change in the habits of the poor inebriate. It was at once discovered, however, that there was something singular in the appearance of the child. When it was three months old, there began to be strange speculations respecting it among the people. At the age of six months these speculations had settled down into a very general opinion, but not a word was said to the disconsolate woman who had also begun to have her own forebodings. At last, as she was one evening looking upon her child, and wondering what could be the reason of its strange conduct, the terrible idea flashed upon her soul—"My child is a natural drunkard!" She shrieked aloud; and her husband, who happened to be within hearing, came to her. She fell upon his neck, and exclaimed, "Dear husband, our little George is born a ——". She could proceed no further, but swooned away in her husband's arms.

From that hour the father of the boy never tasted a drop of intoxicating drinks. The sight of his eyes and the heavings of his heart entirely cured him of his habit. He seldom looks upon his unfortunate little George without shedding a tear over that sin which entailed upon him a life of obscurity and of wretchedness. He has lived, I rejoice to add, so as to redeem his character, and he is now the father of five children, all of whom are bright, and beautiful, and lovely, excepting only the one whose destiny was thus blasted.

This principle of inheriting traits and characteristics,

however, is susceptible of an indefinite number of illustrations. It has become a proverb, and it is sustained by all history and observation, that the offspring of libidinous connections are uniformly marked with tendencies to strong passions. With a world full of such or similar cases, it seems incredible that men and women should longer refuse to investigate the laws of marriage and parentage.

80.

IMPORTANT TESTIMONY OF FATHER ROBINSON.

WAUKEGAN, ILL., *December* 16, 1857.

WE have been lecturing before large audiences for many weeks. . . . . The newspapers, especially those under the management of self-styled Christians, are excessively abusive and malicious. A mass of outrageous charges, made by the editor of the *Waukegan Gazette*, has brought out from Mary's justice-loving father the following reply:—

To the Editor: * * * * * * Read the "Magic Staff" [The Autobiography of A. J. Davis], and there find a truthful relation of his first perilous adventure in this direction, and his reception at the "Robinson House," and among the relatives, the opposition and indignation he had to brave. And why all this? What troubled so many of us? Just what troubles the *Gazette* now, and all other ranting opposers—simply that we were *then* and they are *still* orthodox believers, and Mr. Davis was a disbeliever—infidel, heretic, "moral leper!"

We partook somewhat of this same sectarian prejudice—hence the cold shoulder, almost indignity, which he met with. Nothing else. We had heard of the strange phenomenon down at Poughkeepsie; a young infidel, insinuating infidel doctrines, he would contaminate us all, especially his intended; did not believe in the divine record! *Horrible! Away with him! Crucify him!* His approach to our family was felt to be like that of a huge dragon with seven heads, two tails, and ten horns, about to pitch in among us! and for this reason only—this was the sum of his offending. We knew nothing against him otherwise. He appeared like a gentleman; and I think he must have had his magic staff with him, and used it as he alleges, else he could not have endured his treatment so patiently. . . . . The ground of most, if not all, the opposition to them and their labors, is *religious intolerance!*

Said I to a clergyman here not long since, "Fowler and Combe are great guides on the subject of life and health." He retorted sharply, "They are infidels, disbelievers in the Bible, A. J. Davis with them—all of one school." Hence the inference is that their words and works are worthless. This is the spirit of Bible orthodoxy—of sectarianism. "Work in my harness, or die!" They are afraid to have the claims of the Bible discussed—it must not be—hands off. So, children are taught and made to believe—hence they never put off childish things—orthodoxy and sectarianism are in danger from the new philosophy, and it must be resisted; and where argument fails, a resort to personalities is had, and the believers in the "Father of lies" invent falsehoods to ruin the reputation of reformers, and limit their influence. It is said by this editor that Mr. Davis at a certain time "came near being mobbed." Perhaps it was at the Hartford Bible Convention, the first gathering, I suppose, in this, or any other country, to discuss and question the claims of the Bible, which barely escaped being mobbed by the *Orthodox Bible believers* there assembled—Mr. Davis being a member of that convention.

Mother Earth, by the fruits of this intolerance, is paved with human skeletons, both pagan and Christian, Mahometan and Jew. . . . . Mines of treasure have been expended, in the shape of money, time, and labor, in building temples of worship, educating and supporting a priesthood, all for the soul's eternal interest, after the Bible pattern. Now let this vast tide of wealth take a new direction—be applied more to the bodily comforts—the physical and mental wants of man—to remodel society—reform, refine, and elevate the race—promote and extend the universal brotherhood and sisterhood of man—prepare him to live right here, and the *hereafter* will take care of itself.

C. Robinson.*

* Mary's father, whose entire earthly life was one of physical and mental industry, crowned with truth and honor, has taken up his residence in the Summer Land. If the reader would seek more ample testimony than we have given in the brief extract, it may be found in a little family volume entitled "Father Robinson's Scrap Book."

81.

MURDER COMMITTED BY BIBLE BELIEVERS.

NEW YORK, *December* 14, 1859.

THE religious papers of this country have been filled with horrible stories of dark deeds committed by spiritualists—mere fabrications; while the *Tribune* gives a case of *real* crime committed by full believers in "hell," "devil," and all the great "cardinal" points of orthodoxy:—

The late strange murder at New Haven seems to have grown out of a *religious* delusion very singular in its particular details, but in its general character sufficiently common. The Widow Wakeman, the woman on whose behalf it was perpetrated; Elder Sly, the man who committed it; Justus Matthews, the man who was murdered, and the four other persons who were in the house at the time of the murder, and who if they did not actually assist in it, knew of it, and connived at it, all appear to have been wretched victims of a hallucination falling little if any thing short of insanity.

The Widow Wakeman was believed by her followers, and doubtless believed herself, to be a person who had risen from the dead and had been sent as a special "messenger" to redeem the world. The very existence of the world was indeed believed to be bound up in her life, since it was imagined that immediately upon her death the end of the earth and the "Judgment"—of which these persons seem to have had a great deal—would follow. But with all her supernatural gifts and graces, the Widow Wakeman, as usually happens in such legends, had also a supernatural enemy to encounter—no less a one, indeed, than the "devil" himself, or at least one of his imps. This evil spirit, it was believed, had first taken possession of the body of one Hunt, who, it is alleged, had unsuccessfully tried to poison the "messenger" with arsenic. Next, this evil spirit was supposed to have passed into the person of Justus Matthews, the man upon whom the murder was perpetrated. Having thus become the "man of sin," Matthews was accused, not, indeed, of any overt acts of personal violence, but of bewitching the "messenger" with his eyes, and in that way greatly distressing her, and even endangering her precious life, and thereby the duration of the world. Matthews himself seemed fully to have believed in the fact of his being thus possessed, and of exercising this malign power. He was anxious to have the evil spirit driven out of him, and for that purpose came to Sly's house in New Haven, where the Widow Wakeman lived, and where was the scene of her religious teachings and exercises. He there submitted to be blindfolded and to have his hands tied behind him, keeping himself retired in a room below, apart from the rest, who were singing and praying above. If the witnesses are to be believed, he even expressed a willingness to die if the evil spirit could not otherwise be driven from him, and the precious health and life of the "messenger" secured. Elder Sly appears to have been perfectly satisfied that nothing short of the death of Matthews would answer; and while the others were going on with their religious exercises, he proceeded to murder him, with the full knowledge and consent of the rest, and apparently at the express instigation of the Widow Wakeman.

A bloody tragedy of this sort, enacted under the very eaves, as it were, of Yale College, in the intelligent, enlightened and pious city of New Haven, must strike every one who hears of it with a sudden and creeping horror. Yet the sort of delusion out of which it grew is by no means rare or uncommon. In what did that delusion differ, we should like to ask, from that which has made so many ecclesiastics believe not only that they had power, both in earth and heaven, to bind and to loose, but also that it was their right to deliver over the enemies of the Church to the secular arm to be put to death? In what does this delusion differ except in its bloody catastrophe—nor does even that difference always exist—from that which makes up the staple of the innumerable miraculous legends of the Middle Ages? We have chosen this example, not because the Middle Ages by any means had a monopoly of these delusions, but because it is more agreeable to contemplate the faults of other people than our own.

82.

MISS LIZZIE DOTEN BEFORE THE PEOPLE.

NEW YORK, *October* 17, 1864.

SOMETHING this morning makes me recall that not long since I for the first time saw Miss Lizzie Doten on the platform. . . . . This slender, graceful, spiritual, prophetic-looking woman, whose voice, sweet and clear, rings out fearlessly, is exerting a wide and lasting influence on the thousands who listen to her utterances. She accomplishes more spiritual labor, and endures annually more bodily fatigue, in journeying from city to city, than a phrenologist or a physiologist would consider possible. . . . She is the very soul of earnestness and lucidity in thought, and the author, under inspiration, of numerous poetic compositions, surpassingly opulent in deep truth and excellence, but remarkable, chiefly, for a kind of ethereal penetration into the secret springs of human character, feelings, impulses, and motives. Her pale complexion, black and glossy hair, dark, and singularly-expressive eyes—the entire atmosphere of her face and figure—impress me with the feeling that every word she speaks is the coin of a mind that has thought and struggled in earnest. . . . I do not wonder that so real, and yet shadowy, a genius as Poe, should, from his higher life and still mystic wanderings, seek to impress this serious, logical, metaphysical, poetic mind. . . . . . This brilliant-minded woman, with her earnest and clear perception of truth, is certain to enrich the world. And I hope the world will have wit enough to kindly accept it.

83.

PICNIC EXCURSION OF THE CHILDREN'S LYCEUM.

NEW YORK, *October* 18, 1864.

A FEW days ago I attended the Annual Excursion and Picnic of the children, parents, and members of the New York Society of Progressive Spiritualists. The day was perfect, everybody seemed delighted, and the whole party returned to the city and to their homes, without the least accident or discord to mar the pleasures and memories of the occasion. Fancy, then, my unutterable astonishment, not to say indignation, when, on taking up the *Springfield* (Mass.) *Republican* this morning, I read:—

"At a recent spiritual picnic near New York, seven women were brutally outraged, two men killed, five wounded, and fourteen robbed, not only of their watches and portemonnaies, but of their clothes, so that they were compelled to hide in the woods all night."

The editorial staff of the *Republican* is composed of scholarly and Christian gentlemen. They are members of the churches popularly termed "Orthodox," and they are publishing an influential journal. But is it not a *new* problem in morals, how it is possible for such gentlemen to perpetrate the foregoing absolutely disgusting and horrible falsehood?

84.

THE WORLD BROUGHT TO JUDGMENT.

NEW YORK, *October* 19, 1864.

THE following thrilling "Moral Police" vision was described, as I am informed, by an English gentleman, who has more than once furnished evidence that he is, at times, both a medium and a seer:—

I saw a mighty Spirit traversing the world without rest or pause. It was omnipresent, it was all-powerful, it had no compunction, no pity, no relenting sense that any appeal from any of the race of men could reach. It was invisible to every creature born upon the earth, save once to each. It turned its shaded face on whatsoever living thing, one time; and straight the end of that thing was come. It passed through the forest, and the vigorous tree it looked on shrunk away; through the garden, and the leaves perished and the flowers withered; through the air, and the eagles flagged upon the wing, and dropped; through the sea, and the monsters of the deep floated, great wrecks, upon the waters. It met the eyes of lions in their lairs, and they were dust; its shadow darkened the faces of young children lying asleep, and they awoke no more.

It had its work appointed; it inexorably did what was appointed to it to do; and neither sped nor slackened. Called to, it went on unmoved, and did not come. Besought, by some who felt that it was drawing near, to change its course, it turned its shaded face upon them, even while they cried, and they were dumb. It passed into the midst of palace chambers, where there were lights and music, pictures, diamonds, gold, and silver; crossed the wrinkled and the gray, regardless of them; looked into the eyes of a bright bride, and vanished. It revealed itself to the baby on the old crone's knee, and left the old crone wailing by the fire. But whether the beholder of its face were now a king, or now a laborer; now a queen, or now a seamstress, let the hand it palsied be on the scepter or the plow, or yet too small and nerveless to grasp any thing, the Spirit never paused in its appointed work, and, sooner or later, turned its impartial face on all.

I saw a Minister of State sitting in his closet, and round about him, rising from the country which he governed, up to the eternal heavens, was a low, dull howl of ignorance. It was a wild, inexplicable mutter, confused, but full of threatening, and it made all hearers' hearts to quake within them. But, few heard. In the single city where this Minister of State was seated, I saw thirty thousand children, hunted, flogged, imprisoned, but not taught—who might have been nurtured by the wolf or bear, so little of humanity had they, within them or without—all joining in this doleful cry. And, ever among them, as among all ranks and grades of mortals, in all parts of the globe, the Spirit went; and ever by thousands in their brutish state, with all the gifts of God perverted in their breasts or trampled on, they died.

The Minister of State, whose heart was pierced by even the little he could hear of these terrible voices, day and night rising to heaven, went among the priests and teachers of all denominations, and faintly said:—

"Harken to this dreadful cry! what shall we do to stay it?"

One body of respondents answered, "Teach this!"

Another said, "Teach that!"

Another said, "Teach neither this nor that, but the other!"

Another quarreled with all the three; twenty others quarreled with all the four, and quarreled no less bitterly among themselves. The voices, not stayed by this, cried out day and night; and still among those many thousands, as among all mankind, went the Spirit who never rested from its labor; and still, in brutish sort, they died.

Then a whisper murmured to the Minister of State:—

"Correct this for thyself. Be bold! Silence these voices, or virtuously lose thy power in the attempt to do it. Thou canst not sow a grain of good seed in vain. Thou knowest it well. Be bold, and do thy duty!"

The minister shrugged his shoulders, and replied:— "It is a great wrong—BUT IT WILL LAST MY TIME." And so he put it from him.

Then the whisper went among the priests and teachers, saying to each: "In thy soul thou knowest it is a truth, O man, that there are good things to be taught, and stay this cry."

To which each answered in like manner:—"It is a great wrong—BUT IT WILL LAST MY TIME." And so *he* put it from him.

I saw a poisoned air, in which life drooped. I saw disease, arrayed in all its store of hideous aspects and appalling shapes, triumphant in every alley, by-way, court, back street, and poor abode, in every place where human beings congregated—in the proudest and most boastful places most of all. I saw innumerable hosts, foredoomed to darkness, dirt, pestilence, obscenity, misery, and early death. I saw, wheresoever I looked, cunning preparations made for defacing the Creator's image, from the moment of its appearance here on earth, and stamping over it the image of the devil. I saw from those reeking and pernicious stews, the avenging consequences of such sin issuing forth, and penetrating to the highest places. I saw the rich struck down in their strength, their darling children weakened and withered, their marriageable sons and daughters perish in their prime. I saw that not one miserable wretch breathed out his poisoned life in the deepest cellar of the most neglected town; but, from the surrounding atmosphere some particles of his infection were borne away, charged with heavy retribution on the general guilt.

There were many attentive and alarmed persons looking on, who saw these things too; they were well clothed, and had purses in their pockets; they were educated, full of kindness, and loved mercy. They said to one another, "This is horrible, and shall not be!" And there was a stir among them to set it right.

But, opposed to these, came a small multitude of noisy fools and greedy knaves, whose harvest was in such horrors; and they, with impudence and turmoil, and with scurrilous jests at misery and death, re pelled the better lookers-on, who soon fell back, and stood aloof.

Then the whisper went among those better lookers-on, saying, "Over the bodies of those fellows, to the remedy!"

But each of them moodily shrugged his shoulders, and replied:—"It is a great wrong—BUT IT WILL LAST MY TIME!" And so they put it from them.

I saw a great library of laws and law proceedings, so complicated, costly, and unintelligible, that, although numbers of lawyers united in a public fiction that these were wonderfully just and equal, there was scarcely an honest man among them, but who said to his friend, privately consulting him, "Better put up with a fraud or other injury, than grope for redress through the manifold blind turnings and strange chances of this system."

I saw a portion of the system, called (of all things) EQUITY, which was ruin to suitors, ruin to property, a shield for wrong-doers having money, a rack for right-doers, having none; a by-word for delay, slow agony of mind, despair, impoverishment, trickery, confusion, insupportable injustice—a main part of it. I saw prisoners wasting in jail; mad people in hospitals; suicides chronicled in the yearly records; orphans robbed of their inheritance; infants righted (perhaps) when they were gray.

Certain lawyers and laymen came together, and said to one another:—"In only one of these, our Courts of Equity, there are years of this dark perspective before us at the present moment. We must change this."

Uprose, immediately, a throng of others—secretaries,

petty bags, hanapers, chaff-waxes, and what not, singing (in answer), "Rule Britannia," and "God save the Queen;" making flourishing speeches, pronounced hard names, demanding committees, commissions, commissioners, and other scarecrows, and terrifying the little band of innovators out of their five wits.

Then the whisper went among the latter, as they shrunk back, saying, "If there is any wrong within the universal knowledge, this wrong is; Go on! Set it right!"

Whereon, each of them sorrowfully thrust his hands in his pockets, and replied:—"It is, indeed, a great wrong—BUT IT WILL LAST MY TIME!" And so *they* put it from them.

The Spirit, with its face concealed, summoned all the people who had used this phrase about their Time, into its presence. Then it said, beginning with the Minister of State:—

"Of what duration is *your* time?"

The Minister of State replied, "My ancient family has always been long-lived. My father died at eighty-four; my grandfather at ninety-two. We have the gout, but bear it (like our honors) many years."

"And you," said the Spirit to the priest and teachers, "what may *your* time be?"

Some believed that they were so strong, as that they should number many more years than threescore and ten; others were the sons of old incumbents, who had long outlived youthful, expectants. Others, for any means they had of calculating, might be long-lived or short-lived—generally (they had a strong persuasion), long. So, among the lawyers and laymen.

"But, every man, as I understand you, one and all," said the Spirit, "has his time?"

"Yes!" they exclaimed together.

"Yes," said the Spirit; "and it is—ETERNITY! Whosoever is a consenting party to a wrong, comforting himself with the base reflection that it will last his time, shall bear his portion of that wrong throughout ALL TIME. And, in the hour when he and I stand face to face, he shall surely know it, as my name is JUSTICE!"

It departed, turning its face hither and thither, as it passed along upon its ceaseless work, and marking all on whom it looked.

Then went among many trembling hearers the whisper, saying, "See, each of you, before you take your ease, O wicked, selfish men, that what will 'last your time,' be just enough to last forever!"

85.

REV. J. H. FOWLER ON THE COMPARATIVE AMOUNT OF EVIDENCE.

NEW YORK, *October* 19, 1864.

THE testimony which I have collected with regard to Spiritualism, records this critical and candid "Divinity Student," though not a tithe of what has come under my observation, and in many respects—owing principally to the necessity for brevity—not so complete and convincing as much which I have rejected, is still sufficient to *establish the facts*, AS FAR AS HUMAN TESTIMONY CAN DO IT. The facts must either be admitted, or the testimony of the human senses, however multiplied, pronounced unreliable. If the latter alternative be accepted, then, of course, it applies as well to past ages as to the present, and the New Testament testimony is worth nothing. So all *a priori* objections to the occurrence of any fact, or class of facts, at the present day, would apply with equal force to those of any past age. And all arguments from the wants of mankind, previous prophecies, and arguments of whatever kind, which have been made to render the New Testament accounts probable, will apply with equal force to those of the present day; so that, aside from the amount of testimony, the ancient "miracles" have no advantage.

Let us, then, compare the testimony in favor of each. To facilitate this, we will classify the so-called miracles of the New Testament in the following manner:—

1st. The counteraction of the law of gravitation in the movement of physical objects; the rolling away the stone at the door of the sepulcher of Christ; the opening of the prison-doors to Peter; Christ walking on the water, &c.

2d. Luminous appearances accompanying the manifestations of physical power, and the seeing of spirits—as in the case of Peter's release from prison; the transfiguration of Christ on the mount; the conversion of Paul on the day of Pentecost.

3d. Spirits are seen, recognized and conversed with—as, Moses and Elias; Christ after his death; and others.

4th. Voices are heard—as at St. Paul's conversion; at the baptism of Christ, &c.

5th. Speaking in unknown tongues.

6th. Jesus is taught to read.

7th. A remarkable healing power is exhibited.

8th. Cursing the fig-tree.

9th. Turning water into wine.

10th. Feeding a multitude on less than nothing.

11th. Raising a person from the dead.

12th. Child born with no natural father.

These twelve classes, I believe, comprise all the pretended miracles of the New Testament.

We will first present our testimony to facts precisely similar to, or involving the same principles as, those of the first seven classes, and then consider the other five particular ones. *The reader should now turn to the testimony, and read the cases as they are referred to.* (See his historically excellent pamphlet.)

Witnesses for New Testament miracles are, according to the record, Saul of Tarsus (otherwise called Paul); Peter, a fisherman of Galilee; Luke, Paul's secretary; Mark, Peter's secretary; Matthew, a tax-gatherer of Capernaum; John, a fisherman of Galilee.

Witnesses to modern miracles or manifestations, in this day and hour, can be counted by hundreds of thousands!

86.

CHANGES IN THE RELIGIOUS WORLD HERALDED BY WONDERFUL SIGNS.

NEW YORK, *October* 20, 1864.

AT this moment it seems to me to be an undeniable historical fact, that intimately associated with all religious dispensations have been certain spiritual excitements and awakenings; a certain fertilization and blossoming of the spiritual sentiments of mankind; also, that in keeping with such fertilization and exaltation of the religious feelings, there have been remarkable "manifestations," showing the working of interior causes, potential and intelligent. . . . . . When an old dispensation retires from the stage, a new one is heralded by certain notifications that are striking to the senses—acting directly upon the external and internal nature of man, rousing his intellectual and moral powers to a fresh apprehension of principles. Mankind have called these developments "miracles"—the mysterious operations of yet more mysterious and distant agents. But we now know that it is the inevitable operation of a vigorous vital force within the constitution of man—prophetic on the summit of all human hope and reason, and is what religious people call "God." It is what physicists call the "Law of Nature;" it is what the skeptic calls the natural religious "proclivity of humanity;" it is what the historian calls the testimony of "God speaking through human history." . . . . All human history is alike; repeats itself. It brings unanimous testimony that every dispensation has been heralded by and intimately associated with these mysterious manifestations of spirit-power. It is something grander than a mere question of testimony. There is a genius in human life which indorses this uniformity of spiritual experience. . . . . Inspiration comes from agents once living in flesh, but who, by being subjected to the chemical process called physical death, have been disinthralled, launched on the broad sea of future existence, with the power not only to think better thoughts, and to feel nobler sentiments, but with all their characteristic attractions, which, like telegraphic lines of communication, lead them instinctively and joyously back to the haunts of life on the earth; and thus, wherever in Germany, in Scotland, in Ireland, or in this country, the spirits found a house where the conditions were in harmony with manifestations, they have made them; and so, in spite of human ignorance and superstition there has been, so to say, a sort of apostolic testimony, not only through human history in this life, but from human history in the higher world—the present and future being intimately and indissolubly united! . . . . Now, in modern days, by examining these matters carefully, men become free to reject all irrational supernaturalism; are not fettered with belief in an abstract God—in any power which subverts, or inverts, or transcends, or in any way infringes upon, the well-established order of the natural universe and the great spiritual empire to which all is tending. . . . . . Spiritualism is a great Emancipator! It has a remarkably liberalizing influence; for through facts, well ascertained, we have discovered that our existence after death is not ghostly and ghastly, but is natural, palpable, definable, and most desirable—a relative existence, as much in harmony with objects and substances as the present. Spiritual manifestations are not only a key by which to solve man's spiritual constitution as he is, but they scientifically and prophetically demonstrate his constitution as it is to be.

87.

IMPRESSIONS OF THEODORE PARKER.

NEW YORK, *October* 23, 1864.

NOT since the summer of 1859, while engaged, at Mr. Poole's residence, in the composition of the "Thinker," (Gt. Har., vol. 5*), have I felt the comprehensive presence of Theodore Parker. . . . . True, honest, energetic, reverential, modest, inspired! he is greatly beloved in the Summer Land. . . . . Of him it is wisely said: "His spiritual life had its fountains and its sanctions, not in the traditions and creeds and customs of churches, but in the depths of his own spiritual nature. He lived from within, not from without. No vicarious, artificial, or ceremonial sanctities molded his spirit, controlled his conduct, or prescribed his destiny. His thoughts, beliefs, devotions—his hopes, aspirations, assurances—his yearnings, exertions, sacrifices; his purposes, vows, obediences—were his own: dictated only by his own consciousness, governed only by his own judgment, warranted only by his own nature, consecrated freely to his own salvation. He revered the traditional, but not the dust in which it was enshrined. He loved the ancient saints, not for the titles bestowed

* For the author's estimate of Mr. Parker's character and writings, see the volume referred to.

upon them by the manufacturers of a sinister calendar, but for the radiant virtues that made them strong whilst they lived, and the unquenchable piety that gave them immortality. Prophets he revered, not because ecclesiastical tribunals had pronounced them divine, but because they had borne the testimony of their protests, their sorrows, and their blood to the everlasting justice of God, and to the outraged rights and responsibilities of mankind. He called no man 'master;' but, with the beautiful modesty of true righteousness, he preserved his mind free from every ghostly enslavement, that it might the more purely dedicate itself to the simple services of earth and heaven."

In 1851 I visited Theodore Parker in his study. It was a cold day in Boston. His writing and thinking room looked to me like a book-store, where one could get musty copies of most ancient works by authors long since departed from the world's memory. The four sides of his study were books, books—nothing but books, in all kinds of covers—from floor to ceiling. He, the master, sat very near an old-fashioned kitchen wood stove, with a broad flat top, suggestive of a good place to bake immense buckwheat cakes. . . . Against the wall, near his desk, hung a rusty musket and soldierly gearings, recalling the old revolutionary war. . . . He, an outcast from all the Boston churches, looked gloriously and lovingly, while in speech his heart came tenderly forth; and through plain, short, earnest words, he freely testified his decided interest, almost entire *faith*, in the demonstrations of Clairvoyance and Spiritualism, which he regarded at least as among the many great educational agencies promotive of the world's progress and emancipation. . . . But I could not talk with him! His multitudinous books oppressed me. . . I wished for a walk with him in the woods; possibly, in the great out-doors I might be at home with him.

88.

THE MIRACLE OF RAISING A PERSON FROM THE DEAD.

NEW YORK, *November* 2, 1864.

THIS afternoon a gentleman called at our office, No. 274 Canal Street, to obtain facts and arguments suitable for a discussion of the claims of "modern miracles" as he called them. . . . I handed him my friend J. H. Fowler's admirable essay on this very subject, which he read before the middle and senior classes in Cambridge Divinity School. . . . This circumstance reminds me of the following interesting passage in Mr. Fowler's pamphlet:—

There is only one case of this kind in the New Testament, that of Lazarus. In the other cases there is no certainty that the persons *were really dead*, as any one will readily see by referring to the accounts themselves. Persons are very frequently supposed to be dead, and are sometimes buried, when they are only in a swoon. But I think, in the case of Lazarus, this could not be. It is not at all probable that he could lie in this state *four days*, and in the tomb. I am aware that this account is given more in detail than that of any other miracle in the New Testament. But I will ask any candid person, who professedly believes this narrative given in the writings of only one man, and those of doubtful authorship, but who finds it too great a stretch of credulity to believe "modern miracles" on the testimony of a thousand living witnesses,—I will ask such a person, Could you believe a fact similar to that related in the Gospel of John, if ten *most reliable men should declare they saw it performed?* If not, then may I not infer that you, with me, do not believe this account? I think the other gospel writers did not believe it, or they would have recorded it. For, if it took place, they must have known it, as Jesus was a particular friend in this family of Lazarus. It is a greater miracle than they have mentioned; and I can account for their silence only on the ground that they never heard the story, or did not believe it. I know not why a big story could not grow up from a small matter in that age, as well as in the present age. All, who have read any considerable portion of the church fathers know that the greater the story they could tell, the better; and who can say how early they began to fabricate them, or when the gospel of John was written?

The silence of the other three histories, as to this greatest of all the miracles, looks rather suspicious. It can be accounted for only in one of three ways: either the writers did not hear of the miracle, or they did not believe it, or they did not think it of sufficient importance to be recorded.

The last supposition can not be accepted; for they all three, with John, record several miracles, which we all know, and which *they* must have known, were far less important than this.

Either of the others amounts to the same thing. For, had such a miracle as this occurred in the presence of so "many Jews" (John 11: 45 and 46), it would have been not only extensively known, but well attested. This, and the fact that Lazarus, with his family, were particular friends of Jesus and his disciples (John 11: 11), makes it certain that they all would have known the fact, had it really occurred as related in the fourth gospel. So, if they heard but did not *believe* the story, having the same means of knowing the facts, we must conclude that it was false. The Jews, who did not believe in Jesus, might hear of this or any other work of Jesus, and not believe it; or they might witness facts, and think it a deception or an imposture, as many at the present day, who disbelieve "spirit manifestations," reject any particular fact, though they may have been eye-witnesses to it. But this could not be the case with the disciples of Jesus. They would both have *known* and *believed* the fact, had Jesus raised Lazarus to life, after he had been dead (11: 13, 14), four days in the tomb. Since, then, we are compelled to accept one of those alternatives,—namely, that they did not *know*, or did not *believe*,—we must conclude that the fact did not occur as related.

This reasoning proceeds on the supposition that the first three gospels were written by the immediate disciples of Jesus; but, if they were written by those of a later period, the reasoning, with a slight alteration, will apply with equal force.

And again, as to the miracle of a child being born

with no natural father. How do we know? Somebody said so. Who said so? Supposed to be Matthew and Luke! Who told them? Suppose Paul told Luke, and somebody told Matthew and Paul; for neither of these persons knew any thing about the child or its mother till thirty years after he was born. Suppose, then, the mother of the child told this story, for it must come to this at last. Joseph's dream can not be credited among a people who do not believe in dreams and visions; nor can any of the spiritual communications to Mary, or any of the parties, be relied upon by those who do not believe it possible for spirits to communicate to mortals. We then have the story reported to us at second-hand, at least.

Now, where is the court, in any country, which could accept such second-hand testimony as this, for the most natural event? And could the most credulous Christian judge, upon any bench, but smile with pity upon the unfortunate female who should personally give oath before him that her child had *no* natural father, or that an angel, or a spirit, had begotten him; and would he not be the more surprised, should she solemnly declare that no less a spirit than God himself had done this? Why this goes beyond all the spirit *intercourse* of modern times; though there were many similar stories told, and believed, in those ancient times. The people then did not think it at all strange for the gods to have intercourse with women; and it appears, by the Old Testament, that Jews could credit such stories as well as the heathens.—Gen. 4: 2 and 4.

I am fully aware that those who professedly believe these stories do not receive them on the flimsy testimony which is given in their support, but through their theories of "*the fall*," and "*the plan of redemption*;" else they accept them from tradition and habit, as they do many others, without the disposition or courage to question them. But, should we not be cautious how we build theories upon facts so poorly substantiated? Theories to support the facts—then make the facts support the theories! and this when both the theories and the facts are, in themselves, so monstrous and absurd, if not blasphemous, that human nature revolts at them!

89.

THE LYCEUM.—A NEW THING UNDER THE SUN.

NEW YORK, *November* 24, 1864.

PERHAPS I am too enthusiastic to-day, but sincerely I think that the Children's Progressive Lyceum is really a "new thing under the sun." Its basis is in the twofold organization of the child—the body with its functions, and the soul with its intuitions—both needing and demanding attention, education, and recreation. . . . Thousands of people are superstitious about the day called "The Sabbath." . . . Sunday is not exempt from the operation of physical laws; neither are the moral laws suspended between Mondays and Saturdays. In short, a child is just the same *natural* being on Sunday as on every other day of the week; and the "wing movements," and the harmonious "marchings with the stars and stripes," in the Sunday sessions of the Children's Lyceum, are introduced upon the principle that *there is no difference in days to the body and soul of a child;* and as to men and women, the same principle will apply, for it is, I believe, admitted that they are but "children of a larger growth." . . . The Sunday-Schools of orthodox establishments are universally distasteful to children; because such schools—although conducted by very excellent persons, who are moved by the best intentions—are founded upon false and unnatural doctrines. Take out of popular orthodox Sunday-Schools two influences, and they would cease in less than a year—first, the social attractions, which are very powerful with children; and, second, the fascinations of the library, full of story books! With these influences paramount, any association of young people is bound together firmly, and will sail under any flag of sectarianism; not one in fifty of them knowing or caring a particle about the creed, and the whole congregation thinking next to nothing about the fundamental ideas and cardinal "points of doctrine." . . . The Children's Progressive Lyceum, while it most beautifully provides for the social and literary wants of the young, possesses *inherent* attractions. It begins by classifying the children into "groups" with beautiful titles. Over each group is an officer called a "Leader," who, like the children, is provided with a badge of beauty and significance. The color of each group is unlike that of every other; just as, in the fields, every flower and bud and tree and stone is provided by the Divine Love and Wisdom with adaptations and a color of its own.

As to the plan of education: This differs essentially from popular methods. We have no text-books nor "catechisms" with stereotyped questions and answers. On the contrary, the children in a Lyceum are "educated" to think for themselves, and to select their own "questions," and to bring on the following Sunday their own "answers." How beautifully and perfectly this plan works, can be illustrated by the school better than described in words. The plan will, I am quite sure, receive the approbation of every wise and sincere lover of children and humanity. . . . The Lyceum Manual contains hymns, songs, impressive silver-chain recitations, &c. The children learn to sing the songs of Progress, to chant the hymns of the Summer Land, and to recite the holiest sentiments of thanksgiving and praise. . . . Last Spring, while recovering from a brief illness, the feeling came upon me that I might contribute at least *one* song to the music of childhood. I went directly to writing; and as it was "my first," and in all probability will be "my last," I will make a note of it right here:—

The sun is bright, and its golden light
  Is filling the world with power;
The song-birds fly through the kindling sky,
  And music floods the hour.
This gladsome life, when free from strife,
  Shall fill our hearts with glee,
And falling showers on fields and flowers
  Shall make us happy and free.

CHORUS: Oh! let us drink from Nature's fount,
  Whence love and beauty flow;
Oh, let us walk in Wisdom's ways,
  Where all the angels go.

There are golden beams in laughing streams,
  And music in the trees;
There are heavenly dyes and love-lit eyes,
  And whisperings in the breeze.
The beautiful songs of unseen throngs
  O'erflow this world of ours,
And loving hands from angel-lands
  Bedeck our paths with flowers.

There is no death! for the Father's breath
  Filleth our hearts with youth;
And a heavenly wave destroys the grave
  For him who loveth the truth.
The earth is singing, and time is winging
  Each to another sea;
Then let us love the truths above
  That make us happy and free.

90.

WHAT A SPIRIT THINKS ON THE RIGHTS OF PROPERTY.

NEW YORK, *November* 25, 1864.

ABOUT five years ago, at a hotel in Buffalo, New York, I conversed an hour or so with a retired merchant on the subject of Labor, Poverty, Riches, Monopoly, &c. He was a violent opponent of Charles Fourier and Albert Brisbane, and attributed their public efforts for "Association" to an *insane* wish to disturb and reconstruct the natural order of human society. Seeing that no impression could be made upon his mind in the direction of associated labor, &c., I said: "Will you promise me to take a look into this subject as soon as you can after you pass through death?" He was much amused, but replied: "Yes, I'll study up every thing when I become one of your spirits." Then I added: "Will you, as soon as you find opportunity, come to *me* with your *post-mortem* opinion on the subject of this conversation?" He laughingly promised that "he would," and thereupon in friendship we separated. That was in 1859. . . . . . To-day, as I was contemplatively walking in one of the shady retreats in Central Park, this man (in the spirit body!) came to me, announced his name, refreshed my memory concerning the conversation in Buffalo, his promise, and his readiness to express his new convictions.*

At once, I asked: "Have you yet met Fourier?" He replied that he had not; but now he fully accepted, "as truth, Fourier's fundamental principle of the Right of Property."

I asked him kindly to "define it to me." And he substantially answered:—

"Every individual possesses, legitimately, *the thing* which his labor, his intelligence (or more generally), his *activity* has created. This principle is incontestible, and contains expressly an acknowledgment of the right of all to the soil. For as the soil has not been created by man, it follows from this fundamental principle of property, that it can not belong to any small portion of the human race, who have created it by their activity. Let us then conclude that the true theory of property is founded on the '*creation of the thing possessed.*' "

"Can you," I inquired, "give me what you now think is the *cause* of poverty?"

* I had not heard of the merchant's decease at that time, and was naturally somewhat surprised, but subsequently learned that he died with cholera two years before this interview.

"On all these subjects," he answered, "I have entirely new views," and in substance he thus proceeded:—

"The *cause* of poverty is ignorance, disunion, and monopoly. The *cause* of monopoly is money, and love of power. Money is used to monopolize the soil and other necessaries of life which make men rich. In ages past, when all had to work to provide themselves with the necessaries of life, a few idle ones got together and said to themselves—'How can we get all the good things we want, and do no work?'

"'I have it,' says one of them; 'I will get gold and mold it into beautiful forms, which will please the multitude. I have seen some of them admire gold as it lies in the mine. It is of no use now, but we will make it into glittering coin, and to our advantage. It has been in the earth immured for ages, while by its side iron has been brought forth and made useful to man; and now gold shall be made also useful.'

"They then took the beautiful stuff from the mine, and made it into glittering coin. They showed it to the people.

"'Give us that,' said they.

"'We will, if you will give us bread, clothes, and let us lie in your houses.'

"'We will,' they answered. And then was given birth a curse that is filling the world with want and misery. It is money that enables those who do nothing to extract the comforts of life from those who make all the necessaries of life. To illustrate: If I should go to California and get gold from the mines, and bring it into society, and buy a farm, food, clothing, &c., what would I give in exchange for those things? Why, for the farm I would give something that was earth itself; and for the food give something that has not made any food, and never will. I buy clothes with it, but I do not give the tailor any food or clothes, or any of the comforts of life in return; I only give him some California gold that has lain there a long time doing nothing, and when brought forth and made into money, it is worth nothing; because it is doing nothing. I wish I could say that it has done nothing. It has done much; it has bought up the soil and made a world full of landlords and tenants; it has bought up food, and clothing, and left man to go through the world naked, and starving, when the world was full of food and clothing. It buys men in high and low places. It bought Judas; it bought Arnold; it has made chattel slavery by buying up our brother man, and making him as a beast of burden.

"'Now, these are my new conclusions: To do away with poverty on earth, let those that labor, unite and work for each other only. Let a certain number in every community UNITE their labor and interests; let them create the necessaries of life, and hold them in common, and deposit them in some convenient place, and when any member wants let him go to the place of deposit and get what he wants *without money and without price!* God has given the earth, not to man, or men, but to *humanity;* because humanity is dependent on her for life as much as they are on the air we breathe, or the water we drink. Therefore, governments must give you the land, and then from its bosom take the raw materials, and form all the necessaries of life. The working classes know how to make every thing. Do they not build all the houses, make all the clothing, and prepare all the food? Do they not build all the ships 'that traverse the waters like things of life,' that come and go to all parts of the world, and distribute the comforts of life to all nations? Yes, it is you that do every thing? Then, why should you longer be slaves, when you *know* so much and are so *strong*? Come out of the institutions that you are in, and build up *new ones* that will make you independent, free, and happy. Arise, and take land, and build yourselves houses—not huts, but splendid mansions. Furnish them with the comfortable, the useful, and beautiful. Shear your sheep; gather your flax; and cotton; and set your spinning-jenny in motion; and make such clothing as will adorn and comfort your bodies and homes. Plow your fields, sow your grain, and when the harvest comes, gather from the earth the food you want. Build ships and carry your surplus products to other nations in exchange for such things as you may want. Establish schools, and colleges, and halls of science, and libraries, with useful books in them. Make pleasure-grounds and pleasure-houses. In a word, make all those things that will elevate you and make you happy. There is an abundance of material scattered over the earth to supply all your wants. Be wise; unite; and become rich by the union of labor. *The poor shall cease out of the land.* ASSOCIATION will make you rich. ISOLATION will keep you poor. The past has been *Isolation;* the effect has been discord, poverty, vice, misery, and slavery. The future will be Association: the effect will be harmony, plenty, purity, happiness, and liberty."

The foregoing is the substance of what the "merchant" said, who had now "retired" from the earth not only, but also from all his selfishness regarding property.

91.

MIND YOUR OWN BUSINESS.

NEW YORK, *November* 26, 1864.

MARY and I have been freely and joyously mingling with the Lyceum children to-day. . . . Is there any thing more beautiful than a beautiful soul in a beautiful form? . . . The order of thought, feeling, and will is developed extremely slow in a child; because it is spirit *power*, and not the number of years and sensations, that constitutes the cause of orderly development. . . . This morning I was reminded that there are certain persons who seem only qualified to detect vices in others; while different minds seem *only* to see virtues. . . . "Mind your own business," is a proverb often used and seldom applied. . . . In our national character, which is not yet formed, there are traits of moral laxity, selfishness, fickle-heartedness, with much benevolence and sympathy for suffering. . . . PAUL, in his Epistle to the Philippians (chap. ii. v. 4), said: "Look not every man on his own things, but every man also on the things of others." To follow this rule one can not exclusively "mind his own business." A little mind, having found peace in God, shrivels and shuts itself up from the world. A great mind, having strengthened its life in God's, unfolds and strives to win the world over to His kingdom. . . . How does a little picture look in an enormous frame? How looks a little thought in an immense book? How looks a little soul in a giant body? . . . Let us have proportion—balance, harmony! This is the central idea of our new Religion. Who wonders that it is beloved by *children;* by the aspiring; and by angel-natures throughout the universe?

92.

THE ONE ONLY AND TRUE MARRIAGE.

NEW YORK, *November* 28, 1864.

THIS morning the mail brought a letter full of questions. I have little time to give to these numerous daily arrivals. There is one query which, I think, I have answered a thousand and one times, namely: "Mr. DAVIS:—In the light of your inspiration is 'free love' an inheritance of Spiritualism, or is it an incident which time and truth will divest it of?"

Now, if I do not once more answer, the correspondent will say, "Ah, it's just as I have supposed. I wrote to Mr. Davis, asking a plain, civil question. He don't answer me; therefore, 'silence gives consent;' and I conclude that Spiritualism is the father of Free Loveism, and I shall have henceforth nothing to do with it." To promote truth in his mind I thus replied: Love controlled alone by Wisdom—free from the iniquities of passion, free from the misdirections of sensuality, free from the extremes of blood, free from the inversions of disease—such love is an "inheritance" of Spiritualism. The wise love of the New Dispensation is unselfish—fraternal, unbounded, universal. Behold the love of flower for flower; so pure hearts beat responsive and free.

But that misery-promoting abuse of the conjugal relation, called by us free-passionism, is an "incident" to the development of mankind out of blood into spirit—out of materialism into spirituality—out of prostitution into the divine order of society, when men and women will be but little lower than the angels. In plainer language: There is but one true marriage, namely: *the marriage of the right man with the right woman, forever!* The state of singleness is unnatural. No woman, no man, is naturally a celibate. "Union" is the universal decree of Father God and Mother Nature. Dr. Johnson gives the philosophy of marriage in a few words:—"A married man," says he, "has many cares; but a bachelor has no pleasures. Cutting himself off from life's purest and most exquisite enjoyments for fear of some trifling annoyance, he emulates the sagacity of the wiseacre, who amputates his leg to secure himself from corns." But harmonial philosophers will study to secure the true marriage first.

93.

THE ORTHODOX CHURCH SYSTEM FINANCIALLY CONSIDERED.

NEW YORK, *November* 30, 1864.

FEW considerations (says a writer) are better calculated to awaken attention, at this time, than those of a monetary character. It may therefore be well to examine the "Financial aspects of Christianity."

It has been conclusively demonstrated, that it costs the nation *three hundred millions* of dollars to keep the machinery of the church in operation! Now let us see what it costs the State of New York. By the census of 1855, it appears that the amount of church property in the State is $31,480,000! The salaries paid to the clergymen of the State, amounted to $2,400,000 annually! To this sum add the income from the church property, at seven per cent. interest, which amounts to $2,200,000, and we have an annual expense to the State of *four million six hundred thousand dollars!!* This is for the support of pulpits alone. The additional cost of Sunday-Schools, Bible and Tract Societies, is not so easily determined, though some idea of the expense incurred by the two latter, may be gained by the following statements taken from the reports of the societies.

"The American Tract Society has, since its foundation, thirty-one years ago, issued publications to the number of one hundred and eighty-five million, and expended $5,000,000! Eight million families have been visited, nearly five million books sold, and one and a quarter million given away. Last year the Society employed seven hundred colporteurs, and expended nearly half a million dollars!"

"The American Bible Society has, during the forty years of its operation, issued over eleven million Bibles and Testaments! The receipts last year amounted to almost four hundred thousand dollars!"

In addition to these, there are, in this State alone, some sixty religious papers and periodicals, circulating thousands of pages of religious reading of a Christian character.

Now what is the success of the Christian system in this State, with all these appliances and this immense expenditure of wealth? Why, just this: about *one-third* of the people are induced to attend church! and only *one-fifth* become church members! It is acknowledged that a large number of the church members are not experimentally acquainted with the religion they profess. If so, how small a share of the people of the State are Christianized, notwithstanding the efforts of five or six thousand clergymen, and the vast sums expended.

To show the value of the money thus annually squandered, let us see what might be done with it, if differently appropriated. First, then, the sum paid for "pulpits and pulpit preaching," would comfortably support all the deaf, dumb, blind, insane, and idiotic in the State—over seven thousand persons in all; would provide for our ten thousand paupers, and pay the salaries of the teachers of all the common schools! Or, omitting the charities, the sum would defray the expense of our entire common school system—pay the salaries of teachers, and leave a sum for the purchase of library, apparatus, &c., equal to nearly two hundred dollars for each district every year! Think you, intelligent reader, this sum judiciously applied, would not prove of greater benefit, physically and spiritually, to our citizens than the one hundred or one hundred and fifty sermons preached from each of the five thousand pulpits?

The first cost of the church edifices of the State was six times that of all the school-houses, so that the same capital would rebuild all the school-houses at double the original cost, and erect a "public hall" in every village and settlement, at an average cost of over four thousand dollars! Only think of it! For the sum which we have paid for the "houses of God," which are almost universally closed to all purposes of human good—not even opened for anti-slavery and temperance lectures, and pertinaciously shut against all lectures upon man or Nature—for this sum expended for these edifices—appropriated to the use, every seventh day, of the "Unknown God" who is there "ignorantly worshiped," we might have built a splendid school-house in every district, and erected in every desired locality a spacious and elegant "public hall" for a "People's Lyceum," where *all* the people could every day learn more of themselves, of nature, and "Nature's God," and thus know how to improve themselves, enjoy nature, and glorify God.

Then for the sum paid to the clergy for interpreting the Bible, for our own individual understanding of which—not theirs—are we to be held responsible; every school-house could be supplied with an abundant library, and every "public hall" with a reading-room, library, apparatus, piano, and other articles for amusement and instruction. The provision would be ample, leaving a goodly sum to pay qualified lecturers from a distance for their services. What a dead loss is there to society every year! How great a good do we surrender for an insignificant benefit!

Christian professors are accustomed to undervalue all these instrumentalities to which I have alluded, and award credit to the "grace of God" for the few conveniences and limited accessions to the church in consequence thereof. But I venture the assertion that, could all the thirty thousand pulpits of the land be occupied by Harmonial teachers, all the religious papers be put under the control of Harmonial minds, the incomes of the Bible and Tract Societies be expended in publishing Harmonial works for gratuitous distribution, and last, but not least, could all the Sunday-Schools be appropriated to the promulgation of the truth as it is in the "Harmonial Philosophy," not five years would elapse before there would be a moral revolution in this country unprecedented in history! The immortal life would become an acknowledged fact, intercourse with the spirit world would be universally demonstrated as a verity, and liberty be proclaimed over all the land! The laws of individual harmony being early taught and understood, intemperance and licentiousness would diminish and public morals and private virtue rapidly improve. Once let mankind understand the laws of their being, and learn to know the inevitable consequences of wrong doing, and banish the idea of a way of escape from the penalties of sin, and an effect, blessed and glorious to every friend of goodness, would follow as speedily and certainly as do life and vegetation obey the magnetic influence of the balmy air and bright sunlight of early Spring.

The light of truth has yet scarcely penetrated the clouds of superstition which have been hanging over us from man's earliest infancy; and it is not strange that men should wander from the path of true wisdom, when their highest teachings have been mythological ideas too crude and absurd for intelligent credence.

One thought more and I have done: We all know how zealous the Catholic Church, and especially the priesthood, is to secure the early training of the young. Give them control of the schools, and they ask but little more. The Protestant Church manifests the same desire, and for the same reasons. They both understand the importance of bringing their religious influences to bear upon the susceptible minds of children and youth. Let men grow up to years of mature judgment and discernment, without prejudice, unbiased for or against Christianity, and not one in ten could be brought into the Church. The mass of Christians are such, in fact, from their youth up. This is a truth acknowleged by the best orthodox authority.

I have before me "The Family Christian Almanac for 1838," published by the American Tract Society, which indorses the following statement of Dr. Spencer: "Make up a congregation of a thousand Christians. Divide them into five classes, according to the ages at which they became Christians. Then count each of the five classes separately. Of your thousand Christians, there were hopefully converted under twenty years of age, 548; between twenty and thirty years of age, 337; between thirty and forty, 86; between forty and fifty, 11; between fifty and sixty, 3; between sixty and seventy, 1."

So, then, by their own showing, *more than half* of the hopeful converts to our churches, are made before the subjects have arrived at an age sufficient to render them capable of understanding what they accept as true. *Three-tenths* are converted between the ages of twenty and thirty, and *only one-tenth after they have arrived at thirty years of age!* What a commentary upon the popular system of religious teaching!

Early impressions are lasting, and it is not strange that those who, in their childhood and youth, when the character is being formed, are completely enveloped in orthodoxy, should, as they grow up, pass into the Church and become as rigid and dogmatic as the most bigoted. It is a well-known fact, with rare exceptions, that the persons who embrace Christianity at an advanced period of life, and are very devoted to their faith, zealous and sincere, are persons of weak minds. The "great lights" of the so-called Christian Church, are those who imbibed Christianity with their mother's milk.

True it is that, to-day, the popular sentiment is on the side of the Church. Not only so, but the affairs of the Church are completely interwoven with the business and commercial interests of the country, so that one hazards not only reputation, but business prosperity, employment, and daily bread even, by "denying the faith" of his fathers. Who may tell the number influenced by considerations such as these to attach themselves to a popular church, with powerful advantages of a pecuniary character!

The principal accession to the orthodox churches are those who drift with the current. The merchant, mechanic, or physician soon finds that he must attend church to secure the support of its members. And a perfect success requires, in most communities, that he become a member himself. How easy, therefore, it is for one desirous of business prosperity, to accustom himself to a regular attendance at church, and, ere long, to take advantage of a little revival of religion, to take sides with the Church. Such a course almost inevitably secures a "living business."

The day has gone by when, to profess Christianity involved the burden of the "Cross." It is decidedly the easiest course to take. The Martyrs are those who brave the popular sentiment in religious matters. To *practice* in conformity to the example of Jesus is quite another thing from the "profession of religion," and the two are not necessarily at all connected.

The great majority of church-members furnish no distinctive evidence of their peculiar "separation from the world."

Who can tell, upon taking up a residence in any place, what persons are Christians by profession, and what are not? Will he find the "professors" any less close in driving a bargain? Will he find them any more benevolent to the poor? Will he find them *es*-chewing the filthy weed tobacco, or *chewing* it? Will he find them total abstainers from drinking beer and hot whisky? Will he find them members of the various reform societies, or conservative laggards in every question of human good? Will he find them warning sinners, who they pretend to believe are bound for hell—to repent and "flee the wrath to come," or daily associating with them without one effort to reform them? My own observation teaches me that these latter conclusions are correct ones. Do our orthodox friends really believe all their creeds include? If so can they explain their remissness in personal efforts for the "salvation of souls?"

From such a Church system as I have here faithfully pictured, to the inviting acclivities of "the better way," may we all make swift Progress.

94.

CHILDREN AND FOOLS SPEAK THE TRUTH.

New York, *December* 3, 1864.

There is a good deal of bad feeling in the city pulpits against dramatic and kindred amusements. Why do the ministers of the Church consider theaters so injurious? Is it because theaters compete with the Church? Is there such a thing as "professional envy?" . . . I sometimes think that there is a dead, dogmatical virtue in society, as there is a dead, dogmatical religion in the creeds. . . . "Children and fools speak the truth," is an old proverb; but the truly wise speak the truth too; the former speak it unconsciously or innocently—the latter, because they *know* it and worship it. . . . Do not seek the means of education in far distant parts of the world; for all around thee lie the objects of true education and development. . . . Every moment, in the casual chain of life, do your highest duty. Fill up every moment with good thoughts, good sentiments, and good deeds, and thus you will advance healthily in both body and mind. . . . When the mind elevates itself to higher thoughts and purposes, all forms and uses receive an inner and more profound signification. All life, too, receives a deeper and holier explanation. The exterior world becomes full of divinity from the interior world. . . . To observe and examine and advance is our first and eternal right; not to mimic, and repeat, and follow fashion, as monkeys do. . . . "Yea, yea, nay, nay," are words which do not lead into heaven; but they do lead to the door of what is truly sincere and simple.

95.

THE EFFECTS OF EVIL MARRIAGES.

NEW YORK, *December* 12, 1864.

THE newspapers of the city and country insist that *all* conjugal infidelity is attributable to the teachings of Spiritualism. . . . I wonder whether these journals, mostly *religious*, of the orthodox stamp, expect to bring "the kingdom of heaven on earth" by promulgating falsehoods? In the doctrines of Spiritualists we find "the germ of thoughts that will revolutionize the world." For as surely as there is a God of harmony in the universe, so surely will woman one day become the acknowledged equal and co-worker of man, in *every* department of life; and yet be more truly gentle and affectionate than she now is.

On the surface of society, and seemingly often at its heart, we find corruption, and injustice, and tyranny, festering and eating away, as it were, the very life that is within; yet we see at the same time influences far different in their nature at work, to right these wrongs, to overthrow injustice and selfishness and crime, and to bring about more and more a condition of things where justice, fraternal love, and virtue shall prevail and direct the affairs of men. Let there be ever so little leaven of truth and justice in a cause, and let men only feel and know it, that cause will grow and brave the deadliest opposition; to the strength of truth will be added the strength of numbers, and by-and-by the nations will be found on its side, lifted to a higher and nobler consciousness of life, by virtue of the sacred principles which they have espoused. It is only men who are bound up in creeds, and adapt them to the selfish promptings of social and political atheism, who doubt or deny the divinity in human nature. He who is truthful and free, and everywhere carries with him a heart of love and kindness, measures man, not by the length of his creed, but by the life within and its external manifestation. He weighs circumstances, opportunities, obstacles of ignorance, of social position, of inherited tendencies, and ever finds the God within, however feebly and within however great uncertainty of victory in the short period of earthly life, struggling to the light. In some nook or corner of the spirit, unseen by the superficial and thoughtless, he beholds love and beauty that are immortal and divine. And whether the victory and the reconciliation of life be achieved here or hereafter, this truthful searcher beholds God present in each soul—present now, present for ever.

What, then, with this estimate of woman's nature and of man's nature, are law-makers and law-executors to do with cases of "separation," with the instances of heart-breaking "estrangements," with the "murders," "suicides," "infanticides," "elopements," &c., &c., which occur every day, in all countries the same, whether "divorces" are easy or whether they are forbidden, and in the hundreds of thousands of cases wholly disconnected with the ideas and teachings of Spiritualism? For example, take the case of the marriage of the intelligent Mrs. Heaviside to the celebrated Dr. Lardner, at Paris, both of the parties having resided in this country many years ago, at which time the facts were brought before the public. A brief recital of the circumstances connected with that extraordinary elopement might prove interesting and instructive to lawyers.

The maiden name of Mrs. Heaviside, was Miss Mary Spicer; she was the only daughter of Col. Spicer, of the British Lancers. She was married to Captain Heaviside, of the army, in 1824. He settled upon her the sum of £20,000 at their marriage, and she was also entitled to £13,000 on the death of her father. The marriage was one of affection, and was blessed with three children. Mrs. Heaviside eloped with Dr. Lardner on the thirteenth of March, 1840, sixteen years after her marriage. Now, why did she do this deed ? The following letter, written to her husband two days after the elopement, contains the lady's own frank account of the matter:—

Mrs. Heaviside to her Husband.

Sunday, *March* 15, 1840.

I sit down to the painful duty of fulfilling the promise made in my note of Friday.

I will do it as briefly as the circumstances to be told and the feelings to be expressed will permit. You have observed the continued indisposition from which I have suffered for many years past, and which I have allowed you to suppose proceeded from bodily illness. My sufferings, however, were of a different nature, and arose from a different cause. They originated in the mind and in the heart.

Among the persons introduced to my acquaintance within the last few months, was one, who, unfortunately for me, produced such an impression on my heart as I felt could never be effaced. In the first period of our acquaintance, I flattered myself the sentiments he inspired were those of friendship merely, and I indulged in his society with unguarded, and, as the event proved, most imprudent freedom; as this, however, was no more than was done by other ladies by whom his acquaintance and conversation were eagerly sought, and as I never before had reason to distrust myself, I proceeded, unapprehensive of the consequences.

He departed from Brighton, and the effects of his absence convinced me for the first time of the real state of my heart, and I soon felt that my peace of mind was irretrievably lost. He had never presumed to tell me that I was to him an object of affection. His manner and language were, on the contrary, most deferential and respectful. I had seen, however, indications of his feelings toward me, more convincing and unequivocal than mere words could convey.

In short, without any express communication on the subject,

our feelings became mutually known: we felt that every dictate of duty suggested immediate separation and absence; separation and absence were accordingly tried and continued until I was driven well nigh to madness. I shall not attempt, because the attempt would be unavailing, to describe to you what I suffered; had you been more constantly with me than your avocation usually permitted you to be, the state of my feelings could not have been concealed from you, and it was only by heartrending efforts that I assumed an apparent cheerfulness during the brief and distant intervals you passed with me. You know me too well to doubt my truth when I assure you, that on more than one occasion I was on the point of attempting to rescue all parties from the evil which menaced them, by removing myself to another world by opium.

I struggled—God alone knows how I struggled—to subdue this criminal attachment, and to recover sufficient tranquillity of mind to enable me to perform my duties as your wife. I wrote to him declaring my resolution to conquer my affection for him; his good feeling and real regard for me prompted him to acquiesce in this course, and he expressed his entire approbation of it. I tried it—I failed—the struggle almost cost me my life.

I now became fully convinced that I was forever incapable of discharging toward you the duties and offices of a wife, save by the adoption of a course of systematic dissimulation and unremitting hypocrisy, from which all my better feelings revolted with loathing and disgust. *I felt that the attempt would render my life one continued lie.* No course then remained for me by which I could be rescued from the horrors of my position except, either self-destruction, or to withdraw myself openly from you, and resign myself to him who engrossed all my affections; to have adopted the only intermediate measure by indulging in his society, and secretly committing infidelity to you, while I continued to profess the feelings and perform the duties of a wife, was one of which I was altogether incapable. I therefore, after viewing my situation and examining my heart, determined to abandon a position which I could not conscientiously maintain; and I did accordingly, on Friday last, deliberately and advisedly, and not in a moment of excitement, or from any sudden impulse of feeling, leave my house and placed myself in the hands of him to whom my affections had been surrendered.

Need I assure you that up to the hour I quitted your door I was never guilty of any act injurious to your honor, or incompatible with the vows I had made you? What I have done I have done openly, and have not added the meanness of falsehood and deception to the sin of infidelity. While by this formal confession I place in your hands the power of releasing yourself from the tie which binds you to me, and of preserving the rights of our children from the possible consequences of my act, I am prompted as much by feelings as by duty to declare most unequivocally that what I have done has not been caused by an absence of kindness or affection on your part; that, on the contrary, from the day of our marriage to the day of my departure from you, you have been most kind, most tender, most affectionate; and I am deeply sensible that you have deserved a different return from any that has been in my power to make.

As I believe and trust that my own conduct, as well as that of the person to whom I am now united, has been, up to the hour of my separation from you, such as to afford no grounds for objection, and suspicion, you can not, I presume, have any means of knowing who that person is; it is necessary, therefore, that I should inform you that it is Dr. Lardner. Neither he nor myself desire to offer any extenuation, much less defend our conduct. We feel it, however, to be only justice to ourselves to say, that we are prepared to suffer all the evils attendant upon a total change in pecuniary circumstances as the inevitable consequence of the step we have taken. I have come to him destitute of any means of support, and bring nothing with me but the few articles of dress I had upon my person. He has surrendered a large income, which he has for many years enjoyed, arising from his professional labor. Banished, as he must be, to a foreign country, damaged in character by the very measure which gives me to him, removed from all those connections on which the profitable occupation of his time has hitherto depended, he is at this moment uncertain where or how he may obtain that very small income which will suffice to supply our most moderate wants and wishes. Not foreseeing an exigency like the present, he has not realized any considerable amount of property—nothing, in fact, which can materially aid us in our present position. We were both fully aware of these formidable difficulties and sacrifices; but he felt that any sacrifice, however great, would be most willingly made by him to soften the evils attendant upon the position which I must assume.

Now, in conclusion, allow me to express a hope, that after the first anguish attending this misfortune has been assuaged, you will see that your peace and comfort will be more promoted by losing me altogether; for retaining me, without retaining my affection, would be irksome to you, and you would have the pain of seeing me daily consumed by a hopeless attachment to another, which would eat into my heart until I should be reduced to the mere shadow of myself, and which must, after a brief period, have brought me to the grave. It is not likely that you will feel any disposition to communicate further with me; but as we still have some common interests, I feel that it is my duty to supply you with the means of such communication should it be necessary. Any thing which is addressed to Mrs. Williams, No. 17 Old Burlington Street, will be forwarded to me.

Believe me still your most
Sincere and grateful friend,
MARY HEAVISIDE.

Now, the question arises: What is to be done with such cases? She thought and believed that her new affection was criminal—thought of removing herself to "another world by opium"—was willing to do any thing rather than elope with the celebrated philosopher. She received no hints from Spiritualism, which was not born until *eight years after* her elopement. Or, take the more recent, not less notable and respectable, case of the separation of Mr. Charles Dickens from his very intelligent and excellent wife. He publicly sneers at Spiritualism, attempts to ridicule its philosophy and its facts, yet he takes the very steps and justifies a course which law-makers are now called upon to consider.

96.

DEATH OF THE BODY OF ELIZA W. FARNHAM.

NEW YORK, *December* 15, 1864.

TO-DAY Mrs. Farnham, the reformer, closed her earthly career, and opened her superior life. Her labors for humanity have been many and noble. Her mind was brave, benevolent, intelligent, and progressive; and thus her life for the spheres had a good beginning. Early in the autumn of 1862, she returned from California, with the manuscript of her great work, "Woman and Her Era," well advanced toward completion. An incident connected with her return is worthy of mention, particularly as to it we are indebted for this valuable contribution to Progressive Literature. The narration is thus given in her own words:—

"Being in Santa Cruz, Cal., in the early part of June (1862), and intending to come East during the summer, I one morning stated to my friend, Mrs. K——, in whose house I was visiting, that I had concluded to sail on the 21st of July. While we were talking on the subject, Mrs. Glover, a medium, a resident of the town came in, and was presently influenced by a spirit whom I had known when a child of about ten years, who said:—

"'We do not wish you to go on the vessel you talk of.'

"I did not know what steamer would sail from San Francisco

on the 21st of July, and had not even thought about it at all; but I asked:

"'Why not? Is n't she safe?'

"'They have been overhauling her, but she is wrong about her fire-works.'

"'Won't she get to Panama?'

"'No, she will *never* get to Panama again.'

"'Will she be lost at sea?'

"'No, she will get to the land *somewhere down there*, but half her people will be lost.'"

In consequence of this warning, she did not take passage on the ill-fated "Golden Gate," and her life was prolonged to complete the book, the manuscript of which would have been in her possession, and doubtless lost to the world, had she not been persuaded from following her first intent. One of her public lectures contained ideas somewhat to this effect: It is not in the discovery of new and heretofore unsuspected religious truths, that we expect Progress; but in very unexpected *applications* of the long known and simplest truths of Nature. It is sufficiently difficult to inspire men with the idea of high spiritual truths; but this is much easier than to procure their practical assent to them. Let the absolute requirements of Truth be peremptorily laid upon business, pleasure, social usage, political economy, and the whole of public procedure, and it would be like the letting loose of tornadoes in the forest. Let an angel come down to measure the ways of men, and to change all that disagreed with Justice in the family, in the shop, in the ways of commerce, in social and political life, and the clamor of resistance would fill the heavens! What has been the occasion of all the heat and fury which has gone forth upon the slavery question, but the simple endeavor to procure for a despised class the simplest element of justice? The whole mighty fermentation of England, the irrepressible throes of Italy, are but the result of the simplest truths of Progress. Little by little it leavens the lump. Each encroachment upon embodied and organic selfishness brings on a battle. Behold, indeed, the ax is now laid at the *root;* and every tree which bringeth not forth good fruit shall be hewn down and cast into the fire!

Important changes are to be made slowly. There is too much human happiness involved in every form of social usage to justify rash experiments or sudden changes, which *may* be from bad to worse. Nevertheless, no age will be allowed to shrink from the application of ascertained truths to known imperfections or misusages. Forever to pray "Thy kingdom come," and forever to fight each step of advance as a rash innovation, is the wisdom of conservatism. Some would be glad if God's kingdom would descend, as the rainbow comes, in the air; a thing for the eye; a picture on the clouds, which shines over the world without changing it. Yes! it will come like a rainbow!—the sweep and the scowl of the storm first, which rends and purifies, and then the peaceful bow on the retiring cloud. The coming will be seen in the growing humanity of the public mind; in the application of religious justice to the processes of society; in the eradication of all errors; and the subversion of all hoary evils of established fruitfulness, by which the progress of men in knowledge and goodness has been restrained.

97.

PROFESSOR MAPES ON THE USES OF LIFE.

NEW YORK, *December* 18, 1864.

I AM now recalling the fact that years ago Professor Mapes spent half an hour at our cottage in Hartford. I listened to his accumulated rich treasures of experience in Spiritualism. His refined wife was a very surprising medium for painting exquisite plants and flowers. His memory seemed to overflow with the numerous scientific tests he had instituted. His mind was positive on the subject. He had examined the various New York mediums; and was certain that the spirits *caused* the manifestations.

There was a rather gaudy splendor in his verbal equipage—a kind of artificial luster or exaggeration in some of his statements concerning the uncommon facts in science—but he was frank, reasonable, and unequivocal in all he said respecting the incontestible proofs of Spiritualism. He seemed to love Nature and life like a child. It is a common error, he thought, to find fault with Nature, and to entirely overlook her beauties; and in consequence many suppose that there are no pleasures in this life; that from childhood to old age we are surrounded by sorrows. He held that this is both false and impious.

The Great Creator has given us the means of enjoying life and rendering it one continued source of pleasure; but we must use means. Improve the mind, learn so much of the sciences as to feel an interest in all the natural affairs of life, and for ever afterward misanthropy will leave our doors.

Is it not monstrous to find a full-grown man unacquainted with the principles of the earth's rotations—to view sunrise without knowing the cause—to feel the changes of seasons without ever trying to learn why such changes occur? But how much worse is it to see a being endowed with reason, so besotted with want of mental energy as to be sour with himself and the world. If he be inclined to indulge in moral feeling, instead of an uplifted eye, adoring with a lively and happy heart, thanking God for surrounding pleasures, he talks of his trials, calls our beautiful, happy world, *made by the hand of God himself*, a vale of sorrow, and speaks of the world to come as if he were anxious to leave this. Is not all this the effect of morbid slothfulness? Is it not sinful? Would it not conduce to such a man's happiness to study so much of the sciences as would contribute to his amusement, and enable him to enjoy the beauties which surround him?

The word *science* seems to many as a scarecrow or a bugbear. It simply means knowledge reduced to a system, and so arranged as to be conveniently taught, easily remembered, and readily applied.

Professor Mapes exerted a wide influence in the field of Agriculture; was a genuine American; and a working, as well as a theoretical, farmer.

98.

THE WORLD ACCEPTING THE TESTIMONY OF JUDGE EDMONDS.

NEW YORK, *December* 20, 1864.

THE truly candid editors of magazines and respectable journals are gradually finding out that "there must be something in Spiritualism." To-day one of our best papers contains a clear and candid statement of the "Phenomenal Aspects" of the question. At last, too, the world begins to respect the testimony of Judge Edmonds. One public man, speaking of this distinguished and fearless advocate of Spiritualism, says: "I knew him as a man of finished classical education, a profound lawyer, astute in his investigations and in analyzing testimony, unsurpassed in his legal opinions and in the discharge of his high judicial duties;—and above all, I knew him to be a man of unimpeachable integrity, and the last to be duped by an imposture, or carried away by a delusion."

In 1851 Judge Edmonds spent a Sunday with us in the Hartford cottage. There was a meeting appointed at the public hall that evening, and he had the kindness to attend as a guest; but, in order to fully explain some of my allusions to his remarkable experience, he arose and addressed the congregation. It was a great *event* for the citizens of Old Hartford. The morning papers gave reports of the Judge's remarks; which, in corrected form, were substantially as follows:—

My attention was first drawn to the intercourse by the rappings, then the most common, but now the most inconsiderable, mode of communing. Of course I was on the look-out for deception, and at first relied upon my senses and the conclusions which my reason might draw from their evidence. But I was at a loss to tell how the mediums could cause what I witnessed under these circumstances; the mediums walking the length of a suite of parlors, forty or fifty feet, and the rappings being distinctly heard five or six feet behind them, the whole distance backward and forward several times; being heard near the top of a mahogany door, above where the medium could reach, and as if struck hard with a fist; being heard on the bottom of a car when traveling, on a railroad, and on the floor and the table, when seated at lunch, at an eating-house by the side of the road; being heard at different parts of the room, sometimes several feet distant from the medium, and where she could not reach—sometimes on the table, and immediately after on the floor, and then at different parts of the table, in rapid succession, as to feel the vibration as well as hear the sounds; sometimes when the hands and feet of the medium were both firmly and carefully held by some one of the party, and sometimes on a table when no one touched it.

After depending upon my senses, as to these various phases of the phenomenon, I invoked the aid of science, and with the assistance of an accomplished electrician and his machinery, and of eight or ten intelligent, educated, shrewd persons, I examined the matter. We pursued our inquiries many days, and established to our satisfaction two things:—1st, that the sounds were not produced by the agency of any person present or near us; and 2d, that they were not forthcoming at our will and pleasure.

In the mean time, another feature attracted my attention, and that was the "physical manifestations," as they are termed. Thus, I have known a pine table with four legs lifted bodily up from the floor, in the center of a circle of six or eight persons, turned upside down and laid upon its top at our feet, then lifted up over our heads, and put leaning against the back of the sofa on which we sat. I have known that same table to be tilted up on two legs, its top at an angle with the floor of forty-five degrees, when it neither fell over of itself, nor could any person present put it back on its four legs. I have seen a mahogany table, having only a center leg, and with a lamp burning upon it, lifted from the floor at least a foot, in spite of the efforts of those present, and shaken backward and forward as one would shake a goblet in his hand, and the lamp retain its place, though its glass pendants rang again. I have seen the same table tipped up with the lamp upon it, so far that the lamp must have fallen off unless retained there by something else than its own gravity, yet it fell not, moved not. I have known a dinner bell taken from a high shelf in a closet, rung over the heads of four or five persons in that closet, then rung around the room over the heads of twelve or fifteen persons in the back parlor, and then borne through the folding doors to the farther end of the front parlor, and there dropped on the floor. I have frequently known persons pulled about with a force which it was impossible for them to resist, and once, when all my strength was added in vain to that of the one thus affected. I have known a mahogany chair thrown on its side, and moved swiftly back and forth on the floor, no one touching it, through a room where there were at least a dozen people sitting, yet no one was touched, and it was repeatedly stopped within a few inches of me, when it was coming with a violence which, if not arrested, must have broken my legs.

This is not a tithe—nay! not a hundredth part of what I have witnessed of the same character, but it is enough to show the general nature of what was before me.

Angels speed this noble Judge! He is a man of remarkable integrity, and the very soul of courage. It was truly remarked that this fearless independence has often caused him to war upon popular prejudices, and in no respect has that been more strikingly evinced than in the course he has pursued with regard to the spiritual manifestations. As a man of large and varied experience, and of great practical sagacity, with all the advantages of a long legal, legislative, and judicial training and experience, it would have been difficult to find a man more thoroughly competent to a full and searching investigation into the truth or falsehood of spiritual manifestations than Judge Edmonds.

99.

THACKERAY AND DICKENS LOOKING AT SPIRITUALISM.

NEW YORK, *January* 12, 1865.

IT is a curious fact, that our two leading novelists, each in his own particular periodical, have come out precisely at the same time on the physical phase of Spiritualism.* The battle that has been fought out in America to the great discomfiture of the press, and to the greater growth of Spiritualism, is just beginning here. We congratulate Mr. Thackeray on the manliness and common sense with which he has met the question. He has allowed "a friend of five-and-twenty years' standing, and for whose good faith and honorable character he can vouch," to state plainly the physical phenomena which he has seen in highly respectable private families; on one of which occasions Mr. Home was present, and floated in the air. These phenomena, which strike the press with such profound

* This entire review of Mr. Dickens is taken from the London (Eng.) *Spiritual Magazine* for September, 1860.

astonishment, are merely such as the Americans for the last ten years, and very like what the Chinese for the last three thousand years, profess to have been witnessing, and which we have been detailing to our readers for these many months, on the authority not only of our own eyes and other senses, but also on those of some of the most learned and acute men in the kingdom, some of whom have been previously as determined in their opposition to the belief in these things as Mr. Dickens himself.

We can not but think Mr. Dickens pre-eminently unfortunate. It is not long ago that he knocked his head against the Chestnut ghost, and got a severe rebuff; and now that his able rival has ventured to give a fair field to the statement of the candid observations and perfect convictions of the truth of these psychological facts—he comes forward to announce that he has discovered them to be the most egregious impositions. And where has he discovered these impositions? In the same fair and conspicuous arena as the friend of Mr. Thackeray? Has he gone to the houses of highly respectable and firmly believing private people, who can have no possible motive to deceive, to make his observations? Has he sat down in the circles of persons as educated and honorable as himself, and who have the most serious and sacred conviction of the reality of these phenomena; who would revolt at any imposture, and who would lament, as the shaking of their faith in a most comfortable persuasion, the possibility of any trickery in these *séances?* This, at least, Mr. Dickens should have done before he impugned the high veracity, the honor, and the common sense of hundreds, and of thousands of people in this country, as clear-headed and observant as himself; of millions in America and other parts of the world.

No! Mr. Dickens has thought fit to denounce the physical demonstrations of Spiritualism, upon a single visit to a professional demonstrator or medium, where he paid his half-crown, and where he went with the foregone conclusion that he was about to detect an imposture. Is that, we ask, the way to settle a great question, in which not this single medium, but hundreds of thousands of mediums, and the habitual observers of those mediums, is concerned? Where men and women as able and as highly—and in many instances more highly—educated than himself, and of the most undoubted capacity for determining the truth or falsehood of what they see, are implicated? On the contrary, his conduct has been equally rash, equally foolish, equally capable of immediate exposure, with the senseless acts of the late Dr. Dionysius Lardner, who was repeatedly attempting to prove that steam could never succeed; that it could not get across the Atlantic, and that trains under the utmost possible stimulus could never run more than thirty miles an hour on land. Why will Mr. Dickens so rashly attempt the impossible? If he could prove that the mediums to whom he went—"the one old and the other young"—were impostors, what would he have gained? Nothing! He would not have advanced one step toward the refutation of the claims of Spiritualism, of which these physical demonstrations are but one phase; for at the moment when they read his article, hundreds would laugh at his folly, knowing from years of observation on all sides of them, that precisely the same kind of phenomena, and still more wonderful, are daily taking place in private families of all ranks from very near the throne down to the humblest houses, where no imposture can obtrude itself; where the soul's hopes of immortality and of Christian truth are too deeply associated with what he terms nonsense to suffer them to tolerate it for a moment. Does Mr. Dick ens think that he is the only man possessing a decent share of shrewdness? That he alone is capable of using his eyes and his judgment to the detection of imposture, or the establishment of truth? That his testimony is to be taken in preference to that of millions; to that of judges, physicians, and barristers, and logicians, and experimentalists, who have spent their lives in abstruse inquiry, and in tracing out all the windings and subtleties of chicane? The inference is that of an assumption most preposterous and offensive.

Now our opinion is that, so far from Mr. Dickens being at all qualified for philosophical inquiry, the long habits of his literary life have very much disqualified him for the search after any great truth. Mr. Dickens has not been seeking after the truth so much as after the melodramatic and grotesque in effect. He has mixed so much, in pursuit of material for his fictions, with the lowest and most corrupt and degraded of the London populace; with cadgers, and costermongers, and touters, and swindlers, and artful dodgers, for his Quilps, his Fagans, and Dick Swivelers, that his mind has become nearly ruined for any other department of inquiry. Wherever he goes, he looks for low cunning, and sordid trick, and base motive, and a false and fictitious state of things. It is as great a mistake for him to assume the office of inquiry into the nature and phenomena of Spiritualism, as it was some years ago, for him to attempt an account of Italy in his tour there. Italy with all her grand antiquity, her great and melancholy story, her beauty, her sublime arts, her wonderful evidences of the Pagan and the Christian past; her fragments of temples, and palaces, and amphitheaters, and tombs, and triumphal arches, in which and among which the masters of the world once moved, and the oppressed of the world suffered; and where the proudest of the proud triumphed; and the noblest souls wept tears of blood; and where the groans and aspirations of trodden Christianity are yet perpetuated in mausolea, and in the living clutch of a priestly despotism. Italy, whispering from her deep foundations, from her tawny Campagna, from her mountains, her olive-yards, and her vineyards, of a coming resurrection of liberty and truth,—was not the scene for Charles Dickens. His eyes were still tinged with the vapors of Clerkenwell and Rotherhithe; his senses still inhaled the perfumes of Wapping and Ratcliffe Highway; and he presented his astonished readers, not with the sublime, not with the touching and the beautiful of "The Niobe of Nations," but only with the odd, the vulgar, the flippant, and the grotesque. Let Mr. Dickens adhere to his peculiar province, where he shines. We shall always be glad to have his stories, with all their exaggerations and their mannerism, because they give us as well, real touches of human nature. But let him not deceive himself; we are not likely to adopt him as a pioneer of psychological or theological truth. We appeal from Dickens, indulging in fiction and distortion, to Thackeray and honest and fair inquiry. . . . . . .

But Mr. Dickens has given other examples of his learning. He tells us that these sorts of things have been going on in all ages. Very true. And because this faith in the ministry of spirits, these evidences of spiritual surroundings have so risen up in all ages, spite of ignorance, and atheism, and literary presumption, every sensible man is satisfied that it is a great and eternal truth, underlying all our life, and binding it up with the life to come. It is because it has thus manifested itself in all ages, and in all countries,—to Hesiod and Homer, Socrates and Plato, to the great dramatists of Greece; to Cicero and Seneca and Tacitus in ancient Rome; to all the Christian Fathers; to the Catholic church in all ages; to our own church, which has its ministry of saints and angels; to Fenelon, Luther, Melanchthon, Erasmus, and Tauler; to Fox, and all the Wesleys; to many of our celebrated bishops; to Bacon and Milton, and Addison, and Johnson; to the most eminent leaders of the Dissenters; to Doddridge, and Scott, and Baxter, and Adam Clarke, *cum multis aliis;* that we know that it is a condition of the race, and will live to the end of time, and knock down all the proud and self-inflated Sadducees who shall venture a blow at it.

100.

A SPIRIT DESCRIBING THE EVILS OF CAPITAL PUNISHMENT.

New York, *January* 20, 1865.

At a recent meeting of the "Moral Police Fraternity," an account was given from the spirit of a very noble-hearted gentleman who had innocently suffered "death by hanging." He came to call our attention to the *injustice* of legal strangulations; more especially to remonstrate against ever relying upon what is called "circumstantial evidence." The following case seems to give all the important facts: There was a trial and execution in Dublin, more than a century since, which excited great interest. It was that of a surgeon, well known in society, and esteemed for his amiable character, and remarkable for his humanity to the poor; he lived in a retired street.

It happened one evening that the milk-woman found the street door a-jar, and not being answered when she knocked at it, she made her way to the kitchen. She had no sooner entered it, than uttering a loud shriek, she called loudly for help. The passers-by and persons from the neighboring houses were soon on the spot, and the kitchen was crowded in a short time.

A sad spectacle presented itself. The young woman,

who was servant to the surgeon, was lying dead on the flags, while her dress was stained with the blood which had issued from a wound in the side. In looking about the floor, a surgical instrument was found, which also was stained with blood. A medical man, who was present, ascertained that it was the instrument which had inflicted the death wound. On a further search, a shirt saturated with blood was found, huddled up in the coal-hole; it was marked with the initials of the surgeon's name.

He was immediately seized, and, though protesting his innocence, he was evidently under considerable agitation. The silent witnesses which were brought against him were thought sufficient to prove his guilt, and all attempts to account for their having been found near the unfortunate girl were scouted in the cross-examination. A living witness was also produced in court, an old lady, who deposed that she lived in the house directly facing that where the surgeon resided; that her drawing-room window commanded a view of his premises, and that it was customary with her to watch his movements; she deposed that she had not taken her eyes off his house all that day on which the murder was perpetrated; that no one had left or entered his house that day but himself; that he went home at about four o'clock, his usual hour of returning; and that on knocking at the door it was opened by the servant, who, to the best of her belief, shut it fast when her master went in; that she saw him three or four times pass the windows of his sitting-room; that the last time she saw him was about an hour and a half before the murder; that she observed him look down both sides of the street, and then shut down the window; he held something in his hand, which she thinks may have been a surgical instrument; but this she could not swear.

In summing up the evidence, the horror which the prisoner had betrayed, when looking on the body of his murdered servant, was evidently dwelt on as a crowning proof of guilt. The defense was weak and meager —a bare denial of the crime being its chief substance. A thrill of horror pervaded the court.

The jury retired—a brief space sufficed for deliberation—they returned with a verdict of "Guilty." The judge having donned his black cap, exhorted the prisoner on the heinousness of his crime, and pronounced the fatal sentence.

It is said that the condemned showed much fortitude throughout, and persisted to the last in asserting his innocence. He was brought to the place of execution amidst a vast concourse and the execrations of the people.

We were told by an old gentleman that his father remembered having been held up in his nurse's arms to see the procession to the place of execution. He was often spoken of in the social circle as one who had been held in much estimation. His untimely end was lamented, but there were few who believed it undeserved.

It was after the lapse of several years that some one, who had emigrated to America, returned; he was ill in mind; something lay heavy on his heart and disturbed his conscience; he made his confession to his priest; he had been the "sweetheart" of the murdered girl; she had let him in by the back way, early in the evening, to take tea with her. As they sat side by side, he asked her for a kiss, which he would have snatched, when she denied him; she took up her master's surgical instrument, which she had to clean, and which lay on the table beside her, and she pointed it toward him jestingly; in a struggle, she fell on it, and it pierced her side; he snatched the shirt, which she had in her lap to mend, and stanched the blood which was flowing with it; but life soon ebbed away, and he saw the girl that he loved—who had been laughing and talking with him but a few moments before—lying dead beside him; his agony only gave way to the instinct of self-preservation, when he thought he heard the sounds of approaching footsteps; he thrust the blood-stained shirt into the coal-hole, and setting the hall-door a-jar, he concealed himself behind it, and when the crowd had collected on hearing the alarm, he mingled with it, and then passed into the street, and on to the quay, and getting on board an American ship, he sailed in a few hours. When he learned that the surgeon's life had been forfeited, he was overwhelmed with anguish. The only reparation in his power was to clear his character from the dreadful imputation; but though he felt a relief in this act of justice, yet it could not undo the injury inflicted.

On hearing of such a tragedy, the questions are naturally suggested: May not such have often occurred?—and may they not again?—and is there no remedy?

101.

SPIRITS APPEARING IN THEIR CAST-OFF EARTHLY GARMENTS.

NEW YORK, *January* 22, 1865.

THE great difficulty in explaining the phenomena of apparitions, says an English writer, is to account satisfactorily for the spectral appearance of garments as well as persons. The candid ghost-seer, in relating his experiences is baffled by the scoffing logician, who exclaims, "I have no objection to believe in the apparition of the soul of your grandmother, but don't tell me that you really and literally saw the ghost of her night-cap and apron! Your dead uncle, too, whom you saw drowning when you and he were a thousand miles apart; is his pea-jacket endowed with an immortal spirit?" Our credulous friend is puzzled, and meekly acquiesces in the conclusion—"Well, perhaps it was all a delusion." To meet this difficulty, I venture to offer, as a solution, the following hypothesis: that every significant action of our lives—in the garments we wear, and in the attitudes and gestures of our humanity—is vitally photographed or depicted in the spirit-world; and that the angels, under God's direction, have the power of exhibiting, as a living picture, any specific circumstances or features to those who have the gift of spiritual sight, and who are intended to be influenced by the manifestations. These tableaux may represent still life, or they may be animated by certain spirits appointed for the purpose, or by the identical spirits of the persons whose forms are shown, when the apparitions are the images of those who have departed this world.

What an idea of infinity and divine government does it give us, to suppose that after death we shall move through a grand picture-gallery of our own deeds self-delineated. What a subject of contemplation and awe to those who are debating in their own minds the character of their actions! What a check to those who have not yet quite decided to perpetrate something unworthy of future exhibition! And what a consolation to believe that true repentance for any vicious deeds may secure the removal of the portraits of such deeds from the gallery of celestial art!

This idea of vitally photographing in the spirit spheres the persons and scenes of this world, may be used to explain another curious class of phenomena—those exhibited in what is called "traveling clairvoyance," in which the spirit of the clairvoyant is stated to leave the body and go on journeys, describing events happening at a distance. But in studying this subject, a great difficulty presents itself. The clairvoyant sometimes sees places not as they appear now, but as they existed many years ago, before modern improvements and restorations were effected; and minute events, of which the clairvoyant never had, and never could have had, any knowledge, are narrated as occurring, which really happened perhaps half a century before the time they are seen. Here our Spiritual Photographic Theory comes to our assistance, and helps us to clear up the mystery.

We are at liberty to suppose that the angels unroll before the spiritual sight of the clairvoyant, a grand panorama of past scenes and events in their order of time and sequence of action; so that without leaving the body, the soul can discern literally and faithfully things and persons that have long since disappeared from this world, as well as those that are now actually in existence. Or we may believe, that in the trance, another spirit enters and takes possession of the body of the clairvoyant to perform this discerning and descriptive office.*

102.

INVESTIGATIONS OF ROBERT DALE OWEN.

NEW YORK, *January* 30, 1865.

AFTER Rev. T. W. Higginson and Dr. R. T. Hallock, Dr. H. T. Childs, and others, comes Hon. R. D. Owen. He enters the ranks of Spiritualism after long and thorough investigation. As a thinker and historian he is the embodiment of patience, candor, and completeness. His testimony is perfect. He brings great natural intellectual and moral endowments into the field; and as a scholar, judged by the standard of worldly wisdom, he is second to no person in public life. He comes among Spiritualists with the "pen of a ready

* The foregoing is extracted from Mr. Crosland's very excellent little *brochure* entitled "*Apparitions; a New Theory.*"

writer," and with a mind well acquainted with "the ways of the world." The press and the pulpit have become the creators of public opinion—the agents for good or evil—the promulgators of truth or falsehood. And those powers, when they can be united for truth and goodness in both hemispheres, may, with ease, create, before the termination of this decade, a new public opinion in favor of spiritual ideas, and an irresistible general desire to have them carried, on both sides of the Atlantic, faithfully into practice. I now, in the name of humanity and common sense, call upon Spiritualists in both hemispheres to unite, heart and soul, in this great and good cause. Let the world be regenerated—emancipated from diseases, crimes, and their evils—and the human race, in peace and charity, enabled to enjoy the abundance of the good things of the Spirit, which nature has so lavishly provided for all.

Mr. Owen, it seems to me, is the man whom Spiritualists should elect to fill the "editorial chair" in that *sanctum* from which might emanate the best American Spiritual Magazine. He would sweep out of our ranks all mere frivolity and sensationalism, and the common artificial excitements, which, as every one knows, gradually vitiate the taste and weaken the mind, like deleterious stimulants too long taken into the stomach; and, instead, he would infuse a closer system of investigation, awaken interest in the pure facts of our experience, and so elevate and ennoble a beloved cause.

103.

VISION OF A FRIEND IN GERMANY.

PHILADELPHIA, PA., *October* 18, 1865.

BEFORE this morning session of the National Convention of Spiritualists, to which we came as delegates from the New York Lyceum, I took a clairvoyant observation of Mr. G. C. Wittig, the esteemed and thoroughly-devoted translator of the Harmonial Philosophy into the German language. . . . What I discerned this morning strongly reminded me of a view I had of him, at his home in Breslau, Prussia, about the tenth of September, 1862. . . . There was in the house (as I now recall the facts) a pleasant-faced man, rather below the ordinary stature, talking with Mrs. Wittig concerning one of her two sons. Three girls were in the house, and the person, who was the object of my visit, was just writing on an envelope the name of a book-merchant in Saxony. . . . He seems to have dreamed in youth that, in some sequestered place, near his native village, among the lovely hills, he would find a treasure to enrich and bless his beloved parents. . . . The IDEAS of the Harmonial Philosophy, flashing like stars in the firmament of his reason, are the silver and gold of his dreams. . . . He dreams now that his beloved fatherland will be abundantly enriched by his translations. . . . His translation of Mr. Partridge's chapter on Spiritualism is valuable; but—who will read it? Who, as yet, will purchase and read any one of the translations by this faithful Wittig? . . . But this morning a new light breaks in upon his waiting reason. There is a note from a dear distant friend, conveying tidings of encouragement. May his heart grow stronger, as his mind sees deeper and higher! Very slow will come his reward.

104.

THOUGHTS ON THE CHILDREN'S PROGRESSIVE LYCEUM.

St. Louis, Mo., *December* 14, 1865.

Yesterday, a large number of the enterprising people of this city met in Mercantile Hall. . . . My discourse to them was, in substance, as follows:—

We hold, first, that the Universe is the product of Divine Intelligence, perfect in attributes, harmonious in parts and purposes, and essentially unchangeable.

We hold, secondly, that the human mind is a finite embodiment of the infinite; and that, by much and diligent searching, man can perceive and comprehend much of the nature and operations of the infinite.

Such comprehension is wisdom. It differs from knowledge as much as substance differs from shadow. Wisdom is akin to the intelligence that lives in the life of things, while knowledge reorganizes the shape locality, color, and uses of things, without discerning their ultimate purpose and divine significance. Knowledge is external; wisdom, internal. The intellectual faculties delight in perception and comprehension of "things," while the inmost parts of the mind, its spirit's intuitions, delight in the fellowship and infinite deep of eternal "principles."

Now, the question arises, what is *true* Education? It consists, we reply, in WISDOM. But it is true, also, that no man's education is "complete" unless his mind is stored with *facts*, with knowledge of things, as part of the principles which constitute wisdom.

Memory is an essential of knowledge, as a house is necessary to furniture, or as canvas to the lights and shadows of a picture. Without memory—which is a "recording angel" in the mind's sanctuary—ordinary intelligence is impossible. As the world goes, the tact of memory is paramount to the talent of large reasoning powers. The man of tact is successful in ordinary worldly enterprises, while the man of talent alone will fail; but the latter is victorious in parts and places where the former is defeated and despairing.

Inasmuch as memory is an essential to the acquisition of and progression in knowledge, and inasmuch as *knowledge of things* is more valuable and in greatest demand as the world is now constituted, so we observe that all popular "systems of education" are *based* on the faculty of memory, as though the sum and essentials of a man's mind consisted in what his senses can grasp and his memory retain!

If man's mental organization were a casket merely—a vessel for containing ethereal impressions—then there would be matchless wisdom in the plan of education adopted in the public and other schools of the day.

The possibilities of growth in spirit, independent of memory, are now universally discarded. Hence, the popular institutions of learning are, for the most part, under the control of mechanically-minded men—men who plod and plod like dray-horses through a muddy road, in the vain endeavor to "educate" the young under their charge in the evil and crooked ways of memory.

We, of the Harmonial Philosophy, start upon a wholly different plan. While we admit the value of a "practical education" in the facts and uses of things, and although we perceive and avail ourselves of the "benefits" of knowledge to be derived from the study of books and of external Nature, yet we start with a great, deep, infinite conviction, congenial to whatever is deathless in the human soul, that it is our duty as much as it is our glorious privilege, to "know the HEART of things," to unfold in that Wisdom which can discern

"———The promise of to-morrow,
And feel the wondrous beauty of to-day;"

which comprehendeth the lengthening sweep of immutable principles in the universe of matter and mind; and which, seeing beyond the material night of immaterial shadows, and beyond the enveloping clouds of a seemingly engulphing fate, calmly planteth its feet upon the life-laws of the Divine Intelligence, and steadily advanceth through "ways of pleasantness," and walketh harmoniously in "paths of peace."

Memory, at best, holds but the reflections of shadows. The spirit, which is the great immortal Man, is compounded of the life-essences of the perfect Soul, which, in common language, is called "God."

All true education, therefore, is unfoldment. The inner life unrolls, flower-like, beneath the sun of intellect. Instinctively, we begin with the mind of the young, begin with the physical senses, as the natural method of reaching and developing the inner life. Henceforth the method is deductive (*i. e.*, intuitive and feminine) from the heart, outwardly. Both methods are finally harmonized, and thus the mind of youth is balanced—first, by the acquisition of knowledge *inductively* from without inwardly, which depends on memory for its permanency and value; and secondly, by the development of wisdom *deductively* from within, in accordance with the life-laws of the Divine Intelligence.

The Children's Progressive Lyceum is such an institution. Its methods are, primarily, in the realm of external and physical exercises and attractions. The attractiveness of a thing to a child consists in its physical properties and attributes. The *sound* of music, the *color* of bodies, the *plumage* of birds, the *taste* of fruit and other food, the *smell* of flowers. It would be folly to attempt to interest either children or adults in unbeautiful things. Dry, indeed, is the path of "learning" to most children. Consequently the world, all civilized society, is filled with persons of *little* book-knowledge—persons whose early years were spent in activities out of the school-house—with "education neglected," simply because the school-house, under the jurisdiction of the mechanical and arbitrary schoolmaster, was a place of *unnatural* confinement to both mind and body, as dreadful to little children as is the temple of error to the angels of God.

The mind does not more need, does not more imperatively demand, education at first than the body. The body and its senses first call loudest for true education. The baby-heart is *wiser* than the "learned" college professor. It calls unto God in the midst of "the garden." The eternal Father and Mother, whispering, say to it, "Behold the singing birds, the streams with their many voices, the trees of sweetest fruit, the flowers of finest fragrance; behold these, my child, and go forth out of the cradle and out of the house—go on the full run away from the steady step of thy father and mother; scamper from the school master who teacheth under the tree of evil; run, skip, sing, be as happy as thou art free in the fields of nature, which is boundlessly expanded in the universe without thee."

Hearing and *heeding* this Divine voice, thousands of children "play truant" when sent to the wrongly-constituted school. They will deceive their "doting parents;" will tell a big story to escape detection; will play the hypocrite to perfection—all to obey the voice of God, which is stronger in the bone and blood of a child than is the fear of parents or the lash of the whipping professor of learning. Children will, like adults, go without asking to places attractive to them, which may be most in accordance with their physical and sensuous necessities; and it is the climax of philosophical absurdity, as it is the stupidest exercise of parental authority, to set up barriers against the Divine law that impels to such a course. Instead of quarreling with your children for playing *truant*, better reconstruct your systems of education, and begin with the young as nature begins with them—in the realm of the Senses, with their bodies, gradually reaching their affections and inmost life.

Congratulate yourselves, Spiritualists! Open your hearts to utterance of grateful thanks, because the inhabitants of the Summer Land have reached forth their strong arms to sustain you in the effort to inaugurate a more just, rational, and attractive school for the culture and perfection of the young in your midst. The Lyceum is *progressive* in every true sense of the word. It begins with the senses and deepens inwardly to the soul. It begins with the perceptions of the head and continues into the intuitions of the heart. It begins with amusement and ends with the unfoldment of wisdom. It gains access to the dweller within the temple by kindly and beautiful offices performed in love at the outmost vestibule of personal child-life. Badges with significant colors, corresponding to the color of the station target for each group, will be worn by each child. (All flowers, all birds, all precious stones, every thing, have *colors* or badges significant of their places and purposes in nature.)

The Lyceum children will learn to sing, before they think, the ideas of progress. The plan is so truly simple that "he who runs may read," and without constraint, all may acquire habits of *order*, the art of correct thinking, the freedom of truth, and make progress in whatsoever by Christianity and by good people generally is deemed wise, good, and effective unto salvation from error and other sources of misery to mankind.

105.

REMARKABLE POWERS OF HEINRICH ZSCHOKKE.

CLEVELAND, O., *January* 20, 1866.

ACCORDING to a writer in the London (Eng.) *Spiritual Magazine*, Heinrich Zschokke was a "self-made man" —poet, novelist, schoolmaster, historian, statesman, philosopher, and public instructor. Adventurous, of restless activity, much given to thoughtful speculation, haunted for long years by the phantom of doubt, and tormented with the problems of existence, but attaining in the end to a serene rational Christian faith, his mental struggles and diversified outward and inward experiences peculiarly qualified him for the vocation to which he specially applied himself in his later years— that of a popular religious guide and teacher through the press. Toward the close of life, on looking back, he felt like Stilling, that the wondrous web of his past life had been not the work of his hand, "but of a mightier, an invisible." That he had been "borne along the torrent of events wherein (he says) I had no power but over my own will, hurled without any co-operation on my part into the wide fields of action, I was compelled to find within myself a strength of which I had not been conscious." He was instinctively a spiritualist from his youth up, was well acquainted with the phenomena of rhabdomancy, which, he says, "presented me with a new phase of nature," and which was, moreover, of considerable use to him in his mining operations. He believed in spiritual impressions and presentiments from personal experience, especially as conveyed in dreams; but his most remarkable faculty was what he describes as "a singular kind of prophetic gift, which I called my inward sight, but which has ever been enigmatical to me." The following is his detailed account of it, which he gives, as "it may be an addition to our stock of soul experiences":—

It is well known that the judgment we not seldom form at the first glance of persons hitherto unknown, is more correct than that which is the result of longer acquaintance. The first impression that through some instinct of the soul attracts or repels us with strangers, is afterward weakened or destroyed by custom, or by different appearances. We speak in such cases of sympathies or antipathies, and perceive these effects frequently among children to whom experience in human character is wholly wanting. Others are incredulous on this point, and have recourse rather to the art of physiognomy. Now for my own case. It has happened to me sometimes, on my first meeting with strangers, as I listened silently to their discourse, that their former life, with many trifling circumstances therewith connected, or frequently some particular scene in that life, has passed quite involuntarily, and, as it were, dreamlike, yet perfectly distinct, before me. During this time I usually feel so entirely absorbed in the contemplation of the stranger life, that at last I no longer see clearly the face of the unknown wherein I undesignedly read, nor distinctly hear the voice of the speakers, which before served in some measure as a commentary to the text of their features. For a long time I held such visions as delusions of the fancy, and the more so as they showed me even the dress and motions of the actors, rooms, furniture, and other accessories. By way of jest, I once in a familiar family circle at Kirchberg, related the secret history of a seamstress who had just left the room and the house. I had never seen her before in my life; people were astonished, and laughed, but were not to be persuaded that I did not previously know the relations of which I spoke, for what I had uttered was the *literal* truth; I on my part was no less astonished that my dream-pictures were confirmed by the reality. I became more attentive to the subject, and when propriety admitted it, I would relate to those whose life thus passed before me the subject of my vision, that I might thereby obtain confirmation or refutation of it. It was invariably ratified, not without consternation on their part. I myself had less confidence than any one in this mental jugglery. So often as I revealed my visionary gifts to any new person I regularly expected to hear the answer—"It was not so." I felt a secret shudder when my auditors replied that it was true, or when their astonishment betrayed my accuracy before they spoke. Instead of many I will mention one example, which pre-eminently astounded me. One fair day, in the city of Waldshut, I entered an inn (the Vine), in company with two young student-foresters; we were tired with rambling through the woods. We supped with a numerous society at the *table-d'hôte*, where the guests were making very merry with the peculiarities and eccentricities of the Swiss, with Mesmer's magnetism, Lavater's physiognomy, &c., &c. One of my companions, whose national pride was wounded by their mockery, begged me to make some reply, particularly to a handsome young man who sat opposite, and who had allowed himself extraordinary license. This man's former life was at that moment presented to my mind. I turned to him and asked whether he would answer me candidly if I related to him some of the most secret passages of his life, I knowing as little of him personally as he did of me. That would be going a little further, I thought, than Lavater did with his physiognomy. He promised, if I were correct in my information, to admit it frankly. I then related what my vision had shown me, and the whole company were made acquainted with the private history of the young merchant; his school years, his youthful errors, and lastly with a fault committed in reference to the strong box of his principal. I described to him the uninhabited room with whitened walls, where, to the right of the brown door, on a table, stood a black money-box, &c., &c. A dead silence prevailed during the whole narration, which I alone occasionally interrupted by inquiring whether I spoke the truth. The startled young man confirmed every particular, and even what I scarcely expected, the last mentioned. Touched by his candor, I shook hands with him over the table and said no more. He asked my name, which I gave him, and we remained together talking till past midnight. He is probably still living. I can well explain to myself how a person of lively imagination may form, as in a romance, a correct picture of the actions and passions of another person, of a certain character, under certain circumstances. But whence came those trifling accessories which in *nowise concerned me*, and in relation to people for the most part indifferent to me, with whom I neither had, nor desired to have, any connection? Or, was the whole matter a constantly recurring *accident?* Or, had my auditor, perhaps, when I related the particulars of his former life, very different views to give of the whole, although in his first surprise, and misled by some resemblances, he had mistaken them for the same? And yet, impelled by this very doubt, I had several times given myself trouble to speak of the most insignificant things which my waking dream had revealed to me. I shall not say another word on this singular gift of vision, of which I can not say it was ever of the slightest service; it manifested itself rarely, quite independently of my will, and several times in reference to persons whom I cared little to look through. Neither am I the only person in possession of this power. On an excursion I once made with two of my sons, I met with an old Tyrolese, who carried oranges and lemons about the country, in a house of public entertainment in Lower Hanenstein, one of the passes of the Jura. He fixed his eyes on me for some time, then mingled in the conversation, and said that he knew me, although he knew me not, and went on to relate what I had done and striven to do in former time, to the consternation of the country people present, and the great admiration of my children, who were diverted to find another person gifted like their father. How the old lemon merchant came by his knowledge he could explain neither to me nor to himself; he seemed, nevertheless, to value himself somewhat upon his mysterious wisdom.

106.

BEAUTIFUL SHOWER OF ICE AT ST. PETERSBURG, RUSSIA.

ORANGE, N. J., *March* 2, 1866.

A FEW days since, incidentally to an observation of an object in St. Petersburg, I noticed what might be called "a snow shower," consisting of brilliant icy crystals, which fell on the people as they walked or rode in sledges through the streets. Every crystal seemed to be formed exactly alike, something like a star, with six points of radiation; but I think there were other varieties of structure. . . . It seemed like the breaking up of the winter season; but, perhaps, I was mistaken in this. . . . . It was certainly a new, brilliant, and beautiful exhibition of snow which seemed to be formed just above the city, in the atmosphere—the air being full of these ice-crystals, having all the appearance of snow, and yet they were not flakes of snow, but the finest creations of electricity in the air, which clothed itself and fell in starry figures of pure frost upon every thing.

107.

SUBSTANCES CONVEYED THROUGH IMPENETRABLE MATTER.

ORANGE, N. J., *April* 20, 1866.

YESTERDAY a controversy arose between two investigators, during which one urged his belief that, sometimes, spirits convey material substances through what is deemed impenetrable matter. The other contended that it was not *necessary* to believe that material substances are conveyed, or even can be conveyed, through what is deemed impenetrable matter in order to conceive the possibility of the facts. Take, for instance, the reported case of "the slipper being carried away, the door being closed, and none of the party having moved from their seats, he being directed to look in a leather bag which was lying in another room, where it was found, the bag being locked and the key in his pocket," &c., &c. Is it not possible to conceive that the door might easily be opened and closed so *rapidly* and *noiselessly* that no *natural* eyes could possibly see it? Is it not possible to conceive that the lock of the carpet bag might be opened and closed again by spirits in a non-miraculous manner? Is it not possible to conceive that the laws of motion in matter, and the laws of *natural vision*, have very different degrees of limitation in proportional relations?

These reflections, says Doherty, were excited in my mind some years ago, when I was at a *séance* of the Davenport boys in Buffalo, where I witnessed the operation of tying the two boys to their chairs with a very long and strong rope, by Professor Mapes, who observed that he had been a sailor, and would tie the cords in sailor's knots, which he did in a most complicated manner, occupying what seemed to me some twenty minutes' time, being tediously long in doing it, and unnecessarily multiplying the difficulties of untying the innumerable knots. When the boys had been thus tied to their chairs we all retired to a distant part of the very large room, holding each other by the hand (the father of the boys, myself, Professor Mapes, his daughter, and Mr. A. Brisbane), that none might stir without the others knowing it. The light was turned down so as to make the room almost entirely dark, and the spirits began to untie the ropes, which was accomplished with a noise something like that of running a cord rapidly from a windlass, and in about two seconds, as nearly as I can guess, the cords were thrown heavily in a mass on the ground, and the light immediately turned on again. This feat seemed to me almost miraculous, but on reflection I asked myself, What proportion does the rapidity of material motion of one degree bear to that of another? What relation does the motion of our planet through space bear to that of a bird flying? Where do the limits of human vision begin and end with regard to the motion of material bodies? Can we not conceive, from our knowledge of the rapid motions of the heavenly bodies in space, and the undulations of light, that certain degrees of rapidity are utterly invisible to natural sight?

I need hardly mention the school-boy's peg-top, spinning "asleep," as a familiar example of invisible motion; and a door might possibly be opened and closed as rapidly as the top spins invisibly before our eyes. I do not say the rope scene was or was not a trick of the Davenport boys, but only that invisible motion is neither miraculous nor incredible.

The doctor thus concludes:—I do not know what is possible or impossible, but I can easily conceive that the limitations of power in human vision, motion, sensation, &c., may exclude us from the possibility of being conscious of many kinds of physical phenomena which are supposed to be miraculous, while they may be perfectly natural within limits which transcend our normal powers of sensation.*

108.

MR. W. P. ANDERSON, THE SPIRIT ARTIST.

ORANGE, N. J., *May* 24, 1866.

THE wonderful pictures and portraits by this truly spiritual man, are drawn upon artists' paper with *lead pencils.* It is supposed that they have a much more lifelike expression and effect than might be expected through this simple means. Even the effect of *several*

* The reader is referred to the *Philosophy of Spiritual Intercourse.*

colors can be produced from a black pencil, by the singular combinations of light and shade!—though this is not *ordinarily* attempted. As his labors are of a very fatiguing character, from the exhaustion of his magnetic strength, but a brief time is spent in *continuous* occupation with the pencil, not longer, usually, than half an hour, without rest, under favorable circumstances—oftener less.

Mr. Anderson (see the *Spiritual Magazine*) is clairvoyant, and spirits appear to him, at any time, as substantially as those in the flesh, and converse as free is held with them. While using his pencil he is in a nearly trance or unconscious state, and subject to the *real* artists who are using his organism. The pictures are not in *miniature*, but of *life-size*, and represent the persons, who are the subjects, in all the peculiarities of dress, &c., which belonged to them in life, at whatever time distant they may have lived. A very pleasing feature of these portraits is the lavish display of floral embellishment with which the more elaborate and highly finished ones are adorned. A work which Mr. A. will produce in two or three hours, would occupy artists of the readiest skill many days, and often weeks—by their own admissions—and at the same time it exhibits all the marks of consummate ability in design, in calculation of space, and in perfectness of execution. Portraits are commenced from the lower extremities and wrought *upward* to completion as often as the reverse; especially is this the case when the figure is made to rest upon some elaborate pedestal.

In our Orange home hangs a very exquisite specimen of Brother Anderson's vase and flower-work—a gift from him and his gentle and inspired companion, who is also fast becoming "a spirit artist," and thus more perfectly *one* with her mate.

109.

PSYCHOLOGICAL ARGUMENT FOR IMMORTALITY DEDUCED FROM FACTS.

ORANGE, N. J., *June* 11, 1866.

A BOSTON gentleman, once a clergyman in good and regular standing, writing upon the evidences of individual immortality, comes out thus favorably of Spiritualism: There is one argument for the existence of the spirit after the dissolution of the physical body, to some more convincing than any other. I allude to certain psychological phenomena which have impressed many minds, and which are wholly inexplicable on any other ground than the admission of the soul's immortality. The kind of evidence which I now adduce may be classed among the mystical, but it can not be among the unreal, for the reality is established in numerous minds beyond all possible doubt. I refer to some *appearances* which have been made of the departed. And the evidence which we are now giving will of course strike those minds most powerfully which have realized the same phenomena; nevertheless, I see not how they can fail of carrying a degree of conviction to all. We are not of an imaginative character—those who know us best will entirely acquit us of any such charge. And it is to pure reason, and reason alone, accompanied with palpable fact, that the evidence in question has any importance. The evidence is this: Many persons may be found, of all varieties of dispositions, mental characteristics, and degrees of culture, who, during the common occupations of life, have suddenly been impressed with the presence of absent friends or relatives. Sometimes the vision has been complete. Friends at sea, or at distant parts, have thus been the cause of a distinct and conscious presence to the vision of their friends at home, and after months of time, frequently, the next news of those friends was—*that they had departed from this life precisely at that time!* What could it have been but a spiritual appearance, impossible to be made until the spirit was released from the body? These cases are not uncommon. But they are frequently locked as a secret within the heart, and not related but to a familiar friend, and even then with an injunction to secrecy, for fear of ridicule, or the charge of superstition: so tyrannous is this power of popular opinion, and so sensual is the prevailing philosophy of our day. I have, myself, within but a few weeks, received relations of this kind from persons of unquestioned veracity, and far from an imaginary character, who told me of the presence—the visible, entire form of near relatives and friends, and the next news was, that they died at that time. Perhaps as familiar an instance as could be given of the reality of such spiritual appearances, may be found in "Mrs. Child's Letters from New York."

Scottish legends, she says, abound with instances of second sight, oftentimes supported by a formidable array of evidence. But I have met with only one person who was the subject of such a story. She was a woman of plain, practical sense, very unimaginative, intelligent, extremely well-informed, and as truthful as the sun. I tell the story as she told it to me. One of her relatives was seized with a rapid consumption. He had for some weeks been perfectly resigned to die; but one morning when she called on him, she found his eyes brilliant, his cheeks flushed with an unnatural bloom, and his mind full of belief that he should recover health. He talked eagerly of voyages he would take, and of the renovating influence of warmer climes. She listened to him with sadness; for she was well acquainted with this treacherous disease, and in all these things she saw symptoms of approaching death. She said this to her mother and sisters when she returned home. It was at that home, away from her invalid relative, in the afternoon of the same day, as she sat sewing in the usual family circle, that she accidentally looked up—and gave a sudden start, which immediately attracted attention and inquiry. She replied: "Don't you see cousin?" They thought she had been dreaming; but she said, "I am not certainly asleep. It is strange you do not see him; he is there!" The next thought was, that she was seized with sudden insanity; but she assured them she was never more rational in her life—that she could not account for the circumstance any more than they could; but her cousin was certainly there, and looking at her with a very pleasant countenance. Her mother tried to turn it off as a delusion; but, nevertheless, she was so much impressed by it, that she looked at her watch, and immediately sent to inquire how the invalid did. The messenger returned with the news that he was dead, and *had died at that moment!*

My friend told me (continues the narrator) that at first she only saw the bust; but gradually the whole form became visible, as if some imperceptible cloud or veil had slowly rolled away. The invisible veil again rose, and then that vanished. She said the vision did not terrify her at the time; it simply perplexed her, as a thing incomprehensible. Why *she* saw it, she could explain no better than why her mother and sisters did *not* see it. She simply told it to me just as it appeared to her, as distinct and real as any other individual in the room.

Now, there is one thing in connection with this phenomena which is inexplicable on any other ground than the admission of the spirit's immortality. The *whole* of it is striking and convincing—to any thing but an inveterate sensual philosophy. But there is *one* thing that deserves particular attention. If this appearance, or these appearances, for they are many, took place any time *before* the death of the person, or *after* it, then it might be said that the vision was only imaginary—the effect of a nervous or impressible mind, by mere accident, by a momentary, intense reflection on the absent one. But why should these appearances so frequently happen *at the very time* of the death? Is not this an argument for the disenthrallment of the spiritual body, which, on its release from the flesh, then only had the power to make its appearance in this manner?

110.

HARMONIAL BASIS OF THE CHILDREN'S LYCEUM.

ORANGE, N. J., *June* 12, 1866.

I HAVE just mailed a letter to a very dear friend, now traveling and lecturing, who wants further information concerning the "idea" and the "plan" of the Lyceum. . . . . Of course the Manual contains the sub stance, and much of the detail, of what I have thus far received for the world on this celestial institution. . . . . The Lyceum is based in the fact that ordinarily children are indoctrinated with false theology; that in after years, when such children become men and women, this false theology clings to them and manifests itself in the form of bigotry, uncharitableness, assumed righteousness, and unprogressive conservatism. Furthermore, that the popular mode of religious teaching for the young is unattractive, is chilling and unnatural; therefore injurious to confiding and impressible natures. It is believed that the young should be taught by pleasing and natural methods to love the Beautiful and the Useful, the Just and the Wise. By the Lyceum it is proposed to cultivate and harmonize the *physical*, by teaching and obeying the conditions of life and health; by vocal exercises and strengthening motions under the influence of instrumental music; by singing appropriate songs, marches, and by the practice of those physical movements known as light gymnastics. Next, by the cultivation of the intellectual, by means of legitimate signs and the prime symbols of natural things, to teach *attractively* reading, writing, geography, natural history, arithmetic, grammar, &c. Next, to cultivate the *moral* by the study of the mind, its structure, laws, powers, functions, by interesting mind in mind, inducing the child's spirit to look into itself, through apt hints and suggestions; and by encouraging young minds to think accurately of forms, qualities, uses, relations, and adaptations. And finally, to cultivate and harmonize the *spiritual* by addressing the intuitions and mental powers, beginning with the simplest truths, and thence advancing toward fixed and central principles—the Divine Existence, the works and ways of Father God and Mother Nature. . . . . . Let all remember that true Education is a life-long, yea an eternal, process; therefore, that it is not reasonable to expect that the germs of purity, goodness, and greatness, inherent in the child-spirit, can be rapidly made to unfold.

111.

THEODORE PARKER DEFINES THE TEACHINGS OF SPIRITUALISM.

ORANGE, N. J., *July* 9, 1866.

MOST appropriately to-day—the earth and the sky so golden and glorious in their Summer beauty—Mr.

Parker arrives from the Summer Land, and imparts great, strong, stirring "thoughts" on the question of Spirit and Matter. His definitions are still the same as reported and embodied in the following paragraph. Of true Spiritualism he says :—

"It teaches that there is a natural supply for spiritual as well as for corporeal wants; that there is a connection between God and the soul, as between light and the eye, sound and the ear, beauty and the imagination; that as we follow an instinctive tendency, obey the body's laws, get a natural supply for its wants, attain health and strength, the body's welfare; as we keep the law of the mind, and get a supply for its wants, attain wisdom and skill, the mind's welfare—so if, following another instinctive tendency, we keep the law of the moral and religious natures, we get a supply for their wants, moral and religious truth, obtain peace of conscience and rest for the soul, the highest moral and religious welfare. It teaches that the World is not nearer to our bodies than God to the soul; 'for in him we live and move and have our being.' As we have bodily senses to lay hold on Matter and supply bodily wants, through which we obtain, naturally, all needed material things; so we have spiritual faculties to lay hold on God, and supply spiritual wants; through them we obtain all needed spiritual things. As we observe the conditions of the Body, we have Nature on our side; as we observe the Law of the Soul, we have God on our side. He imparts truth to all men who observe these conditions; we have direct access to Him through Reason, Conscience, and the Religious Sentiment, just as we have direct access to Nature through the eye, the ear, or the hand. Through these channels, and by means of a law, certain, regular, and universal as gravitation, God inspires men, makes revelation of truth, for is not truth as much a phenomenon of God as motion of Matter? Therefore, if God be omnipresent and omniactive, this inspiration is no miracle, but a regular mode of God's action on conscious Spirit, as gravitation on unconscious Matter. It is not a rare condescension of God, but a universal uplifting of Man. To obtain a knowledge of duty a man is not sent away, outside of himself, to ancient documents, for the only rule of faith and practice; the Word is very nigh him, even in his heart, and by this word he is to try all documents whatever. Inspiration, like God's omnipresence, is not limited to the few writers claimed by the Jews, Christians, or Mohammedans, but is co-extensive with the race. As God fills all Space, so all Spirit; as he influences and constrains unconscious and necessitated Matter, so he inspires and helps free and conscious Man."

112.

RALPH WALDO EMERSON AND FREDERICK DOUGLASS.

BOSTON, *December* 19, 1866.

ONE of the standard American journals, the *Atlantic Monthly*, has, in two successive numbers, placed the above names in juxtaposition by publishing an article from the pen of each. In like manner, Boston has placed these two men side by side during the present season, in the course of Parker Fraternity Lectures. Thus, probably without designing it, editors and lecture committees have joined in giving a most striking illustration of the opportunities and tendencies of American life.

Emerson was born amid the conditions of Culture. From earliest youth his mind was elected to thought. A graduate from college while yet under age, he had a distant background of educated ancestry; being, when ordained by the Unitarian Church, the eighth, in orderly succession, of a consecutive line of ministers. Too great for the pulpit, he has become the Plato of modern Athens, and the representative of culture throughout the world of letters.

On the other hand, Frederick Douglass was born a Southern slave! It is only necessary to state this terrible fact, to show that he was, from the first, environed by the worst conditions of ignorance. No grammar school, no college, opened its doors for him—the son of a slave mother, and the chattel of a relentless master. He secretly taught himself to read and write, and, when the hour came, fled from his bonds to the freedom and intelligence of the North. Just then of age, he had graduated, not from a seminary of learning, but from the charnel-house of ignorance and oppression.

And this Man stood in Music Hall last evening, before an immense audience, to teach the American people the principles of statesmanship, to show them the deep and solid foundations of a true government, by first revealing the "Sources of danger to the Republic." Calm, grand, impressive was his utterance, each sentence freighted with convincing truth, till at last argument was merged into appeal, and, flinging himself with passionate earnestness into the cause of his oppressed race, the spirit of outraged justice poured forth through his soul in a flood of eloquence, which streamed like living fire into every heart.

Just one week ago Emerson stood on the same platform, and to the same vast throng, which hung breathless upon his words, announced the eternal verities, under the guise of "The Man of the World." Golden were the thoughts which flowed from the fountain of his wisdom. Welcome to the inmost spirit were the immortal truths which sparkled upon the background of his discourse, like shining stars on the vaulted sky. Exhilarating as a breath of divine air, were the electric sentences which roused every soul to heroic self-reliance and conscious moral power.

Thus the rostrum has become the common ground where meet the utmost extremes of American society, giving us infinite hope that, by means of true American Democracy, the dream of Plato may be more than realized in a harmonial republic and the brotherhood of nations.

113.

SPIRITUALISTIC DOCTRINES CONCERNING PRAYER AND WORSHIP.

ORANGE, N. J., *January*, 29, 1867.

NOT long since a clergyman, writing candidly for information, asked:—

"But when we come to Spiritualism, do you not think that that prominence is not assigned to the religious faculties that ought to be? Are not prayer and divine worship indispensable to the public welfare? . . . . Man, the world over, is a worshipful being. It is as natural to pray as to sing, to cry, or to laugh. . . . But Spiritualism should have its religious, as well as its purely demonstrative side."

Now, to a close and critical thinker (says a respondent), this passage sounds strange, coming, as it does, from the pen of a Christian clergyman. In front of this sentiment, thus candidly and genially expressed, place the following words, said to have been uttered by Jesus, the assumed teacher of all Christian clergymen: "And when thou prayest, thou shalt not be as the hypocrites are, for they pray standing in the synagogues and in the corners of the streets that they may be seen of men. Verily I say unto you, they have their reward. But thou, when thou prayest, enter into thy closet, *and when thou hast shut thy door*, pray to thy Father which is in secret, and thy Father which seeth in secret, shall reward thee openly." Matthew vi. 5, 6.

And when to this clear and express command, we add the fact, that we have no account of an example of public prayer by Jesus, before his assemblies, as a mode of worship, who can resist the conviction that public prayer as a stated mode of public worship, is a direct violation of the teachings and practice of Jesus? If Jesus was a Christian (which he was not evidently in the modern acceptance of the term), then public prayer is *anti*-Christian. The clergy of all Christendom are living in continued violation of this emphatic teaching and practice of the celebrated Nazarene. How can a clergyman, educated by the New Testament, engage in, or recommend, public prayer, unless, indeed, he has become the creature of a habit, practiced by the church without any good authority therefor.

Will it be said that Jesus gave a special form of prayer? I answer that this prayer immediately succeeded the command to *pray only in secret.* It was meant to be heard by no second ear. Matthew, Mark, and Luke, represent Jesus as going away from his disciples, to pray three several times—just before the betrayal of Judas. He would not pray in the immediate presence of his disciples—his dearest friends, even. When he returns to them, he finds then fast asleep. . . . . There is, therefore, an inner and a spiritual side to worship.

There are moments when, after long and severe toil in the work of elevating ourselves and others; when we have fought with beasts, not at "Ephesus" only, but in our own blood and society; when we have opposed the unjust law; when we have labored to save the fallen, to protect the weak, to feed the hungry, and to emancipate woman, and negroes, and labor; then it is that there comes over us the deepening, holy presence of the Divine Spirit; our very souls yearn for more light, love, power, and beauty. *But mark the fact and the law*—such moments do not come to the selfish, self-seeking, hard-hearted, and lazy man, who works for nobody but himself; but only to the self-forgetful toiler for his race. And the soul at such hours lifts itself up toward the seat and center of Divine Sovereignty; its towering aspirations that put out its Spiritual tentaculæ into the ocean of celestial forces, are but the correlative and equivalent of its duty done, the force of heart-love and hand-work for men transformed into power, of soul into consciousness of our Spiritual Unity with God and the Republic of Ideas.

The power to rise up into the Divine beatitudes arises from the just and generous performances of deeds of kindness, of mercy, of justice, of love. It is thus we get re-enforced from higher levels, for other duties which shall come at the right moment. *Yet these need more devotion.* But not devotion in the shape of ecclesiastical performances. The husband needs more devotion to his wife, who has forsaken all for him; and the wife needs more devotion to her husband; and both need more devotion to their children's culture and success as future men and women; and we all need more devotion to justice, liberty, and love. The amount of wind expended in oral prayer, if it could fill the sails of our souls' commerce, would waft us into the harbor of eternal peace and plenty; but it flows from too low levels to accomplish this celestial voyage. To be sure, let us love devotion; but let it be a devotion which will free the Republic, emancipate woman, and open to her a career; which will educate all the children of the land; which will exalt labor and degrade idleness; which will soften the heart; spiritualize the affections; purify marriage and society; develop science, art, philosophy, religion, until the dear old earth shall blaze and brighten under the beams of an actual millennium.

114.

VOICES AND LESSONS OF NATURE.

ORANGE, *July* 29, 1867.

TAKING up the *Republic* this morning, the following inspiration from Miss Wheelock's Oration before the First Spiritual Society of Rock Island, Ill., was read with pleasure :—

"Let us love truth for its own dear sake—Truth, royal and regal as the stars whose constellated glories robe the night in silver splendor, and clothe all hours in solemn awe. Truth, regnant as morning, opens each glorious day with salutations of praise and thankfulness. She walks the fields with stately grace, holding high converse with the stars. She treads the valley glooms, and meadow floors, in sweet communion with streams, and all of Nature's voiceless messengers chanting of God's universal love. She sings her songs in sunlight, or in shadow; at morning, at noontide, or at evening hour; in valleys or on hill-tops. Everywhere Nature's solemn presence inspires to holy utterance—whether silent or voiceful. She prints her lessons on every living thing; upon solid rocks and mottled marble; upon every imaginable form, animate or inanimate. Their glory beams from stars, orbs, and central suns; reflects light into the dark corners of this dark earth; into ocean's treasure-spread floor; upon every wavelet of the sea, and into the soul of all life. She robes earth in everchanging, yet unchanging beauty; she thrills the sky with the stern grandeur of her purpose, and suspended words re-echo her commands. The grand, crowned mountains, uplift her to their bold brave brows, and her eloquence thrills to joy the circling rounds above. Night is vocal with her presence; day, commanding with her majestic soul. Nowhere is there contradiction; nowhere inharmony in Nature's grand oratorio. No false transcript of thy life, O Truth! in the vast universe of Nature. Science demonstrates thee peerless in thy integrity. Facts, weighty and significant, imprint their evidence upon the walls of earth and time. Philosophy, with higher sense, rolls out subjective truths; these too, are epics of the Great Eternal, mingled with mysteries of the celestial spheres. Law, potential with infinite purpose, and positive in its authority, asserts the sovereignty of truth throughout the illimitable bounds of being. O, man! teach thy soul to love truth as Nature loves it; as Spirit loves it; as God loves it; for only through such love can we enter the inner court of the spiritual heavens; only through such love can we establish holiest spiritual communion, like conversings of white-robed angels, on the beautiful shores of the Morning Land; only through such love for truth and equal faithfulness thereto, can we ever attain to spiritual clearness of vision and perfection of eternal principles."

These inspired orations by young women and the beautiful mothers of America, indicate the dawning of better times on earth. Men, hitherto, have monopolized the pulpit and the places of learning, while women, sitting demurely and submissively in the pews, have had their "rights" presented in all sorts of shapes, and illustrated in all sorts of ways; presented in prose and jingled in verse; joked about and preached about; treated lightly and solemnly, sagaciously and nonsensically. But, behold! "The old heavens and the earth" have passed away, and the "end" of one radical error has come. Look all around you: Behold, how in the public places, the "Lords of Creation" sit with dignity and gratitude, listening to the inspired Queens of Nature!

115.

DEATH-BED OF A SPIRITUALIST.

ORANGE, N. J., *November* 12, 1867.

MANKIND have been presented, through orthodox publications, with unnumbered instances of the "Death-bed of a Christian," and with not a few examples of the tragical exit of unbelievers from the stage of life. The people have been warned by earnest and anxious church members that Spiritualism "might do to live by, but not to die by;" but, methinks, there is no more beautiful instance on record of the departure of a spirit from earth than the following touching description of this "quiet and holy passover."

THE TRANSFIGURATION.

Great sorrow has again overtaken us, resulting in

great gain to one of my mother's children. A dear sister, Mrs. D., whom you and M. met at our house some years ago, arrived with her two children from South America about three months since. She had been some months in the tropics, and came home with the fever burning in her veins. Week after week she suffered, until Christmas day, when the weary spirit went home with the waiting angels. I have seen many die, happily, calmly, with faith and hope, willing and resigned; but never before saw I such majesty and glory and strength as sustained my dear sister Carrie in her upward flight. She gave full directions for every thing with a clear, calm realization of her condition; left a message for her far-off husband still in South America; instructed her children, told them she would come to them and care for them, and spoke fully to each one present.

Then she asked us, as Spiritualists, to suggest any thing that might be instructive to her. Remembering some things you have written, I told her not to linger here when free, but go home with her spirit friends and *rest;* then to come, and we would try to be ready to receive her, striving, meanwhile, not to attract her. After conversation at length upon this subject, she asked us to sing "Summer Land;" and broken voices gave forth the sweet song, with chorus accompaniment by the guitar. The sweet little girl, so soon to be motherless, sang, like an angel, the death song. Then the pale sufferer desired to sleep. We adjusted a soft hair pillow beneath her head, put a warm blanket next her, left a window open near, and then sat down to watch: no groans, no sobbings were there; all felt that the passing spirit must be sustained, and not disturbed by our grief. A short time she slept peacefully, then a pause in the breathing, another breath—she was gone! And, now, do we find "ashes on the hearth,' and a "smell of varnish in the house?" Oh, no! We are lifted up. The angels have been with us, and they will come often. They will linger over the little home that shelters an angel's children. I can say but little in a letter, but could not omit a word to tell you how joyful is our mourning, how blessed is our grief, how glorious the light and *knowledge* of our religion in an hour like this.

116.

THE POET TASSO AND HIS SPIRIT FRIEND.

PHILADELPHIA, *November* 18, 1867.

MR. SEYMOUR KIRKUP, of Florence, Italy, in a translation for the *London Magazine*, in 1862, says: Torquato Tasso published nothing respecting his spiritual experiences, and mentioned them to but few of his friends. Among the nearest and most trustworthy of his friends, and second to none, was Giambatista Manso, so acknowledged by Tasso himself in his verses, in his letters, his dialogue, and in the Jerusalem. In a letter by Manso, when Tasso was staying with him at Bisaccio, written to a common friend, the Principe di Conca, High Admiral of the kingdom of Naples, he gives, after the usual compliments, the following account of Tasso:—

"The Signor Torquato has become a great sportsman, and braves the coldness of the season. In bad weather we pass the time in music and singing, and he is especially interested with these improvisatori, and their great facility, in which he says nature has been very sparing to him. Sometimes we dance, which delights him much, with these ladies, but more frequently we sit talking round the fire, and often have fallen on the subject of that spirit, which he says appears to him, and he has so described it to me that I know not what to say, and I doubt sometimes if his illusion (*frenesia*) will not drive me mad. I, who wished to relieve him from what I consider an infirmity, have shown him sometimes with the most severe reasoning, that these visions of his can not be real, but are most likely formed by his imagination, disturbed by vapors of melancholy, which, by causing these vain phantasms, make him see things that are not, and most likely can not be. This spirit of his is not evil, as is proved by a thousand signs, such as its discourse of things religious and devout, and persuading them, and besides naming the most holy names of Jesus and Maria, with reverence for the cross and reliques of the saints, as he himself affirms, and above all, the consolation and comfort which it leaves behind, contrary to the custom of evil spirits. I tell him, on the contrary, that it can not either be an angel, because, although he is a Christian and a virtuous man, and even, for many years past, very spiritual (*spirituale*), nevertheless, these favors of apparitions of angels are not conceded to men of common goodness, but to the perfect and holy (*santi*) only, so that it would be presumption to believe that this, his spirit, were an angel, as it would, on the other hand, be an injustice (*ingiuria*) to consider it was a demon. Wherefore, there not existing any other sort of spirit but angels and demons, and this being neither, it follows that this which appears to him is no real spirit, but rather a deception of the fancy (*fantastica virtù*) represented to him as apparent (*verisimile*), as has happened to many others, and especially to those who are afflicted with fixed ideas (*mirarchia*, a word not in the Crusca) as he has been. To which he replied that such was not the fact (*non vero*), was clearly proved from the length of time that he has seen these apparitions, and from the conformity which he has observed in them, which could not continue if the things he saw were not in themselves real, but only figured by weak imaginations of his fancy. Nor could its reasonings be consistent with each other; as in fantastic visions the powers of the soul do not operate through the intellect, and, consequently, can not have between themselves any consistency (*correspondenza*) or order, as is seen to happen in the apparitions of fixed thinkers (*miriarchiaci*), and in the dreams of fever patients, and the thoughts of drunken men. Likewise he says, that if the things heard and seen by him were fantastic appearances created by his own imagination, they could not be such as to surpass his own knowledge, because the imagination is caused by the returning (*rivolgimento*) of the same fancies (*fantasmi*), and of the kind of things already learned, which are retained in the memory, but that in the long and continual reasonings held with that spirit, he has heard things that he had never before heard, nor read, nor known, and that other men had never known; from which he concludes that these visions of his can not be foolish imaginations of the fancy, but rather true and real apparitions of some spirit, who, whatever be the cause, allows himself to be visibly seen by him. Which things, contradicted and disputed by me, led us one day to such a point that he said to me, 'Since I can not persuade you by reasoning, I will undeceive you by experience, and cause you to see with your own eyes that spirit to whom you will not lend your belief from my words.'

"I accepted the offer, and the following day being together without other company, sitting near the fire, he, turning his eyes towards a window, and keeping them so fixed for a good space of time, so that on my recalling him he answered nothing, at last said, 'Here, behold, is my spirit-friend who has courteously come to converse with me; behold him (*miratelo*) and you will see the truth of my words.' I turned my eyes in that direction immediately, but, however much I strained them, nothing could I see but the rays of the sun, which entered the room through the glasses of the window. And whilst I turned my eyes around discovering nothing, I heard Torquato engaged in the most sublime reasonings, with whomsoever it was, so that although I neither saw nor heard any other but himself, nevertheless his words, sometimes questioning (*proponendo*) and sometimes answering, were such as occur between persons in close reasoning on some important subject; and from what he spoke my intellect easily comprehended what was said to him in reply, although I did not hear it with my ears; and these reasonings were so grand and wonderful for the sublimity they contained, and for a peculiar mode not used in conversation, that I remained under a strange stupor raised within me, and did not dare to interrupt them, nor to ask Torquato any questions respecting the spirit whom he had pointed out to me, and whom I did not see. In this manner we remained for a good length of time, I listening half stupefied and enchanted (*vaghito*), almost without perceiving it; and at the end of which the spirit departing, as I understood from Torquato's words, he, turning to me, said, 'All the doubts will now be removed from your mind.' And I said to him, 'On the contrary, they are increased, for many things I have heard worthy of admiration, but nothing have I seen of what you promised, to make me end my doubts by satisfying my eyes.' Smiling, he answered, 'Much more have you seen and heard than perhaps—' . . . . and here he stopped (perhaps he would have added, Than, perhaps, you will confess); and I, not wishing to importune him with more questions, we here ended this conversation, from which, as yet, I can comprehend nothing more than that which I said at the beginning, namely, that those visions of his or deliriums (*frenesia*) will make me go out of my mind (*da cirvello*) before I can remove from him his opinion either true or imaginary."

The foregoing letter was published in the lifetime of Manso, and of many other witnesses of Tasso's adventures. It is to be found in the 33d vol. of the Opera, Pisa, 1832, in 8vo, p. 172.

117.

BIBLE BELIEVERS ENACTING SCENES OF INDECENCY AND INSANITY.

ORANGE, N. J., *January* 25, 1868.

THE entire religious press of the country has charged to the account of the millions of American Spiritualists the insane and nude performances of some three or four persons, residing in Newark, who claim to believe in mediumship and in the influence of spirits. Justice is slow, but sure. In yesterday's *Tribune* it is recorded that the grossly indecent scene in Mr. Ewen's house, in Newark, on New Year's night, was enacted under somewhat similar circumstances fifteen years ago, in a village near Zurich, Switzerland. An abandoned woman named Reinecke, living in Diesikon, a hamlet near Zurich, connected herself with a sect which had sprung up in the district, professing principles similar to those of the Latter-Day Saints. Some men became attached to this woman, and lived with her in open profligate intercourse. Reinecke becoming pregnant, gave out to these men that she would bring forth a son, who should be the Christ, and called upon them to make this known among the sect to which they belonged. They accordingly declared in the assembly of the Saints that the Old Testament prophecies had not been fulfilled, and that the Virgin who was to bear a Son was the woman Reinecke. Reinecke's child, however, proved to be a girl. Having hidden the infant, Reinecke proclaimed herself the Christ incarnate.

At the woman's request some of the men, who had connected themselves with Reinecke's followers, assembled one evening in her room, bringing large crops of wooden planks, to which they nailed her hands and feet, the woman promising, meantime, that she would remain three days and nights crucified, suffering neither death nor pain; and that on the third night, if they would assemble in the room, she would descend to them from the cross, of her own free will. These madmen complied with Reinecke's directions, and returning on the third evening found her dead on the cross. Some of the men fled from the country, two were incarcerated for life, and one was guillotined. The child who was to have been the man Christ, is a poor servant in a hamlet near Wallisellen.

They have a scandal nearly of similar character in Somersetshire, England. A clergyman named Prince had a parish between Bridgewater and Taunton. He was a scholar and good preacher, as far as delivery and composition go. He sometimes inculcated strange dogmas, and his doctrinal enunciations from the pulpit became more *bizarre* on each succeeding Sunday, until at last the Rev. Mr. Prince announced to his surprised hearers that the Saviour of the world was embodied in his reverend person; that he was the Prince for them; and that those who would believe in him should surely go to heaven. A certain Miss L., an accomplished and beautiful young woman, who had attended this blasphemous divine's ministrations, was the first convert to the new religion. Miss S. soon found a co-religionist in a rich married woman. With the wealth which these infatuated women placed in Prince's hands, this pretender built a large house, with a chapel in the center, and a conservatory, in extensive grounds—naming his paradise the Agapemone, or abode of Love. Into this abode Prince and his converts retired. The conditions of entrance to the Agapemone, and of securing salvation were, that the candidate should be well supplied with the one thing needful to Prince, money, and if they were married men, having their wives, that they should agree to the rules of the house, *i. e.*, to have all things in common. For years the Agapemone flourished, quite a numerous body of Princeites having taken up their residence in this abode of immorality. Married women quit their husbands to follow Prince, and gave him their property, and a few disreputable clergymen and men of property also joined his society. Prince began his establishment in style. The house was furnished luxuriously, and the richest exotics were in the conservatory. He drove in an elegant equipage, with four horses and outriders, two men running by the carriage with spears, and when he left the Agapemone his converts and domestics bowed before him. The Agapemone is now comparatively deserted; the four-in-hand has been replaced by a one-horse brougham; money is scarcer, and women become converted less frequently. Last November a woman who had quit her husband to become a Princeite, was claimed by her husband at the Agapemone. Mr. M. found the iron doors closed, and admittance was denied him. He went to Bridgewater and asked assistance. An indignant populace accompanied him to the Agapemone and assailed the doors with crow-bars, forcing an entrance. Mrs. M. was not found, Prince having gone with his convert on a trip to the South. Mr. M. ascertained his wife's whereabouts about a month after her conversion, at which time her belief in Prince was not to be shaken, and she refused to return to her husband from Prince's Paradise.

118.

AN EPISCOPALIAN CHURCH TRIAL IN NEW YORK.

ORANGE, N. J., *February* 12, 1868.

I HAVE just returned from the great city. . . . New York streets are covered with mud, and I fear the effect thereof is felt by certain great men in the lucrative calling of teaching the Episcopalian *forms* of the "meek and lowly." A young minister, Mr. Tyng, is being put through. The place chosen for the extraordinary trial is graced by the presence of many respectable citizens. It should be known in these parts by the name of "Vatican"—a dingy Vestry Hall beneath the grandiloquent meeting-house of York—wreathed with pictures by the worst masters, on the time-honored and holy art of religious persecution. The princely Pilate of old, with his query, "What is truth?" would grow large with satisfaction within these suspicious and proscriptive courts. Coroners' verdicts, records of ecclesiastical sessions, and frightful indications of every evil deed, seem to fill with poison the atmosphere in the neighborhood of this hall. There is here, too, somewhat of those

> "——Thick and gloomy shadows damp,
> Oft seen in charnel vaults and sepulchers,
> Lingering and sitting by a new-made grave."

Very grand, however, is the upholstered, castle-like sanctuary overhead; from which heavenward soar millions of literary prayers every year in seventh-day installments—*never in violation of the rules of the Prayer-book!* This sacred place (historically speaking) will swim in golden seas of evangelical glory. Visions of eternal conservatism will fall dream-like upon the thronging multitudes who worship there. . . . Every Sunday the great organ peals its thundering tones along the lofty ceiling, and the dim magical darkness shed by the holy lights conspire to fill with enthusiasm the devotee's imagination. Beneath all this grandeur and bewildering beauty history will see a black-painted subterranean "Chamber of Justice," in the presence of one-sided judges and prejudiced ministers. . . . I believe this extraordinary performance is dignified with the appellation of "a church trial." It is worse than a mixed compound of law, physic, and divinity; the stuff generally taken in desperate cases, when all milder medicines fail and "doctors disagree." I, however, should christen this proceeding "an ecclesiastical-civil suit," wholly unsuitable and abominably illegal; and I think Mr. Tyng will come out

NOTE.—In 1859, at the house of Dr. Bartlett, in Aurora, Ill., the author wrote, under the *nom de plume* of "Philo Hermes," a satire in point, entitled, "An Extraordinary Church Trial."

stronger and better. . . . They proceed in due form to set forth, and to call upon him to answer and to refute the grievous sin against their holy religion, and the monstrous infractions and pernicious contempt of the customs and moral well-being of the Episcopal Church! Mr. Tyng! Sir: It is charged that you have officiated at unevangelical places of worship; also declined to ask leave of ministers of the church whether you might perform such Sabbath services: instead whereof, you have taken and do still take every occasion to act independently of the ministry, and to teach our doctrines wrongfully in the Methodist Church!

Mr. Parker, according to the reporter, opened for the respondent: Is he charged with any offense against the laws of God? Is he charged with doing aught to injure the ministers who complain against him? The charge is, that, being a minister of the Gospel, he preached the Gospel; that, being a minister of the Church, he preached the Church; that he carried it, with its Liturgy, to those who, but for him, had it not, or, at least, had it not in the perfection in which he placed it before them. And although he was compelled by the necessities of the occasion not to ask responses from those who had no books with which to make them, and even to omit the Litany, which he would have loved to use before that or any other congregation that might assemble; although compelled to make these omissions from want of the aids to those devotions which the presence of the Book of Common Prayer among our own congregations gives, yet he did not violate the canon to which the learned gentleman who has just closed (Mr. Logan), alluded. He obeyed it—he used the Book of Common Prayer. Take the language of the canon, and analyze it as you will—he performed every thing that was incumbent upon him. Ay, it is for preaching the Gospel, and for carrying the Church with him and preaching it, that he stands now before this court and the country an accused instead of an applauded man. [Applause.] And all the harm that he has done, all the offense he has committed, is that he did not preach the Gospel and the Church with the *consent* of the Rev. Dr. Stubbs, or of the Rev. Dr. Boggs [laughter]—gentlemen, who know that when I mention their names I do it with no disrespect. They are my friends. I can truly say that I love them personally; but I can likewise say that I think that they have here committed a grand ecclesiastical blunder. I can say that to them as churchmen and as men of the Gospel: Had they, instead of taking this course, aided Mr. Tyng in carrying their Church to that congregation of Methodists—ay, aided him, even if they thought that he might be able to do it every Sunday of his life, what would have been the result? But the charge comes back, "You did this; you preached God's Word without first obtaining the consent of Stubbs and Boggs, and thereupon you are an ecclesiastical felon." The first, last, perpetual duty of a minister is to preach the Gospel. When the Church was established it was not for the simple preservation of a conventional politeness between individuals; and if the respondent had courteously applied to the reverend ministry of New Brunswick for permission to preach there, and had been refused, it would still have been his duty to go there and preach. The Saviour did not stand on ceremony when he went to the Synagogue. The counsel denied that respondent had violated the canon; held the offense, if it may be so called, has been committed scores of times; and that never before in seventy-five years has a court been called on to try a similar case. There are thousands of cases in which a minister is called upon to officiate where it would be impossible, or even wicked, for him to wait for the permission of the minister of the parish. Should one of this reverend court be invited by either of the others to officiate for him next Sunday, could he do it without the express permission of a majority? In New Brunswick, Drs. Stubbs and Boggs are the only ministers of this Church. One of them wishes one of this court to preach for him. Can he lawfully do it unless the other likewise consent? One of you has a brother, perhaps, residing in New Brunswick. He falls sick, and desires your services. You long to give them; must you not first run to the house of Messrs. Stubbs and Boggs to get their express permission? [Laughter.] I do not wonder at the laugh, and I am pleased that the chairman agrees with me. When a literal interpretation is given to this canon, *it is sheer nonsense.* [Renewed laughter.] Or perhaps you have a sister there who belongs to the Methodist denomination, and who is about to be married; she desires you to join her in holy matrimony. Must you first get the express permission of Stubbs and Boggs? . . . . . Verily, the "Church" is an institution of the Past—full of Stubbs, Boggs, and obstructions. Amen.

119.

QUESTIONS FOR SUNDAY-SCHOOL ANNIVERSARIES.

ORANGE, N. J., *February* 13, 1868.

THE trial (Episcopalian) now proceeding in New York, brings to mind some very curious way-side notes recorded in 1859:—Rev. Jerusalem Stubbs was next called by the prosecution. He was much fleshy and much excited. Being sworn and interrogated, he said: "Am a minister of the High Church of England; a link in the unbroken chain of calendar Saints; a member of the Divine Order of the Holy Ghost; a believer in the Church's power to work miracles, such as the forgiveness of sins [never committed], the feeding of thousands with five loaves of bread [providing of course the loaves are large enough to go round], and lastly, that the Church can support the finest livery, and may boast of the most accomplished class of purely genteel saints. Am acquainted with philology; can read Hebrew, Greek, Latin, and French." [Of course he expects a bishopric.]

In order to establish the reputation of the worthy Dr. Stubbs, and to add weight to his testimony, the attorney asked him to give some illustrations and references, biblical or otherwise, showing his knowledge to be accurate, classical, and extensive. This permission or question fired the reverend gentleman's breast with new zeal, and he responded: "Perhaps, sir, you have not seen my list of questions, prepared with great diligence and learning, for a Sunday-School Anniversary?" The court signified that it had *not* had that great profit and pleasure. "Then," resumed the witness, "see the Boston Liberator for February 1, 1856, wherein Mr. J. Cushing, of South Hingham, Mass., had the justice to report my scriptural labors as follows:—

If any one doubts that the Church is engaged in a *great* work, let him read the following list of questions, prepared and published for the anniversary meeting of the Sunday-School in a neighboring town:—

1. What was the name of the giant who had twenty-four fingers and toes? 20th Chron.

2. What person had a nail driven through his head? 4th Judges.

3. Who wore a garment that had no seam? 19th John.

4. What distinguished man's sons had bonnets made for them? 28th Exodus.

5. There is only one woman whose age is mentioned in the Bible; what was her name? 23d Genesis.

6. How many pitchers were broken by an army of men? What was in them? 7th Judges.

7. Where in the Bible is there an account of a temperance society? Who belonged to it? 35th Jeremiah.

8. How many persons lapped water with their tongues, like the dogs? 7th Judges.

9. Who plowed with twelve yoke of oxen? 1 Kings, chap. 19th.

10. Who was it had thirty sons and thirty daughters? 12th Judges."

By the distinguished counsel it was held that the foregoing questions must forever put at rest the insinuation that the Episcopal Sunday-School is not doing a mighty work for the redemption of the world. The man who plowed with twelve yoke of oxen, our children should keep in everlasting remembrance; and a family of thirty sons and thirty daughters in our day should excite physiological interest, if nothing more. And then, too, the name of the giant who had twenty-four fingers and toes: how momentous such ancient knowledge!

In order to induce a laudable degree of religious inquiry in Methodist Sabbath-Schools, I will suggest a few questions, perhaps equally important, which may serve them for an anniversary occasion like the one just alluded to:—

1. How old was the Shunamite damsel who ministered to King David's necessities?

2. How much oil did Zadok the priest use in anointing Solomon, after he rode his father's mule down to Gihon?

3. What was the expense of Elijah's board per day, when fed by the ravens at the brook Cherith?

4. What was the name of the man who drew a bow at a venture, and smote the King of Israel between the joints of the harness?

5. . . . . . But, why multiply questions for children in orthodox Sunday-Schools. The Bible and the Catechism are replete with suggestions. . . . .

A little moral may be drawn from the following story,

which may be useful to Sabbath-School superintendents and teachers :—

A boy of more natural brightness than some who are better educated, was asked, "Where do you go to Sunday School, Jimmy?"

"Why, marm, I go to Baptisses, and Methodisses, and the Presbyteriums, but I've been trying the 'Piscopals for two or three weeks."

"You don't seem to belong anywhere, then, Jimmy."

"Why, yes, marm, don't you see, I belongs to 'em exceptin' the 'Piscopals, but I'm going to jine them, too, now."

"Well, Jimmy, wha t's your idea in going to so many?"

"Why, you see, I gits a little of what's going on at 'em all, marm. I gits liberies, and hymn-books, and all that; and when they have picnics, I goes to every one of 'em."

120.

THE SPIRIT OF INVESTIGATION.

ORANGE, N. J., *February* 14, 1868.

THIS morning's mail brings to me a city magazine of some influence, containing quotations from an old assault on Spiritualism, some years ago, published in *Blackwood.* To that very calumnious article I would apply the concluding paragraphs of a rejoinder by the truth-loving William Howitt. In his reply, Mr. Howitt first details *positive facts*, which convinced him that the sprits do cause the real manifestations, and then proceeds :—

These, sir, I think, will be admitted, "according to strict scientific method," to be a complete refutation of the statements of Blackwood & Co.; and in conclusion I will beg to remind these gentlemen of the press, that the very same things which they now assert of Spiritualism were said of Christianity, for above one hundred years after its appearance; ay, far worse things. The Christians were held by the Greek and Latin *illustrissimi*, not only as the grossest impostors, but as the most vile and degraded of men. The practices attributed to them were too revolting for modern language. Christianity was the *superstitio prava* of Pliny the Younger; the *exitiabilis superstitio* of Tacitus; the Christians were the "*homines per flagitiis invisos*" of that historian. Every classical reader can lay his hand on these statements.

These are the calumnies which truth has, in every age, to endure. Take the very highest philosophical authority of Greece—Plato. He makes Socrates, in Eutyphron, say: "And we, too, when I say any thing in the public assembly concerning divine things, and predict to them what is going to happen, they ridicule me as mad; and although nothing that I ever have predicted has not turned out to be true, yet they envy all such men as we are. However, we ought not to heed them, but pursue our own course."

How precisely identical are the truth, and the enemies of the truth, in every age of the world! Sir, I am a man who all my life have hated humbug, and have, at whatever cost, dared to expose it without hiding my head under the anonymous. In my early years I had my blow at priestcraft. I am not one of those who think it wise to jeer at what I do not take the trouble to examine. Some years ago I heard some very wonderful things of gold-finding in Australia. I determined to go and examine how far these fine stories were true. I did not think the way to come at the truth was to shy an article at it from a journal without going near it. I got a real spade, and dug in real earth, and I and my sons found one of the finest gold-fields in Victoria—Nine Mile Creek—in consequence of which my son is at this moment heading a government expedition of discovery in that colony. I got as much gold with my own hands as would have knocked any man down who should have said it was imaginary. Well, I am just as sure of the facts of Spiritualism as I am of those of gold-finding. If I were to go to Lord Campbell and tell him that I knew more about the business of the Court of Chancery than he did, he would laugh at me; and if Lord Campbell came to me and said he knew more about the phenomena of Spiritualism than I do, after years of examination, I should laugh at him; and we should both laugh on the same good grounds at the other talking of things that he had not thoroughly sifted to a man who had.

I have sifted these things for five years. I have witnessed nearly all the varieties of extraordinary things seen in this country, and often in private houses of the highest character where no professional medium was present. The facts of Spiritualism are, therefore, to me, common-places, and as positive as a stone wall. Let the opponents, instead of blustering and talking the sheerest nonsense, sift these things for five years, and then they may cavil if they please. The writer in *Blackwood* thinks Spiritualism the "disgrace of the age;" I, on the contrary, think the disgrace of the age is the want of faith in people's own senses, and the want of courage to make use of them.

Of the higher and more sacred teachings of Spiritualism, and its numerous phases—for this movement of tables is but one, and one of the least—I could say much, but I confine myself here to the refutation of a most transparent calumny.

121.

PRE-EXISTENCE, OR REINCARNATION.

ORANGE, N. J., *February* 16, 1868.

Two hours of this beautiful, crispy, winter morning have been given to conversation with visitors concerning the doctrine of learned French Spiritualists who strenuously inculcate the "eternal *past* individuality of every human being." During the conversation, many historical references were made by way of "great names" and inferential testimony, to substantiate the theory. It was shown that Mede, in chap. III. of his *Mystery of Godliness*, combats the vulgar opinion of a "daily creation of souls" at the time the bodies are produced which they are to inform. He calls "the reasonable doctrine" of pre-existence "a key for some of the main mysteries of Providence, which no other can so handsomely unlock." Sir Harry Vane is said by Burnet to have maintained this doctrine. Joseph Glanvil, Rector of Bath (the friend of Meric Casaubon and of Baxter, and a metaphysician of singular vigor and acuteness), published in 1662, but without his name, a treatise to prove the reasonableness of the doctrine. It was afterward republished, with annotations, by Dr. Henry More.

In 1762, the Rev. Capel Berrow published "A Pre-existent Lapse of Human Souls Demonstrated;" and in the *European Magazine* for September, 1801, is a letter from Bishop Warburton to the author, in which he says: "The idea of a pre-existence has been espoused by many learned and ingenious men in every age, as bidding fair to resolve many difficulties."

Southey, in his published Letters, says: "I have a strong and lively faith in a state of continued consciousness from this stage of existence, and that we shall recover the consciousness of some lower stages through which we may previously have passed seems to me not improbable." Again: "The system of progressive existence seems, of all others, the most benevolent; and all that we do understand is so wise and so good, and all we do or do not, so perfectly and overwhelmingly wonderful, that the most benevolent system is the most probable." Every one is familiar with the traces of belief in this doctrine in Wordsworth's "Ode on the Intimation of Immortality in Childhood," in the lines beginning "Our birth is but a sleep and a forgetting."

In *Chambers's Edinburgh Journal*, No. 93, New Series, this "Sentiment of Pre-existence" is stated to have been first described by Sir Walter Scott; this may be correct as to the *expression*. Scott, it will be remembered, was highly *susceptible* upon psychological matters.* The description is thrown into the mouth of Henry Bertram on his return to Ellangowan Castle: "How often," he says, "do we find ourselves in society which we have never before met, and yet feel impressed with a mysterious and ill-defined consciousness that neither the scene, the speakers, nor the subject are entirely new; nay, feel as if we could anticipate that part of the conversation which has not yet taken place!" . . . . . . We find the following entry in Scott's diary, under the date February 17, 1828:—

"I can not, I am sure, tell if it is worth marking down, that yesterday, at dinner-time, I was strongly haunted by what I would call the sense of pre-existence, in a confirmed idea that nothing which passed was said for the first time; that the same topics had been discussed, and the same persons had stated the same opinions on them . . . The sensation was so strong as to resemble what is called *mirage* in the desert, or a calenture on board a ship . . . It was very distressing yesterday, and brought to my mind the fancies of Bishop Berkeley about an ideal world. There was a vile sense of want of reality in all I did and said.—*Lockhart's Life of Scott.*"

Sir Bulwer Lytton, in his *Godolphin*, thus notices this day-dream:—

"How strange it is that at times a feeling comes over us, as we gaze upon certain places, which associates the scene either with some disremembered and dream-like images of the Past, or with a prophetic and fearful omen of the future! . . . Every one

* In this volume all theorizing, and all mere speculations on disputed points of philosophy, are deemed out of place. Therefore, for the author's impressions on this subject, the reader is referred to his different works, more especially to the "Thinker," Gt. Har. vol. v. Part III, on the "Lawof Immortality.

has known a similar strange, indistinct feeling, at certain times and places, and with a similar inability to trace the cause."

Elsewhere the same writer describes the same feeling of reminiscence as "that strange kind of inner and spiritual memory which often recalls to us places and persons we have never seen before, and which Platonists would resolve to be the unquenched and struggling consciousness of a former life." In fewer words, the feeling may be described as seeing and hearing, apparently for the first time, what we have seen or heard before, though our reason assures us of the contrary. Can any thing be more expressive of the *sameness* of human existence?

In one place Tennyson touches upon a like experience, thus:

"Moreover something is, or seems,
That teaches me with mystic gleams,
Like glimpses of forgotten dreams—
Of something felt, like something here;
Of something done, I know not where;
Such as no language may declare."

Mr. Dickens, an extremely imaginative and tragedy-loving writer, in his *Pictures from Italy*, mentions this instance on his first sight of Ferrara:

"On the foreground was a group of silent peasant girls, leaning over the parapet of a little bridge, looking now up at the sky, now down into the water; in the distance a deep bell; the shadow of approaching night on every thing. If I had been *murdered* there on some former life I could not have seemed to remember the place more thoroughly, or with more emphatic chilling of the blood; and the real remembrance of it acquired in that minute is so strengthened by the imaginary recollection, that I hardly think I could forget it."

It should be remembered that Memory is something more than a mental faculty of registration. The mind is a compound of *eternal* principles, each of which, being from God and of God, is self-intelligent, from which intelligence memory is inseparable. The most profoundly spiritual intellect is blest with the most profound memories (intuitions), and thus the past is, in certain moments, imaged to the consciousness like the feelings and scenes of the present. . . . . . . It seems to me, whenever I hear or read any thing from the pre-existence philosophers, that they would obtain a more rational explanation of their "evidences" by investigating the three forms of mediumship, entitled the "Clairlative," the "Symbolic," and the "Pictorial," hints of which are given in "Present Age and Inner Life," pp. 152, 155, 175.

122.

A STELLAR KEY TO THE SUMMER LAND.

ORANGE, N. J., *February* 18, 1868.

THE Key, Part First, has been in the world about six weeks. . . . . . It was written during the time that I was engaged upon "Arabula;" alternately, an hour at one and an hour at the other; and both were composed while I, with Magic Staff, was slowly ascending the Sixth Mountain. . . . . . Years have elapsed since I began the ascent of Mount Harmony, and although I have for a brief period reached its summit, I find myself, as yet, unable to make it an abiding place. . . . . Still, now and then, I am lifted to "perceptions and feelings far beyond the limits of thought." . . . . . Yet I know, notwithstanding these rare communions and exalted contemplations, that I can not write the *Second Part* of "Stellar Key" until I am spiritually able to remain on the mountain, undisturbed, for at least four weeks. . . . . Yes, there is yet work to be accomplished. . . . Rise, O my soul—rise, to thy Labor!

INTRODUCTION TO HORTENSIA.

I AM impressed to introduce to the reader the translation of Heinrich Zschokke's remarkable story of *Hortensia*, or *the Transfigurations*, which forms in part the Appendix to this volume.

The writer, under the inspiration of truth, and with great beauty of language, portrayed the exalted condition of a person deeply entranced, and the strange contrast between that and the ordinary state. "He builded better than he knew" by showing that, by the beautiful balance of human powers termed "health," the common state might be lifted into the superior condition, and the two be permanently blended.

The picture of Hortensia's gradual growth, from disease and discord into sweet and noble womanhood, clearly illustrates the truth, too often entirely overlooked, that much, *very* much, of the troublous "evil" or "imperfection" in human nature is traceable, not to "innate depravity" or external "demoniac agencies," but simply to a lack of harmonious and perfect balance between the physical and spiritual parts, which condition only is worthy of being denominated "Health of Body and Mind." The gradual cure for this lack, is progression. May this lesson, so essential to universal charity and good will, be deeply impressed on every heart.

APPENDIX.

HORTENSIA;

OR, THE

TRANSFIGURATIONS.

THE charm, elegance, and retirement of the villa, the hospitality of our rich host, Ambrosio Faustino, and the grace of his most lovely wife, contributed not a little to the healing of our wounds, received in the battle of Molito (we were four German officers), but still more the pleasing discovery, that both the generous Faustino and his beautiful wife were of German descent. He was formerly called Faust, and was, by a singular chain of circumstances, induced to settle in Italy and to change his name. The delight of being able, far from our native land, to exchange German words, made us mutually confidential.

I had the liberty of passing my morning hours in Faustino's library. There I found, in magnificent rows, the choicest works, and also some volumes of Italian manuscripts, written by Faustino. They were memoirs of his own life, mingled with observations on painting and sculpture. I asked the favor of being permitted to read them, which Faustino was not only good enough to grant, but also drew out one of the volumes, and pointed out what I should read.

"Read it," said he, "and believe me, however incredible it may appear, it is true. Even to myself, it seems at times a deception of the imagination, though I have experienced it all."

He also imparted to me many smaller circumstances. But this is sufficient for an introduction. Here follows the fragment from Faustino's, or rather Faust's memoirs.

ADVENTURES IN VENZONI.

On the twelfth of September, 1771, I crossed the stream of Tagliamento, at Spilemberg. I approached with firm steps the German confines, which I had not seen for many years. My soul was full of an indescribable melancholy, and it seemed as if an invisible power drew me back. It constantly cried to me to return. In fact, twice did I stop on the wretched road, looked toward Italy, and wished to return again to Venice. But then, when I asked myself, "What argues it? to live! for what?" I again proceeded onward, toward the dark mountains, which rose before me in clouds and rain.

I had but little money in my pocket, scarcely sufficient to reach Vienna, unless I begged on the way, or should sell either my watch, linen, or better clothes, which I carried in a knapsack. The finest years of my youth I had passed in Italy, in order to improve myself in painting and sculpture. At last I advanced sufficiently in my art to discover, in my twenty-seventh year, that I should never accomplish any thing really great. It is true, my Roman friends had often had the kindness to encourage me. Many of my pieces had occasionally sold well. Nevertheless this gave me but little comfort. I could not but despise creations which gave me no satisfaction. I experienced the painful feeling that I was and should remain too weak to call into life, with pencil or chisel, the living conceptions within me. This threw me into despair—I wished not for money—I longed only for the power of art; I cursed my lost years, and returned to Germany. At that time I still had friends there: I longed for a solitude, where I could forget myself. I would become a village schoolmaster, or engage in any humble employment, in order to punish my bold ambition, which had attempted to rival Raphael and Angelo.

The rainy weather had already continued several days, and increased my uncomfortable feelings. The thought frequently awoke in me, if I *could* but die! A fresh shower drew me aside from the road, under a tree. There I long sat upon a rock, looking back with deep melancholy upon the destroyed plans and hopes of my life. I saw myself solitary, amid wild mountains. The cold rain fell in streams. Not far from me a swollen torrent roared through the rocks. "What will become of me?" sighed I. I looked at the torrent to see whether it were deep enough to drown me if I threw myself in. I was vexed that I had not already made an end of my sufferings at Tagliamento. Suddenly an unspeakable anguish, and the pangs of death, seized me. I sprang up and ran on in the rain, as if I would escape from myself. It was already evening, and becoming late.

I came to a single large house not far from Venzoni. The increasing darkness, continued rain, and my own fatigue, induced me to stop at this building, which exhibited the friendly and inviting sign of accommodation for travelers. As I passed the threshold of the door, a violent shuddering and the same mortal agony seized me that I had experienced while sitting on the rock in the wood. I remained at the door to take breath, but quickly recovered myself. I felt lighter than I had for some days, when in the warm public room I again felt the breath of man. Without doubt it had been merely an attack of bodily weakness.

They welcomed me, and I cheerfully threw my knapsack on the table. I was shown a small room where I could change my wet clothes. While undressing, I heard a quick step on the stairs; the room door opened, and some hasty questions were asked about me, such as whether I should remain over night—if I came on foot and carried a knapsack—if I had light hair; and many more of a like nature. The interrogators went away—came again, and another voice asked similar questions. I knew not what it meant.

When I returned to the public room all eyes examined me with curiosity. I seated myself as if I remarked nothing. Yet I was tormented to discover wherefore any one had made such particular inquiries about me. I led the discourse to the weather—from the weather to traveling, and from thence to the inquiry, if any more strangers were in the house. I was informed that there was a noble family from Germany, consisting of an old gentleman and a very beautiful and sick young lady, an elderly lady, probably the mother of the young one, a physician, two servants, and two maids. The party arrived at mid-day, and had been detained, partly by the badness of the weather, and partly by the weakness of the young lady. I learned, besides, that both the physician and the old gentleman had come into the public room, in great haste, and had inquired with some anxiety and astonishment about me. The host was certain that the party knew me well. He urged me to go up, as I should certainly meet old friends and acquaintances, since they appeared to expect me. I shook my head, convinced that there was some mistake. In the whole world I had no noble acquaintances, and least of all could I claim any of the German nobility. What confirmed me still more in this belief was, that an old servant of the count came in, seated himself at the table near me, and in broken Italian called for wine. When I addressed him in German, he was delighted to hear his native tongue. He now related to me all that he knew of his master. The gentleman was a Count Hormegg, who was carrying his daughter to Italy for change of air.

The more the old man drank, the more talkative he became. At first, he seated himself gloomily by me; at the second flask he breathed more freely. As I said to him, that I thought of going back to Germany, he sighed deeply, looked toward heaven, and his eyes filled with tears. "Could I only go with you! could I only go!" said he, sorrowfully and softly to me. "I can bear it no longer. I believe a curse rests on this family. Strange things occur among them. I dare confide them to no one, and if I dare, sir, who would believe me?"

THE MELANCHOLY COMPANY OF TRAVELERS.

By the third flask of wine, Sebald, for so he was called, became open-hearted. "Countryman," said he, and he looked timidly round the room; but no one was present except ourselves; we were sitting alone by the dim burning candles. "Countryman, they can not blind me. Here is a curse under the veil and abundance of riches—here rules the bad spirit himself; God be merciful unto us! The count is immensely rich, but he creeps about like a poor sinner; he is seldom heard to speak, and is never gay. The old lady, companion, governor, or something of that kind to the Countess Hortensia, appears to be in constant fear from a bad conscience. The countess herself—truly a child of paradise—can scarcely be more beautiful; but I believe her father has united her with the devil. Jesu Maria! what was that?"

The frightened Sebald started from his seat and became deadly pale. It was nothing but a window shutter dashed violently to by the wind and rain. After I had tranquilized my companion, he continued:—

"It is no wonder; one must live in constant fear of death. One of us must and will shortly die! That I have heard from the young woman, Catharine. God be merciful to me! May I not, in the mean time, with my comrade, Thomas, refresh myself with wine? Sir, there is no want of what we desire, to eat or drink, nor of money; we fail only in a happy mind. I should long since have run off——"

Sebald's fable appeared to me to be full of his wine.

"From what do you infer that one of you must die?"

"There is nothing to infer," replied Sebald; "it is only too certain. The Countess Hortensia has said it, but no one dares speak of it. Look you—at Judenberg, fourteen days ago, we had the same story. The young countess announced the death of one of us. Being all in good health, we did not believe it. But as we were proceeding on the highway, Mr. Muller, the secretary of the count, a man generally beloved, suddenly fell, together with his horse and baggage, from the height of the road, over the rocks, into the abyss beneath, ten times deeper than the church steeple. Jesu Maria! what a spectacle! Hearing and sight left me. Man and horse lay shattered to pieces. When you pass through the village where he lies buried, the people will relate it to you. I dare not think of it. The only question now is, which of us is to be the next victim? But if it comes to pass, by my poor soul, I will demand my discharge from the count. There is something wrong here; I love my old neck, and do not wish to break it in the service of the God-forsaken."

I smiled at his superstitious distress, but he swore stoutly, and whispered: "The Countess Hortensia is possessed by a legion of devils. For a year she had frequently run over the roof of the castle Hormeggar, as we scarcely could do on level ground. She prophesies; she often, unexpectedly, falls into a trance, and sees the heavens open; she looks into the interior of the human body. Dr. Walter, who is certainly an honest man, affirms that she can not only see through people, as if they were glass, but also through doors and walls. It is horrible. In her rational hours, she is very sensible. But, O God! it is in her irrational hours that she governs us, when those evil spirits speak out of her. Could we not have remained upon the high road? But no! Immediately upon leaving Villach, we must go on sumpter horses and mules over the worst roads and most frightful precipices. And wherefore? Because she so willed it. Had we remained on the great road, Mr. Muller (God be merciful to him!) would still, to-day, have drunk his glass of wine."

ATTEMPT AT AN ENGAGEMENT.

The return of the people of the house, with my spare evening's meal, interrupted Sebald's gossip. He promised when we were again alone to disclose many more secrets. He left me. In his place, a small, thin, gloomy-looking man seated himself, whom Sebald, on going away, called doctor. I knew, therefore, that I had before me, another member of the melancholy travelers. The doctor looked at me, at my supper, for awhile silently. He appeared to be watching me. He then began to ask me, in French, from whence I came, and where I thought of going? When he heard I was a German, he became more friendly, and conversed with me in our native tongue. In answer to my questions, I learned that Count Hormegg was traveling with his sick naughter to Venice.

"Could you not," said the doctor, "give us your company, since you have no particular object in going to Germany? You are more familiar with the Italian language than we are—know the country, the manners, and healthy parts. You could be of great service to us. The count could take you immediately in place of his secretary. You will be free of expense, have a comfortable life, six hundred louis-d'ors salary, and to that added the known liberality of the count."

I shook my head, and remarked, that neither did I know the count, nor the count me, sufficiently to foresee whether we should be agreeable to each other. The doctor now made the count's eulogium. I replied in return, that it would be very difficult to say so much to my advantage to the count.

"Oh, if that is all," cried he hastily, "you are already recommended; you may, therefore, rely on it."

"Recommended! By whom?"

The doctor appeared to be seeking for words, in order to rectify his hastiness.

"Eh, why through necessity—I can promise you, that the count will pay you a hundred louis-d'ors down, if you——"

"No," replied I, "I have never in my life labored for superfluities; only for what is necessary. From childhood I have been accustomed to an independent life. I am far from being rich, yet I will never sell my freedom."

The doctor appeared to be irritated. In truth, I was

serious in what I said. Add to this, that I particularly desired not to return to Italy, in order that my passion for the arts should not resume its power. I do not deny, also, that the sudden importunity of the doctor, and the general behavior of these travelers, were disagreeable to me, though I certainly did not believe that the sick countess was possessed by a legion of devils. As all his persuasions had no other effect than to make me more unwilling, the doctor left me. I then reflected on all the different little circumstances—weighed my poverty against the comfortable existence in the train of the rich count, and played with the little money in my pocket, which was all my riches. The result of these reflections were—"Away from Italy; God's world stands open before you. Be firm! only peace in the breast—a village school and independence? I must first endeavor to recover my individuality. Yes, I have lost all—the whole plan of my life—gold can not replace it."

NEW OFFERS.

My surprise was not a little increased, when, scarcely ten minutes after the doctor's departure, a servant of the count appeared, and begged me, in his name, to visit him in his room. "What in the world do these people want with me?" thought I. But I promised to go. The adventure began, if not to amuse, at least to excite my curiosity.

I found the count alone in his room; he was walking with great strides up and down—a tall, strong, respectable-looking man, with a dignified appearance, and pleasing, though melancholy features. He came immediately to meet me, and apologized for having sent for me—led me to a seat, mentioned what he had heard of me through the doctor, and repeated his offers, which I as modestly, but firmly, declined. He went thoughtfully, with his hands thrown behind his back, to the window, returned hastily, seated himself near me, and taking my hand in his, said: "Friend, I appeal to your heart. My eye must deceive me much, if you are not an honest man—consequently sincere. Remain with me, I entreat you—remain only two years. Count upon my deepest gratitude. You shall have, during that time, whatever you need, and at the expiration of it, I will pay you a thousand louis-d'ors; you will not repent having lost a couple of years in my service." He said this so kindly and entreatingly, that I was much moved, more so by the tone and manner, than by the promise of so large a sum, which secured me, with my trifling wants, a free and independent fortune. I would have accepted the offer, had I not been ashamed to show, that at last I had yielded to vile gold. On the other side, his brilliant offers seemed to me suspicious.

"For such a sum, my lord, you can command much more distinguished talents than mine. You do not know me."

I then spoke to him openly of my past destiny and occupation, and thought by that means, without vexing him, to put aside his offers, as well as his desire to have me.

"We must not separate," said he, as he pressed my hand entreatingly. "We must not, since it is you alone that I have sought. It may astonish you; but on your account only, have I undertaken this journey with my daughter; on your account have I chosen the worst road from Villach here, that I might not miss you; on your account have I stopped at this inn."

I looked at the count with astonishment, and thought he wished to jest with me.

"How could you seek me, since you knew me not? since no one knew the road I wandered? I, myself, three days ago, knew not that I should take this road to Germany."

"Is not this a fact?" continued he. "This afternoon you rested in a wood; you sat, full of sorrow, in a wilderness; you leaned on a rock, under a large tree; you gazed at the mountain torrent; you ran on impetuously in the rain. Is it not so? Confess candidly—is it not so?"

At these words my senses forsook me. He saw my consternation, and said: "Well, it is so! you are, indeed, the man I seek."

"But," cried I, "I do not deny that some superstitious horrors seized me," and I drew my hand out of his. "Who watched me? Who told you of it?"

"My daughter—my sick daughter. I can easily believe that to you it appears wonderful. But the unfortunate one says and sees many strange things in her sickness.

"Four weeks since she declared that only through your means could she be restored to perfect health. And as you now appear before me, so did my daughter describe you four weeks ago. Perhaps about fourteen days since, she declared that you came, sent by God, to meet us, and that we must break up and seek you. We set out. She directed the way we should take—at least the part of the world we should go to. With the compass in the carriage, and the map in hand, we traveled, uncertain where, like a ship at sea. At Villach, she pointed out the nearest way to you, described even the particulars, and that we must leave the high road. From Hortensia's mouth, I learnt this morning how near you were, and at the same time the little circumstances which I have mentioned to you. Immediately after your arrival, Dr. Walter declared to me that, from the description of the host, you resembled exactly the person whom Hortensia, four weeks ago, and since that time almost daily, had described. I am now convinced of it, and since so much has already been fulfilled, I do not for a moment doubt that you and no other can save my daughter, and give me back my lost happiness."

He was silent, and waited my answer. I sat long, uncertain and silent. I had never in my life met with so singular an adventure.

"What you tell me, my lord, is somewhat incomprehensible, and therefore, with your permission, somewhat incredible. I am, or rather I was, nothing but an artist; and I know nothing of medicine."

"There is much in life," said he, "that is incomprehensible to us, but all that is incomprehensible, is not therefore incredible, particularly when we can not put aside the reality, and the phenomenon stands before us, whose cause lies hidden before us. You are no physician; that may be. But the same power which has discovered to my daughter your existence in the world has, without doubt, destined you to be her savior. In my youth I was a freethinker, who scarcely believed in God, and can now, in my mature age, even go as far as any old woman, and consider as possible the existence of devils, witches, specters, and familiar spirits. Hence is explained both my importunity and my offers. The first is very pardonable in a father, who lives in constant anxiety about his only child; and my offers are not too great for the saving of so precious a life. I see how unexpected, extraordinary, and romantic it must all appear to you; but remain with us, and you will be a witness to many unexpected things. Do you wish for an occupation exempt from the care and trouble of a journey. It depends upon yourself to choose. I will impose no labor on you. Remain only as my confidential companion, my comforter. I have before me a heavy hour, perhaps it is very near: one of our company will suddenly and, if I rightly understand, in an unusual manner, die. It may be myself. My daughter has foretold it, and it will happen. I tremble to meet the fatal moment, from which my whole fortune can not redeem me. I am a very unhappy man."

He said still more, and was even moved to tears. I found myself in a singular dilemma. All that I heard excited sometimes my astonishment, sometimes my just doubts. Sometimes I had a suspicion of the right understanding of the count, and sometimes supposed the error was my own. At last, I made the courageous resolution to attempt the adventure, come what would of it. It appeared to me unjust to consider the count an impostor; and in God's wide world I had no employment or living.

"I renounce all your generous offers, my lord," said I; "give me only as much as I have need of. I will accompany you. It is sufficient for me if I may hope to contribute to your happiness and your daughter's recovery, though, as yet, I in no way comprehend the *how*. A human life is of much value; I shall be proud if I have it in my power, one day, to believe that I have saved the life of a human being. But I release you from all that you promised me; I do nothing for money. On the contrary, I will, moreover, maintain my independence. I will remain in your retinue as long as I can be of service to you, or can find my life comfortable in it. If you agree to those terms, then I am at your service. You can introduce me to your invalid."

The count's eyes shone with joy. He inclosed me silently in his arms, and pressed me to his heart, while he merely sighed, "Thank God!" After a time he said, "To-morrow you shall see my daughter. She has already gone to rest. I must prepare her for your presence."

"Prepare her for my presence?" exclaimed I, surprised. "Did you not tell me, a few minutes since, that she had announced my arrival, and described my person?"

"Your pardon, dear Faust; I forgot to inform you of one circumstance. My daughter is like a double person. When she is in her natural state, she is in no way conscious of what she hears, sees, knows, and says in her state of trance, if I may so call it. She does not recollect the smallest trifle that occurred during that period, and would herself doubt that she had spoken and acted as we have related to her, if she had not every reason to place confidence in my words. But in her trance, she remembers all that has passed in a similar state, as well as what she has experienced in her usual and natural life. It is only during her trance that she has seen and described you, but out of that she knows nothing of you, except that we, by repeating her own expressions, have been able to inform her. Let us only wait for one of her extraordinary moments, and I have no doubt she will immediately recollect you."

In a conversation of some hours, I learnt from the count that his daughter had for years, even from a child, an inclination to sleep-walking. In a state of somnambulism, she had, without being able to recollect it afterward, with closed eyes, left her bed, dressed herself, written letters to those present, or played the most difficult pieces on the piano, and executed a hundred other trifles with a skill, which she not only did not possess when awake, but which she could not afterward acquire. The count believed that that which he now sometimes called a trance and sometimes a transfiguration, was nothing more than a higher state of somnambulism, but which enfeebled his daughter almost to death.

A FRIGHTFUL EVENT.

It was late when I left the count's apartment. There was no one but old Sebald in the public room, who was still enjoying his wine.

"Sir," said he, "speak a little German with me, that I may not entirely forget my noble language, which would in truth be a shame. You have spoken with the count?"

"I have spoken with him. I shall now travel with him to Italy, and remain in your company."

"Excellent! It does me good to have one more German face near me. The Italians, as I have heard, are bad birds. Now, with the exception of our possessed countess, you will be pleased with all our company. As you now belong to us, I can now speak more openly of our affairs. The count would be a good man if he could only smile. I believe he is not pleased when one laughs. All that surrounds him has the aspect of the last day. The old lady is also right good, but is easily vexed, if one does not immediately fly here and there according to her motions. I believe she goes to Italy merely on account of the pure burnt water, as she loves a glass of liquor. The sick countess also would not be bad, if she had not, beside her pride, an army of devils in her body. Whoever wishes to be in her good graces must creep on all-fours. Bow yourself diligently before her. Dr. Walter would be the best of us all, if he only knew how to exorcise the devils. My comrade, Thomas, is therefore——" At this moment the host, full of horror, rushed into the room, and cried to his people, "Help! help! there is fire."

"Where is the fire?" asked I, alarmed.

"Up-stairs, in a chamber; I saw the bright flames outside the window."

He ran out; the house was filled with cries and confusion. I was following, when Sebald, white as a corpse, held me by both arms: "Jesu Maria! what has happened?" I told him in German to get water, as the house was on fire.

"Another piece of deviltry!" sighed he, and hurried into the kitchen.

The people ran up and down stairs. It was said the room was fastened, and they sought instruments to break open the door. Sebald was up-stairs even as soon as myself, with a bucket of water. As he perceived the door, toward which all pressed, he cried, "Jesu Maria! that is the chamber of the old lady."

"Burst it open," cried the Count Hormegg, in extreme agony. "Burst it open: Mrs. Montlue sleeps there, and she will be suffocated."

A man soon came with an ax, but it was not without difficulty that he could break the strong, well-mortised oaken door. All pressed in, but, shuddering, bounded back.

The room was dark. Only in the background, near the window, a yellow flame played on the floor, which soon went out. An indescribably sharp stench blew toward us as we opened the door. Sebald made the sign of the cross, and sprang headlong down stairs; some of the maids followed his example. The count called for a light. It was brought. I went through the room in order to open the window. The count directed us to the bed. It was empty and undisturbed, and nowhere any smoke. Near the window the stench was so great it made me sick.

The count called the name of Mrs. Montlue. As he came nearer with the burning candle, I saw at my feet —imagine my horror!—a large black spot of ashes, and near by a burnt head we could not recognize; one arm with the hand; in another place three fingers, and the foot of a lady, partly charred.

"Great God!" cried the count, turning pale, "what is that?" He observed, shuddering, the remains of a human figure. He saw the fingers with the rings, and sprang, with a loud shriek, to meet the doctor, who was entering. "Mrs. Montlue is burnt, yet no fire, no smoke! Incomprehensible!"

He tottered back, in order once more to convince himself of the reality of his discovery. He then gave up the candle, folded his hands, looked fixedly before him, and turning deadly pale, left the room.

I stood petrified, by a so horrible and unheard-of spectacle. All that had happened during this day, the wonders that had been told, had so stupefied me, that I stood, without feeling, gazing at the black dust, the coals, and the disgusting remains of a human form at my feet. The room was soon filled with the men and women belonging to the inn. I heard their whispers and their stealthy steps. It seemed to me that I was in the midst of specters. The nursery tales of my childhood were ripened to reality.

When I came to myself, I withdrew from the chamber, intending to go down into the public room. At that moment, a door at the side opened; a young lady, dressed in a light night dress, came out, supported by two maids, each of whom carried a lighted candle. I remained standing, as if blinded by this new apparition. So much nobleness in figure, movement, and features, I had never seen in reality; nor ever found in the creations of the painter or statuary. The horrors of the preceding moments were almost forgotten. I was only eyes and admiration. The young beauty tottered toward the chamber, where the frightful event had occurred. When she observed the men and women, she stood still, and cried out in the German language, and with a commanding voice, "Drive away this crowd from me." Immediately one of the count's servants executed her commands. He did it with such uncourtly violence, that he forced them all, and me with them, from the gallery to the stairs.

"If there ever has been a fairy, this is one," thought I. Sebald was sitting, quite pale, in the public room, near the wine. "Did not I say so?" cried he. "One of us must go. The possessed, or rather that malicious Satan, so willed it. The one must break his bones and neck--the other, a living body, be burnt. Your obedient servant, I take my leave to-morrow, lest the next turn comes to my insignificant self. Whoever is as prudent as I am will not travel with them to hell. In Italy, even the mountains spit fire. God keep me from going too near. I should certainly be the first roast of Moloch, since I am much too pious, and, nevertheless, at all hours not a saint."

I told him of the young lady.

"That was she," said he; "that was the countess. God be near unto us. She has, probably, desired to snuff up the burnt mess. Go with me to-morrow; let us make our escape. Your bright young life raises my sincere compassion."

"Even the Countess Hortensia?"

"Who else? She is handsome, therefore the chief of the devils has himself bewitched her; but——"

At this time, Sebald was called by the count; he went, or rather staggered, sighing deeply. The accident had filled the whole house with noise. I sat on my chair, amid all these wonders, estranged from myself. Long after midnight, the host showed me a small room, where there was a bed.

ANTIPATHY.

After the fatigues of the past day, I slept soundly until nearly mid-day. As I awoke, the events of yesterday appeared like a feverish phantom, or the illusions of intoxication. I could neither convince myself of their truth, nor yet doubt them. I considered every thing now with greater composure of mind. I no longer hesitated to remain with the count. I rather followed him with pleasure and curiosity, so entirely new and wonderful did my destiny appear. Then also what had I to lose in Germany? What even in life? What could I risk in following the count? At last, it only depended upon myself to break the thread of the romance as soon as its length became disagreeable to me. When I entered the public room, I found it filled with the overseers of the place, police officers, capuchins, and peasants of the neighboring country, who had been drawn thither either from motives of curiosity or by their official duties. Not one of them doubted but that the burning of the lady was the work of the devil. The count, indeed, had the remains of the unfortunate woman buried by his own people. But it was thought proper that the whole house should be consecrated and blessed by the reverend Capuchin fathers, in order that it might be purified from the evil spirit. This was a considerable expense. There was a question, whether we should be arrested and given up to justice; but it was disputed whether we should be delivered to the civil or ecclesiastical authority. The majority were in favor of our being taken to Undine, and brought before the archbishops.

The count, not being master of the Italian language, was glad when he saw me. He had in vain offered a large sum of money to defray the expenses occasioned by the extraordinary circumstances. He entreated me to finish the business with the people in his name.

I immediately drew near the priests and police-officers, and declared to them that, until now, I had as little connection with the count as themselves, and offered two things for their consideration; either the misfortune of burning had happened naturally, or at least without the participation of the count, in which case they would bring much trouble on themselves, by the arrest of so high a nobleman; or he was truly in league with bad spirits, in which case, he could out of revenge, play some bad tricks on them, their cloister, and their village. Their wisest course was, to take the count's money and let him go; they would then have no responsibility or resentment to fear, and in any case would be the gainers. My reasons were obvious. The money was paid. Our horses were given us—we mounted, and rode on. The prospect cleared up.

The countess, with the women and other servants, had gone some hours before; the count, with only one servant, having remained behind. On the way, he began to speak of the frightful event of the past evening. He said his daughter had been very much overcome by it. She had suffered for some hours with cramps and convulsions, after which she had a quiet sleep. She appeared tranquil on awakening; but desired to leave the unfortunate house immediately.

Probably in order to prepare me for my future situation, he added: "I am obliged to pardon and yield much to my sick child. She is of unconquerable obstinacy. From her extraordinary irritability, the least contradiction moves her to anger, and a slight vexation is sufficient to cause many days of suffering. I have announced your arrival to her. She heard it with indifference. I asked if I might introduce you to her. Her answer was, 'Do you think I have so much curiosity? It will be time enough when we are in Venice.' I think, however, we shall have sufficient opportunities on the way. Do not allow the humors of my daughter to vex you, my dear Faust. She is a sick, unfortunate creature, whom we must treat with tenderness, lest we destroy her. She is my only treasure, my last joy on earth. The loss of Mrs. Montlue does not appear to be painful to her, as she had lately, I know not from what cause, taken an aversion to her. Perhaps the slight, certainly not violent inclination of that person to strong drink, was disgusting to her. Dr. Walter affirms, also, that this habit was the cause of her spontaneous combustion. Formerly, she was a very good woman, and much attached to my daughter and myself. I lament her loss very deeply. Dr. Walter related to me other instances which must be extremely rare, of the spontaneous combustion of the human body, by which it is in a few moments reduced to ashes. He endeavored to account for the phenomenon on very natural grounds, but I can not comprehend it. Only this much I know, this burning door of death is one of the most frightful."

Thus spoke the count, and this formed the subject of our conversation to Venice. For the young countess had now the humor, notwithstanding her bodily weakness, and the objections of her father and the physician, to make the journey by long days' rides, and with no other delay than the nightly rest demanded. I had not, therefore, the honor of an introduction. Nay, I must even keep at a distance, since, alas! I had not the good fortune to please her.

She was carried in a sedan chair—servants ran near her on foot. The women rode, and the count, likewise, in his own carriage. The doctor and myself rode on horseback.

As the countess one morning came out of the inn to mount her sedan, she perceived me, and said to Dr. Walter, "Who is that man, that forever and eternally follows us?"

"Mr. Faust, my good lady."

"A disagreeable fellow—send him back."

"You, yourself, have wished for him; it was on his account that the journey was undertaken. Consider him as a medicine which you have ordered for yourself."

"He has the disgusting qualities common to all drugs."

I was near enough to hear this not very flattering speech, and knew not what countenance I put on, though

I well recollect that I was almost vexed, and should immediately have left the whimsical Venus, had not the count been so kind. I could not affirm that I was a handsome man, but I know that generally I did not displease the women. But now, only to be endured as a disgusting medicine, was too severe on the vanity of a young man, especially for one who, had he been a prince or count, would not have hesitated to have joined himself to the adorers of the charming Hortensia.

In the mean while I continued with them. The countess reached Venice without any particular accident, and her medicine followed obediently after. A magnificent palace was hired, in which I had an apartment, and also servants, particularly appropriated to my service. The count lived in great style, as it is called. He had many friends among the Venetian nobility.

THE TRANCE.

We had been about four days in Venice, when one afternoon I was hastily sent for by the count. He received me with an unusually cheerful countenance.

"My daughter," said he, "has inquired for you. Indeed, no day has passed without her speaking of you: she has done so already to-day; but now is the first time that she has desired your presence. Enter her room with me, but very gently; the least noise throws her into dangerous cramps."

"But," asked I, with secret horror, "what does she wish me to do?"

"Who can answer?" replied the count. "Wait for the future. May God direct all."

We entered a large state chamber, hung round with green silk hangings. Two female servants were leaning, silent and anxious, near the window—the doctor sat on a sofa, watching the invalid. She stood upright, with closed eyes, in the middle of the room—one of her beautiful arms was hanging down, the other, half raised, stiff and immovable as a statue. Only the movement of her bosom betrayed breath. The solemn silence which reigned, the goddess-like figure of Hortensia, upon whom all eyes were fixed, filled me with involuntary yet pleasing horror.

As soon as I entered this silent sanctuary, the countess, without opening her eyes or changing her position, said, with an indescribably sweet voice, "At last, Emanuel! why dost thou keep so far off? Oh, come hither, and bless her, that she may be cured of her sufferings."

I probably looked rather foolish at this speech, being uncertain whether or not it regarded me. The count and the doctor motioned me to draw nearer, and gave me a sign that I should, like a priest, make the sign of the cross toward, or else, as blessing her, lay my hands on her.

I approached, and raised my hands over her wonderfully beautiful head. But from extreme respect, had not courage to touch her. I let my hands sink slowly down again. Hortensia's countenance seemed to betray discontent. I again raised my hands, and held them stretched out toward her, uncertain what I was to do. Her countenance cleared, which induced me to remain in that position. My embarrassment, however, increased as the countess said, "Emanuel, thou hast not yet the will to relieve her. Oh, only give thy will—thy will. Thou art all powerful. Thy will can do all."

"Gracious countess," said I, "doubt all, but not my will to assist you." I said this truly, with great earnestness. For had she commanded me to throw myself into the sea for her, I should with joy have done so. To me, it was as if I stood before a divinity. The soft symmetry of her form, and her countenance, which seemed to belong to the unearthly, had likewise disembodied my soul. Never had I seen grace and sublimity so united. Hortensia's face was, as I had before seen it, it is true, only transiently or from a distance, pale, suffering, and gloomy; now it was quite different. An uncommon delicate color was spread over it, like the reflection from the rose. In all her features swam a light, such as a human countenance, under ordinary circumstances, could never obtain, either by nature or art. The expression of the whole was a solemn smile, and yet no smile, but rather an inward delight. This extraordinary state was justly called transfiguration by her companions; but such a transfiguration, no painter in his moments of inspiration, ever saw or imagined. Let one, therefore, figure to himself the statue-like position, the marble stillness of the features, with the eyes closed as in sleep. Never before had I felt such fearful delight.

"Oh! Emanuel!" said she, after a time, "now is thy will sincere. Now knows she, that through thee she will be cured. Thy hair flows in golden flames; from thy fingers flow silver rays of light; thou floatest in heaven's clear azure. How eagerly her whole being imbibes this brilliancy—this health-bringing flood of light."

At this somewhat poetical form of speech, the drugs, with which I had the melancholy honor of being compared to a few days before, involuntarily recurred to me, and I continued silent, taking no notice of the gold and silver rays.

"Be not angry with her in thy thoughts, Emanuel," said Hortensia. "Be not angry that her weakness and distempered wit compared thee with bitter remedies. Be more generous than the thoughtless one, by suffering misled, and often by earthly weaknesses given up to frenzy."

At these words the doctor threw a smiling look on me —I also toward the doctor, but with a gesture of astonishment, not because the proud beauty humbled herself to an apology, but that she appeared to have guessed my thoughts.

"Oh! distract not thy attention, Emanuel!" said the transfigured, quickly. "Thou speakest with the doctor. On her alone turn thy thoughts, and on her safety. It distresses her when thy thoughts for one moment leave her. Continue in the firm desire to penetrate her half-dissolved being with the beneficial power of thy light. Seest thou how powerful thy will is? The stiffened fibers relax and melt, like the winter's frost in the sun's rays."

While she spoke, her raised arm sank. Motion and life animated her figure. She asked for a seat. The doctor brought her one which stood in the chamber, with richly embroidered green silk cushions.

"Not that kind," said she. After a while she continued: "The arm-chair, with a striped linen cover, which stands in Emanuel's chamber, before his writing-table. Bring it here, and leave it forever!"

I had, truly, but the moment before left the arm-chair standing before the table. But the countess had never seen my room. As I reached the key of the room to one of the women, Hortensia said, "Is that the key? I did not understand those dark spots. Thou hast in the left pocket of thy vest, yet another key—put it away from thee." I did so. It was the key of my press.

So soon as the chair was brought, she seated herself in it, apparently with great comfort. She commanded me to stand near before her, with the ends of my fingers toward the pit of her heart.

"God! of what delight is the man capable!" said she. "Emanuel, give her thy word, she entreats thee, not to forsake her till the ruins of her mind have been re-established—till her recovery is perfect. Shouldst thou forsake her, she must die wretchedly. On thee hangs her life."

I promised with delight and pride to be the protector and guardian angel of so precious a life.

"Also, regard it not," continued she, "if she, in the state of earthly waking, mistakes thee. Pardon her—she is an unfortunate, that knows not what she does. All faults are the sicknesses of the mortal part, which cripple the power of the spirit."

She was talkative, and so far from being vexed by my questions, she appeared to hear them with pleasure. I expressed my astonishment at her extraordinary situation. Never had I heard that sickness made a person, as it were, godlike; that she should, with closed eyes, perceive what she had never seen before, and what was far distant from her, and even know the thoughts of another! I must believe that her state, which, with justice, might be compared to a transfiguration, was the perfection of health.

After a minute's silence, which was always the case before she answered, she said, "She is healthy like a dying person, whose material is breaking asunder. She is as healthy as she will be, when her humanity ceases, and the earthly body of this lamp of eternal light falls to pieces."

"The transfiguration," said I, "makes all dark to me!"

"Dark, Emanuel? But thou wilt experience it. She knows much, and yet can not express it; she sees much clearly, much dimly, and yet can not name it. See—man is combined from a variety of beings, which bind and arrange themselves together, as round a single point, and thereby he becomes man. So are all the little parts of a flower held together, whereby it becomes a flower. And as one part holds and binds the other, so the other restrains it in turn; no one is what it would be by itself, since, only ALL can form man, and be otherwise nothing. Nature is like an endless ocean of brightness, in which single solid points are drawn together. These are creatures. Or like an extensive shining heaven, in which drops of light run together and form stars. All that is in the world, has run together from the dissolved chaos, which is everywhere and always imbibing and then dissolving itself again in ALL, since nothing can remain stationary. So is man, out of the manifold substances of the universe, grown around with floating flowers. But in order that man may be, more insignificant beings must place themselves around him, which shall support his divine part.

"The strange things or beings which are placed around us, form the body. The body is only the shell of the heavenly body. The heavenly body is called the soul. The soul is but the veil of the Eternal. Now is the earthly shell of the sick broken, therefore her light flows out, her soul meets in union with ALL, from which it was formerly separated by a healthy shell, and sees, hears, and feels without it and within it. Then it is not the body that feels; the body is only the inanimate casement of the soul. Without it, eyes, ears, and tongue are like stones. Now, if the earthly shell of the sick can not become healthy by thy aid, she will be entirely broken and fall to pieces. She will no longer belong to mankind, since she possesses nothing by which she can communicate with them."

She stopped. I listened as if she brought revelations from another world. I understood nothing, and yet divined what she thought. The count and physician listened to her with equal astonishment. Both assured me afterward, that Hortensia had never spoken so clearly, connectedly, and supernaturally, as at this time; that her communications had been broken, and made often under great suffering; she frequently fell into the most frightful convulsions, or would lie for many hours in a torpid state; that she very rarely answered questions, but now the conversation appeared not at all to fatigue her.

I reminded her of her weakness, and inquired if talking so much did not exhaust her strength? She declared, "Not in the least! She is well. She will always be well, when thou art with her. In seven minutes she will awaken. She will enjoy a quiet night. But to-morrow afternoon, about three o'clock, her sleep will return. Then fail not, Emanuel. Five minutes before three the cramps will begin; then, blessing her, stretch thy hands toward her, with an earnest desire of healing her. Five minutes before three, and by the clock in thy chamber, not by thy watch, which is three minutes different from the clock. Set thy watch exactly by the clock, that the sick may not suffer by their difference."

She also mentioned several trifling circumstances; ordered what they should give her to drink on awakening; what for her supper; at what time she should go to bed, and gave other similar directions. She was then silent. The former death-like stillness reigned. Her face gradually became paler, as it usually was; the animation of her countenance disappeared. She now first appeared to wish to sleep, or actually to be asleep. She no longer held herself upright, but sank down carelessly, and nodded, as is usual with a person sleeping. She then began to extend her arms and stretch herself, yawned, rubbed her eyes, opened them, and was almost in the same minute awake and cheerful, as she had announced.

When she saw me she appeared surprised—she looked around on the others. The women hastened to her, also the count and doctor.

"What do you want?" she asked me, in a hard tone.

"Gracious lady, I wait your commands."

"Who are you?"

"Faust, at your service."

"I am obliged to you for your good will, but desire I may be left alone!" said she, somewhat vexed; then bowing proudly toward me, she arose and turned her back on me.

I left the room with a singular mixture of feelings. How immeasurably different was the waking from the sleeping person! My gold and silver rays disappeared; also her confidential *thou*, which penetrated deep into my innermost feelings—even the name of Emanuel, with which she had enriched me, was no longer of value.

Musingly, I entered my chamber, like one who had been reading fairy tales, and became so absorbed in them that he holds the enchantment for reality. The arm-chair before my writing-table was wanting. I placed another, and wrote down the wonderful tale, as I had experienced it, and as much of Hortensia's conversation as I recollected, since I feared that I might not hereafter believe it myself, if I had it not written before me. I had promised to pardon all the harshness the might use toward me while awake—willingly did I forgive her. But she was so beautiful! I could not have borne it with indifference.

A SECOND TRANSFIGURATION.

THE next day the count visited me in my room to inform me of the quiet night Hortensia had enjoyed, and also that she was stronger and more animated than she had been for a long time. "At breakfast, I told her," said he, "all that had passed yesterday. She shook her head, and would not believe me, or otherwise she said she must have paroxysms of delirium, and began to weep. I quieted her. I told her that, without doubt, her restoration to health was near, since in you, dear Faust, there certainly dwells some divine power, of which hitherto you have probably been unconscious. I begged her to receive you into her society during her waking hours, since I promised myself much from your presence, but could not move her to consent. She asserted that your sight was insupportable to her, and that only by degrees could she perhaps accustom herself to your appearance. What can we do? She can not be forced to any thing, without placing her life in danger."

Thus he spoke, and sought in every way to excuse Hortensia to me. He showed me, as if in contrast to Hortensia's offensive antipathy, self-will, and pride, the most moving confidence; spoke of his family circumstances, of his possessions, law-suits, and other disagreeable circumstances; desired my counsel, and promised to lay all his papers before me, in order that my opinion of his affairs might be more precise. He did so, that same day. Initiated in all, even his most secret concerns, I became every day more intimate with him; his friendship appeared to increase in proportion as the antipathy which his daughter had taken to me augmented. At length I conducted all his correspondence —had also the management of his income, and the government of his household—so that, in short, I became every thing to him. Convinced of my honesty and good-will, he depended on me with unlimited confidence, and only seemed discontented when he perceived, that with the exception of mere necessaries, I desired nothing for myself, and constantly refused all his rich presents. Dr. Walter and all the domestics, as well male as female, soon remarked what extraordinary influence I had, as suddenly as unexpectedly, attained. They surrounded me with attentions and flattery. This unmerited and general good-will made me very happy, though I would willingly have exchanged it all for mere friendship from the inimitable countess. She, however, remained unpropitiated. Her antipathy appeared almost to degenerate into hate. She cautioned her father against me, as against a cunning adventurer and impostor. With her women she called me only the vagabond, who had nestled himself in her father's confidence. The old count, at last, scarce dared to mention me in her presence. But I will not anticipate the history and course of events.

My watch was regulated. It was really three minutes different from the clock. Five minutes before three in the afternoon, neither sooner nor later, I entered, unannounced, Hortensia's room. The witnesses of the day before were present. She sat on a sofa, in a thoughtful position, but with her own peculiar grace, pale and suffering. As she perceived me, she threw a proud, contemptuous look on me, rose hastily, and cried, "Who gave you permission—without being announced——"

A violent shriek and fierce convulsions stopped her voice. She sank into the arms of her women. The chair which she had desired the day before was brought to her. Scarcely was she seated in it than she began in the most frightful manner, and with incredible velocity, to strike herself, both on the body and head, with her clenched fist. I could scarcely support the horrible spectacle. Tremblingly, I took the position which she had prescribed the day before, and directed the finger-ends of both my hands toward her. But she, with eyes convulsively distorted and fixed, seized them, and thrust the fingers with violence many times against her person. She soon became more tranquil, closed her eyes, and after she had given some deep sighs, appeared to sleep. Her countenance betrayed pain. She fretted softly for some time. But soon the pain appeared to subside. She now sighed twice, but gently. Her countenance gradually became clearer, and soon again resumed the expression of internal blessedness, while the paleness of her face was overspread by a soft color.

After some minutes, she said, "Thou, true friend! without thee what would become of me?" She spoke these words with a solemn tenderness, with which angels alone might greet each other. Her tones vibrated on all my nerves.

"Are you well, gracious lady?" said I, almost in a whisper—since I yet feared she might show me the door.

"Very, oh! very, Emanuel!" answered she, "as well as yesterday, and even more so. It seems thy will is more decided, and thy power to assist her increased. She breathes—she swims in the shining circle which surrounds thee: her being, penetrated by thine, is in thee dissolved. Could she be ever so!"

To us prosaical listeners, this manner of speaking was very unintelligible, though to me in no way unpleasing. I regretted only that Hortensia thought not of me, but of an Emanuel, and probably deceived herself. Yet I received some comfort, when I afterward learned from the count, that to his knowledge none of his relations or acquaintances bore the name of Emanuel.

Her father asked her some questions, but she did not hear them—as she began in the midst of one of them to speak to me. He approached nearer to her. When he stood by me, she became more attentive.

"How, dear father, art thou here?" said she. She now answered his questions. I asked her why she had not observed him sooner.

She replied, "He stood in the dark—only near thee is it light. Thou also shinest, father, but weaker than Emanuel, but only by reflection from him."

I then said to her that there were yet more persons in the room; she made a long pause, then named them all, even the places where they were. Her eyes were constantly closed, yet she could denote what passed behind her. Yes, she even remarked the number of persons who were passing in a gondola in the canal before the house, and it was correct.

"But how is it possible that you can know this, since you do not see them?" said I.

"Did she not declare to you yesterday that she was sick? That it is not the body which discerns the outer world, but the soul. Flesh, blood, and the frame of bones is only the shell which surrounds the noble kernel. The shell is now torn, and its vital power would repair the defects, but can not without assistance.

Therefore the spirit calls for thee. The soul, flowing out and searching in the universe, finds thee, and fulfills its duty with thy power. When her earthly waking comes, she sees, she hears, and feels more quickly and acutely; but only that which is external and near—that which approaches her. Now, however, she meets things whether she will or not; she touches not, but penetrates; she guesses not, but knows. In dreams thou goest to the objects, not they to thee; and thou knowest them, and wherefore they so act. Even now, it is to her like a dream; nevertheless, she knows well that she is awake, but her body wakes not; the outward senses do not assist her."

She next spoke much of her sickness, of her sleep-waking, of a long fainting fit, in which she once laid—what had passed within her, and what she had thought while those around wept her as dead. The count heard her with astonishment, since, besides many circumstances of which he was ignorant, she touched upon others which had occurred during her ten hours' stupor, of which no one but himself could have known; for example, how he had in despair left her, gone into his chamber, fallen on his knees, and prayed in hopeless agony. He had never mentioned this, and no one could have seen him, since not only at the time had he fastened the door, but it was also night, and his chamber without a light. Now, that Hortensia spoke of it, he did not deny it. It was incomprehensible how she could have known it in her fainting fit, and yet more so that she could recollect it at this time, as the incident had occurred in her early childhood. She could scarcely have been more than eight years old at the time.

It was also remarkable that she always spoke of herself in the third person, as of a stranger, when she related her own history, or spoke of herself, as she stood in the civil and social relations. Once she said explicitly, "I am no countess, but she is a countess!" Another time, "I am not the daughter of Count Hormegg, but she is."

As her whole exterior appeared in a floating transfiguration, more quiet, more exalted, more beautiful than usual, so was her voice a language in conformity to it. It was, though as soft and clear, yet more solemn than in common life; every expression was chosen, and sometimes even poetical. There was frequently a singular obscurity in her words—often an apparent total want of connection, occasioned partly because she spoke of things, or observed them in a point of view foreign to us. She, however, spoke willingly, and with pleasure, particularly when questioned by me. Sometimes she was in a long and quiet reflection, during which one might read in her features the expression, sometimes of a discontented, sometimes a contented research, astonishment, admiration, or delight. She interrupted this deep silence, from time to time, with single exclamations, when she lisped "Holy God!"

Once she began of herself: "Now is the world changed. It is one great ONE, and that eternal one is a spiritual one. There is no difference between body and spirit, since all is spirit, and all can become body, when they associate together, so that they may feel as a single one. The all (or the component parts) is as if formed from the purest ether; the all, acting and moving; transforming itself; since all will unite; and the one counterbalances the other. It is an eternal fermentation of life, an eternal vibration between too much and too little. Seest thou how clouds move in the clearest heaven? They float and swell, till the mass is filled; then, attracted by the earth, they penetrate it in the form of life or rain. Seest thou the flower? A spark of life has fallen in the midst of a throng of other powers; it unites itself with all that may be of service to it, forms them, and the germ becomes a plant, until the inferior powers overgrow and dislodge the original power. And as the spark is expelled, they fall asunder, since nothing any longer binds them together. She is the formation and decay of man."

She said yet much more, wholly unintelligible to me. Her transfiguration ended like the first. She again announced the period of her earthly waking, likewise the occurrence of a similar state the next day. She dismissed me with the same dark looks as on the first day, as soon as she opened her eyes.

SYMPATHY AND ANTIPATHY.

Thus it continued, always in the same way, for some months. Her extraordinary indisposition experienced only insignificant changes, from which I could neither affirm that they denoted improvement or the contrary. For, if she suffered less from cramps and convulsions—and while awake there was not the slightest trace of uncomfortable feeling, except extreme irritability—her unnatural sleep and transfiguration returned more frequently, so that I was often called two or three times in a day.

I became thus completely the slave of the house. I dared not absent myself even for a few hours. Any neglect might cause serious danger. How willingly did I bear the yoke of slavery! I never faltered. My soul trembled with joy, when the moment allotted to the beautiful miracle came. Each day adorned her with higher charms. Had I but for one hour seen and heard her, I had sufficient remembrance to banquet on for a long time in my solitude. Oh! the intoxication of first love.

Yes, I deny it not, it was love; but I may truly say, not earthly, but celestial love. My whole being was in a new manner bound to this Delphic priestess, by an awe in which even the hope died of ever being worthy of her most insignificant looks. Could the countess have endured me without disgust, even as the most unimportant of her attendants, I should have thought that heaven could have offered no higher happiness. But, as in her transfigured state, her kindness toward me seemed to increase, even so did her aversion, as soon as, when waking, she saw me. This dislike grew at last into the bitterest abhorrence. She declared this on every occasion, and always in the most irritating manner. She daily entreated her father, and always more harshly, to send me from the house; she conjured him with tears; she affirmed that I could contribute nothing to her recovery; and were it so, all the good I could effect during her unconscious state was again destroyed by the vexation my presence caused her. She despised me as a common vagabond, as a man of low origin, who should not be allowed to breathe the same air with her—to say nothing of so intimate connection with her, or the enjoyment of such great confidence from Count Hormegg.

It is well known that women, particularly the handsome, indulged and self-willed, have humors, and consider it not unbecoming if they sometimes or always are a little inconsistent with themselves. But never in any mortal could more contradiction be found, than in the beautiful Hortensia. What she, waking, thought, said, or did, she contradicted in the moments of her trance. She entreated the count not to regard what she might advance against me. She asserted that an increase of her illness would be the inevitable consequence of my leaving the house, and would end in her death. She entreated me not to regard her humors, but generously to pardon her foolish behavior, and to live under the conviction that she would certainly improve in her conduct toward me as her disease abated.

I was, in fact, as much astonished as the others at Hortensia's extraordinary inclination to me during her transfigured state. She seemed, as it were, only through me, and in me, to live. She guessed, indeed, she knew my thoughts—especially when they had any relation to her. It was unnecessary to express my little instructions; she executed them. However incredible it may be, it is not the less true, that she, with her hands, followed all the movements of mine in every direction. She declared that it was scarcely any longer necessary to stretch out my hands toward her, as at the commencement; my presence, my breath, my mere will sufficed to her well-being. She refused, with scorn, to taste any wine or water that I had not, as she said, consecrated by laying my hands on, and made healthful by the light streaming from the ends of my fingers. She went so far as to declare my slightest wishes to be her irresistible commands.

"She has no longer any free will," said she, one day. "So soon as she knows thy will, Emanuel, she is constrained so to will. Thy thoughts govern her with a supernatural power. And precisely in this obedience, she feels her good, her blessedness. She can not act contrary. So soon as she ascertains thy thoughts, they become her thoughts and laws."

"But how is this perception of my thoughts possible, dearest countess?" said I. "I can not deny that you often discern the most secret depths of my soul. What a singular sickness—which seems to make you omniscient! Who would not wish for himself this state of imperfection?"

"It is so also with her," said she. "Deceive not thyself, Emanuel; she is very imperfect, since she has lost the greater part of her individuality; she has lost it in thee. Shouldst thou die to-day, thy last breath would be her last. Thy serenity is her serenity--thy sorrow her sorrow."

"Can you not explain to me the miracle that causes in me the greatest astonishment, and, notwithstanding all my reflections, remains inexplicable?"

She was long silent. After about ten minutes she said: "No, she can not explain it. Come not persons before thee in dreams, whose thoughts thou seemest to think at the same moment with themselves? So it is with her; and yet to the sick one it exists clearly; she is conscious that she is awake. Truly," continued she, "her spiritual part is always the same; but that which united the spirit to the body is no longer the same. Her shell is wounded in that part with which the soul is first and most intimately connected; her life flows out and becomes weaker, and does not allow itself to be bound. Hadst thou not been found, Emanuel, the sick would already have been released. As an uprooted plant, whose powers evaporating, receives no sustenance, if its roots are again laid in fresh soil, will imbibe new life from the earth, put forth branches and become green—thus is it with the sick. Soul and life in the ALL flowing way, finds nourishment in thy life's fullness; forces new roots in thy being, and is restored to thee. She is an extinguished light in a broken vessel; but the dried wick of life nourishes itself again in the oil of thy lamp. Thus the sick, now spiritually rooted in thee, exists from the same powers as thou, therefore has she pleasure and pain, will, and even thought, as thou hast. Thou art her life, Emanuel."

Neither the women nor the doctor could refrain from smiles at this tender declaration of the petulant countess. On the same day, the count said to me:—

"Will you not for a jest make the strongest essay of your power over Hortensia?"

"And how?" replied I.

"Desire, as a proof of her obedience, that Hortensia shall have you called, when she is awake, and voluntarily give you, as a present, the most beautiful of the roses which are blooming in her vases."

"It is too much; it would be indiscreet. You know, count, what an unconquerable aversion she has to poor Faust, as much even as she appears to have regard for Emanuel."

"Even for that reason I entreat you to make the trial, were it only to discover whether your will is powerful enough to have effect out of the state of transfiguration, and in the waking usual life. No one shall tell her what you have wished. Therefore, it shall be arranged that no person except you and myself shall be present when you express the wish."

I promised to obey—though, I confess, rather unwillingly.

THE ROSE.

When I went to her the following morning, as she lay in the slumber which usually preceded her transfiguration—and I never showed myself earlier—I found the count there alone. He reminded me by a look, and with laughing eyes, of the agreement the day before.

Hortensia passed into her transfigured waking state, and immediately commenced a friendly conversation. She assured us that her sickness had almost reached the turning point, when it would gradually diminish; this would be known by her having less clear perceptions in her sleep. I became more embarrassed the more the count motioned to me to bring forward my experiment.

In order to divert or encourage myself, I went silently through the room to the window where Hortensia's flowers bloomed, and with my fingers played with the branches of a rose-bush. Inadvertently, I stuck a thorn rather deep into the end of my middle finger.

Hortensia gave a loud cry. I hurried to her; the count likewise. She complained of a violent prick in the point of the middle finger of her right hand. The appearance of her finger belonged to the witchcrafts, to which, since my intercourse with her, I had been accustomed. In fact, I thought I could remark a scarcely visible blue spot; the next day, however, a small sore developed itself, and likewise on my finger, only mine was sooner healed.

"It is my fault, Emanuel," said she, after the lapse of a few minutes; "thou hast wounded thyself with the rose-bush. Take care of thyself—what befalls thee happens also to me."

She was silent. I also. My thoughts were how I should bring forward my proposition. The wounding appeared the fittest occasion. The count motioned me to take courage.

"Wherefore dost thou not speak out?" said Hortensia; "ask that she should have you called at twelve o'clock to-day, before she goes to eat, and present you with a new-blown rose."

With amazement I heard my wish from her lips. "I feared to offend you by my boldness!" said I.

"Oh! Emanuel, she well knows that her father himself suggested the wish!" replied she, smiling.

"It is, likewise, my ardent wish!" stammered I.

"But will you, at twelve, when awake, remember it?"

"Can she do otherwise?" she replied, with a good-humored smile.

As the conversation on this subject ended, the count went out and brought in the women and the doctor, who were waiting without. After about half an hour, I, as usual, so soon as the transfigured was lost in a real sleep, absented myself. It might have been about ten o'clock.

Upon waking, Hortensia showed the doctor her painful finger. She believed that she had wounded herself with the point of a needle, and was astonished not to find some outward injury.

About eleven she became restless, walked up and down her room, sought out all sorts of things, began to speak of me to the women, or rather, after her usual habit, to pour on me the fullness of her anger, and to attack her father with reproaches that he had not yet dismissed me.

"This obtrusive man is not worth my spending so many tears and words about. I know not what forces me to think of him, and to embitter every hour with the hated thought. It is already too much that I know him to be under the same roof, and that I know how much you esteem him, dear father. I could swear the wicked man has bewitched me. Therefore, take care, dear father, I certainly do not deceive myself. You will have cause, one day, bitterly to repent your good nature. He will deceive you and all of us some day."

"I entreat you, my child," said the count, "do not be forever vexing and fatiguing yourself with speaking of him. You do not know him; you have only seen him twice, and but transiently. How can you then pronounce a condemnatory judgment upon him? Wait till I surprise him in some false act. In the mean while, do you be tranquil. It is sufficient that he dare not appear in your presence."

Hortensia was silent. She spoke with the women on other subjects. They asked her if she was not well; she knew not what to answer. She began to weep. They endeavored in vain to discover the cause of her grief and melancholy. She concealed her face in the cushion on the sofa, and begged of her father as well as her women, to leave her alone.

A quarter before twelve they heard her ring. She directed the woman, who answered her summons, to say to me, that I should come there as soon as the clock struck twelve.

Notwithstanding I anxiously expected this invitation, it caused me great surprise. In part from the extraordinary fact itself, and in part from fright, I was as much perplexed as embarrassed. I went many times before my glass, in order to see if I really had a face made to awaken horror. But—it struck twelve. With a beating heart, I went and heard myself announced to Hortensia. I was admitted.

She sat negligently on the sofa; her beautiful head, shaded with her raven locks, rested on her soft white arm. She reluctantly arose as I entered. With a weak, uncertain voice, and a look which implored her mercy, I declared myself there to hear her commands.

Hortensia did not answer. She came slowly and thoughtfully toward me, as if she sought for words. At last she remained standing before me, threw a contemptuous side look at me, and said:—

"Mr. Faust, it seems to me that it is I who should entreat, in order to induce you to leave the house and train of my father."

"Countess," said I, and the manly pride was a little roused in me, "I have forced myself neither on you nor the count. You yourself know on what grounds your father entreated me to remain in his company. I did so unwillingly; but the heartfelt kindness of the count, and the hope of being useful to you, prevents my obeying your expressed command, however it may distress me to displease you."

She turned her back on me, and played with a little pair of scissors near a rose-bush at the window. Suddenly she cut the last-blown rose off—it was beautiful, although simple—she reached it to me, and said, "Take the best which I have now at hand: I give it to you as a reward for having hitherto avoided me. Never come again!"

She spoke this so quickly, and with such visible embarrassment, that I scarcely understood it; she then threw herself again on the sofa, and as I wished to answer, she motioned to me hastily, with her face turned, to go away. I obeyed.

Even at the moment I left her, I had already forgotten all injuries. I flew to my room. Not the angry, but only the suffering Hortensia, in all her tender innocence swept before me. The rose came from her hand like a jewel, whose infinite worth all the crowns in the world could not outweigh. I pressed the flower to my lips—I lamented its perishable nature. I thought how

I should most securely preserve it—to me the most precious of all my possessions. I opened it carefully, and dried it between the leaves of a book, then had it inclosed between two round crystal glasses, surrounded with a gold band, so that I could wear it like an amulet to a gold chain round my neck.

THE BILL OF EXCHANGE.

In the mean time this event was the cause of much discomfort to me. Hortensia's hate of me spoke out more decidedly than ever. Her father, entirely too gentle, made my defense in vain. His conviction that I was an honest man, as well as my usefulness in the common affairs of his house, and his firm belief that I was indispensable to the saving of his daughter, were sufficient to render him for a long time deaf to all the whisperings which aimed at my downfall. In a short time, he was the only one in the house that honored me with a friendly word or look. I remarked, that gradually the women, Dr. Walter himself, and at last the lowest servant of the family, kept shyly at a distance, and treated me with a marked coldness. I learnt from the true-hearted Sebald, who remained devoted to me, that my expulsion was aimed at, and that the countess had sworn to turn any one out of her service who dared to have any kind of intercourse with me. Her command was so much the more effectual, as, from the physician and steward to the lowest servant in the house, each one considered himself lucky to be a domestic in so rich a house; and while they only considered me as one of their equals, they envied me my unlimited credit with the count.

Such a situation must of course become unpleasing to me. I lived in Venice, in one of the most brilliant houses, more solitary than in a wilderness, without a friend or familiar acquaintance. I knew my steps and motions were watched; nevertheless I endured it with patience. The noble count suffered no less than myself from Hortensia's caprices. He often sought comfort near me. I was the most eloquent advocate for my beautiful persecutor, who treated me during her transfigurations with as much kindness, I might almost say tenderness, as she vexed me, when out of this state, with the effects of her hatred and pride. It seemed as if she were governed alternately by two inimical demons: the one an angel of light, the other of darkness. At last even the old count began to watch me and became more reserved; the situation was insupportable to me. I had only lately perceived how he was tormented on all sides; how particularly Dr. Walter sought to shake his confidence in me, by many repeated little malicious remarks; and what a deep impression a reproach of Hortensia's once made, when she said: "Have we all made ourselves dependent on this unknown man? They say my life is in his power; well, pay him for his trouble; more he does not merit. But he is also to be a participator in our family secrets. We are, in our most important affairs, in his charge; so that, were I even in health, we could scarcely, without disadvantage, send him away. Who is surety for his secrecy? His apparent disinterestedness, his honorable appearance, will one day cost us much. The Count Hormegg will be the slave of his servant, and a stranger, by his cunning, become the tyrant of us all. This common fellow is not only the confidant of the count, whose race is related to princely houses, but the all-doer and head of the family."

In order still more to revolt the pride of the count, the subordinates appeared to have conspired together to fulfill his commands with a certain reluctance and doubt, as if they were afraid of displeasing me. Some carried this artful boldness so far as to express openly the question, whether the command he gave had also my consent. This acted upon the count so much, little by little, that he became mistrustful of himself, and believed that he had overstepped the limits of prudence.

I remarked it, however much he endeavored to conceal his change of mind. This vexed me. I had never forced myself into a knowledge of his circumstances; he had imparted them to me by degrees, craved my counsel, followed it, and always gained by it. He had voluntarily charged me with the whole care of the receipts and expenditures of his income; it was by me, from the state of the greatest confusion, placed in such clearness, that he confessed he never had such an insight into his household affairs. He was now in a situation to make suitable arrangements both of his money and estates. By my advice he had terminated two old perplexed family lawsuits, whose end was not to be seen, by an amicable agreement, and by this compact gained more immediate advantage than he himself hoped to have won, if he had succeeded in his suit. Many times had he, in the excess of his gratitude of friendship, wished to force considerable presents on me, but I had always refused them.

For some weeks I endured to be hated and mistaken by all. My pride at last revolted. I longed to get out of this unpleasant situation, to which no one any longer tried to reconcile me. Hortensia, even she, who was the author of all the mischief, was the only one who, in her transfigurations, warned me incessantly not to regard any thing she might undertake against me in her waking hours. She would despise herself for it; she coaxed me with the most flattering speeches, as if she would in these moments requite me for all the torments which she immediately after, with redoubled eagerness, would cause me.

Count Hormegg had called me one afternoon to his cabinet. He desired me to give him the steward's book, and also a bill of exchange, lately received, for two thousand louis-d'ors, which sum, he said, he wished to place in the Bank of Venice, since his residence in Italy would be continued for the year. I took the opportunity to beg him to confide to another the whole of the business with which he had charged me, since I was determined, so soon as the health of the countess would permit, to leave his house and Venice. Notwithstanding he remarked the irritability with which I spoke, he said nothing, except requesting me not to neglect his daughter and her care; but as to what regarded the other affairs, he would willingly disburden me from them.

This was sufficient. I saw he wished to make me unnecessary to him. I went, out of humor, to my room, and took all the papers, as well those which he had not demanded as those which he had—but I could not find the bill of exchange; I must have mislaid it among some papers. I had a dim recollection that it was inclosed by me in a particular paper, and with some other things put on one side. My search was in vain. The count, hitherto accustomed to see his wishes executed with the greatest promptitude by me, would certainly be surprised that I this time delayed. The next morning he reminded me of it again.

"Probably you have forgotten," said he, "that I asked you yesterday for the steward's book, and the bill of exchange." I promised to give them to him at midday. I looked through the writings, leaf by leaf, in vain. Midday came; I had not found the bewitching bill of exchange. I excused myself with the count, that I must have mislaid a couple of sheets, which hitherto had not happened to me; probably in my anxious hasty search, I had either overlooked some or taken the papers for others, and placed them away. I asked for a delay the next day, since they could not be lost, but only mislaid. The count made, it is true, a discontented face, but yet replied, "There is time enough! Do not hurry yourself."

What time I could spare, I employed in searching. It lasted till night. The following morning I commenced anew. My anxiety increased. I must at last believe that the bill was lost, stolen, or perhaps, in a moment of absence, employed by myself as useless paper. Except my servant, who could neither read nor write, and who never had the key to my sitting-room, no person entered those apartments. The fellow asserted that he never allowed any one to enter while he was cleaning the room, still less had he ever touched a paper.

Except the count, no stranger came to me, since, from my retired life, I had made no acquaintance in Venice. My embarrassment rose to the highest pitch.

THE SINGULAR TREACHERY.

THE same morning, as I went to the countess to remain near her during her transfiguration, and render her, in this state, the accustomed service, I thought I remarked in the countenance of the count a cold seriousness, which spoke more than words. The thought that he suspected my honesty and truth increased my disquiet. I walked before the sleeping Hortensia, and at the same moment it struck me, that perhaps by her wonderful gift of sight, she might inform me where the papers were. It was indeed painful to me to confess, before Dr. Walter and the women, the charge of neglect or disorder.

While I was yet struggling with myself, what I should do, the countess complained of the unsupportable coldness which blew from me toward her, and which would cause her sufferings if it did not change.

"Thou art pained by some disquiet. Thy thoughts, thy will, are not with her," said she.

"Dear countess," replied I, "it is no wonder. Perhaps it is in your power, from your peculiarity of being able to discover what is most concealed, to restore me again my peace. I have lost among my papers a bill of exchange, which belongs to your father."

The Count Hormegg wrinkled his brow. Dr. Walter cried: "I beg you, do not trouble the countess, in this situation, with such things."

I was silent; but Hortensia appeared thoughtful, and said, after some time, "Thou, Emanuel, hast not lost the bill; it was taken from thee! Take this key, open the closet there in the wall. In my jewel casket lies the bill."

She drew out a little golden key, reached it to me, and pointed with her hand to the closet. I hurried there. One of the women, called Elenora, sprang before the closet and wished to prevent the opening of it. "Your lordship," cried she, anxiously, to the count, "will not allow any man to rummage among the effects of the countess." Ere she had yet ended the words, she was with a strong arm pushed away by me; the closet opened, the casket likewise, and behold the bewitched bill of exchange lay there on the top. I went with a face shining with joy to the old count, who was speechless and motionless from astonishment. "Of the rest, I shall have the honor of speaking to you hereafter," said I to the count, and went back with a light heart to Hortensia, to whom I gave back the key.

"How thou art metamorphosed, Emanuel," cried she, with a countenance of delight. "Thou art become a sun—thou floatest in a sea of rays."

The count called to me in violent emotion: "Command the countess, in my name, to say how she came by these papers."

I obeyed. Elenora sank down fainting on a chair. Dr. Walter hurried to her, and was in the act of leading her from the room as Hortensia began to speak.

The count commanded, in an unusually severe tone, silence and quiet. No one dared to move.

"Out of hate, beloved Emanuel, the sick had the bill taken. She foresaw, maliciously, the difficulty, and hoped to induce thy flight. But it would not have happened, since Sebald stood in a corner of the corridor, while Dr. Walter, with a double key, went in thy chamber, took the bill, which thou hadst put in some letters from Hungary, and gave it on going out to Elenora. Sebald would have betrayed it all, so soon as it was known that some papers of importance had been lost. Dr. Walter, who had seen the bill of exchange with thee, made the proposition to the sick to purloin it. Elenora offered her assistance. The sick herself encouraged them to do so, and could scarcely wait for the time when the papers could be brought to her."

During these words, Dr. Walter stood quite beside himself, leaning on Elenora's chair; his countenance betrayed uneasiness; and, shrugging his shoulders, he looked toward the count, and said: "From this, one may learn that the gracious countess may also speak erroneously. Wait for her awaking, and she will explain herself better how the papers came into her hands."

The count made no answer, but calling to a servant, ordered him to bring old Sebald. When he came, he was asked whether he had ever seen Dr. Walter during my absence go into my room.

"Whether in the absence of Mr. Faust, I know not, but it may well have been so last Sunday evening, since he at least unlocked the door. Miss Ellen must know better than I, as she remained standing on the stairs until the doctor came back and gave her some notes, whereupon they talked softly together, and then separated."

Sebald was now permitted to go; and the doctor, with the half-fainting Elenora, were obliged, on a motion from the count, to depart. Hortensia appeared more animated than ever. "Fear thee not from the hatred of the sick," said she many times; "she will watch over thee like thy guardian angel."

The consequence of this memorable morning was, that Dr. Walter, as well as Elenora, with two other servants, were on that same day dismissed by the count, and sent from the house.

To me, on the contrary, the count came and begged my pardon, not only on account of his daughter's fault, but also for his own weakness, in listening to the malicious whisperings against me, and half crediting them. He embraced me and called me his friend, the only one which he had in the world, and to whom he could open himself with unlimited confidence. He conjured me not to forsake his daughter and himself.

"I know," said he, "what you suffer; and what sacrifices you make on our account. But trust with confidence, to my gratitude as long as I live. Should the countess ever be restored to perfect health, you will certainly be better pleased with us than hitherto. Look at me! Is there on earth a more desolate, unfortunate man than myself? Nothing but hope supports me. And all my hopes rest on your goodness, and the continuance of your patience. What have I already gone through? What must I yet endure? The extraordinary state of my daughter often almost deprives me of reason. I know not if I live, or if destiny has not made me the instrument of a fairy tale."

The distress of the good count moved me. I reconciled myself to him, and even to my situation, which was by no means enticing. On the contrary, the ignoble disposition of the countess much weakened the enthusiasm in which I had hitherto lived for her.

FRAGMENTS FROM HORTENSIA'S CONVERSATIONS.

THROUGH the kind and attentive care of the count, it happened that I now never saw Hortensia when awake, for which I felt little inclination. I even did not learn how she thought or spoke of me, though I could easily imagine it. In the house strict order reigned. The count had resumed his authority. No one ventured again to make a party with Hortensia against either of us, since it was known that she would become the accuser of herself and confederates.

Thus I saw the extraordinary beauty only in those moments when she, raised above herself, appeared to be a being of another world. But these moments belonged to the most solemn, often to the most moving of my life. The inexpressible charm of Hortensia's person was heightened by an expression of tender innocence and angelic enthusiasm. The strictest modesty was observed in her appearance. Only truth and goodness were on her lips; and notwithstanding her eyes were closed—in which otherwise, her feelings were most clearly expressed—yet one read the slightest emotion, by the fine play of her countenance, as well as in the varied tones of her voice.

What she spoke of the past, present, or future, so far as the keen prophetic vision of her spirit reached, excited our astonishment; sometimes from the peculiarity of her views; sometimes from their incomprehensibility.

She could give us no information of the *how*, though she sometimes endeavored and sought by long reflection to do so. She knew by actual sight, as she said, all the interior parts of her body, the position of the superior and inferior intestines, of the bony structures, of the ramifications of the muscles and nerves; she could see the same in me, or any one to whom I only gave my hand. Though she was a highly educated young lady, yet she had no knowledge, or only the most confused and superficial, of the structure of the human frame. I mentioned the names of many things which she saw and described exactly; she, on the contrary, corrected my ideas when they were not accurate.

Her revelations upon the nature of our life, interested me most, since to me her absolutely inexplicable state, led me most frequently to question her on it. I wrote down each time after leaving her, the substance of her answers, although I must omit much which she gave in expressions and images not sufficiently intelligible.

I will not mention here all that she spoke at different times, but will only select and place in a better connection what she revealed concerning things which excited my sympathy or curiosity.

As I once remarked, that she lost much in not being

able to recollect in her natural and waking state, what she, during the short time of her transfiguration, thought, saw, and spoke, she replied :—

"She loses nothing, since the earthly waking is only one part of her life, that terminates in certain single ends; it is only circumscribed outward life. But in the true, unlimited, interior, pure life, she is as conscious of what has passed in her waking state.

"The internal, pure life and consciousness continues in every person unbroken, even in the deepest fainting, as in the deepest sleep, which is only a fainting of another kind and from other causes. During sleep, as in a fainting fit, the soul withdraws its activity from the instruments of the senses back to the spirit. One is also then conscious to himself, when without, he appears unconscious, because the lifeless senses are silent.

"When thou art suddenly aroused from a deep sleep, on waking, a dark remembrance will sweep before thee, as if thou hadst thought of something before awaking, or as thou thinkest, dreamt, though thou knowest not what it is. The sleep-walker lies in the fast sleep of the outward senses; he hears and sees, not with eyes and ears; nevertheless, he is not only in the utmost perfection conscious of himself, and knows exactly what he thinks, speaks, and undertakes, but he remembers also every thing of his outward waking, and knows even the place where he, waking, laid his pen.

"The sick knows very well that she now appears to thee perfect; but in fact, the powers of her mind and soul are not more exalted or commanding than formerly, though less bound or crippled by the restraints of the outward senses. An excellent workman works with imperfect tools more imperfectly than he should do. Even the most fluent human speech is tedious and difficult, since it neither can represent all the peculiarities of the thoughts and feelings, nor the rapid changes and course of the ideas, but only single parts of the onflowing current of thought.

"In the purer life, although the tools of the senses rest, there is a more complete and exact remembrance of the past, than in the earthly waking. Since at the earthly waking, the ALL streams through the open doors of perception too powerful—almost stunning. Therefore, Emanuel, thou knowest when we wish, during our earthly waking, deeply and seriously to think, we seek solitude and quiet, and withdraw ourselves, as it were, from without, and neither see nor hear.

"The more the mind can be removed from outward life, the nearer it approaches to its purer state; the more it is separated from the activity of the senses, the more clear and certain it thinks. We know that some of the most remarkable discoveries have been made in the state betwixt sleeping and waking, when the outward doors were half-closed, and spiritual life remained undisturbed by foreign intermixture.

"Sleep is not to be regarded as the interruption of the perfect conscious life; but the earthly waking is to be regarded as such an interruption, or rather as a limitation of it. Since by earthly waking the soul's activity is directed, as it were, to fixed paths and limits, and on the other side, the attractions of the outer world influence it so powerfully, that the remembrance of the pure life disappears; still more so, since on the earthly waking the attention of the spirit itself is distracted, and is attracted to the guarding of the body in all its single parts. Yes, Emanuel, sleep is probably the full awaking of the spirit; the earthly waking, as it were, a slumber or stunning of the spirit. The earthly sleep is a spiritual sunset for the outer world, but a clear sun rise in the inner world.

"Yet, even amid the distractions of the earthly waking, we perceive, occasionally, glimpses of another life we have passed through, though we do not always know how to express it. So one sees from high mountains, on a summer night, the late or early red of a sun, and of a day that has departed, which is the portion of other countries on the globe. Often with wonderful quickness, in extraordinary accidents, thoughts and resolutions occur to men necessary to their safety, without foregone considerations—without reflection. We know not from whence they spring. Connection fails between our previous ideas and this sudden and commanding one. Men usually say it is as if a good spirit, or a divinity, had inspired me with the thought. At other times, we see and hear in our daily life something that we seem already to have seen or heard; and yet we can not fathom how, or when, or where, and we imagine it to be a singular repetition, or some resemblance to a dream.

"It is not extraordinary, Emanuel, that our conscious being never ends; that is, that whether sleeping or waking, it ever advances; since it is so, how can it cease? But wonderful is the change—the ebb and flow—the hither and thither turning of life from the inner to the outward, and from the outward to the inner.

"The spirit, clothed by the soul, as the sun is by its

rays, flying through the firmament of the world, can exist as well without a body, as the sun without foreign worlds. But the worlds without the sun are dead—loosened from their path; the body without the soul is dust.

"The body has its own life, as every plant lives; though the earthly powers of life must first be awakened through the spirit. These rule and move themselves according to their own laws, independent of the soul. Without our will and knowledge, without the will and knowledge of the body, it grows, digests its nourishment, makes the blood flow, and changes in manifold ways its inheritance. It inhales and exhales; it evaporates and draws invisible nourishment for its wants from the atmosphere. But, like other plants, it is dependent upon the outward things, by which it nourishes itself. Its condition changes with night and day, like the condition of every flower; it raises or relaxes itself; its powers of life consume themselves like an invisible fire, which demands fresh nourishment.

"Only by a sufficient supply of the vegetable powers of life, is the body fitted for the soul to enter into a close union with it, otherwise it is a heterogeneous substance. If its powers become too much consumed or exhausted, the spiritual life draws itself back from the outward to the interior part; that we call *sleep*—an interruption of the activity of the senses. The soul returns again into union with the outer parts, so soon as the vegetative department has recruited its powers. It is not the soul which becomes fatigued or exhausted, but the body; the soul is not strengthened by rest, but the body. So there is a constant ebb and flood, an out-streaming and retreating of the spiritual essence in us, perhaps conformable to the changes of day and night.

"The greater part of our existence we watch outwardly; we should do so, since the body was given to us on earth, on condition of our activity. The body and its inclinations give our activity a determined direction. There is something great and wonderful in this economy of God.

"With age the body loses the faculty of re-establishing its powers of life in a sufficient degree to sustain in all its parts its intimate union with the soul. The instrument, formerly ductile and supple, stiffens and becomes useless to the spirit. The soul withdraws itself again into the interior. To the spirit remains all its inward activity, even till all union with the body is impeded; *this arrives only through the destroying* power of age or sickness. The loosening of the soul from the body is the restoration of the first. It frequently announces itself by predictions at the hour of death and other prophecies.

"The more healthy the body, so much the more is the soul entirely united with all parts of the body; and the more closely it is bound to it, so much the less capable it is of predicting; it is then, as if the soul, in extraordinary moments of enthusiasm, unshackled, as it were, sees into futurity.

"The retreat of the soul from the outer world, produces a peculiar state of the human substance. It is the dream. To fall into a slumber, produces the last attraction of the senses, and the first activity of the free interior life. By the waking, the last ray of the inner world mixes itself with the first light of the outward world. It is difficult to disentangle what particularly appertains to the one or the other; but it is always instructive to observe dreams. Since the spirit, even in its inner activity, occupies itself with that which attracted it in the outward life, one can expound the movements of the sleep-walker. Though, when the outward senses of the sleep-walker are again unlocked, he can remember nothing of what he did during his extraordinary state, yet it can return to him again in dreams. So do they bring from the inner world much knowledge to the outer. Dream is the natural mediator, the bridge between the outward and inner life."

CHANGES.

These were perhaps the most remarkable ideas which she uttered, either spontaneously or excited by questions; it is true, not in the order in which they are here placed, but as regards the expressions, very little different from them. Much that she said, it was impossible for me to give again, since, with the connection of the conversation, it lost much of the delicacy of its meaning; much remained wholly unintelligible to me.

It was also my fault that I neglected leading her back at the right time upon many things that remained obscure to me. I soon remarked, that she did not in all her hours of transfiguration discern and speak with equal clearness—that she gradually liked less to converse on these subjects, and at last discontinued them entirely, and spoke almost only of household affairs or the state of her health. This she constantly affirmed was improving, though for a long time we could perceive no traces of it. She continued, as formerly, to indicate to us what she must eat and drink when awake, and what would be beneficial and what prejudicial to her. She showed an aversion to almost all drugs, but, on the contrary, desired daily an ice-cold bath, and, at last, sea-water baths. As the spring approached, her transfigurations became shorter.

I will by no means describe here the history of Hortensia's illness, but will in a few words state, that in seven months after my arrival she was so far restored, that she could not only receive the visits of strangers, but also return them, and could even go to church, theater, and balls, though only for a few hours at a time. The count was beside himself with joy. He loaded his daughter with presents, and formed around her a various and costly circle of amusements. Connected with the first houses of Venice, or courted by them, either on account of his wealth or the beauty of his daughter, it could not fail that every day in the week was metamorphosed into a festival.

He had hitherto in fact, lived like a hermit, depressed by Hortensia's misfortune, and kept in a constantly constrained and anxious state by the miracles connected with her illness. Therefore, he had become confined to an intercourse with me. Besides, from want of firmness of mind, and through my influence over Hortensia's life, and by a kind of superstitious respect for my person, he allowed himself to be willingly pleased with what I directed. He yielded to me, if I may so call it, a kind of government over himself, and obeyed my wishes with a degree of submission which was unpleasant to myself, though I never abused it.

Now that Hortensia's recovery restored to him a mind free from care, and the long-denied enjoyment of brilliant pleasures, his deportment toward me changed. It is true, I continued to hold the direction over his house and family affairs, which he had formerly given up to me, either from blind confidence or for his convenience, but he wished that I should conduct his affairs under some name in his service. As I firmly refused to place myself in his pay, and remained true to the conditions under which I had first engaged with him, he appeared to make a virtue of necessity. He introduced me to the Venetians as his friend; yet his pride not permitting his friend to be a mere citizen, he gave me out generally as being from one of the purest and best of the German noble families. I opposed at first this falsehood, but was obliged to yield to the entreaties of his weakness. Thus I entered into the Venetian circles, and was received everywhere. It is true, the count continued to be my friend, though not entirely as formerly, since I was no longer his only one. We no longer, as before, lived exclusively for and with one another.

Yet more remarkable was the metamorphose in Hortensia on her convalescence. In her transfigurations, she was, as ever, all goodness; but the old hate and aversion, during the remaining part of the day, appeared gradually to disappear. Either more obedient to the admonitions of her father, or from her own feelings of gratitude, she controlled herself so as not to wound me, either by word or look. It was permitted me, from time to time, though only for a few moments, to pay my most respectful homage to her, as a guest of the house, as a friend of the count, and as an actual physician.

I could even at last, without danger of exciting an outbreak of her anger, be in the society where she was. Indeed, this effort or habit proceeded so far that she could at last, with indifference, suffer me to dine at table, when the count was alone or had guests. But even then I always saw her pride through her manners, as she looked down upon me, and except what decency and common politeness demanded, I never received a single word from her.

For myself, my life was truly only half gay, though from my greater freedom I felt more comfortable. The amusements into which I was drawn diverted me, without increasing my contentment. In the midst of bustle, I often longed for solitude, which was more congenial to my nature. It was my invariable determination, so soon as the cure of the countess was perfected, to regain my former liberty. I longed with eagerness the arrival of that moment, since I felt too deeply that the passion with which Hortensia's beauty inspired me would become my misfortune. I had struggled against it, and Hortensia's pride and hatred for me rendered the struggle more easy. To her feelings of high noble birth, I opposed my citizen feelings—to her malicious persecutions, the consciousness of my innocence and her ingratitude. If there were moments when the charms of her person affected me—who could remain insensible to so many? —there were many more in which her offensive behavior entirely disgusted me, and caused my heart a bitterness which bordered on aversion. Her indifference toward me was as strong a proof of the want of grateful feelings in her disposition, as her former aversion. At last I avoided Hortensia more assiduously than she did me. Could she have regarded me with indifference, she must have discovered in my whole behavior how great was my scorn of her.

Thus, during Hortensia's gradual recovery, had the situations between us all, unremarked and singularly enough, wholly changed. I had no ardent wish, except soon to be freed from an engagement which gave me but little joy, and no greater consolation than the moment when Hortensia's perfect health would render my presence unnecessary.

PRINCE CHARLES.

Among those who in Venice connected themselves most intimately with us, was a rich young man, who, descended from one of the noblest Italian families, bore the title of prince. I shall call him Charles. He was of a pleasing figure, with fine manners, intellectual, quick, and prepossessing. The nobility of his features, as well as the fiery glance of his eye, betrayed an irritable temperament. He lived at an immense expense, and was more vain than proud. He served for some time in the French army. Tired of that, he was upon the point of visiting the most distinguished European cities and courts. The accidental acquaintance which he made with Count Hormegg detained him longer in

Venice than he at first intended; for he had seen Hortensia, and joined himself to her crowd of admirers. In pursuit of her, he soon appeared to forget every thing else. His rank, his fortune, his numerous and brilliant retinue, and his pleasing exterior, flattered Hortensia's pride and self-love. Without distinguishing him from the others by any particular favor, she yet liked to see him near her. A single confidential, friendly look was sufficient to excite in him the boldest hopes.

The old Count Hormegg, no less flattered by the prince's addresses, met them half-way, showed him a preference over all, and soon changed a mere acquaintance into a close intimacy. I doubted not for a moment that the count had secretly chosen the prince for his son-in-law. Nothing but Hortensia's indisposition, and a fear of her humors, appeared to prevent both the father and lover from more open approaches.

The prince had heard, in conversations with the count, of Hortensia's transfigurations. He burnt with a desire to see her in this extraordinary state; and the countess, who well knew that this state was far from being disadvantageous to her, gave him, what she had hitherto denied to every stranger, permission to be present at one of them.

He came one afternoon, when we knew Hortensia would sink into this remarkable sleep, as she always announced it in the preceding one. I can not deny that I felt a touch of jealousy as the prince entered the room. Hitherto, I had been the happy one to whom the countess, by preference in her miraculous glorifications, had turned her exterior graces and intellectual beauty.

Charles approached lightly over the soft carpet, moving on tiptoe. He believed that she really slumbered, as her eyes were closed. Timidity and delight were expressed in his features as he gazed on the charming figure, which, in her whole appearance, discovered something extraordinary.

Hortensia at length began to speak. She conversed with me in her usual affectionate manner. I was again, as ever, her Emanuel, who governed her thoughts, will, and whole being; a language which sounded very unpleasing to the prince, and which, to me, was never very flattering. Hortensia, however, began to appear more restless and anxious. She asserted, several times that she felt pains, though she could not tell wherefore. I motioned to the prince that he should reach me his hand. Scarcely had he done so than Hortensia, shuddering violently, cried out gloomily, "How cold! Away with that goat there! He kills me!" She was seized with convulsions, which she had not had for a long time. Charles was obliged instantly to leave the room. He was quite beside himself with terror. After some time Hortensia recovered from her cramps. "Never bring that impure creature to me again," said she.

This accident, which even alarmed me, produced unpleasant consequences. The prince regarded me from this moment as his rival, and conceived a great hatred toward me. The count, who allowed himself to be entirely governed by him, appeared to become suspicious of Hortensia's feelings. The mere thought that the countess might acquire an inclination for me, was insupportable to his pride. Both the prince and count united themselves firmly together; kept me at a greater distance from the countess, except during the time of her miraculous sleeps; agreed upon the marriage, and the count opened the wishes of the prince to his daughter. She, although flattered by the attentions of the prince, demanded permission to reserve her declaration till the complete restoration of her health. Charles, in the mean while, was generally regarded as the betrothed of the countess. He was her constant attendant, and she the queen of all his *fêtes*.

I very soon discovered that I began to be in the way—that with Hortensia's recovery I had sunk into my original nothingness. My former discontent returned, and nothing made my situation supportable but that Hortensia, not only in her transfigurations, but soon out of them, did me justice. Not only was her old aversion toward me changed into indifference, but in the same proportion as her bodily health rebloomed, this indifference changed into an attentive, forbearing respect; to an affable friendliness, such as one is accustomed to from the higher to the lower, or toward persons whom one sees daily, who belong to the household, and to whom one feels indebted for the services they perform. She treated me as if I were really her physician—liked to ask my advice, my permission, when it concerned any enjoyment or pleasure; fulfilled punctually my directions, and could command herself to leave the dance so soon as the hour was passed which I had fixed for her. It occurred to me, sometimes, as if the authority of my will had in part passed over to her waking, since it began to act more weakly over her soul during her transfigurations.

THE DREAMS.

Hortensia's pride, obstinacy, and humor also passed gradually away from her like bad spirits. In her disposition, almost as lovely as during her trance, she enchained not less by her outward charms than by her affection, humility, and grateful kindness.

All this made my misfortune. How could I, a daily witness of so many perfections, remain indifferent? I wished most earnestly that she might, as formerly, despise, offend, and persecute me, that I might the more easily separate from her, and could be able to despise her in return. But that was now impossible. I again adored her. Silently and without hope, I pined away in my passion. I knew, by anticipation, that my future separation from her would take me to the grave. What made my situation worse, was a dream, which I from time to time had of her, and always in the same or similar form. Sometimes I was sitting in a strange room—sometimes on the sea-shore—sometimes in a cave under over-hanging rocks—sometimes on the moss-covered trunk of an oak, in a great solitude, and with a deeply agitated soul; then came Hortensia, and looking upon me with the kindest compassion, said, "Wherefore so melancholy, dear Faust?" and thereupon each time I awoke, and the tone in which she spoke thrilled through me. This tone was echoed to me the whole day. I heard it in the bustle of the city, the crowd of company, in the song of the gondoliers, at the opera, everywhere. Some nights when I had this dream, I waked as soon as Hortensia had opened her mouth to make the usual question, and then imagined that I actually heard the voice without me.

Dreams formerly in the world used to be dreams; but in the strange circle into which I was placed by my destiny, even dreams had an unusual character.

I was one day regulating some accounts in the count's room, and had laid some letters before him for his signature. He was called to receive some of the Venetian nobility, who had come to visit him. Believing he would soon return, I threw myself upon a chair at the window, and sank into a deep melancholy. Soon I heard footsteps, and the countess, who sought her father, stood near me. I was much startled, without knowing wherefore, and respectfully arose.

"Why so sad, dear Faust?" said Hortensia, with her own peculiar loveliness, spiritualizing my whole being, and with the same voice, whose tones sounded so movingly in my dreams. She then laughed, as if surprised at her own question, or as astonished at herself; rubbed thoughtfully her brow, and said, after a while, "What is this? I fancy that it has occurred before. It is extraordinary. I have once before found you exactly as at this moment, and even so questioned you. Is not this singular?"

"Not more singular than I have experienced," said I, "since not once, but many times, have I dreamt that you discovered me, and asked in the same words the same questions which you have now had the goodness to do."

The count came in and interrupted our short conversation. But this, apparently in itself unimportant incident, caused me much reflection: nevertheless, my researches were in vain to divine how the play of the imagination could mingle with the reality. She had dreamt the same as myself, and the dream had been accomplished in life.

These enchantments were yet far from being at an end.

Five days after this event, the god of sleep mimicked before me that I was invited to a great assembly. It was a great *fêtes* dance. The music made me melancholy, and I remained a solitary spectator. Hortensia suddenly came to me from the crowd of dancers, pressed secretly and fervently my hand, and whispered, "Be gay, Faust, or else I can not be so!" She then gave me a look of compassionate tenderness, and was again lost in the tumult.

The Count Hornegg attended a pleasure party on that day, at the country-seat of a Venetian. I accompanied him. On the way he told me that the countess would also be there. When we arrived, we found a large company—in the evening there were magnificent fireworks, and then dancing. The prince opened the ball with Hortensia; it was like the stroke of a dagger to me, as I looked at them. I lost all inclination to participate in the ball. In order to forget myself, I chose a partner, and mixed with the floating beautiful troop. But it seemed to me that I had lead fastened to my feet, and I congratulated myself when I was able to slip out from the crowd. Leaning at a door, I gazed on the dancers, not at them, but only at Hortensia, who moved there like a goddess.

I thought of the dream of the past night; in the same moment a dance broke up, and, glowing with joy, yet timidly, Hortensia approached me, pressed secretly and lightly my hand, and whispered, "Dear Faust, be gay, that I also may be so!" She spoke this so compassionately, so kindly—with a look from her eyes—a look—I lost sense and speech. When I recovered myself, Hortensia had again disappeared. She swept again in the train of dancers, but her eyes constantly sought only me; her looks constantly hung on me. It was as if she had the humor, by her attention, to deprive me of the residue of my reason. The couples separated at the end of the dance, and I left my place with the view of seeking another situation in the room, to convince myself whether I had been deceived, and whether the looks of the countess would seek me there.

Already fresh couples assembled for a new dance, as I wandered over to the seats of the ladies. One of them arose at the moment that I approached her—it was the countess. Her arm was in mine—we joined the circle. I trembled and knew not how it had occurred, since I never could have had the boldness to ask Hortensia to dance, and yet, it appeared to me as if I had done so in my absence of mind. She was unembarrassed—scarcely observed my confusion—and her brilliant glances roved over the splendid crowd. One moment and the music began. I seemed to be unbound from all that was earthly! spiritualized I swept on the waves of sound. I knew not what was passing around me—knew not that we chained the attention of all the spectators.

What regarded I the admiration of the world? At the end of the third dance I led the countess to a seat, that she might rest herself. Whisperingly I stammered my thanks—she bowed, with mere friendly politeness, as to the greatest stranger, and I drew back among the spectators.

The prince, as well as the count, had seen me dancing with Hortensia, and had heard the general whisper of applause. The prince burnt with jealousy—he did not even conceal it from Hortensia. The count was, offended at my boldness in asking his daughter to dance, and reproached her the next day for so thoughtlessly forgetting her rank. Both maintained, like all the world, that her dancing had been more full of soul, more impassioned. Neither the count nor the prince doubted but that I had inspired the countess with an unworthy inclination for myself. I soon perceived, notwithstanding their efforts to conceal it, that I was an object of hate and fear to them both. I was very seldom, and at last not at all, taken into the society where Hortensia moved. I was, however, silent.

Both gentlemen indulged, nevertheless, too much anxiety on this account. The countess, certainly, did not deny that she felt a sense of gratitude toward me, but any other feeling was a reproach, at which she revolted. She confessed that she esteemed me, but that it was all the same to her whether I danced in Venice or Constantinople.

"You are at liberty to dismiss him," said she to her father, "so soon as my cure is perfected."

THE AMULET.

THE count and Charles awaited this moment in pain, to get rid of me, and to bring on the marriage of

Hortensia. Hortensia looked for it with impatience, in order to rejoice over her own recovery, and at the same time to quiet the suspicions of her father. I also expected it with no less desire. It was only far from Hortensia, and amid new scenes and other occupations, that I could hope to heal my mind. I felt myself unhappy.

The countess one day announced, not unexpectedly, as she lay in her strange sleep, the near approach of her re-establishment.

"In the warm baths of Battaglia," said she, "she will entirely lose the gift of being entranced. Take her there. Her cure is no longer distant. Every morning, immediately on waking, one bath. After the tenth, Emanuel, she separates from thee. She sees thee never again, if such is thy will; but leave her a token of thy remembrance. She can not be healthy without it. For a long time, thou wearest in thy breast a dried rose, between glasses, and set in gold. So long as she wears this, inclosed in silk, immediately about the region of the heart, she will not again fall into her cramps. Neither later nor earlier than the seventh hour after receiving the thirteenth bath, yield it to her. Wear it constantly till then. She is then healthy."

She repeated this desire frequently, and with singular anxiety; she laid particular stress upon the hour when I should deliver up to her my only jewel, and of whose existence she had never heard.

"Do you really wear any such thing?" asked the count, astonished, and highly delighted on account of the announced restoration of health to his daughter.

As I answered, he asked further, if I laid any particular value upon the possession of this trifle. I assured him the highest; that I would rather die than to have it taken from me—nevertheless, for the safety of the countess, I would sacrifice it.

"Probably a remembrance from some beloved hand?" observed the count, laughing, and, in an inquiring manner, to whom it seemed a good opportunity to learn whether my heart had already been bestowed.

"It comes," I replied, "from a person who is every thing to me."

The count was as much moved by my generosity as contented that I had resolved to make the sacrifice on which Hortensia's continued health depended, and, forgetting his secret grudge, embraced me,—a circumstance which had not happened for a long time.

"You make me your greatest debtor," said he.

He was most urgent to relate to Hortensia, as soon as I had gone, on her waking, what she desired in her trance; he, moreover, did not conceal from her his conversation with me on the subject of the amulet, which had so great a value for me, since it was the remembrance of a person that I loved above all. He laid great stress on this, as his suspicion still remained, and, in case Hortensia really felt any inclination for me, to destroy it, by the discovery that I, since a long time, had sighed in the chains of another beauty. Hortensia listened to it all with such innocent unembarrassment, and so sincerely congratulated herself upon her early recovery, that the count perceived he had done injustice to the heart of his daughter by his suspicions. In the joy of his heart he was eager to confess to me his conversation with his daughter, and immediately to mention to the prince all that had passed. From that hour, I remarked, both in the manner of the count and prince something unconstrained, kind, and obliging. They kept me no longer, with their former anxiety, at a distance from Hortensia; but treated me with the attention and forbearance due to a benefactor, to whom they were indebted for the happiness of their whole life. Arrangements were immediately made for our journey to the baths of Battaglia. We left Venice on a beautiful summer morning. The prince had gone before, in order to prepare every thing for his intended bride.

Through the pleasant plains of Padua we approached the mountains, at the foot of which lay the healing spring. On the way the countess often liked to walk; then I must always be her conductor. Her cordiality charmed as much as her tender sense of the noble in the human character, and of the beautiful in nature. "I could be very happy," she often said, "if I could pass my days in any one of these beautiful Italian regions, amid the simple occupations of domestic life. The amusements of the city leave the feelings vacant—they are more stunning than pleasing. How happy I could be if I might live simply, unprovoked by the miseries of the palace, where one vexes one's self about nothing; sufficiently rich to make others happy, and in my own creations to find the source of my happiness! Yet one must not desire every thing."

More than once, and in the presence of her father, she spoke of her great obligations to me, as the preserver of her life. "If I only knew how to repay it," said she. "I have for a long time racked my head to discover something right pleasing to you. You must, indeed, permit my father to place you in a situation which will enable you to live quite independent of others. But that is the least. I need for myself some other satisfaction."

At other times, and frequently, she brought the conversation to my resolution of leaving them as soon as she recovered. "We shall be sorry to lose you," said she, good-naturedly: "we shall lament your loss, as the loss of a true friend and benefactor. We will not, however, by our entreaties for you to remain with us, render your resolution more difficult. Your heart calls you elsewhere," added she, with an arch smile, as if initiated in the secrets of my breast. "If you are happy, there is nothing else for you to wish for; and I do not doubt that love will make you happy. Do not, however, therefore forget us, but send us news from time to time of your health."

What I felt at such expressions, could be as little uttered as that I should repeat what I was usually in the habit of replying. My answers were full of acknowledgments and cold politeness; for respect forbade my betraying my heart. Nevertheless, there were moments when the strength of my feelings mastered me, and I said more than I wished. When I said something more than mere flattery, Hortensia looked at me with the clear bright look of innocence, as if she did not comprehend or understand me. I was convinced that Hortensia felt a grateful esteem for me, and wished me to be happy and content, without, on that account, giving me a secret preference over any other mortal. She had joined me in the dance at the ball, from mere good nature, and to give me pleasure. She herself confessed, that she had always expected me to ask her. Ah! how my passion had created presumptuous hopes from it! Presumptuous hopes, indeed; since had Hortensia, in reality, felt more than mere common good-will toward me, of what service would it have been to me? I should only have become more miserable by her partiality.

While the flame silently devoured me, in her breast was a pure heaven, full of repose. While I could have sunk at her feet, and confessed what she was to me, she wandered near me without the slightest suspicion of my feelings, and endeavored to dissipate my seriousness by pleasantry.

THE DISENCHANTMENT.

By the arrangements of the prince, rooms were provided for us in the castle of the Marquisa d'Este. This castle, situated on a hill near the village, offered, with the greatest comfort, the most lovely distant prospect and rich shaded walks in the neighborhood. But we were obliged to resort to the town for the baths—therefore a house was arranged in that place for the countess, where she passed the mornings as long as she bathed.

Her trance in Battaglia, after the first bath, was very short and indistinct. She spoke but seldom, did not once answer, and appeared to enjoy quite a natural sleep. She spoke after the seventh bath, and commanded, that after the tenth she should no longer remain in that house. It is true, she once more fell asleep after the tenth bath, though she said nothing more than "Emanuel, I see thee no more!" These were the last words she spoke in her transfigurations.

Since then she had, indeed, for some days, an unnaturally sound sleep, but without the power of speech in it.

At last arrived the day of her thirteenth bath. Until now, all that she had commanded or predicted in her transfigured hours, had been most punctually fulfilled. Now was the last to be done. The count and prince came to me early in the morning, in order to remind me of the speedy delivery of my amulet. I must show it to them. They did not leave me for a moment the whole morning, as if, that now being so near the long-desired goal, they had suddenly become mistrustful, and feared I might, as regarded the sacrifice, change my mind; or that the relic might accidentally be lost. The minutes were counted as soon as the news came that the countess was in the bath. When she had reposed some hours after her bath, she was conducted by us to the castle. She was uncommonly gay, almost mischievous. Having been told that she was to receive a present from me in the seventh hour, which she must wear all her life, she was delighted as a child at a gift, and teazed me, jestingly, with the faithlessness I committed toward my chosen one, whose present I gave to another.

It struck twelve! The seventh hour had arrived. We were in the bright garden saloon. The count, the prince, and the women of the countess were present.

"Delay no longer," cried the count, "the moment which is to be the last of Hortensia's sufferings and the first of my happiness."

I drew the dear medallion from my breast, where I had had carried it so long, and loosening the golden chain from my neck, pressed, not without a sorrowful feeling, a kiss upon the glass, and delivered it to the countess.

Hortensia took it, and as her look fell on the dried rose, a sudden and fiery red spread over her face. She bowed gently toward me, as if she would thank me—but in her features one discovered a surprise or confusion, which she appeared to endeavor to conceal. She stammered some words, and then suddenly withdrew with her women. The count and prince were all gratitude toward me. They had arranged for the evening a little festival at the castle, to which some noble families from Este and Rovigo were invited.

In the mean time we expected long, and in vain, the reappearance of the countess. After an hour we learnt, that as soon as she had put on the medallion, she had fallen into a sweet and profound sleep. Two, three, four hours passed—the invited guests had assembled, but Hortensia did not awake. The count in great disquiet ventured to go himself to her bed. As he found her in a deep and quiet slumber, he feared to disturb her. The *fête* passed over without Hortensia's presence—though, without her, half the pleasure was wanting. Hortensia still slept as they separated about midnight. And even the following morning she was still in the same sound sleep. No noise affected her. The count was in great agony. My uneasiness was no less. A physician was called, who assured us that the countess slept a sound and refreshing sleep—both her color and pulse announced the most perfect health. Midday and evening came—yet Hortensia did not awake! The repeated assurances of the physician that the countess was manifestly in perfect health, were necessary to quiet us. The night came and passed. The next morning rejoicing echoed through the castle, as Hortensia's women announced her cheerful waking. Every one hurried forward, and wished the restored one joy.

NEW ENCHANTMENT.

Wherefore shall I not say it? During the general joy, I alone remained sad—ah! more than sad, in my room. The duties, on account of which I had entered into an engagement with Count Hormegg, were now fulfilled. I could leave him whenever I chose. I had often enough expressed my desire and intention of doing so. Nothing more was expected from me, but that I should keep my word. Yet only to be allowed to breathe in her vicinity, appeared to me the most enviable of all lots—to receive only one of her looks, the most exquisite nourishment to the flame of life—to live far from her, was to me the sentence of death.

But I thought of her near marriage with the prince, and the fickleness of the weak count—I thought of my own honor—of my necessities—that I was free to die—then my pride and firmness were roused, and the determination remained to withdraw from the service of the count as soon as possible. I swore to fly. I saw that my misery was without end; but I preferred bidding adieu to joy for the remainder of life to becoming contemptible to myself.

I found Hortensia in the garden of the castle. A soft shudder ran through me as I approached her, in order to offer my congratulation. She stood, separated from her women, thoughtfully before a bed of flowers. She appeared fresher and more blooming than I had ever seen her—glowing with a new life. She first discovered my presence as I spoke to her.

"How you frightened me?" said she, laughing and embarrassed, while a deep blush overspread her beautiful cheeks.

"I also, my dear countess, would offer to you my joy and good wishes."

I could say no more—my voice began to tremble—my thoughts became confused—I could not support her looks, which penetrated into the depths of my heart. With difficulty I stammered an excuse for having disturbed her.

Her looks were silently fastened on me. After a long pause, she said: "You speak of joy, dear Faust; are you also gay?"

"Heartily, as I know you to be saved from an illness by which you have so long suffered. In a few days I must depart, and endeavor, if it be possible, in other lands, to belong to myself, since I am no longer connected with any one. My promise is redeemed."

"Is it your serious intention to leave us, dear Faust? I hope not. How can you say that you belong to no one? Have you not bound us to you by all the obligations of gratitude? What forces you to separate from us?" said the countess.

I laid my hand upon my heart; my looks sunk to the earth; to speak was impossible.

"You remain with us, Faust. Is it not so?" said the countess.

"I dare not," I replied.

"And if I entreat you, Faust?" said the countess.

"For God's sake, gracious countess, do not entreat—do not command me. I can only be well when I—— No, I must go hence;" I replied.

"You are not happy with us—and yet what other employment, what other duty, draws you from us?" asked the countess.

"Duty toward myself," I replied.

"Go, then, Faust," said the countess, "I have been mistaken in you. I believed that we also were of some value to you."

"Gracious countess," I replied, "if you knew what your words excite, you would, from compassion, forbear."

"I must, then, be silent, Faust. Go, then, but you commit a great injustice," said the countess.

As she said these words, she turned from me. I ventured to follow her, and entreated her not to be angry. Tears fell from her eyes. I was frightened. With folded hands, I implored her not to be angry.

"Command me, I will obey," said I. "Do you command me to remain? My inward peace, my happiness, my life, I sacrifice with joy to this command!"

"Go, Faust; I force nothing," said the countess. "You remain unwillingly with us."

"Oh! countess!" said I, "drive not a man to desperation."

"Faust, when do you depart?" said she.

"To-morrow—to-day," I replied.

"No, no, Faust!" said she, softly, and approached nearer to me—"I place no value on my health, on your gift, if you—— Faust! you remain, at least, only a few days," she whispered with such a soft, entreating voice, and looked so anxiously at me with her moist eyes, that I ceased to be master over my will.

"I remain," said I.

"But willingly?" she asked.

"With delight," I replied.

"It is well! Now leave me for a moment, Faust. You have quite disturbed me. But do not leave the garden. I only wish to recover myself."

With these words she left me, and disappeared among the blooming orange-trees.

I remained long in the same place, like a dreamer. I had never heard such language from the countess before; it was not that of mere politeness. My whole being trembled at the idea that I possessed some interest in her heart. These solicitations for me to remain—these tears, and, what can not be described, that peculiar something—the extraordinary language in her manners, in her movements, in her voice—a language, without words, yet which said more than words could express. I understood nothing of it all, and, nevertheless, understood all; I doubted, and yet was convinced.

In about ten minutes, as I wandered up and down the garden walks, and joined the women, the countess approached us quickly and gayly. Enveloped in white drapery, and surrounded by the sun's rays, she appeared like a being out of Raphael's dreams. In her hand she carried a bouquet of pinks, roses, and violet-colored vanilla flowers.

"I have plucked a few flowers for you, dear Faust," do not despise them. I give them to you with quite different feelings from those which, during my sickness, I gave the rose. But I should not remind you, my dear physician, how I vexed you with my childish humors. I recollect it myself, as in duty bound, in order to make up for it. And, oh! how much have I to make up! Do give me your arm—and you, Miss Cecilia, take the other," which was the name of one of her women.

As we wandered around with light chat and jokes, her father, the count, joined us, and soon after, the prince. Never had Hortensia been more lovely than on this, the first day of her restored health. She spoke with tender respect to her father—with friendly familiarity to her female companions—with refined politeness and goodness to the prince; to me, never without demonstrations of her gratitude. Not that she thanked me with words, but in the manner in which she spoke to me. So soon as she turned to me, there was in her words and tone something indescribably cordial; in her looks and manner something of a sisterly confidence, good-naturedly solicitous for my satisfaction. This tone did not change either in the presence of her father or of the prince. She continued it with an ingenuousness and sincerity, as if it ought not to be otherwise.

Some delightful days passed by in *fêtes* and joy. Hortensia's manner toward me did not change. I, myself, ever wavering between the cold laws of respect and the flames of passion, found once more in Hortensia's conversation an inward repose and independence, which I had been deprived of since my acquaintance with this prodigy. Her sincerity and truth made me more calm and contented; her confidence, as it were, more fraternal. She did not at all conceal a heart full of the purest friendship for me—still less did I conceal my feelings, though at the same time I did not venture to betray their depth. Yet who could long behold so many charms and resist their influence?

It was the custom for the visitors of the baths at Battaglia, on fine evenings, to sit assembled before a large coffee-house, enjoying the air and refreshments. An unconstrained conversation reigned there. They sat upon chairs in the open street, and in a half circle. To the right and left were heard the sounds of guitars, mandolines, and singing, after the Italian mode. In the great houses, also, music sounded, and windows and doors were lighted. One evening, the prince having left us earlier than usual, the countess took a whim to visit this assemblage of the visitors of the place. I was already in my room, and sat holding the bouquet in both hands, dreaming over my destiny. The light burnt dimly, and my room-door stood half open. Hortensia and Cecilia saw me as they passed. They watched me for some time, and then came softly in. I did not observe them till they stood close beside me, and declared that I must accompany them to the town. They now amused themselves with jests at my surprise. Hortensia recognized the bouquet. She took it from the table where I had thrown it, and, withered as it was, stuck it in her bosom. We went down to Battaglia and mingled with the company.

It happened that Cecilia, in conversation with some

persons of her acquaintance, separated from us, which neither Hortensia nor myself regretted. On my arm she wandered up and down through the moving crowd, till she was fatigued. We seated ourselves on a little bench, under an elm which grew on one side. The moon shone through the branches upon Hortensia's beautiful face, and upon the withered flowers in her bosom

"Will you again rob me of what you have given me?" asked I, as I pointed to the bouquet.

She looked at me long, with a strange, thoughtful seriousness, and then replied: "It always appears to me as if I could give you nothing, and could take nothing from you. Is it not sometimes the same with you?"

This answer and question, so lightly and quietly thrown out, placed me in embarrassment and silence. From respect, I scarcely dared to dwell on the kind meaning. She once more repeated the question.

"Alas! it is often so with me!" said I. "When I see the abyss between you and myself, and the distance which holds me far from you, then it is so with me. Who can give or take from the gods, that which does not always belong to them?"

She opened her eyes, and looked at me with astonishment.

"Why do you speak of the gods, Faust? Even to one's self, one can give or take nothing."

"One's self?" replied I, with an uncertain voice. "You know that you have made me your own property!"

"I do not myself know how it is," she answered, and her eyes sank down.

"But I, dear countess; I know it. The enchantment which ruled over us is not lost, but has only changed its direction. Formerly, in your transfigurations, I governed your will, now you govern mine. In your presence only do I live. I can do nothing—I am nothing without you. If my confession—a crime before the world, but not before God—vexes you, I am not the cause, since it is at your command that I have acted. Can I dissemble before you? If it is a crime that my soul has involuntarily become chained to your being, it is not my offense."

She turned away her face, and raised her hand to denote that I should be silent. I had at the same moment raised mine, in order to cover my eyes, which were dimmed in tears. The upraised hands sank down clasped together. We were silent; thought was lost in powerful feelings. I had betrayed my passion—but Hortensia had pardoned me.

Cecilia disturbed us. We went silently back to the castle. As we separated, the countess said, lowly and sadly: "Through you I have obtained health only to suffer more."

PETRARCH'S DWELLING.

WHEN we met the next day, there was a kind of sacred timidity between us. I scarcely ventured to address her—she scarcely to answer me. In our looks, full of seriousness, we often met. She appeared to wish to look through me. I sought to read in her calmer moments if she were offended at my boldness of yesterday. Many days passed, without our again seeing each other alone. We had a secret between us, and feared to profane it by a look. Hortensia's whole manner was more solemn—her gayety more moderate—as if she did not enter with her whole heart into the customary routine of life.

Nevertheless, I counted too much on her changed manner, after that decisive hour under the elm. Prince Charles had, as I afterward learnt, formally solicited the hand of the countess, which had caused an unpleasing and constrained state between herself, her father, and the prince. In order to gain time, and not to offend them, Hortensia had entreated for time for reflection: and truly, for such an unlimited period, and under such hard conditions, that Charles must almost despair ever to see his wishes crowned.

"Not that I have any aversion to the prince," as she expressed her explanation, "but I wish still to enjoy my freedom. I will, at a future day, of myself and voluntarily, give my yes or no. But if the offer is repeated before I desire it, then I am determined to reject him, even though I may truly love him."

The count knew of old the inflexible disposition of his daughter; though from that reason he hoped the best, since Hortensia had not directly refused the attentions of the prince. Charles, on the contrary, was discouraged. He saw, in this declaration, only the finally rejected lover, without any definite hopes. Yet he had sufficient self-love to believe that, by his constancy, he should at last move Hortensia's heart. Her confidence toward me was at times displeasing to him, not that he appeared to fear it—he even found it so much the more without danger, because it was open and unembarrassed. Hortensia also treated him in the same manner. He had accustomed himself to see me treated as the friend of the house, and confidential adviser both of the father and daughter; and as the count had confided to him the secret of my plebeian descent, he could still less fear me as a rival. He condescended to make me his confidant, and one day related to me the history of his wooing Hortensia's hand, and her answer. He conjured me to grant my friendly services to discover, however distant, if Hortensia had any inclination toward him. I was obliged to promise it. Every day he inquired if I had made any discovery? I could always excuse myself, that I had no opportunity of seeing Hortensia alone.

Probably, in order to facilitate this opportunity, he arranged a little party of pleasure to Arquato, three miles from Battaglia, where the visitors of the baths were accustomed to make a pilgrimage to the tomb and dwelling-house of Petrarch. Hortensia esteemed, above all the Italian poets, this tender and spiritualized songster of pure love. She had long been enjoying the idea of this pilgrimage. But when the moment of departure arrived, Charles, under some light pretense, not only remained behind himself, but contrived also to prevent the count from accompanying Hortensia, promising, however, to follow us.

I conducted the ladies to the church-yard of the village, where a simple monument covered the ashes of the immortal poet, and translated the Latin inscription for them. Hortensia stood absorbed in deep and serious thought before the grave. She sighed, as she remarked, "Thus die all!" and I thought I felt her draw my arm slightly toward her. "Die *all?*" said I; "then would not the life of man be a cruelty of the Creator, and love the heaviest curse of life?"

Sorrowfully we left the church-yard. A friendly old man led us from thence to a vine hill, not far distant, upon which stands Petrarch's dwelling, and near by a little garden. From this spot the prospect of the plain is truly beautiful. In the house they showed us the poet's household furniture, which was preserved with religious faithfulness—the table at which he read and wrote, the chair on which he rested, and even his kitchen utensils.

The sight of such relics always has a peculiar influence on my mind. It annihilates the interval of centuries and brings the distant past prominently before the imagination. To me, it was as if the poet had only gone out, and that he would presently open the little brown door of his chamber to greet us. Hortensia found an elegant edition of Petrarch's sonnets on a table in a corner. Wearied, she seated herself there, rested her beautiful head upon her hand, and read attentively, while the fingers of her supporting hand concealed her eyes. Beatrice and Cecilia went to prepare refreshments for the countess. I remained silently at the window. Petrarch's love and hopelessness were my destiny. Another Laura sat there, divine, not through the charms of the muse, but of herself.

Hortensia took a handkerchief to dry her eyes. I was troubled at seeing her weep. I approached her timidly, but did not venture to address her. She suddenly rose, and smiling, said to me, with a tearful look,

"The poor Petrarch! the poor human heart! But all passes—all. It is centuries since he has ceased to lament. Though they say, that in his latter years he conquered his passion. It is good to conquer one's self. May it not be called destroying one's self?"

"If necessity commands it," I replied.

"Has necessity power over the human heart?" asked the countess.

"But," I replied, "Laura was the wife of Hugo de Sade. Her heart dared not belong to her lover. His fate was solitary to love, solitary to die. He had the gift of song, and the muses consoled him. He was unhappy—as I."

"As you?" replied Hortensia, with a scarcely audible voice.—"Unhappy, Faust?"

"I have not," I continued, "the divine gift of song; therefore my heart will break, since it hath nothing to console it. Countess, dear countess—dare I say more than I have said? But I will continue worthy of your esteem, and that can only be by manly courage: grant me one request—only one modest request."

Hortensia threw down her eyes, but did not answer.

"One request, dear countess, for my quiet," I again said.

"What shall I do?" whispered she, without raising her eyes.

"Am I certain that you will not refuse my prayer?" I asked.

She regarded me with a long, serious look, and, with an indescribable dignity said: "Faust, I know not what you would ask: but how great soever it may be

—yes, Faust, I am indebted to you for my recovery—my life! I grant your request. Speak."

I seized her hand, I sank at her feet, I pressed her hand to my burning lips—I almost lost consciousness and speech. Hortensia stood with downcast eyes, as if from apathy.

I at length gained power to speak. "I must away from here. Let me fly from you. I dare tarry no longer. Let me, in some solitude, far from you, tranquillize my unhappy life. I must away! I disturb the peace of your house. Charles has demanded your hand?"

"I will never have him!" said the countess, hurriedly and with a firm tone.

"Let me fly. Even your goodness increases the multitude of my miseries."

Hortensia struggled violently with herself.

"You commit a fearful injustice! But I can no longer prevent it!" cried she, as she burst into a passionate flood of tears. She staggered, and sought the chair—seeing which I sprang up, and she sank sobbing on my breast. After some moments she recovered, and feeling herself encircled by my arms, she endeavored to loosen my hold. But I, forgetting the old commands of respect, pressed her more closely as I sighed, "A few moments, and then we part!"

Her resistance ceased; she then raised her eyes on me, and with a countenance on which, as formerly, the color of transfiguration glimmered, said: "Faust, what are you doing?"

"Will you not forget me in my absence?" asked I, in return.

"Can I?" sighed she, and threw down her eyes.

"Farewell, Hortensia!" stammered I, and my cheek rested on hers.

"Emanuel! Emanuel!" whispered she. Our lips met. I felt tenderly and gently her reciprocal kiss, while one of her arms rested around my neck.

Minutes—quarters of hours passed.

At length, together and in silence, we left the dwelling of Petrarch, and proceeded in the path down the hill, where we found two servants, who conducted us to an arbor under some wild laurel trees. At that moment, the carriage of the prince rolled by. Charles and the count descended from it.

Hortensia was very serious and laconic in her answers. She appeared lost in continual meditation. I saw that she was obliged to force herself to speak to the prince. Toward me she preserved, unchanged, the cordiality and confidence of her deportment. Petrarch's dwelling was again visited, as the count wished to see it. As we entered the room, which had been consecrated by the mutual confession of our hearts, Hortensia seated herself again on the chair near the table, in the same place, and with the book, as at first, and so remained till we departed. Then she arose, laid her hand upon her breast, cast a penetrating look on me, and hurried quickly from the apartment.

The prince had remarked this emotion and this look. A deep red rose over his countenance; he went out with folded arms, and his head hung down. All joy retreated from our party. Every one appeared desirous to reach the castle soon again. I did not doubt but that Charles' jealousy had guessed all, and feared his revenge less for myself, than for the peace of the countess. Therefore, as soon as I returned home, I determined to arrange every thing for my speedy departure the next morning. I communicated my irrevocable resolution to the count, gave up to him all the papers, and entreated him to say nothing to the countess until I was gone.

MELANCHOLY SEPARATION.

I HAD long since obtained the consent of the count that, in this event, the honest old Sebald should accompany me, who had many times demanded his dismissal, in order to revisit his German home. Sebald twirled and danced round the room for joy, when he heard from me that the moment of departure had arrived. A horse and cloak-bag for each, was our whole equipment for the journey.

I had determined to withdraw very quietly, at the dawn of the following day. No one knew any thing of my departure, except the count and old Sebald, and I desired that no one should know it. I determined to leave behind, for Hortensia, a few lines of thanks and love, and an eternal farewell. The old count appeared surprised, though not discontented. He embraced me most tenderly, thanked me for the services I had performed, and promised within an hour to come to my room, in order to give me some useful papers, which would procure me for the future a life free from care, and which, as he expressed it, was only a payment on account of a debt for life. I would not refuse a moderate sum for traveling expenses, in order to reach Germany—in fact, I was almost without money—but my pride refused to take more.

I packed up as soon as I returned to my room. Sebald hurried out to prepare the horses, and arrange every thing for departing at the moment. In the mean time I wrote to Hortensia. I can not describe what I suffered—how I struggled with myself—how often I sprang up from writing, to relieve my pains with tears. My life until now, had been one full of care and unhappiness—and the dim future to me presented nothing more soothing to the soul. Death, thought I, is sweeter and easier than thus to outlive hope.

I destroyed many times what I had written, and had not finished, when I was disturbed in a manner that I least expected.

Trembling, and almost breathless, Sebald rushed into my room, hastily took up the portmanteau, and cried :—

"Mr. Faust, some mischief has happened : they will drag you to prison ; they will murder you! Let us fly, ere it is too late."

In vain I asked the cause of his fright. I only learnt that the count was in a rage, the prince raving, and every one in the castle roused against me. I replied coldly, that I had nothing to fear, and still less to fly like a criminal.

"Sir," cried Sebald, "one can not escape without misfortune from this unhappy family, over which a bad star rules. This I have long since said. Fly!"

At this moment, two of the count's gamekeepers

came in, and requested me to come immediately to the count. Sebald blinked and winked, and urged me to endeavor to escape. I could not avoid smiling at his terror, and followed the servants. I, however, commanded Sebald to saddle the horses, since I no longer doubted that something extraordinary had occurred, and thought that the prince, probably from jealousy, had projected some quarrel with me.

I had scarcely reached the Count Hormegg, when Charles came storming into the room, and declared that I had dishonored the house, and had a secret intrigue with the countess. Beatrice, the companion of the countess, gained over to the prince, either by his presents or perhaps by his tenderness, had, as she left Petrarch's dwelling with Cecilia, become impatient at Hortensia and myself, and returned and saw us in the embrace of each other. The Abigail was discreet enough not to disturb us, but was prompt enough, so soon as we returned to the castle, to betray the important event to the prince. The count, who could believe any thing but this—since it appeared to him the most unnatural thing in the world, that a common citizen, a painter, should have won the love of a countess of Hormegg—treated the affair, at first, as a mere illusion of jealousy. The prince, for his justification, was obliged to betray his informer; and Beatrice, though much opposed to it, was compelled to acknowledge what she had seen. The anger of the old count knew no bounds, yet the event appeared to him so monstrous, that he determined to interrogate the countess herself upon it. Hortensia appeared. The sight of the pale faces, disfigured by rage and fright, excited her terror.

"What has happened?" cried she, almost beside herself.

With fearful earnestness, the count replied, "That thou must say." He then, with forced tranquillity and kindness, took her hand, and said:

"Hortensia, thou art accused of staining the honor of our name by—well, then, it must be said—by an intrigue with the painter, Faust. Hortensia, deny it—say no! Give honor and tranquillity again to thy father. Thou canst do it. Refute all malicious tongues—refute the assertion that thou wast seen in Faust's arms; it was a delusion, a misunderstanding, a deception. Here stands the prince, thy future husband. Reach him thy hand. Declare to him, that all that has been said against thee and Faust, are wicked lies. Faust's presence shall no longer disturb our peace; this night he leaves us forever."

The count spoke still longer. He did so, in order to give an advantageous turn to the fact—since the alternate redness and paleness of Hortensia, allowed him no longer to doubt of its truth—which might satisfy the prince, and make every thing smooth again. He was prepared for nothing less, than what Hortensia, as soon as he was silent, openly declared. Excited to the most impetuous feelings, as much by the treachery of Beatrice, who was still present, as by the reproaches, and the news of my sudden departure—with her own peculiar dignity and resolution, she turned first toward Beatrice, and said:—

"Wretch! I stand not opposed to you. My servant

must not be my accuser. I am not to justify myself before you. Leave the room and the castle, and never appear before me again."

Beatrice fell weeping at her feet. It was in vain—she must obey, and departed.

"Dear Faust," said she to me—and her cheeks glowed with an unnatural color—"you stand here as one accused or condemned." She then related what had happened, and went on to say: "They expect me to justify myself. I have no justification to make before any one but God, the judge of hearts. I have only here to acknowledge the truth, since my father exacts it, and to declare my unalterable design, since destiny commands it, and I am born to be unhappy. Faust, I should be unworthy of your regard, could I not raise myself above misfortune."

She then turned to the prince, and said: "I esteem you, but I do not love you. My hand will never be yours; nourish no further hopes. After what has just passed, I must beg of you to avoid us forever. Do not expect that my father can force me against my will. Life is indifferent to me. His first act of power would have no other consequences than that he must bury the corpse of his daughter. To you I have nothing more to say. But to you, my father, I must acknowledge that I love—love this Faust. But it is not my fault. He is hateful to you—he is not of our rank. He must separate from us. I annul my earthly union with him. You, my father, can make no change, since any endeavor to do so will be the end of my life. I say to you, beforehand, I am prepared for my death, since that only will terminate my miseries."

She stopped. The count wished to speak—the prince likewise. She motioned them to be silent. She approached me, drew a ring from her finger, gave it to me, and said: "My friend, I part from you, perhaps forever. Take this ring in remembrance of me. This gold and these diamonds shall become dust, sooner than my love and truth shall cease. Do not forget me."

As she said this, she laid her arms on my shoulders, pressed a kiss on my lips—her countenance changed—the blood forsook her cheeks—and pale and cold, she sank with closed eyes to the floor.

The count gave a piercing, fearful shriek. The prince called for assistance. I carried the beautiful body to a couch. Women hurried in—physicians were called. I sank, without consciousness, on my knees, before the couch, and held the cold hand of the senseless one to my cheek. The count tore me away. He was like a madman.

"Thou hast murdered her!" thundered he to me. "Fly, wretch, and never let me see thee again!"

He thrust me out of the door. Upon this sign, the huntsmen seized me and dragged me down the stairs before the castle. Sebald stood before the stable. There I lost all power and sense. I lay, as Sebald afterward said, a full quarter of an hour, senseless on the earth. I had scarcely recovered, when he lifted me upon one of the horses, and we hastened from the castle. I rode as if in my sleep, and was often in danger of falling. By degrees, I gained full consciousness and power. The past was now clear before me. I became desperate, and determined to return to the castle, and know Hortensia's fate. Sebald entreated me, by all the saints, to give up so frantic a design. It was in vain. I had just turned my horse, when I saw a rider coming toward us at full gallop, and heard some one cry, "Cursed assassin." It was Charles' voice. At the same time, some shot struck me. As I grasped my pistols, my horse fell dead. I sprang up. Charles rode toward me with a drawn sword, and as he was about to cut me down, I shot him through the body. His attendant caught him as he fell. Sebald pursued them in their flight, and sent some balls after them. He then returned, and took the portmanteau from the dead horse; I mounted with him, and we hurried on at a quick pace.

This murder had occurred in the vicinity of a little wood, which was soon reached. The sun had already set. We rode through the whole night, without knowing where. As we stopped at daybreak, at a village inn, in order to give our horse some rest, we found him so excoriated by the saddle, that we gave up all hope of using him further. We sold him at a very low price, and continued our flight on foot by a secure road, carrying our baggage by turns.

NEW ADVENTURE.

The first rays of the setting sun, as we journeyed on, fell on the diamonds of Hortensia's ring. I kissed it, and wept over the recollections it brought to my mind. Sebald had already told in the night, that he had heard from one of the servants, while I was lying insensible near the horses in the yard, that Hortensia, who had been considered dead, had returned to life. This news had strengthened and consoled me. I was perfectly indifferent about my own fate. Hortensia's greatness of soul had inspired me. I was proud of my misery. My conscience, free from reproach, raised me above all fear. I had but one sorrow—to be eternally separated from one I must ever love.

When we reached Ravenna, we took our first day's rest. It was a long day's rest—for I, shaken by the late events, and exhausted by my unusual fatigue and exertion, was very ill. For two weeks I lay in a fever. Sebald endured the most painful anxiety, since he feared, and justly, the murder of the prince would necessarily bring us into the hands of justice. He had given us both feigned names, and bought other clothes. My good constitution, more than the science of my physician, at length preserved me, though great weakness remained in my limbs. But as we had determined to go by ship from Rimini to Trieste, I hoped to recover my health on the way.

One evening, Sebald came to me in the greatest fright, and said, "Sir, we can remain here no longer. A stranger stands without, and wishes to speak with you. We are betrayed. He asked at first my name, and I could not deny it. He then asked for you."

"Let him come in," said I.

A well-dressed man entered, who, after the first exchange of politeness, inquired after my health. As I assured him that I was quite well again, he said, "So much the better. I may then give you some good advice. You know what passed between Prince Charles and yourself. He is out of danger, but has sworn to take your life. You had, therefore, better leave immediately. You intend to go to Germany, by Trieste. Do not do so. There is only a Neapolitan vessel that goes back to Naples. When once at sea, you are safe; otherwise, in a few hours, death or a prison. Here is a letter for the Neapolitan captain, he is my truest friend, and will receive you with pleasure. Now go immediately to Rimini, and from thence to Naples."

I was not a little embarrassed at seeing this stranger so well informed. To my question how he acquired his knowledge, he smiled, and only replied, "I know nothing more, and can tell you nothing more; I reside here in Ravenna; I am a clerk of the court. Save yourself." He then suddenly left us.

Sebald affirmed stoutly and firmly, that the man must be possessed by a devil, or he could not have known our secrets. As the stranger spoke with several of the people of the hotel, we learnt afterward, that the unknown so-called court's secretary, was a good, honest man, wealthy and married. It was incomprehensible how our most carefully concealed plan of going to Germany by Trieste, could be so exactly known, as no one but ourselves was privy to it. The enigma was, however, soon solved, when Sebald confessed to me that he had, during my illness, written a letter to his former comrade, Casper, at Battaglia, begging to know whether the prince was dead or not. He expected the answer in vain. Without doubt, the letter had fallen into the hands of Charles or his people, or the contents were betrayed to him.

Sebald was now in the greatest anxiety. He engaged

a carriage for Rimini without delay, and we set out that same night. These untoward circumstances made me not quite at ease. I knew not whether I was flying from, or going to meet the danger. The justice's clerk might be an agent of the prince. In the mean while we not only reached Rimini, but found there the Neapolitan captain. I gave him the letter of the clerk—though I do not deny that I had before opened and read it. I soon agreed with him as to our voyage to Naples. The wind became fair—the anchors were raised. Beside ourselves, there were some other travelers on board; among others, a young man, whose sight at first was not very agreeable to me, as I remembered to have seen him once, though very transiently, at the baths of Battaglia. I, however, became easy, as I judged from his conversation, that he had not observed me, and that I was completely a stranger to him. He had only left Battaglia three days since, and was returning to Naples, where he had carried on a considerable business. He mentioned the acquaintance he had made at the baths, and spoke of the German countess, who was a wonder of grace and beauty. How his remark made my heart beat! He appeared to know nothing of the wounding or death of the prince. The countess, whose name was unknown to him, had gone four days before him, but where, he had not troubled himself to inquire.

However imperfect this news was, it served not a little to tranquilize me. Hortensia lived—Hortensia was in health. "May she be happy!" was my sigh.

The voyage was tedious to all but myself. I sought solitude. Upon the deck, I watched through many nights, and dreamed of Hortensia. The young merchant, who called himself Tufaldini, remarked my melancholy, and took much pains to enliven me. He heard I was a painter; he passionately loved the art, and constantly turned the conversation upon that subject, since nothing but that appeared to interest or make me talkative. His sympathy and friendship went so far, that he invited me to stay at his house in Naples, which I was the less inclined to refuse, as I was an entire stranger in that city, and my own and Sebald's joint stock of gold, particularly after the deduction of traveling expenses, had considerably dwindled away.

NEW WONDER.

The kindness and attention of the generous Tufaldini, in fact put me to the blush. From a traveling companion he made himself my friend, though I had done little or nothing to gain or merit his love. He introduced me as his friend to his aged and respectable mother, and his charming wife. They prepared the best chambers for Sebald and myself, and treated me, from the first day of our arrival, like an old family friend. But Tufaldini did not rest here. He introduced me to all his acquaintances, and orders soon came for pictures. He was as eager to make me known as if it were for his own advantage. He consented at last to receive payment for my board and lodging, though he was at first much mortified by my offering it. But when he saw my determination to leave his house, if he would not accept any remuneration, he took the money, though more to gratify me than indemnify himself.

I was, above all expectation, fortunate in my works. My pictures were liked, and I was paid what I demanded. One finished order brought on another. Even Sebald found himself so comfortable in Naples, that he forgot his home-sickness. He thanked God for having escaped from the service of the count with a sound head, and would, as he expressed it, rather serve me for bread and water, than the count for a whole bowl of gold.

My plan was to gain sufficient by my labors to enable me to travel to Germany, and there settle myself. I was industrious and economical. So passed one year. The love which I enjoyed in Tufaldini's house; my quiet life in the dissipated city; the charm of the soft climate, and then, that I was without a vocation, without friends in Germany, induced me to forget my first design. I remained where I was. Joy bloomed for me as little in Germany as in the Italian soil; only the thought that perhaps Hortensia dwelt on the estate of her father, that I might then have the consolation to see her once more, though at a distance; this thought alone sometimes drew my desires toward the north. But then I recollected the parting hour and the words she spoke: *I annul my earthly union with him!* as before her father she solemnly, and with such heroic greatness renounced me: I again roused my courage, and determined to suffer all and cheerfully. I was an oak, which the storm had shattered, without branches, without leaves, solitary, unregarded, and dying in itself.

It is said that time's beneficent hand heals all wounds. I myself had believed the saying, but found it untrue. My melancholy continued the same—I avoided the gay. Tears often gave me relief, and my only joy was to dream of her—when I again saw her in her greatness and loveliness. Her ring was my holiest relic. Had it fallen into the depths of the sea, nothing should have prevented my plunging in after it.

The second year passed, but not my sorrow. A faint gleam of hope sometimes refreshed me even in my darkest hour, that perhaps an accident might bring me in the vicinity of my lost chosen one, or that at least I should have some news of her.

It is true, I did not see the possibility of it. How could the distant one know, after years, where the solitary one dwelt? It was all the same. What has hope to do with impossibilities?

But at the end of the second year, I gave up this hope. Hortensia was dead for me. I saw her no longer in my dreams, except as a spirit shining in the rays of a glorified being.

Tufaldini and his wife had often asked me, in our confidential conversations, the cause of my melancholy. I could never prevail on myself to violate my secret. They no longer inquired, but they were the more careful of my health. I felt that the powers of my life were sinking—and the thoughts of the grave to me were sweet.

All was suddenly changed. One morning Sebald brought some letters from the post. Among them were some new orders for pictures, and a little casket. I opened it. Who can imagine my joyful fright? I saw Hortensia's image—living, beautiful—but dressed in mourning—the face softer, thinner, and paler than I had actually seen it. On a small piece of paper, in Hortensia's hand, were written three words: "My Emanuel, hope."

I reeled through the room like an intoxicated person. I sank down speechless on a chair, and raised my hands prayerfully to heaven. I shouted—I sobbed. I kissed the picture and the little paper which her hand must have touched. I knelt, and with my face bowed to the floor, weeping, did I thank Providence.

Thus Sebald found me. He thought I was deranged. He did not err. I feel that man is always stronger to bear misfortune than happiness; while against the one he always approaches more or less prepared, the other comes upon him without preparation or foresight.

Again my hopes bloomed out youthfully, and in them my health and life. Tufaldini and all my acquaintances were delighted at it. I expected from day to day fresh news from my dearly beloved. There was no doubt she knew my residence, though I could not comprehend how she had acquired the intelligence. But from what part of the world did her picture come? All my researches and inquiries on that subject were in vain.

THE SOLUTION.

At the end of eight months, I received another letter from her. It contained the following lines:—

"I may see thee, Emanuel, only once more. Be in Leghorn the first morning of May, where thou shalt receive further information from a Swiss mercantile house, if thou inquirest for the widow, Marian Schwartz. Tell no one in Naples where thou goest; least of all speak of me. I belong no longer to any one in this world, except, perhaps, for a few moments to thee."

This letter filled me with new delight, but at the same time with an anxious foreboding, on account of the sad secret which seemed to pierce through it. Nevertheless, again to see the most perfect of her sex, though only for a moment, was sufficient for my soul. I left Naples in April, to the great sorrow of the Tufaldini family. Sebald and every one believed that I was going back to Germany.

I arrived at Gaeta with Sebald. We had here an unexpected pleasure. In passing by the garden door of a villa, before the city, I observed, among many other young ladies, Miss Cecilia. I stopped, sprang down, and made myself known. She led me into the circle of her relations. She had been married for three months. I learnt from her that she had left Hortensia about a year since. She knew nothing of the residence of the countess, only that she had gone into a nunnery. "It is already a year," said Cecilia, "since Count Hormegg died. From the sudden contraction of his accustomed expenditure, I soon remarked that he had left his affairs in a sadly confused state. The countess diminished her train of domestics to a very few persons. I had the favor of remaining with her. As she soon after, by an unfortunate lawsuit, lost all hopes of preserving any thing from the paternal estates, we were all discharged. She retained only one old attendant, and declared she would end her days in a cloister. Oh, how many tears did this separation cost us! Hortensia was an angel, and never more beautiful, never more charming, never more exalted, than under the heaviest blow of destiny. She resigned all her accustomed splendor, and divided, like a dying person, all the riches of her wardrobe among her dismissed servants—rewarded all with a princely generosity, which must certainly have placed her in danger of want, and only begged us to include her in our prayers. I left her in Milan, and returned home here to my family. She has declared her intention of traveling to Germany, and there seeking the solitude of a cloister."

This relation of Cecilia quickly solved the enigma in Hortensia's last letter. I also learnt from her that Charles, who was severely but not mortally wounded, had immediately on his recovery entered into the service of the Order of Malta, and soon died.

I left Gaeta in a pensive, yet happy mood. Hortensia's misfortune and the loss of her father excited my compassion, but at the same time gave birth to a bolder hope than I had at any time ventured to conceive. I flattered myself that I might be able to change her determination for a cloister life, and, with her heart, perhaps, win her hand. I was dizzy with the thought of being able to share the fruits of my labors with Hortensia. This was my only dream the whole way to Leghorn, which I entered one fine morning, eight days before the allotted time.

I did not delay a moment in seeking out the Swiss commercial house to which I was directed. I ran there in my traveling dress, and asked the address of the widow Schwartz, in order that I might learn whether the countess had yet arrived in Leghorn. A menial servant conducted me to the widow, who lived in an obscure street, and in a very simple private house. How great was my vexation to learn that Mrs. Schwartz was gone out, and that I must call in two hours. Every moment of delay was so much taken from my life. I returned again at the appointed hour. An old servant woman opened the door, led me up stairs and announced me to her lady. I was invited to enter a simply furnished, but neat room. Opposite the room door, on a couch, sat a young lady, who did not appear to notice my entrance, or to return my salutation, but covering her face with both hands, endeavored to conceal her sobs and tears.

At this sight, a feverish shudder ran through me. In the figure of the young lady, in the tone of her sobs, I recognized the form and voice of Hortensia. Without deliberating or assuring myself of the fact, like one intoxicated, I let hat and cane fall, and threw myself at the feet of the weeping one. O God! who can say what I felt? Hortensia's arms hung round my neck—her lips met mine. The whole past was forgotten—the whole future seemed strewn with flowers. Never was love more beautifully remunerated, or constancy more blissfully rewarded. We both feared, simultaneously, that this moment was merely a dream of felicity. Indeed, on the first day of our meeting, so little was asked or answered, that we separated without knowing more of each other than that we had met.

On the following day, one may easily believe that I was ready in good time to take the advantage of the bewitching Hortensia's invitation to breakfast with her. Her servants consisted of a cook, a housemaid, a waiting-maid, coachman, and footman. All the table service was of the finest porcelain and silver, although no longer with the arms and initials of the old count. This appearance of a certain opulence, which was quite contrary to my first idea, and went far above the powers of my own fortune, was very humbling to the dreamy plans I had indulged in during my journey from Gaeta to Leghorn. I expected, yes, I even wished to find Hortensia in a more limited situation, in order to give courage to offer my all. Now, I again stood before her the poor painter.

I did not conceal, in our confidential conversations, what I had heard at Gaeta from Cecilia, and what feelings, what determinations, what hopes had been awakened. I described to her all my destroyed dreams, and hoped that she, perhaps, would give up her cruel design of burying her youth and beauty in a cloister; that she would choose me for her servant and true friend; that I would lay at her feet all that I had saved and all that my future industry might gain. I described to her, with the colors of loving hope, the blessedness of a quiet life, in some retired situation—the simple house, the little garden near it, the work-room of the artist, inspired by her presence. I hesitated—I trembled—it was impossible to proceed. She threw her bright eyes upon me, and a heavenly color flew over and animated her countenance.

"Thus have my fancies reveled," added I, after some time, "and shall they not be realized?"

Hortensia arose, went to a closet, drew out a little

ebony casket, richly studded with silver, and handed it to me, together with the key.

"In order to deliver you this, I requested your presence in Leghorn. It belongs not in part, but in completion of your dream. After the death of my father, my first thought was to fulfill the duties of my gratitude to you. I have never lost sight of you since your flight from Battaglia. A fortunate accident brought into my hands the letter of your servant, written to one of his friends in my service, from Ravenna, giving your traveling plans. Mr. Tufaldini, of Naples, was persuaded by me, in a secret conference, to take care of you himself, forever. He received a small capital to defray all expenses, and even, if necessary, for your support. I would, also, willingly have rewarded him for his trouble, but it was with the greatest reluctance the good man would accept from me the most trifling present. Thus I had the pleasure of receiving, every four weeks, news of your health. Tufaldini's letters were my only comfort after our parting. On the death of my father, I separated myself, as regards fortune, from my family. Our estates must remain in the male line, all the rest I converted into gold. I no longer thought of returning to my native country—my last refuge should be a cloister. Under the pretence of impoverishment, I avoided all the old vicinities of my father, parted with my former domestics, and took a private station and name, in order to live more concealed. It was not until I had accomplished all this, that I summoned you, in order to finish the work, and redeem the vow which I had made to Heaven. The moment is at hand. You have related to me your beautiful dreams. Perhaps on yourself, more than on any other, now depends their realization."

She opened the casket, and drew out a packet of papers, carefully secured and directed in my name; she broke the seal and laid before me a deed prepared by a notary, in which, partly as a payment of a debt, partly as accrued interest which belonged to me, and partly as being heir to an inheritance, left by the widow Marian Schwartz, an immense sum in bank-notes of different countries, was made over to me.

"This, dear Faust," continued the countess, "is your property—your well-earned, well-deserved property. I have no longer any share in it. A modest income is sufficient for me at present. When I renounce the world and belong to a cloister, you will, also, be heir to what I possess. If I am of any value to you prove it by an eternal silence as regards my person, my station, and my true name. Yet more, I desire you to say not a syllable which can indicate refusal or thanks for this, your own property. Give me your hands to it."

I listened to her speech with surprise and pain, laid down the papers with indifference, and replied:

"Do you believe that these bank-notes have any value for me? I may neither refuse, nor yet be thankful for them. Be not fearful of either. When you go into a cloister, all that remains, the world itself, is superfluous to me. I need nothing. What you give is dust. Ah! Hortensia, you once said that it was my soul which animated you; were it still so, you would not pause to follow my example. I would burn these notes. What shall I do with them?—destroy you and your fortune also! Oh! that you were mine! Hortensia, mine!"

She leant tremblingly toward me, clasped one of my hands in both of hers, and said passionately, and with tears in her eyes:—

"Am I not so, Emanuel?"

"But the cloister? Hortensia!"

"My last refuge—if thou forsakest me!"

Then made we our vows before God. At the altar, by the priestly hand, were they consecrated. We left Leghorn, and sought the charming solitude, in which we now dwell with our children.

HISTORY

OF THE INTRODUCTION OF

THE HARMONIAL PHILOSOPHY

INTO GERMANY.

COMPILED BY MARY F. DAVIS.

WHILE the truths of the New Dispensation were making rapid strides in America, thoughtful and receptive minds in the Old World also felt the throbbings of "the electric chain," and awoke to action. Two noble-spirited Germans undertook the work of translating American publications of a progressive character —chiefly works on the Harmonial Philosophy—into the German language. One of them, the distinguished Botanist and Philosopher, Professor Christian G. Nees von Esenbeck, devoted the closing years of his life to the philanthropic labor, which was continued by his friend and pupil, Gregor Constantin Wittig, of Breslau. The following are extracts from the first letter received by the author from the translator:—

MR. WITTIG TO A. J. DAVIS.

BRESLAU, *June* 28, 1860.

. . . .

Your *Revelations* reached me at Breslau, through a dear friend and patron whom I can never forget—the President of the Imperial Leopold Academy of Physicists, at Berlin—the celebrated botanist and natural philosopher, Christian G. N. Esenbeck—having been sent to him, in the latter part of the year 1856, by the hand of some unknown frind in Bremen. It was destined to solace the last days of his laborious life with the fulfillment of his anticipations and hopes for the progress of natural science and the free religion of Humanity. The profound importance of Magnetism, and its flower, Clairvoyance, for the future advance of the mind—an importance which he had long before anticipated and proclaimed—was in this work disclosed to him in all its fullness. Moreover, as a physician he was acquainted with your *Physician;* as an instructor he prized your *Teacher;* as a prophet of a fairer future for the German people, through political and religious unity, he appreciated your *Seer;* and his daily increasing enthusiasm he shared with me, who enjoyed the confiding intimacy of his last remaining days, and was his true disciple in philosophy and religion. . . . In the advanced years of this gray-headed man of science, it had become impossible for him to execute alone so great a work as the *German translation* of the three volumes of your *Great Harmonia*, and he therefore chose me for his assistant, and, dying, confided to me the completion of the enterprise. Until the day when he retired to the couch of his last sickness, with eyes dimmed with age, he labored upon his portion of the sublime philosophy of God—when the Angel of Death bore him to the higher vision of the Deity, on the sixteenth of March, 1858. In this last period of his life, in consequence of political persecution for my intercourse with the leaders of the Free Religious movement in Breslau, I lived in banishment in the town of Striegau, seven German miles from that city. . . . There I finished the manuscript left to my care by my friend, as well as my own translations, when, near the end of the year 1858, by marriage with a lady who is a free citizen of Breslau, I regained my privilege of residence there. In my present situation, as secretary of a judicial functionary, I still find leisure for the performance of my favorite and self-imposed task of translating all your remaining writings, of which I may be able to become the possessor. . . . .

With feelings of unchangeable regard, I remain henceforth,

Your true and most devoted,

GREGOR CONSTANTIN WITTIG.

Among the friends of Spiritual Progress in New York was a cultivated German, Heinrich Schlarbaum, who felt a deep interest in the work of Mr. Wittig. Mr. Schlarbaum corresponded directly with the translator, offering his sympathy and aid, and in due time received a reply from that earnest friend of truth.

MR. WITTIG'S LETTER TO H. SCHLARBAUM.

BRESLAU, *August* 16, 1862.

ESTEEMED FRIEND AND BROTHER:— . . . Your friendly letter has the old charm for me, as it brings me news of the person who has for five years so deeply interested me, for whom I have so strong a sympathy, and whose spiritual rays are destined to bless all nations with light and knowledge. You are fortunate that you are so near him. Do not imagine that the regard I feel for him is a transient excitement, and therefore exaggerated in expression. His Philosophy is that golden treasure of the enchanted land of which I was wont to dream with such yearning, when a boy, among the hills of my native village, and with which I longed to gladden the hearts of my poor parents. At last I have found it. But I long to dispense it with full hands to my friends and acquaintances and the German people. Of the "Divine Revelations" I have translated sections, which I have styled "Cosmology" and "Geology," and its "Principles." "The Physician," "The Teacher," "The Seer," and "The Reformer," are translated and ready for the press. The smaller works are nearly so, viz.: "The Philosophy of Special Providences," and "Free Thoughts on Religion; or Nature *versus* Theology." The "Chart of the Approaching Destiny of the Human Race" is sketched out, and the "Magic Staff" begun. Do you not think here is wealth to make the lasting happiness of our German world? But, alas! I am in want of the gold and silver in which to set my sparkling gems, and without such setting I can not intrust them to the hands of others. Is it not hard to think that the "Harmonial Philosophy" has been compelled to go begging among German publishers for two years? But I have adopted a plan which will, perhaps, meet with success. I intend to prepare a Prospectus, at my own expense, of all of Mr. Davis's works which I have translated, and to circulate it among all the principal establishments, through a dealer here. I may thus obtain a publisher. I have also some faint hopes of making a loan, that will enable me to publish them myself. This would be the best plan, but it would, at the same time, be for me the most difficult. Where can the generous heart be found that would voluntarily tender thousands of dollars for so useful and noble an enterprise! Such hearts there are, but how can they be found? I would gladly renounce all reward for myself, if I might but obtain a wide dissemination for these glorious truths.

September 4, 1862.

—I had written thus far, August 16, when I was prevented from bringing my letter to a conclusion. I am still alone in my enterprise for the publication of my translations. But the printed Prospectus dispatched to you with this letter, will show you the exertions I am making. The time has come when I must find a publisher at any cost. If I possessed the means, I would myself have the teachings of the Harmonial Philosophy printed in golden letters upon silken sheets. My views on this point I have set forth at greater length in my Prospectus, and also in an article for the *Herald of Progress*, sent with this letter to Mr. Davis. It is full two years since I have written him. During this period ten of his works have been translated, and the manuscript is ready for the printer. "The Philosophy of Spiritual Intercourse" has already been taken in hand for the new series, and will be ready in October. Thus I continue to labor at my great and beautiful task, striving after my glorious ideal, though I may never reach it.

Your valuable letter of September 3, 1860, contains so many interesting particulars, that I can not but desire to hear further from you. You say: "To see the works of Davis, Edmonds, Tuttle, and others, translated into German is my ardent desire; should your future labors take that direction, you may rely upon my sympathy and assistance." I accept this friendly offer, and would thank you, in your next, to give me such information in regard to the works mentioned as will enable me to obtain them. Beside Davis's works, I have taken up the excellent treatise of Mr. Partridge on "Spiritualism," and am not disinclined to translate other good works into German, after completing those of Mr. Davis. Every thing from the Beyond seems to me as homelike as a greeting from some fairer German Fatherland.

And yet how much that is mournful has occurred within these two years in your now *dis*-United States! I await with trembling and fearful expectation the final issue. Now, for the first time, the disasters of war seem really to have fallen upon the armies of the North. May the spirit of Freedom grant them the courage and the power for a most glorious victory! It is for your country to deal the death-blow to Slavery, and brutality, and the old order of things generally. France has not sent her legions to Mexico without a purpose, and if the Union fall, the new French Emperor would in Europe tread us, too, beneath his feet. Yet I know that the Redeemer for the people of Freedom is already born, and that he will rule over all nations! *Wisdom*, the flower of Reason, by means of this terrible struggle of human passions, will prescribe the laws of her eternal state to the purified Union. Unity is the fundamental principle of all natural and political life, and this *unity* is the Divine law of movement for all struggling forces. The thought of unity with us in Germany, too, is again awakened, and finds expression in the Schiller and Fichte Festivals, and the Rifle and Turner Unions. Who knows what may happen here among us, even in the course of one short year? . . . . . Your friend,

G. C. WITTIG.

In another letter of the same date, addressed to A. J. Davis, Mr. Wittig said that he had sent his Prospectus to the publishing house of F. F. Weber, Leipsic, and that he should continue his efforts to find a publisher. He had even taken some steps toward undertaking the publication of the Harmonial works on his own account, in the event of being disappointed in all his expectations. He had sent a letter, with the Prospectus, to Weber, giving a brief survey of the tendency and bearings of the Harmonial Philosophy. Comparing it with German speculation, he wrote :—

A new Philosophy opens its victorious career in the writings of Mr. A. J. Davis, which, in the consciousness of its own harmony, does by no means seek to exalt itself by pride and contempt over the philosophic systems of other nations, but seeks to render them all fruitful, falling upon their closed calices like the pollen of flowers. That this is true, that this Philosophy really possesses the sublime quality of universality, is shown by its severe and beautiful simplicity, and its endeavor to give to *Nature, Reason, and Intuition* their highest scientific value, thus securing to itself the stamp of the standard system for all time. In order, however, to reveal this character of spiritual perfection, it was necessary that its expounder should bring to bear more improved means and instruments of thought than had hitherto been within the reach of philosophic minds. With the German mind, speculation had already won its highest triumphs in Kant, Fichte, Schelling and Hegel. The power of the merely logical faculty had in the last-mentioned philosopher attained its most varied culture, and the materialism of the senses had thus reached its highest development. German speculation also had already reached the limits of the profoundest problems, and the search for the *interior essence of things*—the so-called *things in themselves*—had been pushed to the utmost in their investigations. But the speculation of logic and the senses could not pass its own sensuous limit; it was like the unarmed eye, to which the wonders of the universe, of great and little magnitudes, that are unvailed only by the telescope and microscope, remained concealed from deficiency of vision and a lack of the power of discrimination.

This philosophic telescope and microscope of a faculty that penetrates the *innermost being*, deeper than the senses, is now found in the gift of magnetic *clairvoyance*, and in that spiritually-perfect *rational intuition and illumination* which have raised the author of the works named to be the philosophical Gallileo of our day. . . . . These books form, as it were, a new *Gospel of Wisdom*, the teachings of which will be seized upon with avidity, and even with transport; for they are addressed to the most interior and secret thoughts and emotions of the human mind, and stir with quiet power that endless yearning for knowledge, which we see so gloriously embodied in Goethe's "Faust."

Responsive to the enthusiasm of his gifted countryman, and inspired with like ardor in the service of Truth, Mr. Schlarbaum wrote the following timely appeal, which was published in the *Herald of Progress*:—

MR. SCHLARBAUM'S LETTER TO A. J. DAVIS.

NEW YORK, *September* 26, 1862.

DEAR SIR:—I have translated for you the letters of Mr. Wittig. He is full of energy for a good cause. Our duty, it seems to me, would be to take hold of the facts as they present themselves, and make the best out of them for the good of our German brethren. Wittig is thoroughly imbued with the importance of your writings. And the opposition he everywhere meets has made him earnest and anxious. . . . . .

Two years ago, when I got the first letter from Wittig, the thought struck me that the dissemination of works like yours should not be made to depend on the motives of mere tradesmen; the society of generous Americans should lend a helping hand, and bless the rising and future generations with them. Humanity needs it. . . . .

I think your *Herald* should lay the matter before American men of Progress. Let an "European Publishing Association" for these works be formed; let its committee regulate and prepare matters; let a call for means—$1,000 to $1,500 is enough to begin with—go through the world; let us do our best; then the poor, hard-working Wittig can be assisted just in such a way as will serve best for a happy issue. . . . . . It is admitted that one-quarter of our army is of German descent! Much hard, bloody work, is done by the immigrated people; let us, therefore, make a glorious gift to that freedom-loving nation—the people of Germany.

Truly yours,

H. SCHLARBAUM.

In accordance with the suggestion an informal meeting was held in New York, and a committee was chosen, of which the members were William Green,

Eliza W. Farnham, Mary F. Davis, H. Schlarbaum, and C. M. Plumb. A Circular was issued, asking contributions to "The European Harmonial Publishing Fund," which, in addition to the appeals of the *Herald*, was circulated far and wide among American Spiritualists. Tidings of the movement brought responsive words from progressive Germans in our midst; and, among others, the following communication found way to the editorial sanctum:—

LETTER FROM DR. PHILIP SCHULHOF.*

NEW YORK, *March* 30, 1863.

A. J. DAVIS—DEAR SIR:—My heart leaps for joy, for I see in the *Herald of Progress*, of March 28, an article headed: "The European Harmonial Publishing Fund." My soul responds in anticipation of the diffusion of light and happiness by means of publishing a translation of the works of Mr. A. J. Davis, and other Spiritual writings, by Herr G. C. Wittig, of Breslau, Germany, a gentleman of enthusiasm, love, and knowledge.

I see already not only the millions of inhabitants of Germany, but also the German population of our beloved United States, and of every inhabited part of this globe, imbibing the principles of the Harmonial Philosophy, through the simple medium of laying before them these very principles in their native tongue, and such teachings will obtain an easy entrance into their hearts, as they are mostly prepared for the reception of truth.

I am able to testify from my experience that Germans, as a whole, are industrious, sober, honest, charitable, free from bigotry, cheerful, and art and science-loving. See their May-feasts, Sangerbunds, Turner Societies, and Operas. Song, music, gym-

* This spiritual-minded and steadfast friend of the Harmonial Philosophy, passed on to his home in the Summer Land, in June, 1867. He was a cordial supporter of, and leader in, the Children's Progressive Lyceum of New York.

nastics, and order prevail there. They not only practice, but love science, art, music, and, above all, liberty and full freedom of thought. They will and do fight for it. They showed their appreciation of human rights in emancipating the women—their mothers, wives, and daughters—from the thralldom of slavery, at a time of barbaric darkness. At a time when the most enlightened nations of the world lived in bigamy, the followers of Herman would not countenance the multiplicity of wives.

Volumes could be written on this subject, but I can not trespass on your time and patience to indulge in further elucidations in respect to the German nation, since all of this is known to you as well.

But of one thing I am certain, and that is, the great monumental benefit such a publication will be to the progress of the people of America; for there are multitudes of Germans living in this country who will, with open hearts, accept any thing good coming from the beloved Fatherland. Why? It is recognized by German scientific men and published by celebrated book-selling houses there; wherefore they will put more trust in it, and consequently read it. And how vastly will our dear country gain by the awakening of such an increase of Spiritual elements, which at present lie hidden and latent, scarcely perceived or supposed, in those hearts, an inheritance from their ancestors. But you can see its manifestations in their tenderness of feeling, hospitality, and kind friendship. Oh! what a foundation for Harmonial development! Therefore, I do wish you God speed. Go on; arouse our friends and brothers in Progress; have them contribute their material aid; it requires but a little money to effect such a great and sublime end.

I, for one, do pledge my hearty co-operation as far as my means will allow, and when we unitedly put our shoulders to the wheel success will crown the effort, and happiness be diffused over the world at large.

I see by intuition how this New Dispensation spreads like wildfire over the continent of Europe, from plain to hill, from hill to mountain, there to shine as a beacon to the world. It spreads from the Hartz to the Alps—over the Giant Mountain to the Carpats—and a host of warriors for the truth it will awaken from their slumbers, and rouse laborers in the vineyard of Harmony by thousands and hundreds of thousands. Wherefore my heart rejoices, and I thank you for the taking in hand of such an important enterprise as the support and aid of publishing Spiritual writings in the German tongue.

Yours, for Progress,

DR. PH. SCHULHOF.

Encouraging words came also from many warm and earnest American hearts, accompanied, in some instances, by contributions for the work. Hudson Tuttle, who had done noble service in the production and dissemination of spiritual literature, and whose "Arcana" was already translated into German, wrote a letter to the *Banner of Light*, urging Spiritualists to give their aid and influence to the good cause.

EXTRACTS FROM HUDSON TUTTLE'S LETTER.

WALNUT-GROVE FARM, *April* 12, 1863.

The German world is as yet almost ignorant of the blessed literature of Spiritualism. They are only acquainted with the physical phenomena, and but partially even with them. The first volume of the *Arcana* was the first ray of light they received. It was not, however, published ostensibly as a spiritual work, but as a new and scientific exposition of the system of Nature, and was in this manner, and by the high standing of its translator, borne into favor.

It is now proposed to raise a fund by which the glorious writings of Davis and others can be at once presented to the thinkers of Germany. The Germans are proverbial for their belief in spiritual mysteries, and for a century have been laying the foundations of Spiritualism. There is no doubt if the new philosophy is presented to them, they will seize it with avidity, and the greatest good will grow out of it. . . . . .

The directors of the movement are men noble and generous, who have their whole hearts in the glorious work, and will at once receive the entire confidence of the friends of the cause. Than H. Schlarbaum, a more devoted Spiritualist, a more generous and noble-souled man, does not exist. A German, he has the deep spiritual nature of the Teuton, sharpened and Americanized by a long residence in our country. He has not, however, forgotten Germany and the millions of brothers he has left, and with an energy and devotion worthy of the object, he has determined to send light into their darkness. . . .

The eminent scholar, Herr Wittig, with indefatigable industry, has translated all of Davis's works, and is now going on translating other works on Spiritualism. Patiently he awaits the response of the New World, asking no other pay for his labor but the diffusion of the truths he so dearly loves.

Personally, I have no interest at stake; but as a believer in the Divine Philosophy of spiritual intercourse, I can but feel deeply anxious for the success of this movement, which I consider of more consequence than all the tracts and bibles distributed to the heathen for the last hundred years—of more consequence, because a great and enlightened nation are to be convinced and brought to the knowledge of the light. It is not savages whom we wish to enlighten, savages who are not as well off with a book as a fishing-net, but a nation of the deepest thinkers, the most scientific and spiritual of the Old World.

HUDSON TUTTLE.

While these events were transpiring in America, inspirations were ripening to purposes in a European mind, which were destined to bring great results. In distant Russia, a lonely student, "a child of that great Slavonian race, which is so highly distinguished for its mystical tendencies, and its fondness for spiritual facts and questions," was earnestly seeking avenues for the promulgation of spiritual truth, and longing for association with kindred minds. This was Alexander Aksákof, a nobleman of St. Petersburg. The following letter, which failed of its destination, but of which a copy has been lately received, will show better than any description some of the beautiful qualities and divine impulses of this truth-inspired nature:—

LETTER FROM ALEXANDER AKSÁKOF.

Moscow, *April* 12, 1864.

Mr. Andrew Jackson Davis:—

My Well-beloved Brother and Friend:—You wish to obtain the name, residence, and occupation of every individual who identifies himself, in public and practice, with the cause of spiritual and material progress. (Progressive Annual, 1862, page 43.)

I could not satisfy your demand before, for I obtained that Annual only in January, 1864. Since my youth, I always felt attracted to researches of truth concerning the internal nature of man; or, in other words, Philosophy and Theology were studies of my decided predilection. In 1851, at nineteen years of age, having completed my studies at the Imperial Lyceum, at St. Petersburg, I became acquainted with the doctrines of Swedenborg, your guide and friend in the spirit-world. Dazzled by the light of his writings, and young yet, I accepted his doctrines with grateful enthusiasm, for they were to me the highest expression of religion. To perfect myself in the science of correspondences, I studied Hebrew, occupying myself afterward to read the internal, spiritual sense of the Evangel of St. John. A work resulting therefrom was published in 1864, at Leipsic, under the title: "Five Chapters of the Evangel of St. John, with an Exposition of the Spiritual Sense, according to the Science of Correspondences."

But the study of Hebrew was only a philosophical recreation, but no progress; and the more I advanced in the exegesis of St. John, the more weaknesses I perceived; that is to say, the poverty and arbitrariness of the internal sense by correspondences became more and more apparent. Following my researches in the domain of unknown forces in Nature, I occupied myself with assiduity in homeopathy and magnetism, and in order to use to better advantage the attained convictions, I studied medicine and kindred sciences. At this time, I translated into Russian the "Magneto-therapy" of Count Szapary, which was published at St. Petersburg, in 1860.

The great news of the facts of American Spiritualism did not find me skeptical or indifferent. Notwithstanding the difficulties caused by the Russian Censure, I obtained the majority of the books and journals that treated of the great question. I read the "Principles of Nature" in 1855, and afterward all your other works as fast as I obtained them. I enjoyed with delight the perfume of truth. I had loved Swedenborg. I had much studied him. I had made him disciples that became my friends. But in proportion as I studied your writings the weak sides of his doctrines came more and more to light; by degrees the rest of religious dogmatism left me, and to-day I belong with body and soul to Spiritualism and the Harmonial Philosophy.

After ten years of study I got ready for the work. But how was I to act? What was to be done? You know that we have here no freedom of the press—no public speech!

In 1860, I made a voyage to Paris. I hastened to make the acquaintance of the French Spiritualists, but found myself greatly disappointed. The accredited system was the Spiritism of Mr. Kardec, that teaches the reincarnation of the soul. Their researches went more after facts than for doctrine; and respecting the things that transpired outside of France, they were simply not informed. Poverty in facts, in science, and in ideas—this is what I found in Paris. They knew your name, it is true, but nobody had read your works. I knew that their translation in Russian was forbidden at home, but as French books can circulate there with more facility, I resolved to publish in Paris a French translation of your works. Popularizing your doctrines in

France, I expected to transplant them to my own country. I found a good translator, but could not procure a single copy of the works, either in Paris or in London! I had to return to Russia, finding myself compelled to abandon my project. At the present time, Miss Guerin, in Paris, and Mr. Petters, at Frond, in Belgium, are occupied in translating you into French.

After my return to Russia, I resolved to print a Russian translation that I had made of Swedenborg's "Heaven and Hell." This being a very systematic and nearly orthodox book, I thought it useful to serve as a transition to the novel ideas. The book was published, 1863, in Leipsic, with a preface that contained a rapid glance at Spiritualism and its doctrines. I presented Swedenborg in it, not as the founder of a Church, but as a Spiritualist and medium. Among other things, I said in that Preface, "that modern facts have proved the truth, though relatively, of his revelations to the world, and therefore his work, 'Heaven and Hell,' can be read to-day with so much the more confidence and profit." You must remember that the works of Swedenborg are forbidden here. My translation experienced the same fate. It circulates through my hands, but the public at large can not obtain it. The printing of the work has, therefore, not given me any result whatever. Its Preface directed against me the most violent recriminations from the small number of New Jerusalemites that live here, who did imagine that I had thrown stones against Swedenborg; that I had poisoned his book; that I gave myself over to Satan, &c.; and some that called themselves my friends did abandon me. I had to endure, in the circle of my intimate affections, very painful sacrifices.

During this winter, I have written a *critique* of Swedenborg's system. In the shape of objections and contradictions, I have exposed not only the weak sides of his doctrines respecting the origin of evil and the freedom of man, but also the internal sense of the word as a proof of his divine inspiration. By this means I hope to revive the research for truth. If the disciples of Swedenborg begin to doubt the infallibility of their master, they may, perhaps, leave that enchanting circle which blocks up their intellectual progress and leads them to fanaticism. But as this *critique* is but a polemical work, it is only negative, and can not produce much positive good. A system can only be assailed by a system, and evil should be overcome by good.

In view of all this the translation of your writings into Russian has the greatest interest for me. You know that Russia is just now on the highway to reform, and we may soon get even the freedom of the Press! (Remark in 1867: this hope has not been realized.) The materialism of the German school, preached by Voigt and Buckner, makes, under the garb of science, rapid progress here. Lately the English book—"Vestiges of Creation"—has been translated into Russian. I will try to use it as a kind of pedestal to introduce the translation of the "Principles of Nature." Next winter I expect to go to work. Meanwhile the publication of your works in French or German is of equal interest to me. In the Annual of 1863, you say, page 74, "Several volumes of the Harmonial Philosophy have been already translated in Germany, and await the advent of a publisher." Inform me of the name and address of the translator, and I will immediately open correspondence with him, proposing with pleasure to be the editor of his translations. It is partly this news that prompted me to address you to-day. The *Revue Spirite* of 1861, page 153, announces nearly the same fact, naming Mr. Wittig, of Breslau. I have written under that direction, but no such person has been found. Mr. Hornung (who wrote the German book, "New Secrets of the Day," on Spiritualism) whom I saw in Berlin, in 1862, and who died since, could not tell me any thing positive respecting a German translation of your works.

In general, Spiritualism is very little known in Russia. The few that claim it received it as the Spiritism of Kardec, which fact explains itself, as the French literature being so poor on the subject leaves only the books of Kardec. I am not aware of a single person here who occupies himself with Spiritualism as a means of reform and progress. From the bookstores of Moscow and St. Petersburg I know that I am the only person that received your books and others of the spiritualistic literature of America. Thus in this immense country I am alone studying and loving your doctrines—alone in this large field of labor, hoping for better days when freedom of press and speech shall prevail. . . . .

You will greatly oblige me by answering this in the columns of the *Herald;* but not being very sure of always receiving it, it would make me very happy indeed to have your direct answer. I thank you from the depth of my soul for all the good, moral and intellectual, that you have done me, and for the freedom that I attained through you. I greet you as a brother and friend.

ALEXANDER AKSÁKOF.

Unfortunately, as the above communication miscarried, the writer was for two years longer baffled in his efforts to find the devoted Wittig. At last, however, the following letter reached the translator, and opened the way to welcome association, mutual interest, and joint fraternal labors for the advancement and elevation of Humanity :—

FROM ALEXANDER AKSÁKOF TO G. C. WITTIG.

DRESDEN, SAXONY, *January* 15, 1866.

DEAR SIR :—From the Journal *Psyche*, edited by Dr. C. A. Berthelen, at Zettau, a German publication devoted to science and spiritual knowledge, and from the editor's letters to me, I learn that you have translated three volumes of A. J. Davis's "Great Harmonia," without finding a publisher for them.

I am a Russian Spiritualist, and an admirer of Mr. Davis's writings. I perceive with great satisfaction that Germany will soon have facilities for becoming acquainted with the Philosophy of Spiritualism. Please inform me what you have already translated, what you are going to take in hand, and what the prospects of publication are. I am connected with the publisher, Franz

Wagner, in Leipsic, who issued my Russian translation of Swedenborg's "Heaven and Hell," in 1863, and will shortly publish my translations of Hare's and Edmonds's works. It might be arranged that Mr. Wagner would also publish your translations. Please inform me what conditions you propose for it. Inform me, also, respecting Professor Nees von Esenbeck, who translated, with you, some of Mr. Davis's writings. Have you the third volume of "Great Harmonia," the "Seer," completely and literally translated, or merely parts of it? Expecting your earliest answer,

I remain, with much esteem,

A. Aksákof.

New hope thrilled the heart of the translator on the reception of this letter. He had placed the precious manuscripts, over which he had so long and patiently toiled, in the hands of a publisher. But the results of red-handed war were pressing on the American people. Contributions for the "European Publishing Fund" came in slowly, and enthusiasm declined when the *Herald of Progress* was no more. Then came from a distant, despotic realm, a liberty-loving, truth-adoring Brother, who, in the spirit of noblest beneficence, pledged his pecuniary aid for the publishing of all the German translations! Alexander Aksákof became the bosom friend and wise counselor of the loving-hearted, noble-minded Wittig. The manuscripts were rescued, much defaced and mutilated, from the publishing office where first deposited, revised, and placed in the hands of Franz Wagner, of Leipsic, Mr. Aksákof's faithful publisher.

In the *Religio-Philosophical Journal* of August 4,

1866, appeared the following communication from Mr. Schlarbaum, announcing these changes and encouraging prospects:—

MR. SCHLARBAUM'S REPORT.

MANY of your readers will remember the attempt made in 1862, by the *Herald of Progress*, to raise funds for the publication of Harmonial works in German. A number of noble souls responded to the calls made, and contributions were handed over to the Treasurer of the German Publishing Fund, by which the committee was enabled to assist the translator of Mr. A. J. Davis's works in his arduous labors. The amounts raised were not sufficient, however, to go forward very energetically, mainly, perhaps, on account of our war, which disheartened and encumbered so many of us; and when, finally, the *Herald of Progress* was discontinued, the Fund lost its organ, and the committee was compelled to restrict its labors to what little it could do. All the funds, however, have been sacredly devoted to the ends contemplated by the donors. Encouraged and strengthened by the assistance from America, Mr. Wittig, in Breslau, in Prussia, the translator, has persevered in his exertions for the good cause. He has lately had the good fortune to become acquainted with a Russian gentleman of wealth and distinction, a true nobleman, who could not help making the Harmonial Philosophy his own in word and action, and with his munificent help the publication of *all* of Davis's works seems now to be secured to the German nation. The first eight proof-sheets of the fourth volume (The Reformer) of the Great Harmonia, printed at Leipsic, by Wagner, are in my hands. Our German friends concluded to begin with this fourth volume, as being better calculated to secure the attention of the German people. "The Magic Staff," adorned with Mr. Davis's steel engraving, the "Divine Revelations of Nature," and all the other parts of the "Great Harmonia," will follow in quick succession, being ready for the printer these last three years. Steps are now being taken to secure the extensive sale of this German edition here. If many educated Germans residing among us felt attracted to the principles of the Harmonial Philosophy, even if presented to them in the dress of the English language, the ability to bring it home to their searching minds in their own mother tongue will greatly facilitate the widest dissemination of it. The peculiar organization of the German book-trade will serve a like end. All the publishers in the "Fatherland" are united in a certain manner, and whatever book is published in any large or small German city is sent broadcast all over the land "for inspection," and finds its way to the study of every inquiring mind, before even a purchase of the book is made. This German publication will do a great deal for the proper appreciation of Harmonial views in Europe; and just now, this time of commotion, war, and future reconstruction, seems to be the best moment for it.

H. SCHLARBAUM.

It is with wonder and admiration that we trace the life-lines of these two European Reformers, now united to the vanguard of Progress in this country by all spiritual and imperishable ties. Each struggled in loneliness for many years, hemmed in by obstacles that would have been insurmountable to any but heroic souls. To both Heaven sent an inestimable blessing in the sympathy, kindred faith, and loving co-operation of those who bear the sacred name of wife; but aside from that, each toiled on in utter social isolation, until the happy moment came which united their lofty endeavors. We who have the utmost freedom of expression by tongue and pen; who have unlimited access to books, periodicals, and free platforms; who have the advantage of gathering *en masse* for free Conventions; and who enjoy the high privilege of social converse with multitudes possessing kindred ideas and faith, may well summon our powers anew when we behold the moral energy, love, patience, trust, and devotion of these transatlantic brethren under the weight of social and governmental restrictions. The following letter, received during the past year, shows the present *animus* of the movement:—

ALEXANDER AKSÁKOF TO A. J. DAVIS.

No. 6 Nevsky Prospect,

St. Petersburg, *October* 13, 1867.

Beloved Brother and Friend:—I am happy that I have now a letter from you, doubly happy at the idea that it will not be the last one, and that a more or less animated correspondence may be established between us. All my past efforts to reach you have failed. In 1858 I wrote you my first letter, dated from Nizney Novgorod; in 1864 I dated my second from Moscow, and here now I am writing my third, which I am sure will reach you sooner or later.

Your letter of July 26, N. Y., reached me September 16, nearly on the borders of Asia, at the City of the Department, Alexandrooka, where, having an estate near Bougoulma (Government of Samara), I ordinarily spend my summers. I did not come home to St. Petersburg till September 30, which explains the lateness of my answer. Now, my friend, as my words finally have reached you, let me press you to my heart; let me thank you from the bottom of my soul for the good that you have done me. You have made me free in the whole immense signification of this word, by teaching me how I was *not* free. You have taught me to make my peace with myself and my fellow-man. You made it impossible for me to complain against Providence, by giving me an understanding of the stern justice of the cause and its effect. I learned from you what evil is, and how to enjoy the present day. I have experienced heavenly joys and earthly griefs also. After many temptations and defeats, happy days, days of glory have come; and Truth, after having commenced on me its work of redemption, brings me every day new joys and consolations.

As Swedenborg had formerly effected his work of intellectual and moral emancipation in me—having translated his works, prompted by a feeling of deep thankfulness and an ardent desire to let all humanity participate in the boon of possessing truth—so it is in the present days. While, to my present convictions, the Harmonial Philosophy comes nearest to the truth, I feel myself prompted by the same desire to return my tribute of thankfulness by disseminating its teachings, if not in my own country, at least among another European people. I try to be free from illusions. I do not expect to see, while I live here, that enthusiasm in others which I have for the source of happiness—the adequate solution of the profoundest aspirations of my soul. I know very well that the negative side of your teachings may not be quite new for the German rationalist, while the positive side of them, connecting the external intuition with the internal, and thus reconstructing a system of natural religion that might be called a spiritualistic rationalism, will be treated by men of science with sarcasm and disdain, almost as if they were offended by speaking of their own immortality. But this does not intimidate me. Happily we have to do, not alone with men of science, but with men in general; we offer them not a new science alone, but a new life; and if among them there is found one single soul that understands and heeds your writings—a soul that derives the same amount of good from them as I have done, and is thus born to new life, my efforts will be amply rewarded, and I shall have the consolation of not having been *égoïste* in my happiness.

No, my friend, I will not hesitate to pursue the work that we have begun. What is commenced we expect to finish at an early day; for, although yet young, my health is not firm, and I dislike to close my existence here without the conviction of having been of some good on earth. . . . .

It is sad, that, in serving the cause of Spiritualism and the Harmonial Philosophy, I have to operate on a foreign soil. All that treats of Spiritualism, including your works, is proscribed here; the books of Kardec alone enjoy an exception. Thus all my efforts in this line are in vain. But I do not lose courage. I understand very well that the state of affairs in Russia does not accord with the publication of the religious and philosophical works of Spiritualism. As a movement of general reform it is too radical; it can only have its right "to be" in a free country. Our public press, and speech, and action, being under the control of the Government, it can not take root, nor have any effect whatsoever. I submit to these circumstances, seeing clearly that it would be labor lost to act in opposition to the conditions of time.

But there is no reason, I think, why the phenomenal part of Spiritualism should remain unknown. The sensuous demonstration of the immortality of the human soul, this decisive victory won over materialism, is a fact that can not but do service to any Christian doctrine. From this point of view, I will continue to battle against all opposition, using every effort to give the deserved publicity at least to the facts of Spiritualism. After the defense of the doctrine, the history of the doctrine can and should be known also.

In 1865, I laid before the public censors the manuscript of my translation of the experimental part of Prof. Hare's work, but they forbade the printing of it. In 1866, I had it printed at Leipsic, in Germany, and did all that lay in my power to enter it into the Russian book-trade, but all in vain. They found in it a few sentences which Russian Orthodoxy could not tolerate. But I will repeat my efforts with Hare's, Edmonds's, and De Morgan's works, taking care to dwell strictly on facts, without entering at all the domain of doctrine.

Do you approve, dear friend, my reasoning and projects? Could you advise me how to serve our cause in any other way in a country that is strictly orthodox, and void of all public freedom? What I painfully regret, besides, is that I am quite alone here in my interest for Spiritualism and its works. We have, it is true, a small number of Spiritists, of A. Kardec's school, but I am very little acquainted with them, and, besides, Spiritism differs from Spiritualism, and still more from the Harmonial Philosophy. Among the members of that circle, I met but one person who reads and understands English. What chances, then, are left me to be united with others, or to live and act in this community, while all my interests concentrate in the grand movement of universal reform in America? Among men of science, I know only the Professor of Philosophy of the University of Moscow, who is interested in the subject. He understands the whole bearing of this Spiritualistic movement, and takes the most lively interest in the publication of your works, being fully impressed with their full value. He is the only person with whom I may seriously speak on the subject, and yet, all he has read is the "Reformer," in German. . . . . .

Accept, my friend, the sentiments of deep gratitude, esteem, and affection, which unite me to you.

ALEXANDER AKSÁKOF.

The "Reformer" and the "Magic Staff" have been issued in excellent style, in the German language, by the enterprising publisher, Wagner; and Mr. Wittig writes, under date of December, 1867, from St. Petersburg, where he was enjoying a visit with Mr. Aksákof: "With the greatest satisfaction I am enabled to send you the joyful news that the munificence of our friend will help along the publication of 'Nature's Divine Revelations' in such a wise, that the printing will begin soon after my return." The Spiritualists of America will enshrine in their heart of hearts the names of those who have proclaimed to the German nation the "glad tidings of great joy," thus opening for the European continent the golden gateway to Light, Love, Wisdom, and Liberty.

THE END.

PROSPECTUS

der

von dem amerikanischen Seher und Verkündiger der "Harmonischen Philosophie"

ANDREW JACKSON DAVIS

in der

Reihenfolge ihrer Veröffentlichung in Nord-Amerika erschienenen und mit Autorisation ihres Verfassers

eines Theils von

dem im Jahre 1858 verstorbenen

Präsidenten der Kaiserlich Leopoldinisch-Carolinischen Akademie der Naturforscher zu Breslau,

Professor Dr. Christian Gottfried Nees von Esenbeck,

und andern Theils von

dessen Mitarbeiter und Herausgeber

Gregor Constantin Wittig,

aus dem Englischen in's Deutsche übersetzten Werke.

These volumes, as fast as translated into the German language, will be forwarded to America, and can be obtained at the offices of

WILLIAM WHITE & CO.,

158 WASHINGTON STREET, BOSTON, MASS., OR,

544 BROADWAY, NEW YORK.

NOW READY AND FOR SALE.

THE HARMONIA, 4th vol., "***THE REFORMER.***"

ALSO

THE MAGIC STAFF, an Autobiography.

Price of each, $2.75. Postage, 32 cts.

www.ingramcontent.com/pod-product-compliance
Lightning Source LLC
LaVergne TN
LVHW020916110826
845150LV00004B/686